GREAT BASEBALL FILMS

GREAT BASEBALL FILMS

FROM RIGHT OFF THE BAT TO A LEAGUE OF THEIR OWN

Rob Edelman

A CITADEL PRESS BOOK
Published by Carol Publishing Group

A CITADEL PRESS BOOK
Published by Carol Publishing Group
CITADEL PRESS is a registered trademark of
Carol Communications, Inc.
Editorial Offices: 600 Madison Avenue, New York, NY 10022
Sales & Distribution Offices: 120 Enterprise Avenue, Secaucus,
    NJ 07094
In Canada: Canadian Manda Group, P.O. Box 920, Station U,
    Toronto, Ontario M8Z 5P9
Queries regarding rights and permissions should be addressed to
Carol Publishing Group, 600 Madison Avenue, New York,
    NY 10022

Carol Publishing Group books are available at special discounts for
bulk purchases, for sales promotions, fund raising, or educational
purposes. Special editions can be created to specifications. For
details, contact: Special Sales Department, Carol Publishing Group,
120 Enterprise Avenue, Secaucus, NJ 07094

Designed by Andrew B. Gardner

Manufactured in the United States of America

10 9 8 7 6 5 4 3 2 1

Library of Congress Cataloging-in-Publication Data

Edelman, Rob.
    Great baseball films: from Right Off the Bat to A League
of Their Own / Rob Edelman.
        p. cm.
        "A Citadel Press Book".
        ISBN 0-8065-1479-5 (pbk.)
        1. Baseball films—History and criticism. I. Title.
PN1995.g.B28E44
791.43 655—dc20   93-44148
                                                   CIP

DEDICATION

*For Audrey, Anne, and Sam,
and John Garfield
(who never made a baseball
movie)*

ACKNOWLEDGMENTS

Many individuals and organizations deserve grateful thanks for their assistance during the preparation of this book. They are: the Amsterdam Free Library, Amsterdam, New York; Monty Arnold; Arlene Balkansky and Mark Stein; Richard W. Bann; David Bartholomew; Wendy Beck; Spencer Berger; Gordon Berkow and Lois Floersch; Nadine Bloom; the Bohman-Fannings; Dr. Bobby Brown; Joe L. Brown; Gary Carter; Claire of Eddie Brandt's Saturday Matinee; Rick DeCroix; Dan DiNicola; Ginny Donnelly and Dick Phillips; Karen and William K. Everson; Scott Eyman; Al Gionfriddo; Alex Gordon; Henry Griffin and Pamela Wintle; Fred Guida; Dan Jury and the staff of Home Film Festival; Michael Kerbel; Ralph Kiner; Howard and Elaine Kolodny; Bob Lemon; Jim Limbacher; Leonard Maltin; Marian Masone; John McCarty; Tim McCarver; the Museum of Modern Art; the National Baseball Library and Archives, National Baseball Hall of Fame and Museum, Cooperstown, New York; the New York Public Library at Lincoln Center; Karen O'Hara; David Parker; Mel Parnell; Johnny Pesky; Phil Rizzuto; Eli Savada; Phil Serling; Bobby Thomson; Inge and Dr. Alex Zimmerman; and my mother-in-law, Rae Kupferberg. Special thanks go to John Cocchi for his one-of-a-kind knowledge of faces in the movies; Rick Scheckman for his generosity; Dennis Doros and Amy Heller for their input; Madeline Matz, Reference Librarian, Motion Picture, Broadcasting and Recorded Sound Division, the Library of Congress, for her friendliness and dedication to film scholarship; Alvin Marill for his encouragement and advice; Allan J. Wilson for giving this project a go; and my wife, Audrey Kupferberg, for her support and love.

PHOTO CREDITS

ABC Films; American International Pictures; Bonaire Films; BTDS Partnership; Capital Cities/ABC; Castle Rock Entertainment; CBS Television; Cineplex Odeon Films; Columbia Pictures; Fine Line Features; Hal Roach Studios; Harold Lloyd Corp.; HBO Pictures; Jerry Lewis Productions; Kings Road Entertainment; Loews, Inc.; Lorimar Productions; Lucasfilm, Ltd.; MGM; Miramax Films; Morgan Creek Productions; Orion-Nova Twelve Angry Men; Orion Pictures; Paramount Pictures; Platypus Productions; Republic Pictures; RKO Pictures; the Samuel Goldwyn Company; *The Sporting News*; Taft Entertainment Pictures/Keith Barish Productions; Tartan Enterprises; Time-Life Television; Tri-Star Pictures; Troma; Turner Entertainment; Twentieth Century-Fox; United Artists; Universal City Studios; Viacom/Prism Entertainment; Warner Bros.; Walt Disney Productions; York Pictures Corp.

CONTENTS

Meet John Doe: Gary Cooper (right) as Long John Willoughby, Walter Brennan as the Colonel.

INTRODUCTION

n Frank Capra's populist allegory/political satire *Meet John Doe*, scrappy newspaper columnist Ann Mitchell (Barbara Stanwyck) is fired from her job because her pieces lack pizzazz. In her final column, she fakes a letter from "a disgusted American citizen, John Doe": an unemployed man who promises to jump off the City Hall roof at midnight on Christmas Eve. The story causes a hubbub, and Mitchell convinces the paper's new top honcho (James Gleason) to produce a John Doe. They interview candidates, one of whom is a long-unemployed hobo named Long John Willoughby (Gary Cooper).

"I used to pitch...til my wing went bad. . . . [I played in the] bush leagues, mostly," Long John explains.

"He's perfect," observes the writer. "A baseball player. What could be more American. . . . They'll believe him."

What could be more American, indeed. Across the decades, in good times and bad, baseball has (with sincere apologies to pigskin lovers) endured as the Great American Game. Long John Willoughby starts out as a man looking only for a meal; he has no opinion on taxes, foreign relations, or government corruption. But he is ever-so vocal, and refreshingly American, when it comes to baseball. Long John is unable to express emotion until Mitchell riles him by asking how he would feel if one of his pitches cut the heart of the plate, and the umpire called it a ball.

Baseball as a mirror of Americanism has long been depicted in the movies, and particularly in films like *Meet John Doe*, in which the sport otherwise plays a Class D-level role.

George Stevens's classic American comedy *Woman of the Year* was released in 1942, when the country was digging in for the duration of World War II. It was also the first celluloid union of Katharine Hepburn and Spencer Tracy. Hepburn plays Tess Harding, an influential newspaper columnist who is as much a newsmaker herself as an observer of world politics. Tess may speak a hundred languages, but none is the language of baseball. "I really don't know anything about American sports," she casually, shamelessly admits. To her, a runner's sprint from base to base "seems like a frightful waste of energy." Why, Tess Harding would lobby for the banning of baseball until Hitler and Tojo are licked. Her attitude rankles sportswriter Sam Craig (Tracy). "Say, look, we're concerned with a threat to what we like to call our American way of life," he complains. "Baseball and the things it represents is part of that way of life. What's the sense of abolishing the thing you're trying to protect?" After a battle of words in their columns, Tess and Sam declare a truce, and he invites her to a New York Yankees–Philadelphia Athletics clash in the House That Ruth Built.

Young April, a 1926 romantic comedy-drama, may be as obscure as *Woman of the Year* is celebrated,

1

Douglas Croft, cast in *Remember the Day* as a baseball-loving youngster who grows up to run for President, also played Lou Gehrig as a boy in *The Pride of the Yankees.* Here, he is coached by Babe Ruth, who played himself in the latter.

but its relationship between baseball and country is equally telling. Bessie Love plays Victoria Sax, an orphan who has been exiled in America since childhood. Saxheim, her homeland, is annexed by the Kingdom of Belgravia; Victoria becomes a Grand Duchess, and is ordered home to wed her new king's son. "Me leave the U.S.A. to be a duchess? No, sir!" exclaims this spunky Americanized miss, who prefers to be known as plain old "Vic." But words are not needed to establish her sympathies. During her initial appearance in the story, her Americanism is instantly validated because she is seen playing softball with her schoolmates. Similarly, *Hitler's Children*, released in 1943, when the United States was in the depths of World War II, is set in the Berlin of a decade earlier. Kent Smith, playing a teacher in an American school, comes upon some of his charges brawling with their German counterparts. The latter are members of a Hitler Youth group, who have been taught that "it is our birthright to rule" and "to die for Hitler is to live for Germany"; the former had been playing baseball, which certifies their Americanism.

An aging Sultan of Swat displays his batting style for William Bendix, star of *The Babe Ruth Story,* and other cast members.

In *The Best Years of Our Lives,* which came to theaters in 1946, after the war's end, a trio of veterans (Fredric March, Dana Andrews, Harold Russell) return to their hometown of Boone City. They share a taxi, drive past the local ballpark, and query the cabdriver about the fate of the Boone City Beavers. "Sixth place" is the sour response. The point is that ex-GIs now can devote their full attention to the fate of their favorite baseball teams, rather than killing Germans and Japanese. They have won the all-American right to "root, root, root for the home team," and grouse when it is inept.

In *Remember the Day,* a 1941 slice of Americana, a bright twelve-year-old boy, Dewey Roberts (Douglas Croft), is the star pitcher of the Auburn Grammar School baseball team. In class, Dewey

Black Legion: The title Ku Klux Klan-type organization separates Humphrey Bogart from his wife (Erin O'Brien-Moore), his son, and the positive kind of Americanism represented by baseball.

is absorbed not in his textbook but in a volume by Christy Mathewson on how to pitch. In preparation for the Big Game against Rome, he practices hurling by throwing an eraser into a wastebasket; predictably, he is the centerpiece of the contest, a spirited affair played to a throng of avidly cheering children. Unfortunately, our hero wrecks his knee while sliding into third base. This all-American boy, who loves baseball and boats, may not grow up to be Christy Mathewson. But he does mature into a nominee for the United States presidency. If a man is to be president, we are told in *Remember the Day,* one of the prerequisites is a love of baseball.

This still perfectly depicts how baseball can be used as a visual metaphor for the American family and father-son bonding. It is from *Hide in Plain Sight,* the story of a dad, Tom Hacklin, Jr. (James Caan), whose ex-wife marries a hood who has ratted on his superiors and is swept up in the government's Witness Protection Program. As a result, Hacklin's children disappear, and he sets out to find them. Pictured is the Hacklin clan as it should be: father, two cute children, and one family pet. Note that only the males wear baseball caps.

Simple Men: William Sage (left) and Robert Burke set out to find their father, a Brooklyn Dodgers' all-star shortstop turned bomb-throwing anarchist.

The Pride of the Yankees: Gary Cooper as Lou Gehrig.

In the 1993 fantasy *Dave*, Kevin Kline stars as Dave Kovic, a simple, sincere presidential looka-like who is drafted into impersonating the real Commander-in-Chief when the latter is felled by a stroke. First, baseball is metaphorically used to communicate Dave's essential goodness. As the character is introduced, you know he is an all-American guy because he has a ball and glove stashed in his office desk drawer. Later on, garbed in a warm-up jacket with PREZ stitched on the back, President Dave throws out the major-league season's first pitch: a role this everyman especially relishes as he burns his toss down the heart of the plate, right into the glove of the catcher (real-life Baltimore Oriole backstop Jeff Tackett).

In the 1984 comedy *Protocol*, Goldie Hawn plays Sunny Davis, a wide-eyed, all-American Washington, D.C., cocktail waitress whose quick action thwarts a presidential assassin. At a press conference, she explains that she is going to visit her family back in Oregon. She will check on her father and his latest wacky inventions. She will eat her mom's huckleberry pie. Her grandmoth-

Black Legion, a Depression-era social drama from 1936, is the saga of Frank Taylor (Humphrey Bogart), the quintessential impressionable working stiff. His disappointment at losing a promotion to a coworker named Joe Dumbrowski allows him to be coerced into joining the title organization: a Ku Klux Klan–like outfit whose members parade around in hoods and bully anyone they deem to be less than "100 percent American." Taylor is first depicted as an average guy with "the sweetest wife and kid in the world." Young Buddy Taylor (Dickie Jones) is an all-American boy who loves to play baseball, and read Frank Merriwell–-type sports books. After Dumbrowski and his father are terrorized and booted out of town, Taylor becomes foreman—and promptly buys Buddy a new Louisville Slugger. If only the father's national identity manifested itself in a manner more befitting his son's fondness for baseball, whose presence here serves as a symbol of a positive kind of Americanism.

Field of Dreams: Kevin Costner as Ray Kinsella.

er, she notes, is a volunteer school crossing guard. Her grandfather, she adds, used to pitch for the Salem Rockets, in the "Double A League." He was MVP two years running, "and we're really proud of him." A reporter asks Davis if she is a Republican or Democrat. "I consider myself to be just an American," she responds.

There are rare exceptions to this unabashed linking of baseball and flag waving. The 1992 release *Simple Men*, one of many contemporary independent films with a distinctive sensibility, offers an unconventional take on a ballplayer. You won't find William McCabe, the Brooklyn Dodgers' all-star shortstop during the 1950s, invited to any Old Timers games. After his playing career ended, McCabe—who is not to be confused with Pee Wee Reese—became an anarchist. He allegedly tossed a bomb at the Pentagon during the late sixties, killing seven people, and spent twenty-three years on the run. McCabe was captured and promptly escaped, and his two sons set out to find him. "I saw your father play with the Dodgers back in 'fifty-six," an old cop tells the younger son. "He was the greatest shortstop who ever lived, no matter what anyone says about him."

Writer-director Hal Hartley offers no clues on McCabe's political evolution. "I thought it would be interesting to have this all-American hero type fused with this anarchist," Hartley explained, "which is something not too many Americans could identify with."

Bull Durham: Kevin Costner as Crash Davis.

It Happens Every Spring: Ted de Corsia as Dolan, Paul Douglas as Monk Lanigan, Ray Milland as Vernon Simpson (left to right).

Americans can more readily identify with the content of *Protocol*, or *Young April*, or *Woman of the Year*, films that link baseball and patriotism across the decades. In an ever changing, ever more complex world, these films show how the sport has remained integral to the American scene.

In election after election, many a citizen has mindlessly voted for the politician with the slickest ad campaign, without considering the candidate's true nature or stand on issues; it took a major recession in 1992 to convince the electorate otherwise. But ask John Q. Public about the voting for Most Valuable Player. He is always sure to have a knowledgeable viewpoint. Ask him about the prospects for his favorite team. Who was the greater home run hitter, Babe Ruth or Hank Aaron? Does Pete Rose deserve enshrinement in the Hall of Fame? What about George Steinbrenner? Hasn't he tainted the legacy of the Bambino, the Iron Horse, Joe D., and the Mick?

If your team is an also-ran, there always will be tomorrow. Wait 'til next year. Wait until you see this

Slide, Kelly, Slide: William Haines as Jim Kelly.

kid outfielder, ripening down on the farm with the Durham Bulls or New Britain Red Sox, who is the reincarnation of twenty-one-year-old Mickey Mantle. There may be Black Sox scandals, drug probes, or contract disputes; the faces on the ballfield and names in the box scores may change. But there always are nine players in the field and nine innings per regulation game; three outs per team per inning, and three strikes and yer out.

The baseball season begins at a time of rejuvenation, when the snow is melting and flowers are bloom-

ing, just as the title of a 1949 baseball movie tells us: *It Happens Every Spring.* To an American fan, it is irrelevant that the winner of the *World* Series only can be a team from San Diego or St. Louis, Minnesota or Milwaukee (and, as must be acknowledged after the 1992 season, Toronto or Montreal). America is the world, if only because America is baseball.

While baseball has been a constant in American movies, there are few if any baseball films that rank in the pantheon of all-time screen greats. One might respectively dub *Bull Durham, The Pride of the*

The Jackie Robinson Story: Richard Lane as Clay Hopper, Ruby Dee as Rachel Robinson, Jackie Robinson as himself, Minor Watson as Branch Rickey (left to right).

6

The Pride of St. Louis: Dan Dailey as Dizzy Dean, Joanne Dru as Patricia Nash Dean.

type. How many baseball movies open by showing their subjects as young boys who are denied their places on the sandlots by bigger, louder kids, but when given their chance will immediately smash baseballs through windows (as does young Lou Gehrig in *The Pride of the Yankees*) or make solid fielding plays (as does young Jackie Robinson in *The Jackie Robinson Story*)? In the Billy Wilder comedy *A Foreign Affair*, set amid the rubble of postwar, American-occupied Berlin, a congressman notes, while watching some German kids play baseball, "One thing they don't have to worry about around here is breaking windows." The cliché is repeated as recently as *The Babe*, in which young George Herman Ruth is cruelly chided by his fellow inmates at the St. Mary's Industrial School for Boys. The first time he handles a baseball bat, he swings awkwardly. The other boys' derisive laughter compels him to instinctively begin belting pitch after pitch for Ruthian

Yankees, and *Field of Dreams* the *It Happened One Night, Citizen Kane* and *It's a Wonderful Life* of baseball films. But one never would think to reverse the comparison.

The reason for this is inherent in the genre. Whether they be wonderfully entertaining and moving or trite and boring, baseball films rarely are distinguished by originality. This is so from their opening moments. Too many baseball films begin with a rendition of "Take Me Out to the Ball Game." More than a few start with some sort of homage to the game or its great players; typically, *Slide, Kelly, Slide* is "Dedicated to the great American game—Baseball— and to the memory of Frank Chance . . . Eddie Plank, Christy Mathewson, and their immortal legion." Or, a narrator will wax nostalgic about how the film will tell the simple, American story of a boy and his dream of playing baseball, or about how the ballclub depicted in the scenario (whether it be the Pittsburgh Pirates or the Secaucus Cockamamies) might be any team, in any American town.

The typical celluloid diamond hero (whether fact- or fiction-based) has long ago become a stereo-

The Winning Team: Doris Day as Aimee, Ronald Reagan as Grover Cleveland Alexander.

7

The Bad News Bears: Tatum O'Neal as Amanda Whurlitzer, Walter Matthau as Morris Buttermaker.

distances. His last hit, of course, smashes a church window.

Baseball movie heroes grow to manhood and become living legends. But first they must be shown as young pitching prospects or junior Sultans of Swat, usually small-town boys with big-time talent. Major-league scouts watch intently as they whiz fastballs or bash home runs for their high-school or semipro teams. "C'mere, kid," the scout will say after the game. "I represent the New York Yankees/St.Louis Cardinals/California Angels. I think you've got what it takes to be the greatest baseball player in history." The kid, as long as he is neither Dizzy Dean, a Babe Ruth caricature, nor any character played by Joe E. Brown, will respond with a shy, "Ah, gee whiz, wow. D'ya really mean it?"

After enjoying Hall of Fame careers, these jocks must contend with their athletic twilights. A simple, graceful retirement will not suffice. They either face premature demises (most notably Lou Gehrig, in *The Pride of the Yankees* and the television movie *A Love Affair: The Eleanor and Lou Gehrig Story*), becoming bigger heroes in death than in life. Or they will reject the fact that their careers have peaked, alienate their wives while resorting to gambling and drinking, and eventually regain their self-respect either as wily veteran pitchers with one last great ballgame in their arms (Grover Cleveland Alexander, in *The Winning Team*) or in new, baseball-related careers (Dizzy Dean, who becomes a homespun baseball broadcaster in *The Pride of St. Louis*).

Then there is another type of baseball movie hero: the career minor leaguer. He is aging and has just had the proverbial cup of coffee in the Show, but he is as devoted to the game as any Babe Ruth or Dizzy Dean. Occasionally he is set to establish a record that will go unnoticed by all but himself because it is a minor league mark, and he is just a forgotten ballplayer. In *Bull Durham*, catcher Crash Davis is about to hit more homers than any other minor leaguer; in *Pastime* (which, appropriately, was originally titled *One Cup of Coffee*), pitcher Roy Dean Bream is ready to reach a plateau for game appearances. Bream can brag that he once struck out Stan Musial; Morris Buttermaker, the broken-down ex—minor leaguer and Little League coach in *The Bad News Bears*, did whiff Ted Williams twice. These feats occurred not during World Series or All-Star games, but in meaningless spring training exhibitions.

There are other clichés, some of which are derivations of the above: the rookie who is talented but awkward and eager-to-impress, and who will need to gain mental and physical maturity; the veteran utility player, struggling to maintain his spot on the roster; the rising star, on the brink of greatness; and the aging star, who's been around the bases a couple of thousand times and who smartly employs his experience and poise to replace his diminishing skills. Typically all are united by their preference for hotdogs over filet mignon, ketchup to caviar. They will represent the ways of the masses, the fans whose fannies warm seats in the bleachers (and who shell out their hard-earned wages for movie tickets), rather than the corporate types with seasons' tickets behind home plate (who, more often than not, are the villains of the story).

The standard baseball-movie scenario has the hero struggling to show the world that he is adept at playing the game. After making the team, he catches splinters on the bench, and then gets into a crucial contest by happenstance. He comes to bat in the ninth inning—always the ninth inning—representing the winning run. A couple of runners edge off the bases. The opposing pitcher bears down. He winds up, fires the ball. Perhaps the hero will sock the first pitch over the fence, or maybe this will happen on a three-and-two count. But inevitably it *will* happen. If the film is a comedy, the round-tripper will be an inside-the-park job, allowing the star to acrobatically slide into home plate just under the catcher's tag. If the hero is a hurler, he invariably will strike out the opposing team's heaviest hitter with two down in the ninth inning, to win the game and the glory.

Along the way, our hero might dispose of the villains (who, if not the swell-chested braggarts on the opposing team, will be fat cat capitalists or gamblers intent on throwing the Big Game). He will always win the girl, who at first expresses disdain for ballplayers (who, she thinks, are dimwitted louts). If the heroine's attitude is not the issue, then it is that of her father, who has forbidden her to see him because, after all, he is a ballplayer and a bum. Now that our hero has become this moment's Mr. Baseball, he is fit

Edward G. Robinson (right) and Jeff Richards in *Big Leaguer:* the crafty old-timer is mentor to the gifted but raw prospect.

Safe at Home!: Roger Maris as himself, William Frawley as Bill Turner, Bryan Russell as Hutch Lawton, Mickey Mantle as himself (left to right).

enough to be welcomed into the family. All will live happily ever after.

These scenarios date from the beginnings of baseball movies. Take *Somewhere in Georgia*, a drama starring Ty Cobb and released in 1916. The film features, according to *Variety*,

> the usual excitement [that] attends the baseball game in which Cobb cops the climax with his playing and wins the girl in the end. There's a deep-dyed villain and the subsequent denouement at the finale, with Cobb stealing a kiss from his prospective wife behind a baseball glove.

The scenario is "one of those Frank Merriwell stories, with Ty doing the Merriwell stuff that catches the young folks." Even more to the point, *Somewhere in Georgia* "has a good wholesome atmosphere and a real, live-blooded, cleanlimbed athlete for a hero."

Then there is the finale of *The Busher*, a 1919 comedy-drama starring

9

Angels in the Outfield: Janet Leigh as Jennifer Paige, Donna Corcoran as Bridget White, Paul Douglas as Guffy McGovern.

players descend upon a midwestern cornfield. In *Angels in the Outfield*, angels appear in old Forbes Field, stand behind each Pittsburgh Pirate, and transform the Bucs from also-rans to winners. In *Damn Yankees*, the devil converts a middle-aged Washington Senators zealot into a strapping rookie who will lead the perennial second-division team to triumph against the hated New York Yankees.

The baseball movie-as-cliché is deftly captured by Billy Wilder, Charles Brackett, and D.M. Marshman Jr., in their screenplay for *Sunset Boulevard*. William Holden stars as Joe Gillis, "a movie writer with a couple of B pictures to his credit," who is struggling to create a script that will sell. He has pitched a story idea to Sheldrake (Fred Clark), a big-shot Paramount producer. "It's about a baseball player," Gillis tells Sheldrake,

Charles Ray. His character, as described in *Variety*, "does the usual 'save the game in the ninth' by slamming out a homer and sending home a couple of the gang that were on the bags." In Ray's *The Pinch Hitter*, released two years earlier, *Variety* notes that, "at the last minute [the hero is] forced into the [big] game through an accident and, working up a good lot of suspense, he wallops the ball for a homer and wins the approval of dad and the girl, and develops enough self-confidence to propose."

The final baseball-movie cliché is one of magic and fantasy. Only in a baseball movie will an average joe find himself in the presence of a baseball idol. In *Speedy*, a baseball-loving cabdriver picks up none other than Babe Ruth, on his way to the house he built. In *Safe at Home!*, a dreamy Little Leaguer makes his way to the New York Yankees spring training site and lands in the company of the M & M boys, Mickey Mantle and Roger Maris. In *Max Dugan Returns*, an inept, obscure high-school ballplayer has famed hitting coach Charlie Lau as his personal instructor.

There may be an element of outright otherworldliness. In *Field of Dreams*, the spirits of Shoeless Joe Jackson and other long-deceased

"a rookie shortstop batting .347. This poor kid was once mixed up in a holdup, and he's trying to go straight, except there are a bunch of gamblers that

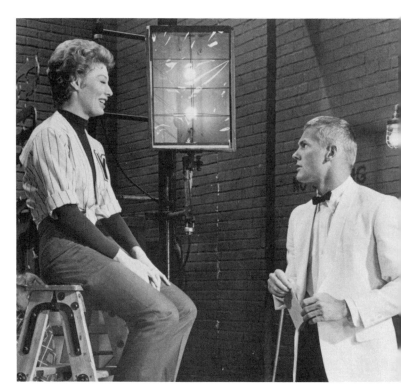

Damn Yankees: Gwen Verdon as Lola, Tab Hunter as Joe Hardy.

Rita Hayworth might have been the perfect actress to star in *It Happened in the Bullpen: The Story of a Woman*, the baseball movie pitched by Joe Gillis in *Sunset Boulevard.* Here she is, behind the plate in *Girls Can Play*, her second credit as a young Columbia Pictures contract player.

won't let him." The title is *Bases Loaded.* "Can you see Ty Power as the shortstop?" the writer continues. "Ya got the best man for it right on this lot. Alan Ladd. Big change of pace for Ladd … And there's a great little part for Bill Demarest. One of the trainers. An old-time player who got beaned. Goes out of his head sometimes." Unfortunately for Gillis, a drone from the readers department (Nancy Olson) reports that she found the script "flat and trite." Observes Sheldrake, with subtle sarcasm, "Of course we're, uh, we're always looking for a Betty Hutton. Do you see it as a Betty Hutton? Now wait a minute. If we made it a girls' softball team, put in a few numbers. Might make a cute musical. *It Happened in the Bullpen: The Story of a Woman.*" Such is a sample of the creative process in Hollywood.

Clichés aside, it can be argued that baseball is not an ideal celluloid subject because the game, with all its subtlety, lacks the visual fireworks of boxing or auto racing: sports that are much more common to the movies. So perhaps the most diverting depictions of baseball on screen are those World Series compila-

tion films highlighting Carlton Fisk's dramatic game-winning home run in 1975, or Reggie Jackson's three consecutive homers in 1978, or Mookie Wilson's grounder trickling under Bill Buckner's glove in 1986. In the latter contest, the Boston Red Sox came within a strike of winning the game—and the series—*four times.* With two outs and the bases empty in the last of the tenth inning, the New York Mets prevailed on three singles, a passed ball, and Buckner's miscue. Such scenarios are high histrionics for the diehard baseball fan, as much the stuff of lore as the climactic moments of *Casablanca* or as chilling and riveting as the shower scene in *Psycho.*

How can any scriptwriter better conjure up the tension of a real-life ballgame in which the tying runs are on base with two outs in the ninth inning and Nolan Ryan or Roger Clemens are on the mound, firing ninety-mile-per-hour fastballs at Ken Griffey Jr., or Kirby Puckett? On any given day between April and October, similar scenes will be played and replayed on baseball diamonds across America.

Would a screenwriter dare create heroes like Mark Lemke, Brian Doyle, Al Gionfriddo, Sandy Amoros, Ron Swoboda, or Dusty Rhodes: obscure

Joe E. Brown.

ballplayers whose timely hitting or clutch fielding transformed them into World Series legends? Or Francisco Cabrera, who spent most of the 1992 season in the minors but came off the bench to put the Atlanta Braves in the World Series with one swing?

If a screenwriter would concoct a team like the New York Mets, who in 1962 lost more games than any ballclub in history but by the end of the decade were world champs, critics would label his scenario cornball, and most improbable.

How could a writer create a name for a ballplayer that is more solidly all-American than Mickey Mantle? Or more colorful than Choo Choo Coleman, Coot Veal, Turk Lown, Blue Moon Odom, Vinegar Bend Mizell, Oil Can Boyd, Catfish Hunter, Wildfire Schulte, Sibby Sisti, Rabbit Maranville, Sherman Roadblock Jones, Dutch Dotterer, Mudcat Grant, Hippo Vaughn, Boom Boom Beck, Sloppy Thurston, Gabby Hartnett, Bobo Newsome, Peanuts Lowrey, Puddin' Head Jones, Birdie Tebbetts, Dazzy Vance, Dizzy Dean, and Yogi Berra?

How could a screenwriter create a character who

Death on the Diamond: Robert Young (left), as Larry Kelly, looks appropriately perplexed. With him is Pat Flaherty, cast as a St. Louis Cardinals' coach, who also is the film's technical adviser.

is more symbolic of his generation than Joe DiMaggio? Or more hard-nosed than Pete Rose? Or more heroic than Jackie Robinson? Or more larger-than-life than Babe Ruth, Casey Stengel, Rube Waddell, Billy Martin ... and Dizzy Dean and Yogi Berra?

Furthermore, a majority of the actors who have impersonated ballplayers have not been able to cut it on the diamond. Gary Cooper may have deserved his Academy Award nomination for playing Lou Gehrig in *The Pride of the Yankees*, but he was so honored for his acting opposite Teresa Wright and his reading of the Iron Horse's legendary Yankee Stadium farewell. On the ballfield, Cooper simply does not look the part of a ballplayer, let alone one of the calibre of Lou Gehrig. It is not so much that Cooper admittedly knew little about baseball; or was right-handed (as opposed to Gehrig's being a lefty); or even that the actor was so uncomfortable favoring his left hand that he had to be filmed as a righty, with the Yankee name reversed on his uniform and the negative reversed in the editing room. Lefty O'Doul, former major-league outfielder hired to tutor Cooper on baseball basics, pinpointed the problem in his assessment of the actor: "He threw the ball like an old woman tossing a hot biscuit." Compare Cooper to the real Iron Horse, in his role in *Rawhide*, a B western. At one point, when

The Pinch Hitter: Glenn Hunter is more believable as a bumbling farmboy than the college baseball hero he is destined to become.

Gehrig spontaneously bats a baseball through a window, you know you are seeing a real, natural, graceful athlete.

There are exceptions here. LeVar Burton, star of the television movie *One in a Million: The Ron LeFlore Story*, looks like an athlete as he stands in the Tiger Stadium batting cage whacking pitches during the depiction of LeFlore's tryout, or when he leads off first base, tense with anticipation as he sets to steal second. Kevin Costner, cast as Crash Davis in *Bull Durham*, also displays a ballplayer's movements. The actor playing Jackie Robinson in *The Jackie Robinson Story* is thoroughly believable on the ballfield because, well, that actor is Mr. Robinson himself. Certainly, Joe E. Brown, a devoted baseball fan who as a young man played minor-league ball, is more than believable on the field in his three baseball films, *Fireman, Save My Child*; *Elmer the Great*; and *Alibi Ike*. In particular, as he takes his first batting practice in *Elmer the Great*, his athletic ability is ever so apparent.

Fear Strikes Out: Anthony Perkins (right), playing Jimmy Piersall (and pictured with Adam Williams and Norma Moore), is a far more effective actor off the ballfield.

No cinematic trickery is necessary to make Brown appear to be a quality ballplayer. This is not so in *Death on the Diamond*, in which the film is speeded up just as pitcher Robert Young is set to heave the ball, in an attempt to create the illusion that he is burning pitches to home plate. The resulting effect, though, simply looks silly. Dan Dailey, cast as Dizzy Dean in *The Pride of St. Louis*, may convincingly capture the backwoods bravura and charm of his character, but the long shots of Dailey pitching, or tumbling to the ground while trying to field a bunt, are done by a double. In *Fear Strikes Out*, gangly Anthony Perkins (playing Jimmy Piersall) is most effective in the scenes in which he is called upon to capture the ballplayer's growing torment, and the tension inherent in his relationship with his father. But he tosses a baseball awkwardly, as if he is lobbing a block of cement.

Ronald Reagan, who played a young college ballplayer in *Brother Rat* and Grover Cleveland Alexander in *The Winning Team*, may have had a sports background: back in the 1930s, the future president was known as "Dutch" Reagan and worked as a

The Babe: The Sultan of Swat (John Goodman) and his famed "called shot"; note the lemons (as well as photographer) on the playing field.

play-by-play announcer for the Chicago Cubs. But in *The Winning Team*, his pitching motion is akin to that of a novice athlete. The sequences in which Alex's pitches whiff batters are filmed in long shot, or are of his back so that a double may be used who can more realistically fire fastballs at the plate. In *The Babe*, John Goodman may offer a well-rounded, emotionally valid performance as the Bambino. However, he joins the legion of actor-nonathletes who flounder in their attempts to resemble real-life Hall of Famers. Goodman labors to master the Babe's motions, from his swing to his distinctive home run trot. Yet he remains a pale imitation of a major leaguer, let alone one as Ruthian as Babe Ruth.

Baseball films also shamelessly toy with history. The facts behind the long-standing feud between Babe Ruth and Lou Gehrig, the reasons for Ruth's dis-

Mel Allen.

obeying Yankee manager Miller Huggins, and the character of Gehrig's mother are among the biographical data divergently depicted from bio to bio. A now famous story about the Bambino's promise to bash a homer for a sick boy named Johnny has become an integral part of the ballplayer's legend. According to Robert Creamer, Ruth's biographer,

> His most famous, or at least most publicized, hospital visit came in the 1920s, when the uncle of a seriously injured youngster named Johnny Sylvester arranged for Ruth to autograph a baseball for the boy. Ruth later visited the hospital, and the papers were soon filled with sob-sister stories about the Babe promising to hit a home run for a dying boy and then saving his life by actually hitting one, the excitement of the fulfilled promise having brought new life to the poor sick kid. Ruth apparently did say he would try to hit a homer, something he said

Aunt Mary: Jean Stapleton as Mary Dobkin, pictured with her Dynamites.

14

The Stratton Story: James Stewart as Monty Stratton, June Allyson as Ethel.

often, and he did come through. But while Johnny Sylvester's injury was serious, he was not dying. In any case, he recovered, and his name became embroidered in Ruth's legend.

It is fascinating to note how the specifics of this story vary from film to film. In fact, in *The Pride of the Yankees*—Lou Gehrig's film, rather than Ruth's—Gehrig is shown to one-up his teammate by delivering on a promise to belt *two* dingers!

Most inexcusable of all, baseball movies are sometimes sloppily researched. In *Pastime*, the players wear batting helmets even though the film is set in 1957, years before they were employed by professionals. Additionally, a public-address announcer doesn't just report batting orders, pitching changes, upcoming promotionals and the like, but comments on events in a game as would a radio or television play-by-play person. The scenario of *Blue Skies Again* ignores the fact that pitchers never attempt to go the distance in the first exhibition game of spring training. In *The Pride of the Yankees*, Lou Gehrig is taken out of a Yankee-Tiger contest, thus terminating his consecutive-games-played streak. Yet such a streak does not end if a player is removed from a game in which he already has appeared. In the climactic sequence of *The Stratton Story*, one-legged Monty Stratton hobbles safely to first base after cracking a single. He is

removed for a pinch runner, yet re-enters the game to pitch when his team returns to the field. In a well-publicized gaffe in *Field of Dreams*, Ray Liotta, cast as Shoeless Joe Jackson, bats right-handed and throws left-handed; the real Shoeless Joe was a left-handed hitter and right-handed thrower.

In *The Babe Ruth Story*, longtime Yankee announcer Mel Allen is the man behind the mike during the 1927 game in which the Babe belts homer number sixty against the Washington Senators' Tom Zachary. But Allen, a 1936 University of Alabama graduate, did not become a Yankee broadcaster until 1939. In *The Babe*, the Bambino is shown calling his home run in the 1932 World Series against the Chicago Cubs. Even though it remains unclear

The Natural: Robert Redford as Roy Hobbs.

15

Major League: Corbin Bernsen (left) as Roger Dorn, Charlie Sheen as Rickie Vaughn.

whether Ruth actually predicted the dinger, there is nothing wrong with choosing to depict him doing so; but there is plenty wrong with showing the game being allowed to continue while the Cubs' fans pelt the field with lemons.

There is a major chronological flaw in *Aunt Mary*, a made-for-television movie. The film is set in 1954: at one point, sandlot baseball coach Mary reads a newspaper headlined DIMAGGIO WEDS MARILYN MONROE. Yet earlier on, her kids serenade her by lip-synching the Diamonds' "Little Darlin'," a hit record in 1957. In the television remake of *The Kid from Left Field*, a young, alleged baseball trivia buff notes that Jackie Robinson was rookie of the year in 1948, yet the ballplayer debuted in the majors the previous season. The boy talks about how Willie Mays made a "remarkable, over-the-shoulder catch in 1951 against the Brooklyn Dodgers." As any of the baseball fanatics in *City Slickers* could tell you, the year was 1954 and Mays's grab came in the World Series, against the Cleveland Indians' Vic Wertz.

While researching this book, one question constantly arose: What are the all-time best and worst baseball movies? Who better to query on this than real-life major leaguers. Among older films, *The Pride of the Yankees* is the favorite of Johnny Pesky, Phil Rizzuto, and Bob Lemon, and is cited on the lists of Ralph Kiner and Gary Carter. Kiner's top film is *Angels in the Outfield*; Lemon and Rizzuto also list *The Stratton Story*. Among newer titles, *Field of Dreams*

heads the list of Bobby Thomson (who notes, "I haven't seen others"), Dr. Bobby Brown (who adds that "I do not see many baseball films") and Carter, and is second on the list of Mel Parnell. *The Natural* tops the list of Parnell, and is cited by Tim McCarver, Rizzuto, and Kiner. *Bull Durham* tops the list of McCarver, and is cited by Rizzuto. Carter also lists *Major League* and *The Babe*.

The Babe Ruth Story is cited by Pesky as the worst all-time baseball film. McCarver notes, "*The Babe Ruth Story* with William Bendix was the second worst movie I have ever seen. The worst was *K2*." Rizzuto dislikes "all the ones they tried to make about Babe Ruth, who saved baseball after the scandal with the Black Sox," and suggests, "They should have ex-ballplayers, groundskeepers [and] newspapermen to make [the films more] realistic." Concludes Al Gionfriddo, "I do not care to go and watch baseball movies. I believe most of them are done very poorly."

"I've seen most all of the baseball movies," reports Joe L. Brown, son of Joe E. Brown and long-time Pittsburgh Pirates general manager. "Most were not good. Some may have been enjoyable, but they were not very realistic. The most true-to-life ones have been made in recent years. *Bull Durham* was good, but I didn't like all the profanity. Some of the incidents in it seemed outlandish, but there was truth to it as it showed some of the experiences kids have in the lower minor leagues. *Field of Dreams* was well done. It captured the emotional feelings the fans have for the game. *The Natural* was good, even though it was unrealistic, a fantasy. Among the older films, I liked *The Pride of the Yankees*. It was a lovely picture. But it was more about two people, their love affair, and tragedy than about baseball."

Brown describes *The Babe Ruth Story* as "one of the worst pictures ever made. The people who made it didn't know much about the game." And he adds, "My father's pictures were good and true, but they were out-and-out comedies. He had a great feeling for the game because he was around it his entire life, but he was making comedies."

However, for all their faults, baseball movies can effectively, vividly convey a kind of emotion not found in World Series compilation films: one that is more

16

interior, more personal, whether it be a minor leaguer's dream of a cup of coffee in the Show or a major leaguer's anguish as his athletic skills erode. In the comedy-drama *It's My Turn*, Michael Douglas plays the self-assured but sensitive Ben, a recently retired ballplayer, who commences a romance with Kate (Jill Clayburgh), a math professor. There is a sequence at an Old Timers game at Yankee Stadium in which the camera pans Mickey Mantle and Bob Feller and Whitey Ford as they sing the National Anthem. In decades past, they were lean young men in their twenties playing a boys' game. In baseball, you are past your prime when you are past thirty-five. These Hall of Famers now sport gray hair and pot bellies.

It's My Turn may primarily be a film about the crisis of a modern woman as she realizes she is no longer a child in her father's house, and learns that she wants in her life the emotional depth of a two-who-*really*-live-as-one kinship. But if you have ever wondered what Michael Douglas would look like on a baseball card, this is the movie for you.

And baseball movies, at their best, can sum up the sheer poetry of the game. Woody Allen's most poignant baseball reference is in his mock-documentary *Zelig*, in which he stars as a man with so little self-esteem that he has lost his personality and become a chameleon: a "miraculous changing man" and a phenomenon of the 1920s, as famous as Charles Lindbergh. One of Leonard Zelig's first public appearances is recorded by Hearst Metrotone News at a New York Yankees training camp in St. Petersburg. A strange player is seen in the on-deck circle, as Babe

It's My Turn: Michael Douglas as Ben Lewin, Jill Clayburgh as Kate Gunzinger...and Douglas/Lewin's baseball card.

Ruth swats at warm-up pitches. "He's listed on the roster as Lou Zelig," intones the announcer, "but no one on the team has heard of him."

There's the Babe on screen; inserted into the picture is Woody/Leonard, garbed as a Yankee and leaning on a pair of bats as he awaits his turn at the plate. Observes Professor John Morton Blum, historian and author of *Interpreting Zelig*, "He was the kind of man who preferred watching baseball to, uh, reading *Moby Dick*." While under the care of psychiatrist Eudora Fletcher (Mia Farrow), Zelig opens up. "I love baseball," he says. "You know, it doesn't have to mean anything. It's just very beautiful to watch."

Christy Mathewson.

THE EARLIEST BASEBALL FILMS

ntil the financial success of *The Natural* (1984, Tri-Star), *Bull Durham* (1988, Orion) and *Field of Dreams* (1989, Universal), baseball films had mostly struck out at the box office. Nonetheless, the sport on celluloid dates as far back as *The Ball Game* (1898, Edison), made up of shots of an amateur team from Newark, New Jersey, battling an unnamed rival. That same year, American cavalrymen who soon were to fight in the Spanish American War were captured on film playing baseball at a training base. Typical short films from the century's first decade are as varied as *Play Ball on the Beach* (1906, Biograph), in which a bunch of ballplayers become angered at an umpire's call; a series featuring stars of the game—a typical title is *Christy Mathewson and the New York National League Team* (1907, Winthrop), in which there is a repeated sequence of Matty winding up and firing the ball; *His Last Game* (1909, Independent Motion Picture Company), about a baseball star on an all-Indian team who refuses a bribe from a pair of cowboy gamblers; and *Bumptious Plays Baseball* (1910, Edison), starring a comedian known as Mr. Bumptious.

Between 1916 and 1917, Universal released a series of "Baseball Bill" one-reelers directed, written and/or produced by and starring the comic Smilin' Billy Mason, who had previously perfected a vaudeville routine as a one-person ballclub. Titles in the series included *Baseball Bill, Baseball Madness* (featuring seventeen-year-old Gloria Swanson), *The Black*

Nine, and *Strike One.* Not to be outdone, Selig in 1917 marketed the "Mudville" baseball comedy shorts, featuring Lee Morris and John Lancaster. In *The Bush Leaguer,* Morris plays a pitcher who, with the aid of a hypnotist, psychically induces his opponents into committing ballfield blunders; in *Baseball at Mudville,* Lancaster and his teammates are temporarily fooled when their opponents garb themselves as the Milligan Bloomer Girls.

A couple of additional early baseball shorts are *Love, Dynamite and Baseballs* (1916, Mutual), about a pitcher (Jack Dillon) who conspires with criminals; and *Home Run Ambrose* (1918, L-Ko Motion Picture Kompany), with portly Mack Swain in the title role.

The first notable feature-length baseball films were glorified travelogues. The economically named *The Giants–White Sox World Tour* (1914, Eclectic Film Co.) is, according to *Variety,* a "long reeled picture of the baseball players' trip around the world the past winter. . . . with here and there snatches of a baseball game played between the natives and the teams in foreign countries. The well-known ballplayers who went along are shown individually at different times, with Germany Schaefer [a journeyman who, the previous season, had hit .320 in fifty-two games for Washington] always in the foreground whenever the camera was working. . . . A sort of story is attempted through 'The greatest bug in the world,' a baseball fan who is broke [and decides] to travel with the teams, upon reading the announcement of their going. . . . 'Matty' [Christy Mathewson] is there with his young

19

son, and there are other famous players. The scenic and action views are interesting in a way. . . . "

None of these early films were made as historical records, as they might be viewed today. The movies were as much a business in 1909 as 1993, and so ambitious entrepreneurs were devising other ways to market baseball on celluloid. In 1908, Essanay began filming the World Series and condensing its highlights into one- (and, later, two-) reelers that were advertised as the one and only "authorized World Series films." According to the October 4, 1913 edition of the *New York Times,*

> Within three hours after the last man is out in each game in New York next week in the world's baseball series between the [New York] Giants and the [Philadelphia] Athletics the fans who failed to see the battles on the diamond will be able to take in the game on the moving picture screens of Marcus Loew's nineteen theaters in New York and Brooklyn. By an arrangement completed yesterday with Manager [John] McGraw, Manager [Connie] Mack, and the National Commission, Loew obtained the rights to the films, paying $8,000 into the fund which will go to the players for the privilege. This sum was paid for the New York City rights alone. The moving pictures will pay many times that amount for their rights. The cameras in the Polo Grounds will begin to take pictures early each afternoon, and just as soon as each 200 feet is reeled off it will be rushed to the developing and printing room. In this manner as early as 7 o'clock each evening after the game there will be a supply of films ready for showing at the theaters, and by the time the early reels have been thrown upon the screens the late films will have come out of the dark room.

3

CHARLES RAY

Easily the best of the early baseball features is *The Busher* (1919, Famous Players-Lasky). It stars Charles Ray, then at his peak playing country bumpkins who, in the final reel, would transcend their oafishness to earn admiration from their peers and win the heroine. Ray is most appealing in this comedy-drama as Ben Harding, the "baseball pride of Brownsville," a fireballing hurler who, when he pitches, has "got more curves than a stovepipe." Ben strikes out the toughest hitter of the St. Paul Pink Sox in an exhibition, resulting in a call to the major leagues. After being exposed to big-city life, Ben is transformed from rube to dandy. He becomes involved with a gold-digger and even snubs his neighbors and his girl, Mazie Palmer (Colleen Moore), when they come to see him play.

Harding's high living soon adversely effects his pitching, and he is released by the Pink Sox. Months pass, and "the lesson of many hardships brings the prodigal's return" to Brownsville. At first, the now-penniless hurler proclaims that he will never again toss a baseball. But when Brownsville is set to play Centerville in a game that "means everything to local pride," Harding pitches his team to victory and hits the game-winning home run. His rehabilitation now is complete. He is no longer a conceited, self-pitying jerk. More important, he has come to appreciate the love and dedication of Mazie, and the simple, real, and lasting values she represents.

The Busher celebrates an America that once was:

The Busher: Charles Ray as Ben Harding.

The Pinch Hitter: The Williamson College pitcher is injured; he will be replaced by Joel Parker (Charles Ray), pictured second on the left.

a nation of small towns and small-town types, unaffected by the ecological perils of the industrial revolution. This was a time in the movies when going off to the city meant going off in search of sin. When he plays for the Pink Sox, Ben Harding loses his innocence. He becomes a morally corrupted spendthrift, and must be humbled in order to find redemption. In *The Busher*, money equals arrogance; John (then billed as Jack) Gilbert does a notable supporting turn as a spoiled rich kid who attempts to buy Mazie's affection. But no amount of money or fame can replace love. Among the most effective sequences in the film are the pastoral country scenes highlighting the affection between Ben and Mazie, his small-town girl.

The premise of *The Busher*—hero allows success to swell his head, with near-tragic consequences—was to become a cinematic staple for years to come. A half decade later, when America was well into the Roaring Twenties and becoming increasingly urbanized, a film like *The Busher* would be considered laughably outdated: not so much for the cliché of Harding's changing character or his ballfield heroics as for the film's small-town values. It also was for this

reason that Ray's popularity was soon to fade.

Two years prior to *The Busher*, Ray starred in *The Pinch Hitter* (1917, Triangle). Despite its title, the film is devoid of baseball until its second half. Typically, the actor is cast as Joel Parker, a shy, gawky farmboy from Turkey Creek, Vermont, who is described as "orful bashful and sorta dummified. He don't take no interest in plowin' nor nothin' worth a man's while." Parker's father (Joseph J. Dowling), an old codger, believes his son to be doomed to failure. The lad's salvation comes in the form of a letter from Williamson College, informing him that he has been accepted for enrollment. His father allows him to go only because it was his mother's dying wish.

With his ill-fitting clothes and thrown-together suitcase, the forever droopy and forlorn Joel Parker finds himself mercilessly chided by his fellow students. Abbie Nettleton (Sylvia Bremer), owner of the Students Progressive Cream Puff Parlor, is his sole supporter. "You're going to be a great man someday," she tells him. "Begin now. Fall in love with yourself like the rest of them do." How can Parker not resist falling in love with her?

22

The Pinch Hitter: Joel Martin (Glenn Hunter) as baseball star.

The Pinch Hitter: Joel Martin (Glenn Hunter) as inept athlete.

Parker tries out for the Williamson baseball team. Athletically, he is inept; "He plays ball like a sick oyster on stilts," remarks the coach, "but he is such a boob that he ought to bring us luck." So Parker is named to the team, but as its mascot. During an important game against Bensonhurst College, Parker as always warms the bench. In the ninth inning, with the score 7–6 in Bensonhurst's favor, the Williamson pitcher injures his hand and is unable to come to bat in the bottom half of the inning. Wouldn't you know that the Williamson bench is depleted. Wouldn't you know that the tying run leads off third base. Wouldn't you know that Parker is ordered to grab a bat. Wouldn't you know that, incredibly, he wallops the game-winning homer. Joel Parker, campus fool, is now Joel Parker, Hall of Famer.

Two aspects of *The Pinch Hitter* were to remain popular in movies during the 1920s: its college campus setting and depiction (particularly in comedies) of losers who become winners by exhibiting physical prowess. The film was remade, albeit far less successfully, in 1925 by Associated Exhibitors. The remake stars Glenn Hunter and Constance Bennett, and the scenario is identical to its predecessor except that Joel's last name is Martin, his father is now his uncle, and he wears an *R* (rather than *W*) across his baseball jersey. Its premise was reworked more famously by Buster Keaton, whose character attempts to master a variety of athletic skills in *College* (1927, United Artists), and by Harold Lloyd, whose sport is football in *The Freshman*.

23

Swell-Head: Mike Donlin (as Brick Baldwin) thumbs out Wallace Ford (in the title role).

4

MIKE DONLIN

A number of ex-major leaguers have over the decades gone on to careers in show business. Chuck Connors, who had one at-bat for the Dodgers in 1949 and played in sixty-six games (hitting a forgettable .239) two seasons later for the Cubs, became a film actor and the star of TV's *The Rifleman*. In *Three Stripes in the Sun* (1955, Columbia), he is cast as a GI, stationed in Japan, who pitches in a game between Americans and Japanese. Before the contest, as per custom, the Japanese players remove their caps and bow; they are followed by the umpires, and then the Americans. After the ritual, Connors's character comments, "What would Durocher say if he saw this?"

John Beradino, Dr. Steve Hardy on the TV soap *General Hospital*, played as Johnny Berardino for the Browns, Indians, and Pirates between 1939 and 1953; he has supporting roles in the baseball features *The Kid From Cleveland* (1949, Republic) and *The Kid From Left Field* (1953, Twentieth Century-Fox), and the made-for-television movie *Don't Look Back: The Story of Leroy "Satchel" Paige* (1981, ABC). As a publicity stunt, Cleveland Indians owner Bill Veeck insured his face for $1 million.

Joe Garagiola, who caught in the majors for the Cardinals, Pirates, Cubs, and Giants between 1946 and 1954, has been a popular baseball announcer, *Today Show* regular, and *Tonight Show* guest. While he is fond of denigrating his athletic skills—unlike his childhood buddy Yogi Berra, he is no Hall of Famer—

Garagiola *did* hit .316 in the 1946 World Series.

Bob Uecker was on the roster of the Braves, Cardinals, Phillies, and Braves (in both Milwaukee and Atlanta) between 1962 and 1967. He has parlayed his talent as a raconteur into success as a baseball announcer and star of "Lite Beer" commercials and the sitcom *Mr. Belvedere*; he is a sometime movie actor, appearing as the baseball announcer in *Major League* (1989, Paramount). Uecker, whose lifetime batting average is .200, relishes self-parody. In a television version of "Casey at the Bat," which premiered in 1985 as a segment of *Shelley Duvall's Tall Tales & Legends*, he and Howard Cosell portray Joe and Ernie, a pair of baseball announcers. As Joe asks Casey (Elliott Gould) what it feels like to hit a baseball, Ernie notes, "That's something Joe never experienced in his life."

Pat Flaherty, a supporting actor in scores of films from the thirties through the fifties, was the beneficiary of Hollywood hype. In various volumes of the *International Motion Picture Almanac,* his "who's who" listing includes the following, misleading data: "From 1919, prof. baseball (Boston Red Sox, New York Giants) ... " Yet Flaherty is not mentioned in *The Baseball Encyclopedia,* which features an alphabetical listing of every major-league player from 1876 to the present. He did, however, play minor-league ball, and knew the game well enough to be the technical adviser of *Death on the Diamond* (1934, MGM), *Meet John Doe* (1941, Warner Bros.) and *The Babe Ruth Story* (1948, Allied Artists). Flaherty played supporting

Three Stripes in the Sun: Ex-major-leaguer Chuck Connors (bottom left) plays an American soldier who pitches in a ballgame in Japan. His fallen teammate is Aldo Ray; his catcher is Dick York.

Chuck Connors (standing), in one of his many post-*Rifleman* acting roles; in 1949, he played in one game for the Brooklyn Dodgers.

roles in all three; in *The Babe Ruth Story*, he was cast as longtime Boston Red Sox catcher-manager Bill Carrigan. He also appeared in *It Happened in Flatbush* (1942, Twentieth Century-Fox), *The Jackie Robinson Story* (1950, Eagle-Lion) and *The Winning Team* (1952, Warner Bros.), in the latter as Hall of Fame umpire Bill Klem; and in such Hollywood classics as *Twentieth Century, My Man Godfrey, Mutiny on the Bounty, A Star Is Born,* and *Sergeant York.*

But the original baseball basher turned Hollywood actor is Michael Joseph "Turkey Mike" Donlin, an outfielder who compiled a .333 average

John Beradino as Dr. Steve Hardy on *General Hospital.*

Bob Uecker (left) and Christopher Hewett, the stars of *Mr. Belvedere.*

Outfielder Mike Donlin Makes Hit as a Real Actor Man

Period newspaper art related to Mike Donlin's dual career as actor-athlete.

while playing for a host of teams between 1899 and 1914. Donlin's nickname derived from the turkey step and hat-tossing routine he would perform on the ballfield after one of his heroic feats. Before commencing his screen career, and even while still playing in the majors, Donlin starred in vaudeville with his actress wife, Mabel Hite. In 1909, Mike and Mabel performed a sketch titled "Stealing Home."
"It is a great sketch," reported one reviewer,

> and made a tremendous hit with the baseball fans, who were present in goodly numbers. Mike has a bad day on the diamond, he plays like a novice, and New York goes down to defeat before Pittsburg [*sic*]. Mike starts home, and had to steal in order to avoid the berating of his wife for poor playing, but he gets caught, however, and has an awful time trying to explain the reasons for his poor playing and the loss of the game. . . .

(Several paragraphs later, the

MICHAEL DONLIN
C. F. NEW YORK (N. L.)

Mike Donlin in his playing days, pictured on an American Caramel baseball card.

reviewer notes, "As a juggler W. C. Fields has few if any equals. He is an artist in his especial line and provokes much mirth with some of his juggling stunts." So, back in 1909, Donlin and Hite rated a more prominent notice than W.C. Fields.)

That same year, Donlin discussed his show business career with a writer from the *New York Review.*

"Baseball, boy, baseball," said Mr. Donlin. "Baseball first and show business second. Maybe we'll switch that order pretty soon, but right now your little playmate is mighty interested in the big game." Donlin was not bothered by his transition from ballplayer to actor. He later noted, "You see when a man's been playing baseball out in front of 30,000 people, and a lot of them of the critical sort, and mighty free with their remarks at that—well, it gives him a little assurance, enough, anyway, to let him get by when he faces an ordinary audience in a theater. So I'm not afraid on that score."

Donlin also appeared in vaudeville with Marty McHale, a hurler whose lifetime record (12–30, pitching for Boston, New York, and Cleveland in the American League between 1910 and 1916) does not reflect his

27

In the time of Mike Donlin, ballplayers regularly appeared on stage during the off-season, and baseball-related skits could be found on bills in vaudeville programs. Here is a very young El Brendel, humorously garbed in baseball attire for one such sketch; Brendel began in vaudeville in 1913, then went on to Broadway (in 1921) and the movies (in 1926).

abilities as a high baritone tenor whom *Variety* dubbed "The Baseball Caruso." McHale worked in vaudeville for twelve years, for five of which he was paired with Donlin. He recalled in a 1963 interview with Lawrence S. Ritter, then researching his classic oral history, "The Glory of Their Times," that he and Donlin were

> doing a double-entendre act called "Right Off the Bat"—not too much singing, Mike would only go through the motions—and we played the Keith-Orpheum circuit: twice

in one year we were booked into the Palace in New York, and that was when it was the Palace . . . They had nothing but the big headliners. When Mike left for Hollywood, I went back to doing a single. He made a bunch of pictures out there, and that's where he died.

A year after Donlin's major-league swan song, he starred in the appropriately-titled *Right Off the Bat* (1915, Arrow). He plays himself, and the film, according to *Variety,* is

> devoted to his experiences as a semi-professional ball player and his subsequent entrance into the national league, where he stood as a prominent star for a number of years and from which he retired with an envious record and a reputation that should assist materially in making "Right Off the Bat" a financial success.

Right Off the Bat chronicles Donlin's ascent to major-league stardom. Though devoted to baseball, he takes work as a machinist because of his shaky financial situation. Even though he has saved his beloved, Viola Bradley (Claire Mersereau), from drowning, Donlin is considered a poor marital prospect by her mother. He becomes a bush-league star; refuses to take a bribe to throw the championship game; is assaulted and locked in a room; arrives (with the aid of Viola) at the ballpark in time to score the winning run; and signs a New York Giants contract. Finally he has earned the right to wed Viola.

Commenting on his *Right Off the Bat* performance, *Variety* noted,

> Mike was a distinct surprise and, contrary to custom, could pass as a film lead on ability alone, despite the professional reputation which is his principal asset in this effort. Mike registered the various required points exceedingly, displaying emotion, joy and disappointment with a perfected ease . . .

Also cast in the film is Rita Ross Donlin, playing Viola's friend. She was Donlin's second wife, Mabel Hite having died in 1912.

While Turkey Mike never became a star, he did enjoy a steady, varied screen career. His roles include Crawshay in the John Barrymore crime drama *Raffles, the Amateur Cracksman,* and Flask in Barrymore's *The Sea Beast*; a movie studio gateman in the Colleen

Madison Square Garden: Mike Donlin, Jack Johnson, Billy Papke, Tommy Ryan, and Tod Sloan (left to right) are standing; Tom Sharkey, Jack Oakie, and Stanislaus Zbyszko (left to right) are seated.

Moore romantic comedy *Ella Cinders*; the Union General in Buster Keaton's *The General*; and Bill in *Beggars of Life*, supporting Wallace Beery, Louise Brooks, and Richard Arlen. Donlin appears as himself in, and is the technical adviser of, the baseball melodrama *Slide, Kelly, Slide* (1927, MGM), and he has roles in other baseball features, including *Hit and Run* (1924, Universal), *Warming Up* (1928, Paramount), *Hot Curves* (1930, Tiffany), and *Swell-Head* (1935, Columbia).

Donlin's most revealing late-career screen role is in the programmer *Madison Square Garden* (1932, Paramount). The film is a sports buff's find. A number of legendary scribes, among them Damon Runyon, Grantland Rice, Paul Gallico, and Westbrook Pegler, make cameo appearances, and Donlin and other famous athletes of his era appear as themselves. They include jockey Tod Sloan, wrestler Stanislaus

Zybyszko, and boxers Tom Sharkey, Billy Papke, Tommy Ryan, and, most intriguingly, the legendary Jack "The Great White Hope" Johnson. All the ex-jocks portray low-level Garden employees; Johnson, who a decade earlier had appeared in *As the World Rolls On* (1921, Andlauer Productions), in which he teaches baseball to a small but plucky young man who goes on to play for the Negro League Kansas City Monarchs, is reduced to impersonating a bug-eyed porter.

Donlin is cast as an usher. By now, he is showing his fifty-four years—he was to die in Hollywood a year after the film's release—but he has a pleasant speaking voice and an at-ease manner before the camera. With flagrant disregard of the Ruths, Cobbs, Tris Speakers, Honus Wagners, and other Hall of Famers of Donlin's day, Turkey Mike is introduced as "the greatest ballplayer of all time."

Ty Cobb.

5
COBB, MCGRAW...
AND BABE RUTH

Scores of real-life nonactor ballplayers have been cast in movies as far back as *Hal Chase's Home Run* (1911, Kalem); *The Baseball Bug* (1911, Thanhouser), with Chief Bender, Jack Coombs, and Rube Oldring; *Baseball's Peerless Leader* (1913 Pathé), starring Frank Chance; and *Home Run Baker's Double* (1914, Kalem). The list goes on and on, all the way to Satchel Paige's appearance as a black army sergeant in the Robert Mitchum Western *The Wonderful Country* (1959, United Artists); Bo Belinsky's casting as "Bo-Bo" along with Bobby Vee, Jackie De Shannon, Eddie Hodges, Patsy Kelly, and John Ireland, Jr., in the musical drama *C'mon, Let's Live a Little* (1967, Paramount); Vida Blue's role in the blaxploitation actioner *Black Gunn* (1972, Columbia); Bucky Dent's appearance as a character named Kyle Jessup in the made-for-television movie *Dallas Cowboys Cheerleaders* (1979, ABC); and Willie Mays's bit in the comedy *When Nature Calls* (1985, Troma). The Say Hey Kid appears onscreen when an

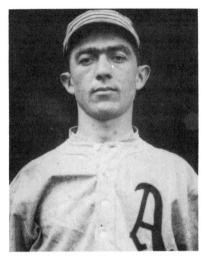

(Top) Home Run Baker. (Bottom) Hal Chase.

Indian observes that "maize" is his word for "corn."

The *Variety* review of *Somewhere in Georgia* (1916, Sunbeam), a feature scripted by Grantland Rice and starring Tyrus Raymond Cobb, the Georgia Peach, sums up the purpose of casting real-life ballplayers in movies:

> As expected, it is a production that aimed at one thing and that was to present the celebrated Ty Cobb in camera action and give the smalltown boys a chance to see 'more of him' ... and save them the long Sunday excursion trips to some of the big league towns to see him play.

Cobb stars as a bank clerk who vies with a sniveling cashier for the love of their boss's daughter. In typical fashion, he is scouted for the Detroit Tigers, makes the major leagues, is temporarily thwarted by some hooligans hired by his rival, and wins both the climactic game and the girl.

Dozens of ballplayers have appeared in movies, either playing themselves or cast in character roles. Here, in *The Stratton Story*, Jimmy Dykes (center) plays himself, in his capacity as Chicago White Sox manager; at left is Frank Morgan, and at right is James Stewart.

Breaking into the Big League: This brief series featured John McGraw and Christy Mathewson.

Before Babe Ruth, the feisty, legendary New York Giants skipper John McGraw appeared most often in fictional baseball scenarios. He starred with his Hall of Fame hurler Christy Mathewson in *Breaking Into the Big League* (1913, Kalem), consisting of two one-reelers, and is prominently cast as himself in a pair of silent features: Mike Donlin's *Right Off the Bat*, and *One Touch of Nature* (1917, Edison). The latter is the story of William Vandervoort Cosgrove (John Drew Bennett, an actor who looks a bit long in the tooth to be playing a college boy "in the midst of his third year at Yale, where he is known by the vulgar appelation of 'Battling Bill' ... "). A major-league scout comes to evaluate the boy's play. "This guy Cosgrove is so fast," he reports to McGraw, "he can lay down a bunt and be sitting on third before the catcher gets the ball."

Cosgrove falls in love with Leonora O'Brien (Viola Cain), a plumber's daughter who heads up a vaudeville dog act under the name Madame de Montignon. This displeases his father, the eminent pork packer E.P. Cosgrove (George Henry), and snooty mother (Helen Strickland). "Battling Bill" is signed to play second base for the Giants. The old man, who in his heart is a baseball nut, is proud; while refusing to go see his son play in the World Series, he phones the press box to check on the score and exudes jubilation upon hearing that Bill has smashed a triple and stolen home. E.P. can no longer contain himself, and he heads off to the game. Here, *One Touch of Nature* becomes downright silly. The old man purchases a seat right in front of Leonora and her father. Inexplicably, E.P. doesn't respond when Bill comes to the plate and waves his way. This upsets the ballplayer, who is an easy out. "Battling Bill" may be responsible for the Giants' sole run, but he is now solidly booed by the fans, and is almost pinch-hit for by McGraw. With two strikes on him, E.P. begins to cheer furiously, and the boy crashes a home run. The Giants win. And everyone lives happily ever after.

Despite its cornball theatrics, *One Touch of Nature* is a must for baseball fans mostly for the presence of John McGraw. The skipper is depicted as being not only a fine manager but a fine man; there is nary a hint of the legendary toughness that earned him the nickname Little Napoleon. One of the film's

Babe Ruth.

William Bendix in *The Babe Ruth Story*.

running gags is that, at the least bit of excitement, old man Cosgrove pops heart pills as if they are jelly beans. After doing so yet again when McGraw informs him that his son has married, the Giants skipper is seen smiling—as much, perhaps, at the silliness of the movie as at the old man's hysteria.

But the captain of any cinema all-star nine has to be Babe Ruth. Relatively speaking, the Bambino's figure was as big in movies as it was on the ballfield. What other baseball player (or, for that matter, star of any sport) has been the subject of three celluloid biographies: *The Babe Ruth Story*, released the year of the Bambino's death, with William Bendix in the title role; and more recently, *Babe Ruth* (1991, NBC), a television movie starring Stephen Lang, and *The Babe* (1992, Universal), featuring John Goodman? What other sports star has been portrayed on celluloid, either overtly or covertly, as often the Bambino? Art La Fleur plays him in *The Sandlot* (1993, Twentieth Century-Fox), and Ramon Bieri plays him in the telefeature *A Love Affair: The Eleanor and Lou Gehrig*

Story (1978, ABC). He has been caricatured in films ranging from *Casey at the Bat* (1927, Paramount) and *Slide, Kelly, Slide* to *The Natural*. He even surfaces as a character (played by Michael McManus) in the television movie *Dempsey*, a biography of the Manassa Mauler.

Ruth himself appears in a clever cameo in the Harold Lloyd comedy *Speedy* (1928, Paramount); in a series of slimly plotted, one-reel photoplays, known as the "Babe Ruth Baseball Series" (1932, Universal) and incorporating athletic instruction, with such titles as *Just Pals*, *Perfect Control*, *Fancy Curves*, *Over the Fence*, and *Slide, Babe Slide*; in a short titled *Home Run on the Keys* (1936, Vitaphone), in which he is the houseguest of a pair of songwriters; and (with Mark Koenig, Bob Meusel, and Bill Dickey) in the Lou Gehrig biography *The Pride of the Yankees* (1942, RKO-Radio). His larger-than-life, overgrown teddy-bear personality registers well on screen. If he had not been a ballplayer, he might have made an effective sidekick or foil for any number of screen comedians. One can imagine the Three Stooges being rechristened the Four Stooges, with Moe, Larry, and Curly being joined by Babe as they gleefully hurl pies at one

John Goodman in *The Babe*.

Ramon Bieri (left) as Babe Ruth in *A Love Affair: The Eleanor and Lou Gehrig Story;* he is pictured with Edward Herrmann, playing Gehrig.

Stephen Lang in *Babe Ruth*.

another, tweak each other's noses, and knock each other with mallets.

Ruth's most prominent screen roles are in two silent features: *Headin' Home* (1920, Kessel & Baumann), a comedy-drama in which he stars as a character known simply as "Babe"; the name is lengthened to "Babe Dugan" for his part in the comedy *Babe Comes Home* (1927, First National). When the latter was released, Ruth's off-the-field carousing had become such public knowledge that *New York Times* sportswriter/columnist John Kieran could casually refer to him as the "Playboy of Baseball" in a piece written the day after the Bambino hit his record-breaking sixtieth home run.

But back in 1920, Ruth still could be cast as a clean-living, mother-loving all-American boy. The "Babe" in *Headin' Home* is a character who, off the field at least, is quite unlike the man who played him: a simple, humble chap, residing with his mother and kid sister in the small town of Haverlock. Babe passes his spare time chopping down trees and fashioning them into baseball bats. He prefers quiet evenings enjoying his mother's home-cooking to attending town socials; his shyness prevents him from expressing his feelings to the girl he loves, Mildred Tobin (Ruth Taylor), a banker's daughter. He lofts a game-winning home run in a local exhibition contest; rescues Mildred from the clutches of a crook; rises to fame in the Big City as a home-run-hitting baseball

star; sets Mildred's playboy brother straight after he is suckered by a vamp; returns home a hero; and, at the finale, homers in front of the Haverlock population, who have come out to see him play. *Headin' Home* is at once an ode to the sanctity of motherhood and the wholesome joys of small-town life and small-town love.

Even as early as 1920, Babe Ruth was so popular that a mere movie palace was insufficient for a screening of *Headin' Home*. Instead, the film was booked into Madison Square Garden. According to *Variety,*

> Just as the crowds get up and leave the Polo Grounds [this was before the Babe "built" Yankee Stadium] satisfied, after watching the big slugger bury one in the top of the grandstand, just so they were satisfied at the Garden when Babe won the game for the home club after wandering through countless scenes dressed in street attire and toting a piece of hickory from which he was supposedly fashioning the bat that later on was to make him famous. There is a story running through the picture and so many minor characters that it

34

would take a computing machine to record them all without the aid of a program. None of the latter were on sale, but everything else was, from Babe Ruth phonographic records to the Babe Ruth song, "Oh You Babe Ruth," which was sung and played by Lieut. J. Tim Bryan's Black Devil Band, who accompanied the picture.

The *Variety* critic may not have liked *Headin' Home*, but he understood the Babe's appeal.

The picture has been thrown together to capitalize [on] Ruth's tremendous popularity and as such it will do a success. Ten thousand people sat patiently through the dreary preliminary scenes waiting for their idol to reach his specialty which is the promulgation of home runs. This is an age of specialists and as a picture star Ruth qualifies as the greatest batsman that baseball has ever developed.

In *Babe Comes Home*, Ruth enacts a role that is more reflective of the real Bambino: a baseball star with an affinity for dirtying his uniform with tobacco stains. Anna Q. Nilsson plays Vernie, the laundress

The Bambino (right) portrayed himself in *The Pride of the Yankees;* at center is Harry Harvey, playing Joe McCarthy; at left is Bill Dickey, cast as himself.

who must clean his uniforms, and who sets out to change him. Predictably the pair become engaged; the ballplayer attempts to reform in the name of love, but slumps badly and is benched. After coming to understand the Babe's need for tobacco, Vernie relents and gives the big guy a plug of the stuff during an important game. Babe is revitalized, just as Popeye the Sailor is after chugging down a can of spinach, and he wins the contest with a homer. There is a point to the scenario: if the Babe were not allowed to be, well, the Babe, he just might not have been able to bash all those real-life home runs.

Ruth's show biz link was not limited to film, as he was featured in vaudeville and on radio. The September 18, 1936, New York *Daily News* reported that

The Kate Smith premiere was distinguished by the first appearance of Babe Ruth as a professional radio comedian. He bandied dialogue with the big gal in a skit entitled, fairly enough, 'Babe and Kate' . . .

Babe Comes Home: Babe Ruth, as Babe Dugan, steps up to the plate.

I don't believe the Babe will ever threaten the crowns of Fred Allen, Jack Benny, or Ed Wynn. But considering his training, he read his lines surprisingly well.

The ballplayer also played an unlikely role in the history of the Broadway musical. He began his major-league career in 1914 as a pitcher for the Boston Red Sox. Ruth was a twenty-game winner in 1916 and 1917, but his abilities with a bat made him more valuable to the team as an everyday player. After Ruth's winning nine and losing five in 1919—and hitting a then major-league-record twenty-nine homers while playing 111 games in the outfield—Boston owner Harry Frazee, intent on raising enough cash to produce *No! No! Nanette!* on stage, sold his goldmine to New York for $125,000 and a $300,000 loan. By 1923, eleven of his Bosox had joined Ruth in New York. While *Nanette* was to become one of the most successful musical comedies of its time, for Bosox fans from the era of the Babe to Boggs this transaction ranks with the treachery of Walter O'Malley's moving the Dodgers out of Brooklyn.

Babe Comes Home: Anna Q. Nilsson as Vernie, Babe Ruth as Babe Dugan.

36

BABE RUTH BIOGRAPHIES

"The man was so vast, so complex and so totally incredible," wrote *New York Times* sports columnist Arthur Daley two days after the death of George Herman Ruth in 1948, "that he makes mere words so puny and insufficient. ... No Hollywood scenarist would dare borrow fragments of the Babe's life for use in a plot. They would seem much too fantastic for belief." Obviously, Daley had not yet seen *The Babe Ruth Story*. While the scenario does borrow these "fragments," the result is the *Titanic* of baseball movies: an astonishingly awful, revisionist film that plays like a 106-minute-long press release while offering the complexity of a jigsaw puzzle designed for a five-year-old.

The scenario dutifully covers the bases of the Babe's life: his youth on the Baltimore waterfront and years at St. Mary's Industrial School for Boys, where Brother Matthias (Charles Bickford), a kindly priest, exhibits paternal concern for young George Herman; his becoming a star pitcher with the minor-league Baltimore Orioles, whose manager, Jack Dunn (William Frawley), inadvertently nicknames him upon observing, "Wait'll my boys get a look at this Babe"; his meeting his future wife Claire (Claire Trevor)—there is no mention of his first wife Helen in the scenario—when she diagnoses the cause of a pitching slump; his falling obsessively in love with her, and her

(Right) The Bambino offers batting tips to William Bendix on the set of *The Babe Ruth Story*.

reluctantly falling in love with him; his major-league stardom with the Boston Red Sox; his conversion from ace hurler to home-run-hitting outfielder; his coming over to the New York Yankees; his numerous athletic feats and records; his on-field decline upon falling victim to father time; and, finally, his being inflicted with a fatal illness.

Beyond this skeleton of a plot, the film paints a ridiculously obvious, unashamedly rosy portrait of the ballplayer. Young George's boyhood troubles stem from innocently bashing baseballs through storefront windows and having to face an unfairly stern bartender-father. At St. Mary's, he is depicted as an awestruck, obedient youth; at his peak, he is an affable jokester and self-confident sports star. In no way is this Babe brash. His legendary propensity for overindulgence is glossed over, as he never crosses the line between clowning and boorishness.

At his worst, Ruth is portrayed as a well-meaning soul whose good intentions occasionally obscure his good judgment. His troubles with his manager, Miller Huggins (Fred Lightner), according to *The Babe Ruth Story*, were the result of the skipper's misunderstanding of the Babe's concern for others. "You've broken every rule in the book and laughed it off," Huggins tells Ruth after the Babe absentmindedly misses a game to help a boy and his injured dog. Ruth then is

The Babe Ruth Story: William Bendix in the title role.

fined and suspended, and is referred to in a newpaper as the "Bad Boy of Baseball." He is approached by a pair of gamblers, who offer him cash to throw a game. Ruth socks both in the face, and summarily is arrested for beating up "two innocent bystanders." The Babe cannot shake this unjust reputation. When he is fatally ill, he grimaces in pain after being lightly slapped on the back in a friendly gesture. An elevator stops, and its operator jokes that the Babe must have had "one too many."

Ruth staunchly defends the game even after being gypped out of a vice-presidency with the Boston Braves. It is suggested that he sue baseball. "That would be like suing the church," the Bambino responds, in astonishment. At another point in the film, he is offered a spot as manager of the Yankees' minor-league club in Newark. The Babe declines, because it would mean the firing of the team's present skipper. Could this incident be a variation of the one described by Robert Creamer in his biography, *Babe: The Legend Comes to Life*? "The [Jacob] Ruppert estate sold the Yankees to a syndicate headed by [Larry] MacPhail," Creamer reports,

and [Ed] Barrow was no longer running the team. Ruth phoned MacPhail and asked

The Babe Ruth Story: Claire Trevor as Claire Ruth, William Bendix as Babe Ruth.

him for the job of managing the Yankees' Newark farm club. It was an embarrassing retreat from his long-held position that he was a big leaguer who did not have to go back to the minors as an apprentice, but he was being realistic. MacPhail said he would get back to him. There was no answer for a few weeks and then a letter came. "That's bad news," Ruth said. "When it's good news, they telephone."

Babe Ruth never did manage, at any level of professional baseball.

Other than the nameless gamblers, there are no villains in *The Babe Ruth Story*. At first, Miller Huggins is portrayed as a shrimp who unfairly disciplines the Babe without determining the facts. But he is quick to defend the ballplayer in a long-winded speech when Ruppert (Matt Briggs) complains about the team's seventh-place finish in 1925. Of course, Ruth makes "the most phenomenal comeback in the history of baseball" when he hits sixty home runs in 1927. He repays Huggins during another of the film's low points, in a speech over the manager's corpse that ends with an emotional "Whatever team you're playing on now, Hug, I know they'll be winners. Goodbye, Hug."

Ruth's teammate, Lou Gehrig, is conveniently absent from the film. There is a sole reference to the Iron Horse—"Lou Gehrig's gone," the Babe observes, while in retirement—and no mention of the pair's famous feud, which resulted in their not being on speaking terms. In the prelude of *The Babe Ruth Story*, a bunch of kids visiting the Baseball Hall of Fame lower their heads on cue upon learning of Gehrig's fate. This acknowledgment seems tacked onto the film, as if to undo the embarrassment of Gehrig's absence in the scenario's main section.

The Babe Ruth Story features another misrepre-

The Babe Ruth Story: Miller Huggins (Fred Lightner) is flustered by the Babe's youthful exuberance.

sentation. For decades, Ruth's legendary called home run off the Chicago Cubs' Charlie Root in the 1932 World Series has been a subject of controversy. Did the ballplayer actually point to the stands? Eyewitnesses have disagreed over what actually happened. But according to *The Babe Ruth Story*, the Bambino not only called the shot with an elaborate, exaggerated gesture but did so because he had promised a desperately ill boy that he would "sock a home run into the centerfield bleachers," an "addition" to the story that is pure fantasy. During the game, Claire yells to the Babe, "Don't forget Johnny." He summarily tips his cap and points to the stands. He gestures again after taking two strikes, and then fulfills his promise. This evokes a smile from Johnny, who has been listening to the game on radio.

In the Lou Gehrig biography *The Pride of the Yankees*, the Iron Horse is treated with similar deference, but that film's artistry makes its scenario seem palatable. However, the simplistic script of *The Babe Ruth Story* results in unintentional comedy. There is an embarrassing lack of subtlety in the playing of a scene in which a crippled boy miraculously lifts him-

The Babe Ruth Story: The Bambino, with Pee Wee and his master.

the cancer with an experimental new drug, a synthetic relative of folic acid, part of the vitamin B complex. . . . His dramatic improvement was apparently only a temporary remission of the cancer, and he continued painfully ill." On the evening of July 26, 1948, Ruth attended the premiere of *The Babe Ruth Story.* "He was very uncomfortable watching the film," writes Creamer, "and left well before it was over." The ballplayer died on August 16.)

William Bendix, an otherwise fine actor, is unconvincing as the Sultan of Swat. The burly, New York City–born character performer's involvement with the game preceded his show business career. "When he wasn't playing broomstick baseball on the city streets," reported the September 2, 1944, edition of the *Saturday Evening Post,*

> [Bendix] hung around the Polo Grounds, worshipping the players. At thirteen, he got a job as turnstile boy for fifty cents a game, plus free admission. Later, he was advanced to locker boy at $1.25 a day. "Remember the time Babe Ruth went to the hospital with acute indigestion?" Bendix recalled proudly. "Well, I'm the guy who got him the thirty hot dogs, twelve bottles of pop and all the peanuts and chocolate he et during the game!"

But he is so miscast as Ruth that director Roy Del Ruth (who is no relation to the Bambino) might

self up after being greeted by the Babe, who has just smacked a six-hundred-foot home run while in Tampa during spring training. "They said he'd always be an invalid," says the lad's incredulous father. "Spend his life on his back. Now look at him. Just look. Oh, God bless that man. God bless him." Next comes the hilariously awful sequence in which the Babe lines a batting practice pitch which hits the little dog, named Pee Wee, who has run onto the field. "Don't let my little dog die," pleads Pee Wee's pint-sized, freckle-faced master. The ballplayer implores a doctor in a "human" hospital to operate on the pooch. "Ah, gee, Babe, you're wonderful," the boy tells the Babe after the operation's success.

Finally, there is the Babe's fatal illness. To the very end, he is depicted as being awash in humility. Upon his hospitalization, he is the recipient of "so much mail, [it] makes me feel important." Ruth's disease and treatment are unnamed. He is offered a new, experimental serum, that has only been tested on animals and that might hasten his demise. "Does that mean if I take it and it works it might help other people?" he asks. He is told that it will, and responds, "Okay, doc, let's go." (Ruth was afflicted with cancer and, according to Robert Creamer, he "never was told he had cancer, but he certainly knew it, at least toward the end." Creamer notes, "By June 1947 the pain had become so bad that his doctors decided to treat

The Babe Ruth Story: Ruth nears the end of his playing career with the Boston Braves.

better have played the role. Bendix, forty-two when he made the film, is most ludicrous when impersonating "Big George," an eighteen-year-old St. Mary's student. He was not the first choice to play Ruth. "I wanted Paul Douglas for the part," wrote Bob Considine, the film's co-scripter, in his "On the Line" column in the New York *Journal-American.* "He looked a little like an earlier form of the Babe, knew Babe, knew baseball, and moved like an athlete. He . . . wanted the part so badly he would have played it for nothing." Perhaps it was to Douglas's benefit that he lost the role.

Observed Robert Creamer (prior to the release of *Babe Ruth* and *The Babe*), "For thousands of people, maybe millions, William Bendix in a baseball suit is what Babe Ruth looked like. Which is a terrible shame because lots of men look like William Bendix but nobody else ever looked like Babe Ruth."

The Babe, compared with *The Babe Ruth Story,* is the equivalent of *Casablanca, Citizen Kane,* or *Gone With the Wind.* On its own, *The Babe* is an ordinary sports biography, as easily liked as disliked but undeniably uplifted by the engaging presence of its star, John Goodman, and its dazzling period production design. Unlike *The Babe Ruth Story,* the scenario highlights all of the Bambino's legendary overindulgences, along with his failed first marriage, his troubled relationships with Miller Huggins and Jacob Ruppert, and his unfulfilled desire to manage the Yankees.

The Babe is most noticeably set apart from *The Babe Ruth Story* and other, Production Code–influenced biographies in that it reports all the warts of its subject. Here, the ballplayer has a Ruthian erotic appetite. Early in his first marriage, he and his wife have sex three times in one day, with the Babe hungry for a fourth. He sleeps with his second wife before his divorce from his first, and makes headlines by cavorting with a sixteen-year-old. He frequents prostitutes; at one point, he passes a night in a French Quarter brothel with four women. Ever the coarse jokester, Ruth's bag of gags include a routine in which he asks a woman to pull on his finger. After doing so, the Bambino loudly passes wind.

The Babe is "based on true events" in Ruth's life occurring between 1902 and 1935. The scenario traces the familiar biographical data: young George Herman's incarceration at St. Mary's; his signing by Jack Dunn (J.C. Quinn); his years with the Red Sox and Yankees, and his astounding ability to belt baseballs farther than any ballplayer ever had before; his

overindulgences, as well as fondness for children; his rushing to the hospital bed of Johnny Sylvester, and delivering on a promise to belt two dingers for the lad; the legendary "pointed" home run; and his final three big-league dingers, hit during one game at Pittsburgh's Forbes Field while a member of the Boston Braves. The Braves' owner considers the fading athlete "a circus act, a sideshow" who is on the last-place club strictly as a gate attraction. But these three smashes, described as "the first balls ever hit out of

The Babe Ruth Story: The fatal illness.

this massive park," allow Ruth to bow out from the majors with a touch of grace. As he walks off the field, he is ever-so-conveniently approached by a now-grown-up Johnny Sylvester. "I'm gone, Johnny. I'm gone," Ruth tells him. (The Babe actually uttered a variation of this line to his friend, Jumpin' Joe Dugan [played in the film by Bruce Boxleitner], several weeks before his death, during the twenty-fifth anniversary celebration of the opening of Yankee Stadium. When Dugan asked the Babe how he was feeling, Ruth responded, "Joe, I'm gone. I'm gone, Joe.")

In *The Babe,* Ruth's first wife Helen (Trini Alvarado) is shown to be like the character of Claire Ruth in *The Babe Ruth Story*: she is unimpressed by

Babe's celebrity, but is won over by his ingratiating personality. Because Helen is a modest young woman who likes animals, gets a charge out of feeding chickens, and detests the spotlight and her husband's after-hours life-style, their marriage is doomed. The Claire Ruth in *The Babe*, as played by Kelly McGillis, is a worldly woman far more suited to his personality: a Ziegfeld Follies showgirl who is acquainted with Al Capone and Johnny Torrio, and is not at all bothered by Ruth's life-style. She accepts the man, loves him, and understands him perhaps better than he understands himself. "You have two speeds, Babe," Claire astutely observes. "Fast and stop." She remains loyal, even when the rest of civilization views Ruth as a clown and has-been.

In its favor, *The Babe* does not sentimentalize either its hero or his sport. Ruth's childhood is one of

The Babe: The Sultan of Swat (John Goodman), in some of his favorite company.

The Babe: Babe Ruth (John Goodman), pictured with his two wives. At top is Claire (Kelly McGillis); at bottom is Helen (Trini Alvarado).

abject cruelty. Unlike in *The Babe Ruth Story*, St. Mary's is portrayed as a grim environment, a combination military school and jail. George Herman is taunted by the other boys for being "too fat and ugly"; when he lashes back in self-defense, he is beaten mercilessly by the Brothers. Early on, Claire asks Babe if he has a dream. He responds that he wants to be the Yankees' manager. "Someday," he says, "I want to be the one in charge." In 1932, Jacob Ruppert (Bernard Kates) promises Babe that if the Yankees beat the Cubs in the World Series he will one day be the team's skipper. The Yankees win, but Ruth never does manage the Yankees, or any other major-league team. Later on, Ruppert tells Ruth, "How can you manage a team when you can't even manage yourself?" The ballplayer may have matured, but he is unable to transcend his reputation for lacking self-discipline. Still, the Babe asks the Yankee owner, "Ty Cobb is managing. Tris Speaker. Why not Babe Ruth?" Ruppert then offers him the job as Newark skipper, a position that Ruth declines (because he considers the proposition an insult, not because of his concern for another man's unemployment). "You don't offer a captain a waiter's job," Claire Ruth tells Ruppert. When she declares, "That overgrown child saved baseball after the Black Sox scandal," she is

Jumpin' Joe Dugan; several weeks prior to Babe Ruth's death, the Bambino told his old friend, "Joe, I'm gone. I'm gone, Joe."

stating a fact, not hyping her husband's accomplishments. In *The Babe*, Ruth does not receive the deference deserving of one of the game's elder statesmen. This, too, is no misrepresentation. At the finale, after hitting his three homers, Babe removes his Braves cap and drops it at the feet of the team's owner. This act is reminiscent of sheriff Gary Cooper's dropping his badge into the dust at the end of *High Noon*: a disrepect for hypocritical authority that, given what has transpired, is a fitting finale to both scenarios.

Resenting the restrictions placed on him by Miller Huggins (Joe Ragno), Ruth rebels and finds himself fined and suspended. But there is no forgiveness, no eulogizing, when the Mighty Mite dies in 1929. Huggins simply disappears from the story; their volatile relationship is not tempered by Huggins's death. Ruth is shown to dislike Lou Gehrig (Michael McGrady) from the latter's days as a rookie, because he senses that the home-run-hitting first baseman will steal his spotlight as the Yankees' premier slugger. Babe also derisively refers to Gehrig as "momma's boy." Perhaps Ruth resents Gehrig (whom he insults, intentionally or not, by calling "Gallagher") because Gehrig has a mother who is so attentive; Ruth's parents, after all, abandoned him at St. Mary's, and his mother died during his stay there. But this is never overtly explored. Neither is Ruth's love of children and special concern for kids in orphanages and hospi-

tals directly related to his childhood. Nor is his desire to be manager, to be the "one in charge," contrasted to his treatment by those in charge of St. Mary's. *The Babe* never means to be a psychological portrait of Babe Ruth. It just depicts the events in the man's life, the quirks of his personality, and his triumphs and disappointments.

Robert Creamer's biography serves as the source material for *Babe Ruth*, the television movie that premiered several months before *The Babe*. The scenario differs from those of *The Babe* and *The Babe Ruth Story* in that it focuses on the Bambino's life from his sale to the New York Yankees; the major variation is that, in the television movie, not once is the ballplayer seen at the bedside of a deathly ill child. All three films are alike in that the did-he-or-didn't-he controversy surrounding Ruth's called World Series home run remains unacknowledged. The Babe is shown to call the shot, and hit the homer.

Stephen Lang effectively plays the Babe as a boisterous, overgrown child who earns respect for his on-field exploits but never learns how to behave as an adult. Also of note is the clever casting of Pete Rose, the man who would smash Ty Cobb's lifetime record for career base hits, in a cameo as the Georgia Peach.

The Babe: Bruce Boxleitner as Jumpin' Joe Dugan.

RUTHIAN CARICATURES

Slide, Kelly, Slide and Casey at the Bat each came to movie theaters in 1927, when Babe Ruth already had earned the status of living legend. With a sly wink at the audience, the characters played by William Haines in the former and Wallace Beery in the latter have within them more than a bit of the Bambino.

Take Jim Kelly, the hero of *Slide, Kelly, Slide*. He is an ace pitcher *and* home run hitter. He is an overgrown boy and practical joker. He has no regard for authority, in that he is constantly disobeying his manager just as the Babe fought with Miller Huggins. He has an eye for attractive women; even though he is in love, Kelly thoughtlessly flirts with a girl on a train. But he is a fan favorite, and he adores kids (in the person of a homeless ragamuffin, who is a clone of the Jackie Coogan character in Charlie Chaplin's *The Kid*).

As if to disguise Kelly's alter ego, the character is named for another notorious real-life diamond legend: Michael Joseph "King" Kelly, one of the nineteenth-century's greatest ballplayers. Between 1878 and 1893, Kelly compiled a .307 average while catching and playing outfield (and occasionally all four infield positions) for a variety of teams. Kelly, who made the Baseball Hall of Fame in 1945, was a daring baserunner, and is credited with originating the hit-

Mike Kelly.

and-run play. His exploits on the basepaths caused fans to cheer him on with chants of "Slide, Kelly, Slide." Yet Kelly was as equally known for his love of straight whiskey. According to baseball historian Harvey Frommer, "'King Kel' could outdo any man moving from base to base or bar to bar."

The scenario of *Slide, Kelly, Slide* further blends fact, fiction, and myth. The team for which Jim Kelly plays is called the New York Yankees, and real-life Bronx Bombers Tony Lazzeri and Bob Meusel are introduced as they train for the upcoming season in Delano, Florida. However, there are no Ruths or Gehrigs on this club, but rather a veteran catcher named "Pop" Munson (Harry Carey); a typically likable but dumb, lumbering jock, Swede Hansen (Karl Dane); and a brash, overconfident rookie, Jim Kelly.

Kelly, who has come to the Yanks from the Pottstown Wildcats, is an obnoxious braggart whose mouth is as big as his talent. He shamelessly boasts that he can pitch two balls at once. He hands out business cards introducing himself as Jim "No Hit" Kelly. He passes around exploding cigars and wears a water-squirting carnation. He even practically date rapes the girl he loves, "Pop" Munson's pert daughter Mary (Sally O'Neil). Still, you know Kelly can't be all bad because of his fondness for little Mickey Martin (Junior Coghlan), who has ridden the rails to Florida and who

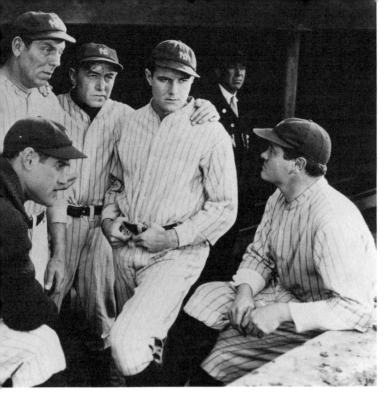

Slide, Kelly, Slide: Warner Richmond as Cliff Macklin, Karl Dane as Swede Hansen, Harry Carey as "Pop" Munson, William Haines as Jim Kelly, Paul Kelly as Dillon (clockwise).

becomes the Yankees' mascot. "Gee, Mr. Kelly," little Mickey tells him, "you're the most regular guy in the world."

Eventually, Kelly's behavior alienates his teammates, his girlfriend, and even little Mickey. In one game, the ballplayer shamelessly clowns while leading off third base. He tries to score on a sacrifice fly; his manager, Cliff Macklin (Warner Richmond), yells at him to "slide, Kelly, slide," but he doesn't—and is called out. Kelly reaches his nadir when he gets soused on the night before he is scheduled to pitch. He calls "Pop" Munson a has-been, and Macklin a four-flusher. He leaves the team, which goes on to win the pennant and battle the St. Louis Cardinals to a draw in the first six games of the World Series. By now, the Yankees mound staff is overtired, and their prospects for winning the decisive game are dim.

Wouldn't you know that Mickey will be hit by a car? Wouldn't you know that, in his delirium, he will ask that Kelly be allowed to pitch—and Macklin will agree? Wouldn't you know that Mickey will be wheeled into the ballpark, his head in bandages, just in time to offer a prayer: "It's Mickey that's askin' you, God. Just a little

bingle for Jim. . . . please!"? Wouldn't you know that Kelly will toss a courageous game and smash the game-winning inside-the-park homer? This time, as he dashes toward the plate, he will slide. Head-first, no less. The umpire will call him safe. Wouldn't you know that Mary will be there to fall into his arms?

Slide, Kelly, Slide features a couple of characters with prophetic names: a Yankee catcher named Munson, and a boy named Mickey Martin (who would have been just a few years older than a pair of future prominent Yankees, Mickey Mantle and Billy Martin). Plus, the film's hero was not the only fictional baseball champion called Kelly. There is Tom Kelly, played by Thomas Meighan in *The New Klondike* (1926, Paramount); and Larry Kelly, played by Robert Young in *Death on the Diamond.* In *It Happens Every Spring* (1949, Twentieth Century-Fox), Ray Milland stars as college professor Vernon Simpson. After successfully trying out for the St. Louis ballclub, he is asked his name. Wishing to maintain his anonymity, he blurts out that he "hadn't thought of it," and then comes up with Kelly. As Simpson begins winning ballgame after ballgame, he quickly earns the moniker "King" Kelly.

Slide, Kelly, Slide: Jim Kelly (William Haines, center) is adored by Mary Munson (Sally O'Neil), but alienates manager Cliff Macklin (Warner Richmond).

Jim Kelly is joined as a Ruthian caricature by Mike Xavier Aloysious Casey (Wallace Beery), hero of *Casey at the Bat*, a slapstick adaptation of Ernest Lawrence Thayer's famed poem that chides the cliché of last-second ball-field heroics. Thayer details the fate of Casey, star batsman of the Mudville nine. Casey comes to the plate in the ninth inning of an important game. His team is down by two runs. There are two men on base, and two outs. The self-confident ballplayer lets two strikes go by. Then, instead of smacking his usual heroic homer, "Mighty" Casey strikes out.

This expansion of the poem features humor as simple as a Three Stooges farce. It is "a story of 'The Gay Nineties,' when a woman's skirt started at the ankles and a man's thirst stopped at the corner." The setting is Centerville, a "baseball-crazy burg in the Plow and Pitchfork League." Casey is a boisterous, none-too-bright junkman and star of the local baseball team, which is "made of 'Home-Run' Casey—and a chorus of eight." A stranger by the name of O'Dowd (Ford Sterling) arrives in town; word on the street is that the "Noo York Giants" have dispatched him to sign their hero. At the finale of the Centerville nine's battle against

Casey at the Bat: Wallace Beery as Mike Xavier Aloysious Casey.

Hillside, Casey lumbers up to the plate. He smiles and clowns for the crowd as the pitcher winds up and fires two quick strikes. Casey gets set for pitch number three, which he belts for a homer that sails for miles—right into the path of O'Dowd, who is riding to the ballpark in a horse-drawn cab.

Casey is signed and quickly becomes "'Home-Run' Casey, the man who owns Broadway."

Newspaper headlines announce, "Casey's Bat Ties Pennant Race." But the content of a subhead is prophetic: "Gamblers Suspiciously Active on Eve of Tomorrow's Deciding Game." O'Dowd and Casey's hometown nemesis, Elmer Putnam (Sterling Holloway), convince the ballplayer that he is too ill to play in the game. He learns of the deception around the fourth inning, as word spreads through the stadium that the contest has been thrown. "Don't talk to me about Casey—he's a crook," is the word on the Giants bench. Casey makes it to the ballpark with two outs in the ninth inning, the bases loaded, and the Giants trailing, 4–1. He comes to the plate as a pinch hitter, and he takes his customary two called strikes, with his back toward the pitcher. "Just to show I ain't lost my battin' eye," Casey proclaims, "I'll foul one into the

Casey at the Bat: Casey (Wallace Beery) and his junk wagon.

Casey at the Bat: Casey (Wallace Beery) gets set to belt one of his patented four-baggers.

Casey at the Bat: "Home Run Casey" (Wallace Beery, front row center) and his teammates; O'Dowd (Ford Sterling), his nemesis, sits to his left.

stands!" And so he does, right into the lap of the shifty O'Dowd, who with Elmer has been betting heavily against the Giants. Casey now gets set in the batter's box. The runners lead off the bases. The scorekeeper is ready to put up a 4 on the scoreboard. The pitcher serves up a fastball. Casey swings. And misses.

His teammates, manager, and fans walk by a disbelieving Casey, brushing him off. "I never tried harder in my life, sonny," he tells a newspaperboy, while symbolically standing in the pouring rain. But there is a happy ending. Casey uncovers the treachery of O'Dowd and Putnam, who at the end are led away by the police. Plus, Casey's manager discovers that the final, catastrophic pitch was thrown with a trick ball. He tells Casey, "You couldn't have hit this educated ball with an iron-board!"

Wallace Beery's slapstick, larger-than-life performance is the entire show in *Casey at the Bat.* In Ruthian manner, Beery's Casey swats gargantuan home runs and possesses a hefty appetite for beer and chorus girls. He does not simply swig a stein of hops; after the game against Hillside, as his teammates enjoy the brew in normal-size glasses, Casey pours himself a pitcherful. Once in New York, rather than rest up for the big game, Casey drinks champagne and relishes the Floradora girls as they parade across a stage. But he is primarily a comic creation, so he also haplessly rips his trousers on the side of his junk

wagon and sits in limburger cheese. After his success, he remains little more than an illiterate rube. Garbed in his fancy New York suit, with its oversize buttons, Casey resembles a clown.

The baseball sequences in *Casey at the Bat* are anything but realistic. As Casey hits against O'Dowd during a tryout, he does so with bat in one hand and pitcher of beer in the other—and he promptly belts a country-mile homer. Nevertheless, Casey does display a Ruthian responsibility toward the game and his young fans. When he is approached about throwing the pennant-deciding game, Casey for the first time becomes serious. "If I'd strike out today," he snarls, "every kid in America would know I done it a-purpose. Now get out!"

Elmer Putnam, first introduced as Centerville's village Romeo and chicken inspector, vies with Casey for the affections of the lovely Camille (Zasu Pitts). As foolish as Casey acts, you know he is in no danger of losing Camille to Putnam because the latter is played by lanky Sterling Holloway, most at home in the role of a soda jerk. So with Putnam and O'Dowd's attempt to defame the ballplayer a failure, Casey and Camille are reunited. One can only assume that Casey's appetite for showgirls has finally been sated.

Casey and Jim Kelly are angels when compared with the Ruthian caricature in *Warming Up.* He is McRae (Philo McCullough), a prankster and home run king who, according to *Variety,* is "supposed to be a prototype of Babe Ruth" but actually is the heavy. The film's happy ending is not his to savor: McRae not only is whiffed by the hero, rookie pitcher Richard Dix, in the deciding World Series game, but loses heroine Jean Arthur to the hurler.

Egomaniacal ballplayers continued to be depict-

48

ed on screen. Certainly, Joe E. Brown played his share during the 1930s. Wallace Ford is the star of *Swell-Head*, a forgettable B film in which he portrays the title character, Terry McCall, a narcissistic home run king. As Jim Kelly, McCall is idolized by a young boy, Billy (Dickie Moore), his girlfriend's kid brother. The ballplayer quarrels with his teammate and rival, a pitcher called the Rube (Frank Moran), who is summarily traded. The teams meet in an important game. McCall jeers the Rube when he comes to bat. He crowds the plate, resulting in his being hit in the head by a pitch.

Poor Terry! He has suffered a concussion, and he goes blind. The heartbroken ballplayer disappears, and Billy catches the flu while searching for him in a rainstorm. McCall learns of Billy's illness and visits him, which inspires the boy's recovery. A famed surgeon operates on McCall, restoring his sight. The now humbled ballplayer resumes his career.

The Natural: Joe Don Baker as the Whammer, the Ruthian slugger fanned on three straight pitches by Roy Hobbs (Robert Redford). Barbara Hershey, cast as Harriet Bird, is at right; umpiring is Robert Duvall, playing sportswriter Max Mercy.

Swell-Head: Wallace Ford (left) as Terry McCall, Dickie Moore as Billy; like Jim Kelly in *Slide, Kelly, Slide*, McCall enjoys a close relationship with an adoring child.

The Whammer (Joe Don Baker), a slugger who is struck out on three pitches by Roy Hobbs (Robert Redford) in *The Natural*, is an obvious Ruthian inspiration. According to the March 3, 1982, *Variety,* TV writer-producer-director Garry Gross had announced plans for his first theatrical feature, to star Baker and be titled *The Babe Ruth Story*: a project that did not materialize. "I never saw two people who look so much alike," Gross was reported to have said, regarding Baker and Ruth. Indeed, of all the actors who have played the Babe (or Babe Ruth types) over the decades, none resembles the Sultan of Swat as does Joe Don Baker.

Perhaps the saddest caricature may be found in the murder mystery *Deadline at Dawn* (1946, RKO-Radio). The character is a minor one: Babe Dooley (Joe Sawyer), a slobbering drunk who prowls the city streets in the wee hours in search of a dame named Edna. A pair of cops arrive to investgate the disturbance he is causing. Their mood changes from gruff to friendly once they discern the identity of the drunk. "Hey, it's the Babe, Babe Dooley," one of them observes. "Nothin's too good for the Babe," adds the other. "Are we gonna' cop the pennant this year, Babe?" But the ballplayer is interested only in copping another "drinkie." Notes another character, tough-guy Joseph Calleia, "There's a fat ballplayer who some night will die in the streets."

DeWolf Hopper.

CASEY AT THE BAT

n forty-five years, DeWolf Hopper, Broadway matinee idol and husband of gossip columnist/actress Hedda Hopper, recited "Casey at the Bat" perhaps ten thousand times. The poem was first printed in the *San Francisco Examiner* on August 13, 1888; Hopper initially performed it a year later, when the New York Giants and Chicago White Stockings were guests of the management at Wallacks Theatre, at Broadway and Thirteenth Street in New York City. Hopper was acting with the McCaull Opera Company in *Prince Methusalem.* "I interpolated Casey in a scene in the second act," he recalled. "It was, I presume, the first time the poem was recited in public. On his debut Casey lifted this audience, composed largely of baseball players and fans, out of their seats. When I dropped my voice to B flat, below low C, at 'the multitude was awed,' I remember seeing Buck Ewing's gallant mustachios give a single nervous twitch. And as the house, after a moment of startled silence, grasped the anticlimactic denouement, it shouted its glee."

Hopper also was quoted in the November 14, 1925, edition of the *Saturday Evening Post,* "No bronze memorial tablet marks the site [of Wallacks Theatre], yet the day may come. Lesser events have been so commemorated."

The initial celluloid *Casey at the Bat* (1899, Edison) is a comedy shot on the lawn of Thomas Edison's estate in West Orange, New Jersey. The film is short and primitive: a batter swings wildly at a pitch, striking out; he and the other players and umpires quickly end up in a brawl, and a jumble of bodies are piled up at home plate.

Hopper himself starred in *Casey at the Bat* (1916, Triangle), a feature-length drama that is an expansion of the poem. Casey, a grocery clerk and "the baseball hero of Mudville," is devoted to his niece (May Garcia). On the day of an important game against Frogtown, she injures herself while climbing a tree, and he refuses to leave her side. The yells of the fans convince Casey to come to the rescue of his team in the ninth inning, but he strikes out as he notices a messenger in the ballpark whom he thinks has arrived with bad tidings about the child. Hopper, then in his fifties, was entirely too old to play Casey. According to *Variety,* the film is

> just another good idea gone wrong. "Casey at the Bat" has been a standby of Mr. Hopper's in recitative form for many years. It should have made a corking subject for a comedy picture, but William Everett Wing, who adapted the scenario, saw fit to make a cheap mushy heart thriller of the story and the result was that the tale, coupled with Mr. Hopper, who failed utterly to look the part, and who acted it extremely badly, did not turn out at all in the manner one assumed it would from the title.

Happily, there is a filmed record of Hopper actually reciting *Casey at the Bat.* Six years later, he did so in a DeForest Phonofilm, utilizing the sound-on-film

Make Mine Music: Casey approaches the plate.

Make Mine Music: Casey strikes out.

technology developed by Thomas Case, and the result is a fascinating, unintentionally funny curio. Hopper, garbed in a tuxedo, a slightly askew bow tie, and the most obvious hairpiece, emerges from behind a curtain. "I am very glad that 'Casey at the Bat' has been asked for," he tells the camera, boastfully adding that if he "should forget a line or two here or there ... most anyone could prompt me." He then recites the poem, becoming so involved in its emotion that his eyes close and pop open at the appropriate dramatic

moments. Hopper orates as if trying to reach the patron in the last row of a theater balcony; back in 1922, sound-on-film was revolutionary and actors knew nothing of playing down to the camera. But to say that Hopper chews the curtain behind him is an understatement. He trills his *r*'s and *wr*'s; at the finale, as he describes how there is no joy in Mudville, he is practically bawling. After completing the recitation, Hopper bows slightly, smiles, and disappears behind the curtain.

Hopper's hamminess did not strike out *Casey at the Bat* as a cinematic subject. Jerry Colonna recites the poem to comic effect in the ten-part animated feature *Make Mine Music* (1946, Disney-RKO-Radio). This cartoon Casey's chest swells with ego; the "gladdened multitude" watching the game consists of several pretty damsels, who swoon at the sight of their hero. Casey struts to home plate, where he stands with his left arm at his side and his right hand almost daintily resting the bat on the ground. Pitch number one is a called strike, which whizzes by Casey; he extends his thumb, as if wishing to hitch a ride on the speeding ball. Pitch number two, which crosses the plate for a strike, finds Casey engrossed in a copy of the *Police Gazette*. Now, he is set to send Pitch number three into the stratosphere, but swings haplessly and misses. The mighty Casey goes crashing, rear-end first, into the mud.

In *Slide Donald Slide* (1949, Disney), baseball fan Donald Duck has tuned in a World Series game on the radio. Garbed in a baseball cap, he pantomimes the contest, becoming pitcher, batter, and catcher on the same play. Unfortunately, Donald's fun is sabotaged by a troublesome little bee who is intent on listening to a symphony. When "Home Run Casey" belts a long one, an exuberant Donald dashes around some imaginary bases. Casey is thrown out at the plate, ending the ballgame, and Donald slides right into the bee's stinger. The poem also is the centerpiece of an installment of *Shelley Duvall's Tall Tales & Legends*. Elliot Gould stars as Casey Frank, slugger for the Mudville Hogs. Casey's climactic strikeout in the championship game against the Boston Beaneaters inadvertently makes him a hero. It thwarts a scheme of the villainous Boss Undercrawl to turn the Hogs' ballpark into a sludge dump.

Among other versions of the poem, there is *Casey at the Bat* (1913, Vitagraph), a one-reeler featuring Harry T. Morey, Norma Talmadge, Harry Northrup, and Kate Price; and the animated *Casey Bats Again* (1953, Disney), in which Casey organizes

Casey at the Bat: Elliott Gould as Casey Frank.

Casey at the Bat: Elliott Gould as Casey, and Carol Kane.

his daughters into a girls' baseball team and dresses in drag to enter the game and drive in the winning run. On television, it was presented as *The Mighty Casey* (1955, Omnibus), a one-act opera with music by William Schuman and libretto by Jeremy Gury; and "The Mighty Casey" (1960, *The Twilight Zone*), about a pitcher who is really a robot and who loses the desire to win after receiving a heart. Lauren Bacall recited the poem in her 1953 television debut, on Ed Sullivan's Sunday evening variety show. Noted *Variety,* "Miss Bacall, of the long frame and deep voice, was given an offbeat assignment but she carried it off with flying colors. Her recitation of 'Casey at the Bat' was delivered as if she were a Mudville rooter herself. It was a socko performance."

Nonetheless, according to Hedda Hopper, the poem "has been recited by every generation since (its publication), but no one has ever been able to interpret it quite like Wolfie."

The real Lou Gehrig, as he is honored at Yankee Stadium.

A Love Affair: The Eleanor and Lou Gehrig Story: Edward Herrmann, as Gehrig, declares that "today I consider myself the luckiest man on the face of the earth."

The Pride of the Yankees: Joe McCarthy (Harry Harvey, center) hands Lou Gehrig (Gary Cooper) a plaque, prior to the Iron Horse's legendary farewell speech.

LOU GEHRIG

As in so many baseball movies, a spirited rendition of "Take Me Out to the Ball Game" plays over the opening credits of *The Pride of the Yankees*, a biography of New York Yankees Hall of Famer Lou Gehrig. But the presence of the tune is deceptive. The music quickly turns sentimental, in keeping with the fact that the film is not so much a drama of baseball as a deeply felt, tragedy-tainted love story about Gehrig and his devoted wife, Eleanor. The essence of *The Pride of the Yankees* is captured in the lyrics of Irving Berlin's "Always," the film's main theme, a tug-at-your-heartstrings song that promises a true, pure love that will transcend the boundaries of time.

The Pride of the Yankees is a film of its time: it was released in July of 1942, seven months after Pearl Harbor. As Damon Runyon notes, in the film's preface, this is "the story of a gentle young man who . . . faced death with that same valor and fortitude that has been displayed by thousands of young Americans on far-flung fields of battle . . ." The script is unashamedly patriotic, with America constantly referred to as a "wonderful country, where everyone has an equal chance." But *The Pride of the Yankees* is also of its era in that, in this nation where everybody is equal, the only African-Americans shown are porters and shoeshine boys.

Gary Cooper, then past forty (which, unless you are Nolan Ryan, is ancient for a ballplayer), may seem an unlikely choice to play Gehrig, particularly when

he is seen as a starry-eyed college student bussing tables in a Columbia University fraternity house. From a physical standpoint, Cooper's decidedly unathletic posture makes his on-the-field scenes seem quite inauthentic. But how can you not like him as Gehrig? Cooper acts the role with his distinctive ease and charm, and he *is* more believable in the role than is Edward Herrmann, who plays the Iron Horse in the television movie *A Love Affair: The Eleanor and Lou Gehrig Story* (1978, ABC).

The Pride of the Yankees chronicles Gehrig's stardom at Columbia, where he is labeled "The Babe Ruth of the Colleges"; his discovery by a sharp sports reporter (Walter Brennan, then frequently appearing in Cooper's films); his recall from Hartford to the Yankees, where he is awed by Babe Ruth, Mark Koenig, Bob Meusel, and his other teammates; his taking over at first base for Wally Pipp, and his tripping over some bats and being dubbed "Tanglefoot" by a pretty voice from the stands: Eleanor Twitchell (Teresa Wright, who plays the role as every all-American boy's wholesome dream-wife), soon to be Eleanor Gehrig. The pair court, marry, and share pure love and fun. Lou rises as a Yankee star, earning a reputation as a "guy who does his job, and nothing else." He plays in a record 2,130 straight major league games. He is stricken with amyotrophic lateral sclerosis, the malady that will kill him just short of his thirty-eighth birthday. At the finale, he delivers his famous farewell speech before sixty-two thousand fans at Yankee Stadium, in which he eloquently concludes,

The Pride of the Yankees: Teresa Wright as
Eleanor Gehrig, Gary Cooper as Lou Gehrig.

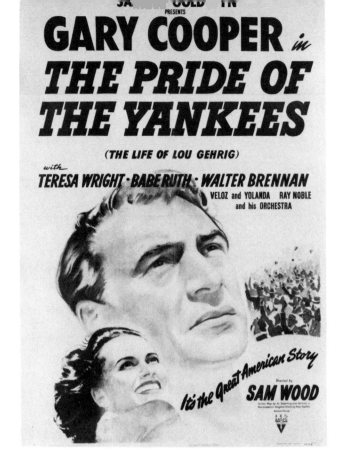

The Pride of the Yankees: Babe Ruth and Bill Dickey as themselves,
Gary Cooper as Lou Gehrig (left to right).

"People all say that I've had a bad break. But today . . .
today I consider myself the luckiest man on the face
of the earth."

Babe Ruth appears as himself in *The Pride of the
Yankees*, along with fellow Bronx Bombers Mark
Koenig, Bob Meusel, and Bill Dickey, and announcer
Bill Stern. The Babe is portrayed as a big, overgrown
clown, who relishes horsing around in the locker
room. He loves to eat. He loves to hit home runs. But
the film is Gehrig's show. The Babe may promise a
bedridden boy that he will smack a homer in the
World Series, and indeed he does, but the Iron Horse
is manipulated into predicting that he will hit two
dingers. And indeed *he* does. Incidentally, the infamous, long-standing feud between the two players is
never seen here, but is symbolically acknowledged in
the banter between Walter Brennan's sportswriter
and a snide colleague (Dan Duryea).

There is one other conflict in the film. Gehrig's
mother (Elsa Janssen) is depicted as a stubborn immigrant lady who labors as a cook and desires that her
son become an engineer. "I want you to be somebody," she tells young Lou. "In this country, you can
be anything you want to be." Her "anything" is a
white-collar professional; Lou's "anything" is a
ballplayer. Eventually she becomes her son's biggest

The Pride of the Yankees: Bill Dickey (left) as himself, Gary Cooper as Lou Gehrig.

fan. Mama is Lou's "best girl" before Eleanor comes along, but she soon accepts this new Mrs. Gehrig and learns not to be a meddling mother-in-law.

The Pride of the Yankees is the story of an authentic American hero: a true-blue guy who works hard and becomes the best that he can be; loves his mother; enjoys a perfect marriage; adores children; and, as millions of Americans were learning to do back in 1942, smiles in the face of catastrophe because, as he observes, "All the arguing in the world can't change the decision of the umpire."

While *The Pride of the Yankees* and *A Love Affair: The Eleanor and Lou Gehrig Story* focus on the couple's relationship, the latter film features nary an on-field heroic. It is a 100-hundred-percent romance, filtered through the sensibilities of Eleanor Gehrig. If ever there was a baseball movie told from the point-of-view of a devoted baseball wife, *A Love Affair . . .* is it.

The film opens with an elderly Eleanor (Blythe Danner) sitting in an empty ballpark, alone with her memories of cheering crowds—and her Lou. She has been collaborating on a book with *New York Times* sportswriter Joseph Durso. "I don't want this to be another baseball story," she explains. "Even though Lou was one of the greatest . . . I waited a long time to tell this story. . . ." The scenario then flashes back to the time in which Gehrig was diagnosed with amyotrophic lateral sclerosis, and from that point jumps

The Pride of the Yankees: Lou Gehrig (Gary Cooper, foreground) can no longer hide the amyotrophic lateral schlerosis that will eventually kill him.

back even further to chronicle their life together.

As a young, single woman, Eleanor believes that all ballplayers are "arrogant musclemen," a view that forever changes upon meeting Lou. He is a nice guy who is shy, devoted to his mother, "is not much for parties" and "doesn't drink much." Lou is more at home around first base than in the company of women. He likes Eleanor, but is incapable of properly courting her. "There were so many feelings inside him that were waiting to get out," the elderly Eleanor recalls. "He was sensitive, vulnerable, and hungry for beauty." Eventually, they acknowledge their love, which is as sweet as a Shakespeare sonnet. Early in their marriage, Eleanor declares that she is not yet ready to have children because, she tells Lou, "I don't want to share you with anybody yet." "El, I love you so," Lou tells her. "And me, you," is her response. She nicknames her beloved Luke, because "Lou Gehrig belongs to the Yankees. Luke belongs to me." The lovers talk of spending thirty, forty, fifty years together. Little do they know . . .

NEW YORK YANKEES
1939
WORLD CHAMPIONS

Edw. G. Barrow
Pres.

Geo. E. Ruppert
Vice-Pres.

Top row (left to right) — Bill Dickey; Charles Ruffing; Joe Di Maggio; Oral Hildebrand; Steve Sundra; Paul Schreiber; Johnny Murphy; Lefty Gomez; Atley Donald; Tom Henrich; Arndt Jorgens.

Center row (left to right) — Joe Gordon; Bump Hadley; Monte Pearson; Marius Russo; Lou Gehrig; George Selkirk; William Knickerbocker; Doc Painter.

Front row (left to right) — Warren Rosar; Charles Keller; Spurgeon Chandler; Jake Powell; Art Fletcher; Manager Joe McCarthy; Coach Earl Combs; Coach Dutch Schulte; Red Rolfe; Babe Dahlgren; Frankie Crosetti; Mascot Tim Sullivan (center).

The New York Yankees: Bill Dickey, who plays himself in *The Pride of the Yankees*, is first on the left in the top row; the Iron Horse himself is fourth on the right in the middle row; Joe McCarthy is seated in the center of the first row.

Several incidents depicted in *The Pride of the Yankees* are replayed here: Eleanor and Lou's rushed wedding ceremony, as movers are carrying furniture into their new home; and Lou's arriving home from the ballpark with a gigantic horseshoe around his neck on the day he plays in his two-thousandth straight game. But these are two wholly different films, and not only because of the focus on Eleanor. In the first film, Lou's mother is a loving if overprotective matron who is stubbornly but innocently jealous of her son's wife. Here, the elder Mrs. Gehrig is a viper, a mean-spirited "old country" woman (played with icy coolness by Patricia Neal) who tells Eleanor with finality, "I know how to take good care of Lou, and

you do not." She also browbeats Mr. Gehrig, whose presence is barely acknowledged. (In *The Pride of the Yankees*, Papa Gehrig is portrayed as being sweetly ineffectual.) In both films, Eleanor realizes that her marriage will be imperiled by her mother-in-law's attitude. The Mama Gehrig in *The Pride of the Yankees* softens up and comes to accept Eleanor; the mother-in-law in *A Love Affair . . .* is not as romanticized, and only acknowledges Eleanor's wifely fitness when Lou is in the throes of death.

The scenario, more than in *The Pride of the Yankees* or any of the Babe Ruth biographies, reflects on the complexities of the relationship between Gehrig and the Bambino. The Babe (Ramon Bieri) is

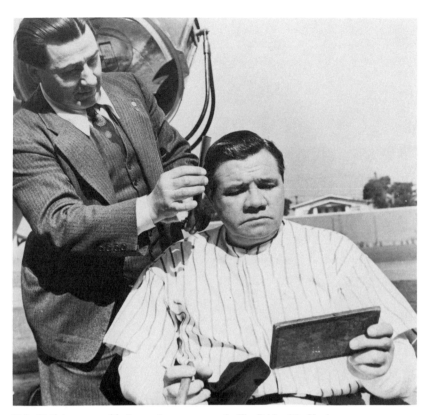

Babe Ruth is groomed before going on camera in *The Pride of the Yankees*.

A Love Affair: The Eleanor and Lou Gehrig Story: Blythe Danner as Eleanor Gehrig, Edward Herrmann as Lou Gehrig.

depicted as an aging hero who is awash in overindulgence. Lou at first makes excuses for his teammate. Then the pair feud. According to Eleanor, tension had erupted between Lou's mother and Babe and Claire Ruth. While on board a ship sailing to Yokohama during an all-star tour of Japan, Claire (Georgia Engel) clues Eleanor in on the facts, and the women conspire to patch things up between their husbands. Eleanor, Claire, and the Babe get high on champagne. Eleanor goes to meet Lou, who is angry at her for disappearing. Enter Claire and the Babe, who tells his team-

mate, "Hey, look, let's bury the hatchet." But Ruth mistakes Lou's foul mood, and there are no further peace overtures.

A Love Affair . . . ends not with Gehrig's farewell speech at Yankee Stadium, but with Eleanor watching Lou die. "We had six years of joy, and two of anguish," she recalls, "and I wouldn't trade it for forty years of lesser joy or lesser anguish." Why didn't she remarry? "I'd already had the best," is Eleanor Gehrig's simple, eloquent response.

Rawhide: Smith Ballew (left) as Larry Kimball, Lou Gehrig as himself.

BASEBALL OUT WEST

aseball and B Westerns come together most intriguingly in *Rawhide* (1938, Twentieth Century-Fox), a Smith Ballew sagebrush saga. Costarred is none other than Lou Gehrig, playing himself, who after a baseball season settles out West on a ranch with his fictitious sister (Evalyn Knapp): a plot device that enabled the Iron Horse, a devoted married man, to enjoy an unromantic relationship with the heroine. That is left for Ballew, cast as a two-fisted singing lawyer who joins the ballplayer in a battle against a racketeer bilking money from ranchers.

Gehrig displays an impressive physical presence and genial charm before the camera. In one scene, he even sings the lyrics, "... I traded [my bats] for riding boots and seven gallon hats. I played the major leagues for years with versatility. I seldom missed the flies I chased, but now the flies chase me ... " Noted Ray Robinson, in his Gehrig biography, *Iron Horse,* "It was clear that he represented little threat to matinee idols Clark Gable and Robert Taylor. However, up there on the black-and-white screen he did come off as a boyish Bronx cowboy, showing as little fear of the varmints as he had batting against the fastballs of Bob Feller." As the scenario unfolds, Gehrig employs his diamond skills as he throws billiard balls with pinpoint accuracy at the noggins of the bad guys during a robust pool-hall fight, and bats a ball through a window to disrupt a contract signing.

In retrospect, *Rawhide* is unintentionally, sadly ironic. At the beginning of the film, Gehrig is catching a train at Grand Central Station. "Lou Gehrig Goes West," reads a newspaper headline. The Iron Horse tells reporters, as one presents him with a cowboy hat, "... I'm gonna wallow in peace and quiet for the rest of my life. I'm gonna hang up my spikes for a swell old pair of carpet slippers." (Not to fear: this is a ploy in a contract dispute. In the final scene, Lou receives a telegram that reads, "Your terms acceptable. Report at once for spring training," and the ballplayer is as happy as a kid on Christmas morning.) Noted *Variety,*

> Gehrig, not just posed as most 'freak' outsiders are when put into pictures, can act and, should his baseball career come to an end, he might develop into a Bill Boyd or Buck Jones type. Photographing well, he has both the personality and the voice to insure a stamp of approval by producers as well as audiences. He's the accepted western type.

In 1938, no one could have known how soon Gehrig really would be hanging up his spikes, or how short the rest of his life would be.

Rawhide does not stand tall in the saddle as the sole Western with a baseball motif. Tom Mix dons a baseball mitt in *Stepping Fast* (1923, Fox), and Gene Autry hits a baseball through a window in *The Last Round-Up* (1947, Columbia). Then there is Hoot Gibson's *Hit and Run.* Gibson was an unusual western hero, if only because his films stressed comedy over gunplay and his characters rarely ever sported

Hit and Run: Hoot Gibson (left, foreground) as Swat Anderson, DeWitt Jennings as Joe Burns.

weapons. *Hit and Run*, in fact, can hardly be classified as a western. It may open in a desert town, but the scenario is played out in a big city. Gibson's character is no law-and-order-man, but a ballplayer whose heroics are confined to belting home runs.

The ubiquitous Mike Donlin is cast as Red McCarthy, a Blue Sox scout who is scouring the bushes for talent. He arrives in a western burg and takes in the game being played in the middle of the prairie between the Desert Twirlers and Sagebrush Rats. McCarthy is impressed with Swat Anderson (Gibson); even though the ballplayer is a thoroughly inept fielder, he can hit a baseball so far that it must be retrieved on horseback. The scout signs Anderson to a professional contract, so that he will be able to play "real baseball." This product of the wild and woolly, who is used to belting balls while garbed in cowboy boots and ten-gallon hat, becomes the talk of the game. "I wish that fence was further away," Anderson observes, after impressing the Blue Sox during his first practice. "I like to see 'em bounce." But he is not bragging. Swat Anderson is just a cowboy, stating a simple truth.

With Anderson in the lineup, the Sox are sure to win the championship. On the night before an important game, the bad guy (who also is fond of McCarthy's daughter Joan, who has become Anderson's girl) hires a bully to break Swat's arm; when this fails, his cronies kidnap Anderson and Joan, tie them up, and place them on board a train. The pair

escape and scurry to the ballpark, just in time for Anderson to pinch-hit the game-winning homer.

There is one major plot hole in *Hit and Run*. Anderson is the epitome of the bad-field, good-hit ballplayer. As an outfielder, it is noted that he "couldn't catch the measles." So wouldn't his inept fielding impact upon his reputation as a hitter? Anderson is reminiscent of Dick Stuart, a first baseman who lasted in the majors for ten seasons beginning in 1958, who was not nicknamed "Dr. Strangeglove" because he smacked forty-two home runs for the Boston Red Sox in 1963.

Cowhide-bashing and cowpunching also come together in *Out of the West* (1926, FBO). The star is Tom Tyler, popular western hero of the 1920s and 1930s; the film, according to *Variety*, "looks like the old Merriwell stuff with the home run hero at the bat. This may not sound like a 'western,' but it is a western crowd that plays [ball]; all cowhands with Tom Tyler, the big hero."

Tyler plays Tom Hanley, a cowboy who has come to work on a ranch. His formidable athletic ability allows him to play on his boss's baseball team, but he must contend with an unscrupulous foreman who has been throwing games and with a rival rancher who schemes to dispose of our hero. Hanley is kidnapped, but escapes with the help of his young sidekick (Frankie Darro, a regular in Tyler's westerns). This enables him to—you guessed it—hit a game-winning homer.

BASEBALL AND RACE

aseball films highlighting the struggles of African American ballplayers are collectively well-meaning and conciliatory. They acknowledge the reality of racism, but then point out that in America fairness will prevail. For every exclusionary bigot there is a Branch Rickey, the real-life Brooklyn Dodgers' powerbroker who initiated the integration of professional baseball; and a Roy Dean Bream, the fictional, aging career minor leaguer who befriends and tutors a young, promising black rookie in *Pastime* (1991, Miramax). As a nod to the changing face of America, movies have been remade with black actors in roles previously played by white ones. Witness *Brewster's Millions* (1985, Universal), with Richard Pryor, and the television version of *The Kid from Left Field* (1979, NBC), starring Gary Coleman and Robert Guillaume.

Baseball movies have chronicled chapters in the life of Jackie Robinson, the man who in 1947 broke the major-league color line, and have depicted how his accomplishment allowed the likes of Roy Campanella and even an aging Satchel Paige to savor the limelight of playing in the Show. With talent and dedication, even a ghetto kid like Ron LeFlore can transcend his roots and make the majors.

The one baseball movie which serves as an ode to the great black ballplayers of an earlier era is *The Bingo Long Traveling All-Stars & Motor Kings* (1976, Universal), a curiously lighthearted comedy given that its characters are victims of racism. Billy Dee Williams stars as Bingo Long, a charismatic, good-

natured Negro League pitcher in the mold of Satchel Paige. James Earl Jones plays Leon Carter, a big, tough, Josh Gibson–like catcher-slugger who is Long's on-field opponent and off-field crony. Their rivalry is friendly but intense. As pitcher faces hitter, they chide one another, hoping to achieve the edge that will result in a strikeout (if Bingo triumphs) or a home run (if Leon perseveres). Had these ballplayers been white, this face-off would be akin to Babe Ruth facing Carl Hubbell, or Mickey Mantle waving his bat against Sandy Koufax.

The villain of the story is a black man: Sallison Potter (Ted Ross), an arrogant fat cat who owns the team on which Bingo Long plays. Potter docks some of the ballplayers' salaries to cover the expenses of an injured teammate. He knows that, if the athletes are not toiling for him, they would be stuck with "nigger work"—Potter's phrase—and that would not entail wearing a suit or sitting behind a desk. For this reason, Potter is able to practically enslave the ballplayers.

Carter believes that, if they ever are to earn respect, the players will have to rise up and overthrow the owners. "Ever since I was ten years old picking turnips," he says, "I wanted to be my own man." Long has a brainstorm. Why not "shake the slave masters" by forming his own team, called the "Traveling All-Stars and Motor Kings?" He contacts the best of the Negro League ballplayers, and soon they all are barnstorming through the country, playing games against all comers.

"We gotta ruin that team before they ruin us,"

63

The Bingo Long Traveling All-Stars & Motor Kings: The team name is spelled out on the ballplayers' jerseys.

pronounces Potter. He and his fellow owners conspire to cancel the All-Stars' bookings. Their emissaries beat up Rainbow (DeWayne Jessie), one of the All-Stars, and steal the team's money. They seriously injure the right fielder, Charlie Snow (Richard Pryor, in a supporting role; he was then on the edge of celluloid superstardom). Eventually Potter pits a Negro League team against the All-Stars. If Bingo and his boys win, they can return to the league as their own franchise. Potter's thugs kidnap Carter and lock him in a coffin. He escapes just in time to pinch-hit the game-winning home run.

Unlike the "blaxploitation" films of the 1970s, *Bingo Long ...* is no superficial story that exploits the emotions of black moviegoers by depicting all whites as racists, and blacks as victims who rise up to "get whitey." At the same time, you never get to see the ugly face

The Bingo Long Traveling All-Stars & Motor Kings: James Earl Jones as Leon Carter.

of racism. There is almost a nostalgic air for the "good old days" of Long and Carter. They represent the older guard of black ballplayers, who tolerate their exclusion from the major leagues. The lone exception is Charlie Snow, who expresses his desire to play in the "white league": an idea that seems as absurd to his teammates as landing a man on the moon. He comically schemes to change his name to Carlos Navarro and pass himself off as Cuban. Later on, he has his hair cut Mohawk-style, as if he will be accept-

Nevertheless, in *Bingo Long . . .* there is no real insight into the lives of the characters, of what it meant to have been black and a baseball player in the era before Jackie Robinson. The film essentially is a lighthearted, episodic entertainment with two larger-than-life heroes, plenty of comic repartee, a car chase, and a bouncy banjo-and-trombone Dixieland score. Bingo Long realizes that he and his players are not perceived of as athletes but as funsters, so he has them parade down the Main Street of each town in

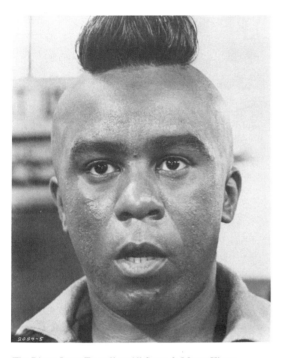

The Bingo Long Traveling All-Stars & Motor Kings: Richard Pryor as Charlie Snow.

The Bingo Long Traveling All-Stars & Motor Kings: James Earl Jones as Leon Carter, Stan Shaw as Esquire Joe Calloway, Billy Dee Williams as Bingo Long (left to right).

ed as the new Jim Thorpe.

But there is a new breed of ballplayer present in the person of nineteen-year-old Esquire Joe Calloway (Stan Shaw), a young Willie Mays who is courted by a major-league scout. The interest in him symbolically foretells the breaking of the color line, and the demise of the Negro Leagues. "Ain't no black folks gonna pay to see us play no more," Carter observes, after hearing of the Brooklyn Dodgers' desire to sign Calloway, "not when they can see kids like Esquire play with the white boys . . . " While this is wonderful for Esquire, and for Willie Mays, Henry Aaron, Frank Robinson, and other young black athletes, it was tragic for the Bingo Longs and Leon Carters of the Negro Leagues, who were born too early to see their names in big-league box scores.

which they are booked. He pitches while garbed in a gorilla suit. Even the scene in which thugs attempt to knife Charlie Snow while he is in bed with a prostitute is played as slapstick. As a result, there is little emotional impact when Snow needs to use the bathroom during a game, and is repeatedly forced to the rear of the line.

Baby-boomer baseball fans will note the presence in *Bingo Long . . .* of one of the more distinctively nicknamed major leaguers of the 1960s: Leon Lamar "Daddy Wags" Wagner, cast as one of the All-Stars.

A trio of made-for-television biographies chronicle the struggles of famed African-American ballplayers. The first to be aired was *It's Good to Be Alive* (1974, CBS), the poignant story of Roy Campanella (Paul Winfield), the Brooklyn Dodgers' Hall of Fame

65

catcher. Campy was a sturdy, indestructible athlete, a winner of three Most Valuable Player awards, who seemingly would never be slowed by age. But on the night of January 28, 1958, his career was ended at age thirty-six by an auto accident; his battle is neither with poverty nor racism, but with the resulting paralysis that rendered him a paraplegic.

The scenario focuses not on Campanella's on-field heroics but the aftermath of the mishap, his relationship with both his family (notably his first wife, an alcoholic, played by Ruby Dee), and a dedicated physical therapist (Louis Gossett, Jr.). In one memorable sequence, his inability to swat a fly emits a wail of pent-up fury. But the key to the story is Campanella's learning to overcome his rage and live with his paralysis. His life is traced through his being honored a year-and-a-half after the crackup at the Los Angeles Coliseum, when ninety-three thousand fans celebrated the man and his fortitude. At the finale, Campy, in his wheelchair, reveals to the crowd that, indeed, "It's good to be alive."

It's Good to Be Alive was followed by *One in a Million: The Ron LeFlore Story* (1978, CBS), a thoughtful film that traces the life of its subject from troubled punk on the mean streets of inner-city America to admired celebrity and All-Star outfielder for the Detroit Tigers. As the film opens, LeFlore (LeVar Burton) is shown visiting the old neighborhood, talking to street kids—and remembering his youth. For young Ron, Christmas is just a season in which you

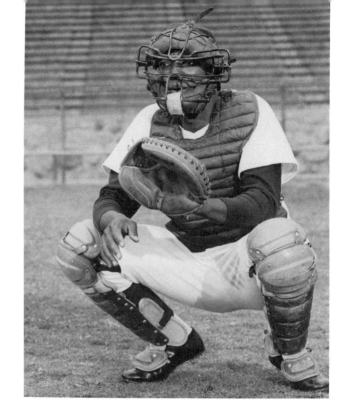

It's Good to Be Alive: Paul Winfield as Roy Campanella.

"freeze your tail." His home life is troubled; his father is embittered because his older brother, a boxer, was killed. He has been thrown out of every school in which he has been enrolled, and is faced with the constant threat of violence from the neighborhood "dudes."

Ron may be angry and alienated, but he is a decent guy who counsels his kid brother Gerald (Larry B. Scott) to stay in school and keep cracking the books. Nonetheless, he and two pals stick up a bar. Ron is busted and sentenced to five to fifteen years in the slammer. "I don't need nobody takin' care of me," is his attitude upon arriving in jail. However, he soon realizes that he is locked up in a "place for losers," and that he has been "nothing but a fool."

Ron senses that Gerald is falling victim to the streets, and determines to find an angle that will get him out of jail. Jimmy Karalla (James Luisi), a fellow inmate, tells him, "The way out . . . is being a jock." So he takes up baseball, and he is soon on the prison ball team where he bashes

The Bingo Long Traveling All-Stars & Motor Kings: Billy Dee Williams, as Bingo Long, leads the Stars on a parade through a town in which they will be playing.

One in a Million: The Ron LeFlore Story: LeVar Burton as Ron LeFlore.

Roogie's Bump: Roy Campanella (right), who appears as himself in the film, is pictured with fellow Brooklyn Dodgers Russ Meyer (left) and Carl Erskine (center), and young Robert Marriot (playing Roogie).

hits, steals bases, and makes snazzy catches in center field. Karalla pushes "Ronnie" to work hard and hone his skills, telling him that he is "one in a million." Through a contact, a bar owner who is a friend of Detroit Tigers' manager Billy Martin, Karalla arranges for the skipper to visit the prison. Subsequently, Ron tries out for the Tigers during a one-day furlough; signs a contract and does some more time, but here it is in the minors, in Clinton, Iowa, and Evansville, Indiana; arrives in the majors when Tigers outfielder Mickey Stanley breaks his hand; struggles at first but soon legs out base hits ... and leads off the bicentennial All-Star game with a hit off the San Diego Padres' Randy Jones.

LeFlore constantly preaches to Gerald about staying straight, which becomes the film's message to young people. But to its credit, *One in a Million* ... does not simplify the issue by illustrating that it is easy to "just say no." Ron tells Gerald, "You can't change the streets, but you can change you"; at the end of the film, he advises a little boy, "Listen to your folks, man, not the streets." Still, Gerald becomes a junkie, and he is shot to death during an argument about drugs. Ron's fate, to be sure, might have been the same had he not discovered athletics. While the film has a happy ending in that Ron survives the streets long enough to become a baseball star, and a symbol to his fellow prisoners, *One in a Million* ... remains sobering in that it illustrates how its subject is the exception, not the rule.

Unlike so many actors cast as jocks, Burton actually looks the part of an athlete. Billy Martin, cast as himself, is relaxed and unmannered before the camera. He doesn't walk through his scenes, but acts the role of Billy Martin. Plus, it is a pleasure to see Tigers veterans Al Kaline, Norm Cash, Bill Freehan, and Jim Northrup up close, in brief bits.

The third TV film, *Don't Look Back: The Story of Leroy "Satchel" Paige*, is an insightful, workmanlike biography of the legendary Negro League moundsman (played by Louis Gossett, Jr., with the real Paige appearing as himself at the film's beginning and end). The scenario follows Paige's career from his days as a teenage semipro player to his barnstorming years with various Negro League teams during the twenties and thirties; his relationships with his mother (Tommie Stewart) and the woman who eventually became his wife (Beverly Todd); and his camaraderie with other Negro League greats, most prominently Josh Gibson (Ernie Barnes) and Cool Papa Bell (Clifton Davis). His friendly rivalry with Gibson is particularly intriguing in view of the similar manner in which their fictionalized counterparts are depicted in *The Bingo Long Traveling All-Stars & Motor Kings*.

Unlike Bingo Long, Paige is obsessed with playing for the New York Yankees, Chicago Cubs, or St. Louis Cardinals, rather than the Homestead Grays, Kansas City Monarchs, or Pittsburgh Crawfords. As a young man, he believes that his ability alone will force at least one big-league team to sign him. As he grows

One in a Million: The Ron LeFlore Story: Billy Martin, the Detroit Tigers' skipper, as himself.

older, he learns otherwise. He heads a Negro League nine that plays an exhibition game against an all-star squad organized by Dizzy Dean. Paige chalks up twenty-one strikeouts against the likes of Lou Gehrig, Rogers Hornsby, Charlie Gehringer, Jimmy Foxx, and Pepper Martin. "We're finally going up to the major

Don't Look Back: The Story of Leroy "Satchel" Paige: Louis Gossett, Jr., as Satchel Paige.

The Kid From Cleveland: Satchel Paige, who plays himself in the film, pictured with Rusty Tamblyn.

leagues," he shouts. But he and his teammates are patronizingly told to keep "playing among yourselves." What will happen to them when they are too old to play? Like the black ballplayers before them, even the best will end up with menial jobs, washing dishes or pushing brooms.

After Jackie Robinson breaks the color line, Bill Veeck signs Paige to a contract with the Cleveland Indians. At forty-two, he becomes baseball's oldest rookie and contributes to the Indians' 1948 pennant drive; at the finale, he tosses his first pitch in the World Series. While Paige never got to pass his prime where he belonged, dueling Babe Ruth and Lou Gehrig in Yankee Stadium, he regretted nothing because, as he explains, he refused to "look back."

Another television movie, *The Court-Martial of Jackie Robinson* (1990, TNT), unspools prior to its subject's professional stardom, telling the story of a little-

A Soldier's Story: Art Evans (seated) as Private Wilkie; William Allen Young (center) as Private Henson; David Harris (right) as Private Smalls.

known incident in Robinson's life. During World War II, while in the United States Army and stationed at Camp Hood in Texas, an attempt was made to court-martial Robinson after he refused to move to the back of an army bus. It is a battle Robinson had to fight prior to his battle to integrate baseball, which was depicted forty years before in *The Jackie Robinson Story*.

Robinson (Andre Braugher) first is seen as a UCLA all-American who is contemplating quitting school because he feels that even a college degree will not enable a black man to attain a decent job. His girlfriend, Rachel (Kasi Lemmons), and mother (Ruby Dee, who played Rachel in *The Jackie Robinson Story*) implore him to remain in school. This debate becomes academic after the Japanese bomb Pearl Harbor, and Robinson is drafted into the army.

The Jackie Robinson portrayed here is a proud, hot-tempered man who refuses to conform to life in a segregated, racist military. He does not accept being called "nigger." He will speak up clearly and loudly when confronted with any sort of discrimination, even after he is transferred to Camp Hood, where traditions die hardest and "Jim Crow reigns supreme."

Joe Louis (Stan Shaw) is a character in *The Court-Martial of Jackie Robinson*. He is the ballplayer's mentor, an intelligent man whose status as heavyweight champion does not exclude him from racism. Louis deals with his anger while in the ring, by hitting his opponent first, faster, and harder, a lesson Robinson will remember once he begins playing pro ball. Black journalist Wendell Smith (J.A. Preston), who is not depicted in *The Jackie Robinson Story*, is

A Soldier's Story: Larry Riley as C.J. Memphis.

Jackie Robinson.

ter cannot deny Robinson's athletic ability, but still is the vilest of racists.

The point of *The Court-Martial of Jackie Robinson* is simple and, for any intelligent person, irrefutable: racism is heinous and idiotic. If a black soldier is prepared to die for his country, he should have the right to sit side-by-side on a bus or at a dinner table with his white counterpart.

Life in the segregated United States Army during World War II is also depicted in *A Soldier's Story* (1984, Columbia), scripted by Charles Fuller from his Pulitzer Prize–winning play. The narrative is set amid an all-black army company that is "basically a baseball team—most of the guys played in the Negro League." The team had been winning all of its games, and there was talk that it soon would be playing an exhibition against the New York Yankees. Instead, their final game was against "a sanitation company." The point is

Jackie Robinson in action.

portrayed as a leader who aggressively lobbies the baseball establishment for the game's inevitable desegregation. Smith is contrasted to the Brooklyn Dodgers' scout who eventually signs Robinson (played by Bruce Dern, with a fictional name). The lat-

70

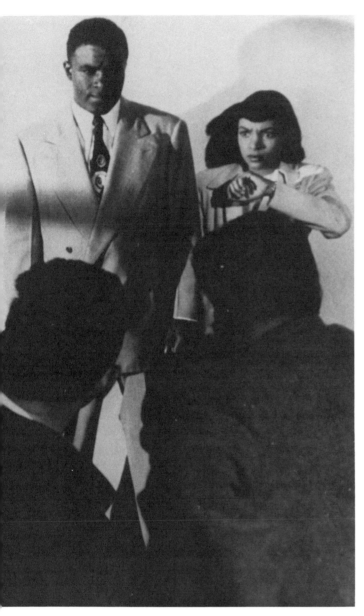

The Jackie Robinson Story: Jackie Robinson, as himself, and Ruby Dee, as wife Rachel, symbolically face the hostility of those who would rather not see the ballplayer at his first spring training.

of its era and a valuable social history. Back in 1950, the year in which *The Jackie Robinson Story* came to theaters, Hollywood was belatedly beginning to acknowledge its biased depiction of African-Americans. Previously the industry had consistently demeaned its black characters, trivializing them as stereotypical mammies, Pullman porters, and shoeshine boys who would fracture the English language. In 1949, a quartet of films—*Intruder in the Dust*, *Lost Boundaries*, *Home of the Brave*, and *Pinky*—attempted to portray blacks not only as victims of a racist society but as three-dimensional characters, as complex or tormented as white roles were allowed to be. No matter that the films were designed for white audiences. No matter that Sidney Poitier, who during the 1950s became the first black to achieve full-fledged Hollywood stardom, had to embody the one-dimensionally exemplary black man for the next two decades: the same superhuman American as the Jackie Robinson depicted in this film.

Robinson is cast as himself, and he gives an awkward but affable performance. As the scenario unfolds, Jackie grows into manhood; stars in football, basketball, and track-and-field at UCLA; plays for a while in the Negro Leagues; is scouted by the Dodgers' Clyde Sukeforth (Billy Wayne) and signed by the team's legendary master builder, Branch

that, in 1944, these Negro League players, described as "the finest baseball team in the entire United States Army," were not allowed to compete against a military team composed of white major leaguers, let alone the Bronx Bombers.

All of these films are preceded by *The Jackie Robinson Story*, which opens with a narrator proclaiming, over the image of a young black lad walking down a road, "This is the story of a boy and his dream. But more than that, it is the story of an American boy, and a dream that is truly American."

The scenario is simple and direct, at once a relic

The Jackie Robinson Story: Minor Watson (left) as Branch Rickey and Pat Flaherty as Karpen, a fictional Dodger pitcher who would like to keep Robinson off the Brooklyn team.

The Jackie Robinson Story: A number of Brooklyn Dodgers at first prefer not to play with Robinson, but come to accept him as a teammate and equal; Drew Allen, Pat Flaherty, and Billy Wayne (as Clyde Sukeforth) are pictured, starting at right.

Rickey (Minor Watson). He sublimates his anger during his year in Montreal, playing for the Dodgers' top farm club, and in his first major-league season, as racists threaten him with beatings and toss black cats on the ballfield. "I want a ballplayer with guts enough not to fight back," Rickey tells him. Jackie is to do his

The Jackie Robinson Story: After his rookie season, Robinson is finally allowed to "fight back" by testifying in Washington that "democracy works for those willing to fight for it."

talking with singles and doubles, speed on the basepaths, and sparkling fielding.

The scenario is overloaded with fair-minded white men, as if to stress that not every white American is a racist. A couple of whites acknowledge young Jackie's ability and give him his first baseball glove. An athletic department honcho at UCLA declares, "Colored boys are all right with me if they're the right color. I like a good, clean American boy with a B average. [If] that's the kind of a boy you're talking about, his colors are blue and gold." A former athletic rival recognizes and happily greets Jackie's brother Mack (Joel Fluellen), himself a talented athlete who finished second to Jesse Owens in the two-hundred-meter run at the 1936 Olympics in Berlin. The Dodgers first baseman offers Jackie pointers on playing the position, even though it might mean his demotion from the starting lineup. Many of those who are against Robinson—Montreal manager Clay Hopper (Richard Lane), and a loud-mouthed baseball fan (played by character actor Jack Carr, cast in a similar role in the baseball sequence in *Woman of the Year*)—come to favor the ballplayer once they see he is willing to dirty his uniform.

Then there is Branch Rickey, the scenario's moral backbone. Throughout the film, he spouts lines like "You know, a box score is really democratic, Jackie. It doesn't say how big you are or how your father voted in the last election or what church you attend. It just tells you how good a ballplayer you were that day. . . . It's all that ought to count, and maybe some day it's all that will count." Rickey's goal is not just winning pennants. "We're tackling something big here, Jackie," he says. "If we fail, no one'll try again for twenty years. But if we succeed . . . We're dealing with rights here. The right of any American to play baseball, the American game." Even when Robinson expresses doubts about this "experiment," Rickey is staunchly in favor of persevering.

It is easy to criticize *The Jackie Robinson Story* for idealizing its subject. The justifiable anger of the man as portrayed in *The Court-Martial of Jackie Robinson* is completely absent here, with the ballplayer presented as nothing short of a candidate for sainthood. At the finale, when he is established enough for Rickey to allow him to speak out on issues, Robinson does not lambaste racism but testifies in Washington about how "democracy works for those who are willing to fight for it, and I'm sure it's worth defending. . . . I'm certain that I and other Americans of many races and faiths have too much invested in our country's welfare to throw it away or to let it be taken from us."

Despite his athletic prowess and college degree, Mack Robinson toils as a street sweeper. He is satisfied, because at least it is a "good, steady job." Still, there is the irony and idiocy of Mack Robinson's situation. Louise Beavers, cast as Mack and Jackie's mother, does get to speak proper English, unlike her usual role as thick-witted maid who would utter such lines as "He ain't like the other men you done made history of" (spoken about Cary Grant, to Mae West, in *She Done Him Wrong*). There is a telling glimpse of life in the Negro Leagues, where ballplayers would toil for low pay and suffer through arduous bus rides and

Spike Lee, director-star, as he appears in *Do the Right Thing.*

then be prohibited from eating inside restaurants.

Without a couple of decades' worth of movies like *The Jackie Robinson Story*, Spike Lee would not be so often photographed wearing Brooklyn Dodgers caps, let alone be making films about Malcolm X, or interracial romances (*Jungle Fever*), or racial tensions in the very New York City borough abandoned by the Dodgers (*Do the Right Thing*).

A pair of trivia notes about *The Jackie Robinson Story*: Also in the cast is Kenny Washington, Jackie's UCLA gridiron teammate, playing a baseball manager. Robinson was a member of the Negro League Kansas City Monarchs when Clyde Sukeforth first saw him play. Here, the name of his team is the Black Panthers!

The Pride of St. Louis: Dan Dailey as Dizzy Dean, Joanne Dru as Pat Nash Dean.

BASEBALL BIOGRAPHIES

Jackie Robinson, Satchel Paige, Roy Campanella, Ron LeFlore, Lou Gehrig, and Babe Ruth are not the only ballplayers whose stories have been recorded on celluloid. Other biographies have told of the lives of diamond legends whose heroics earned them plaques at Cooperstown, or whose afflictions did not exclude them from hurling or hitting baseballs.

The Pride of St. Louis (1952, Twentieth Century-Fox), chronicling the career of Dizzy Dean, is a virtual clone of another baseball biography that opened in movie houses a scant six weeks later: *The Winning Team*, the story of Grover Cleveland Alexander. In each, a talented young pitcher comes out of rural America and enters professional baseball. He rises to the major leagues, leading his team to victories and pennants. After his career has peaked, he falls victim to self-pity and alcohol. His wife leaves him. He is derided for being over the hill. But before the finale, he is resurrected. He regains his self-respect. His mate is back at his side. He learns that stardom on the mound is secondary to living with dignity, and living with love.

The Pride of St. Louis opens with a title that reads, "This is a true story. A story of a few years in the life of one of the most colorful figures of our time. His name is Jerome Herman Dean. His story starts in the Ozarks—in 1928." In typical fashion, a scout watches young Diz pitch. "Hey there, young man," he tells the boy (who is played with a mile-wide smile by

thirty-eight-year-old Dan Dailey). "Right now, our deal is for you to report to the Houston club of the Texas League for a look-see. And, if you make good, the National League is the next stop. St. Louis. The St. Louis Cardinals. That's as far as anybody can go."

True to legend, Dean is portrayed as a good-natured, down-home country boy prone to boastfulness about his and kid brother Paul's athletic talents. He practices his pitching motion in a mirror, as much to admire himself as to hone his skills. He is quick to tell other hurlers how to throw, even those whose stats are leading the league. While pitching for the Houston Buffs, Dean starts an exhibition game against the Chicago White Sox. He promptly tells the lead-off batter that a pitch will be "high, fast, and inside," and whizzes the ball by for a swinging strike. Later in the game, the Pale Hose third base coach implores a hitter to "knock this dizzy kid out of the box. ... Let's drive this busher dizzy. ... Let's get busy on dizzy." And so a nickname is born. All through this, Diz is never truly obnoxious or unlikable. He is just, well, a character: one of the colorful characters of baseball.

While in Houston, he purchases clothes that he attempts to charge to the ballclub and falls for the store's acting credit manager, pert Pat Nash (Joanne Dru). Despite her protests over his pushiness, he charms his way into her heart. In his St. Louis debut, Diz comes on in relief, takes no warm-up pitches, and promptly surrenders a sharp single. He relays a "not-to-worry" message to Pat, who is watching in the

The Pride of St. Louis: Dan Dailey (right) as a stubborn, self-assured Dizzy Dean, with Hugh Sanders as Horst, the scout who discovers the hurler.

The Pride of St. Louis: Dan Dailey (left) as Dizzy Dean, Leo T. Cleary as Houston Buffalos manager Ed Monroe.

stands, and induces the next batter to rap into a double play. Soon Diz is burning up the majors, winning eighteen, twenty, thirty, twenty-eight, and twenty-four games in consecutive seasons for the Cards. He is joined on the team (which during the 1930s was affectionately known as the Gas House Gang) by brother Paul (Richard Crenna), who has been nicknamed Daffy. The pair cavort in the stands, ushering fans to their seats, or greet customers from the ticket office.

This boyish enthusiasm has its downside when Diz, pitching in an All-Star game, is hit in the left foot by a batted ball. He insists on completing his stint on the mound, but the injury eventually disables him. When he comes back, he is forced to put extra weight on his toe while throwing and his pitching motion is permanently marred. Diz is unwilling to accept a doctor's diagnosis that his arm is beyond reclamation. He is traded to the Chicago Cubs for $185,000 and three players; the Cubs do the deal because they think Dean will be a drawing card. Soon, the "old master" is back in the minors, pitching for Tulsa in the Texas League. He is released after one season.

The Pride of St. Louis: Dizzy Dean (Dan Dailey, center) and teammates (including Richard Crenna as Paul Dean, second from right) toy with a tiger; Dizzy and Daffy each won two games against the Detroit Tigers in the 1934 World Series.

Diz drinks. Diz gambles. Some card hustlers call him a "has-been." Pat leaves him. But he finds his salvation as a baseball play-by-play man, where his colorful game descriptions and infectious love of baseball

The Pride of St. Louis: Dan Dailey (right), as Dizzy Dean, shares a broadcasting booth with Chet Huntley, playing a fellow radio sportscaster.

assure his popularity with listeners. He voluntarily decides to give up broadcasting when some heads of parents and teachers organizations lobby for his ouster, feeling his desecration of the English language is negatively affecting schoolchildren. On his final broadcast, Dean tells the kids—his listeners—to get the education that he was denied, so that they may be able to speak proper English. "Each time you're up at bat," he adds, "give it everything you've got. And be sure to tag all the bases, all the time." Now, Diz finally has grown up. His rewards: Pat returns to him and the protesters drop their complaints, allowing Dean to continue in the broadcast booth.

The real Dizzy Dean, along with his brother, can be glimpsed in *Dizzy & Daffy* (1934, Warner Bros.), a two-reel comedy. They are billed as "Jerome and Paul Dean," and the scenario's first half features them playing on a bush league nine, the Farmer White Sox. Joining them for a contest against the Shanty Town No Sox is half-blind big league hurler Lefty Howard (Shemp Howard), who walks into walls, squabbles with a stuttering umpire (Roscoe Ates), and remarks, "The only Dean I ever heard of is Gunga." The brothers then are shown as St. Louis Cardinals pitching stars who lead their team to a World Series triumph against the Detroit Tigers. They are depicted as quiet but self-assured Southern boys who let their pitching do their talking. Dizzy's fastball hums into the plate so fast that it singes the catcher's glove. His next pitch deflates umpire Ates's chest protector.

The Winning Team opens with a title that is virtually identical to the one in *The Pride of St. Louis:* "This is the True Story of Grover Cleveland Alexander."

The Pride of St. Louis: Richard Crenna (left) as Paul Dean, Dan Dailey as Dizzy Dean.

Dizzy & Daffy: Paul Dean (left) and Dizzy Dean, cast as themselves.

The Winning Team: Ronald Reagan as Grover Cleveland Alexander.

Grover Cleveland Alexander.

The Hall of Famer starts out as a smalltown Nebraska boy (played by forty-one-year-old Ronald Reagan) whose fiancée is a smalltown girl, Aimee (Doris Day). He is employed as a telephone lineman, but plans to marry as soon as he can raise enough cash for the down payment on a farm. The fact that he has "been

The Winning Team: Doris Day as Aimee, Ronald Reagan as Grover Cleveland Alexander.

pitching ever since I can remember. When I wasn't throwing a ball, I was throwing a rock" does not endear him to Aimee and her practical-minded papa. Alex hurls for Central City against a team of barnstorming major leaguers, and shuts out the big boys on three hits. But his future father-in-law lambastes him for being "a fellow who wants to play," and Aimee accuses him of not wanting to get married and "settle down." She tells him, "I don't care if you play baseball once in a while, but it shouldn't be your whole life."

Of course, baseball *will* become Alex's life. He is offered one hundred dollars a month to play pro ball. Despite Aimee's protests, he joins the Galesburg team; you know she will come around to her beloved's view when she absentmindedly sings a few bars of "Take Me Out to the Ball Game" while doing household chores. Meanwhile, Alex is hit in the face with a ball and knocked unconscious. When he comes to, he sees double. His career seems over, and his contract is sold to Indianapolis; Aimee (who by now has become Mrs. Alexander) is told that Grover "could have been the greatest pitcher baseball ever had." Inexplicably, the Philadelphia Nationals pur-

78

The Winning Team: Ronald Reagan (left) as Grover Cleveland Alexander; Doris Day as Aimee; Gordon Jones as Glasheen, the man who initially notices Alex's talent.

The Winning Team: Ronald Reagan as Grover Cleveland Alexander, and Doris Day as Aimee; double vision prevents Alex from pitching, and he acts out his frustration by hurling a rock.

chase Alex's contract. One morning Alex awakens—symbolically, as the sun rises—and, glory behold, he no longer sees double. He can throw a pinpoint strike. Aimee, who has revealed that she has been jealous of Alex's love for baseball and was secretly happy when he was injured, sees how devastated Alex is at not being able to play ball. So she tells him that, now, they have got to head south for spring training. The year is 1911.

Alex strikes out Eddie Collins to lead off an exhibition game, and earns twenty-eight victories in his first big-league season. In a few years he is one of baseball's standout moundsmen. One day he pitches against a raw rookie named Rogers Hornsby (Frank Lovejoy). The scuttlebut is that, if he strikes out once again, Hornsby will be heading back to the bushes. Alex does the kid a favor by grooving in a pitch, which Hornsby smacks for a hit. The implication is that, because of Alex's kindness, Rogers Hornsby was able to stay in the major leagues and become a Hall of Famer.

After being sold to the Chicago Cubs, Alex is drafted to fight in World War I. He now hurls grenades instead of baseballs; after an explosion, he is knocked dizzy and, upon returning to the Cubs, falls ill one day in the locker room. While pitching, he passes out on the mound. A doctor—not the Cubs'

team physician—tells him that, if he expects to live out his normal life, he will have to give up baseball. That night, Alex passes out from drink in a bar. Word gets out that his ills are the result of booze. His play becomes erratic, but he tells no one—not even Aimee—the true cause of his trouble.

Soon, Alex really is drinking. Aimee leaves him. He becomes a "stumbling has-been" who boozes him-

The Winning Team: Ronald Reagan as Grover Cleveland Alexander; at left is James Millican, playing Bill Killefer, Alex's friend and teammate for eleven major-league seasons; at right is Billy Wayne, cast as Red Dooin, Alex's manager during his first four big-league seasons.

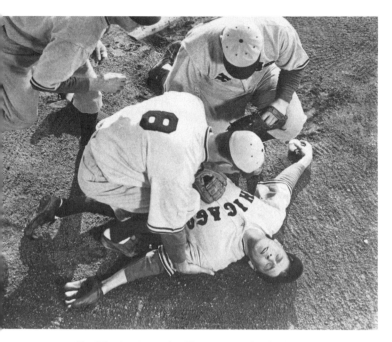

The Winning Team: An ailing Grover Cleveland Alexander (Ronald Reagan) passes out on the mound.

The Winning Team: Ronald Reagan (left) as Grover Cleveland Alexander, and Frank Lovejoy as Rogers Hornsby, who was responsible for resuscitating Alex's career.

self out of the major leagues, then a disheveled drifter scrapping for twenty-dollar bills in pickup games. Aimee learns the truth from the doctor who examined Alex, and finds him toiling as a carnival sideshow attraction. Rogers Hornsby, now manager of the St. Louis Cardinals, signs him to a contract, and soon Alex is making "the most amazing comeback in sports history." "Old Alex Wins Another," reads a newspaper headline. In the 1926 World Series, against the New York Yankees, this "forgotten man of baseball" wins two games, compiling an 0.89 ERA. He tells Aimee, "I've been stealing strength from you all season ... every game ... every pitch ..."

Back in 1952, Ronald Reagan was past his prime as a box-office commodity, while Doris Day was a rising Warner Bros. star. Even though this is the biography of Grover Cleveland Alexander, Day is billed above Reagan. In addition to "Take Me Out to the Ball Game," a musical number featuring Day happily singing about Old St. Nicholas is worked into the script.

If *The Pride of St. Louis* and *The Winning Team* tell the stories of ballplayers whose troubles come after earning their Hall of Fame stripes, *Fear Strikes Out* (1957, Paramount) details the whys and hows of the mental breakdown of a ballplayer at the outset of his career. He is Jimmy Piersall (Anthony Perkins), whose seventeen-year major-league stay commenced

in 1950 with the Boston Red Sox.

The key to the story is Jim's complex relationship with his father, John (Karl Malden). The elder Piersall is depicted not as mean-spirited or evil but as misguided, a man with an obsession that his son realize his own thwarted dream of athletic stardom. "Nothin' comes easy, and you know it," he tells his wife. "If we work hard enough, he can be a great

Fear Strikes Out: Norma Moore as Mary Teevan Piersall, Anthony Perkins as Jimmy Piersall.

Fear Strikes Out: Perry Wilson as Mrs. John Piersall, Karl Malden as John Piersall, Anthony Perkins as Jimmy Piersall (left to right).

while playing for Scranton, he is the third-leading hitter in his league, but his father's response is, "Well, it isn't first." All the while, Jim never complains, internalizing his physical and psychological pain.

While in Scranton, Jim shyly courts a nurse, Mary Teevan (Norma Moore), whom he marries. Mary's love has a stabilizing effect on Jim, but it is no solution to his problems. Finally Jim is told that he can make the Red Sox, but only if he learns to play shortstop during spring training, as the team is loaded with outfielders. From this point on, Jim is paranoically convinced that a conspiracy exists to thwart his goal. "They want to get rid of me," he says. "I don't want to go to spring training. . . . I don't want to be hurt." His dad's response: "You want them to call you yellow?"

Jim does make the team. After hitting an inside-the-park home run, he yells at his father in the stands, "How was that? Was it good enough?" Then, he has a nervous breakdown, using a bat as a weapon against his teammates before he is subdued. Jim withdraws so deeply that no one can make contact with him. As

ballplayer." So John Piersall throws a ball so hard at his son that the boy's hand becomes sore. As Jim grows up, and becomes a high-school baseball star, his father ignores his exploits while emphasizing any mistake, any lapse. Jim is signed by the Red Sox;

Fear Strikes Out: Jimmy Piersall (Anthony Perkins) is pressured yet again by his father, John (Karl Malden).

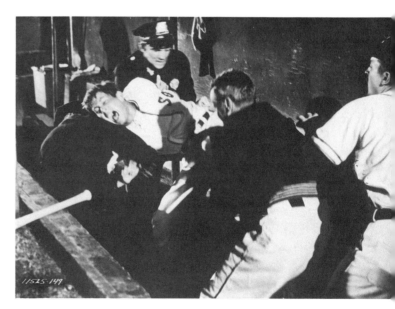

Fear Strikes Out: The crack-up.

81

Pete Gray.

a result of the patience of a dedicated psychiatrist, he comes to realize why he had the breakdown. "You couldn't satisfy that man," he exclaims, during an instant of self-discovery. The senior Piersall learns to love Jim for the person he is, and to accept the fact that Jim may not succeed on the ballfield. Jim is reunited with Mary, and he soon returns to the Red Sox.

Fear Strikes Out has less in common with other baseball films than with *The Snake Pit* and *The Three Faces of Eve*, scenarios that chronicle an individual's mental breakdown and subsequent recovery. The film offers the urban, kitchen-sink realism typical of such 1950s dramas as *On the Waterfront*, *A Hatful of Rain*, *The Bachelor Party*, *The Catered Affair*, and *Marty*, each rooted in either the headlines of the day, the theater, or live television. Piersall's story originally was staged on TV in 1955 in the dramatic anthology "Climax," with Tab Hunter cast as the ballplayer.

Trivia Note: one of the Red Sox personnel who scouts Jim is named Sekulovich; Karl Malden's real name is Mladen Sekulovich. Similarly, in *On the Waterfront*, released three years before *Fear Strikes Out*, in which Malden appears as a priest, Sekulovich is the name of one of the underlings of crooked waterfront union boss Johnny Friendly (Lee J. Cobb).

Jimmy Piersall's problems were purely psychological; those of Pete Gray were purely physical. The latter's story is told in a heartwarming television movie, *A Winner Never Quits* (1986, ABC). The hero (Keith Carradine) is a one-armed outfielder who briefly played for the St. Louis Browns during World War II. The scenario emphasizes the humility and determination of Gray, depicted as a modest fellow who only wants an athletic career. Clearly, Gray could not have achieved his dream without the unwavering support of his loving immigrant parents (Dennis Weaver, Fionula Flanagan) and his older brother (Ed O'Neill), who teaches him the basics of the game and toughens him up for all the naysayers with whom he will have to contend. The essence of the story is revealed as young Pete asks his father why he had to lose his arm. Dad responds, "You had an accident, but you lived. That's the important thing." "It's not fair," Pete complains. "Not everything is, even in this great country of America," Dad explains. "Can't be a major-league baseball player," the boy laments. "Can't play in Yankee Stadium with one arm." His father then tells him, "Don't give up. Things happen. You just never know." As the scenario progresses, Gray offers similar advice to Nelson Gary, Jr. (Huckleberry Fox), a young boy whose arm is amputated, and to whom he becomes a combination baseball coach/role model/friend. "Guys like you and me," he tells Nelson, "we have to try ten times harder than other people."

By the time he befriends Nelson, Gray has been signed by the Memphis Chicks, the Browns' top farm club. He is regarded by the team's front office as a "one-armed geek," a Barnum and Bailey sideshow who will bolster the team's attendance. But after hitting .330, leading the Southern Association in steals and earning league MVP honors (as well as becoming romantically involved with a spunky waitress, played by Mare Winningham), Gray is called to the majors.

The fact remains that Pete Gray would not have played for the Browns if World War II had not depleted baseball of so many able bodies. The statistics compiled in his one major-league season are unspectacular: seventy-seven games played, no home runs, and a .218 average. But the fact that he did make the majors, ahead of players with two arms, is special: a feat that would prove inspirational to all the boys returning from the war as amputees. The film ends

A Winner Never Quits: Keith Carradine as Pete Gray, flanked by his screen parents (Dennis Weaver, Fionnula Flanagan).

with the triumph of Gray realizing his dream to play in Yankee Stadium. He is told that he will be benched for a player with a higher batting average. The latter is injured while making a catch, and is replaced by Gray. In the seventh inning, with the game knotted at 5–5, he comes up to bat and lines a single to center, driving in the go-ahead run. Then, he steals second base, and he scores the eighth Browns run. In the ninth inning, he makes a sparkling, game-saving catch in left field. The film closes with a postscript: "In 1958, Nelson Gary, Jr., was named to the San Fernando Valley All-League baseball team. Pete Gray's glove is now in the Baseball Hall of Fame in Cooperstown."

Thirty-seven years before *A Winner Never Quits*, James Stewart starred in the biography of an athlete in a similar situation to Pete Gray's: *The Stratton Story* (1949, MGM). Monty Stratton is shown to be a Texas farmboy/sandlot pitcher who, at the urging of Barney Wile (Frank Morgan), a baseball has-been who recognizes his talent and becomes his mentor, tries out for the Chicago White Sox. He fails to make the majors, puts in time in the minor leagues, and eventually becomes one of the Sox' more promising hurlers; in his best seasons, 1937 and 1938, he posts 15-5 and 15-9 won-lost records. Those are Stratton's last major-league seasons, as his career is scuttled when he

loses part of his right leg in a hunting mishap. With the support of his loving wife, Ethel (June Allyson), and mother (Agnes Moorehead), and despite the burden of an artificial leg, Stratton overcomes self-pity and despair and aspires to resume playing ball. As she catches her husband's practice pitches, Ethel Stratton is the epitome of the supportive baseball wife. After Stratton stumbles and falls while winding up, she rushes to his side and offers him affection. "Hey," the ballplayer notes, "that's the first time (I've) ever been kissed by a catcher."

The essence of the film can be found in its final sequence, in which Stratton takes the mound for the Southern All-Stars. He comes to bat, grimacing in pain as he swings at and misses a pitch. Then he belts a solid liner and hobbles safely to first as the lead run scores. He winks at Ethel, who watches approvingly from the stands, and she returns his wink. Now he must pitch the ninth inning, to secure the victory. The rival manager tells his lead-off hitter, "I hate to do this, but we gotta get on. Bunt him." He does so, for a hit. The second batter also bunts safely. "Well, I'll just have to get off the mound quicker. That's all," Stratton tells his catcher. The third hitter bunts and, reports the radio play-by-play man, "Monty was off the mound with the pitch, and nailed that man at first. But he's not out of the woods yet. The runners advance to

The Stratton Story: James Stewart as Monty Stratton.

second and third, [with] only one out." The opposing skipper employs a new strategy, ordering his next batter to hit away. Stratton promptly strikes him out. Coming up to the plate is "the power hitter of the league, big Johnny Lindell" (who then was a real-life New York Yankee outfielder). Lindell smacks Stratton's first pitch for a line drive, which the pitcher knocks down, stretches to pick up, and, while in a prone position, heaves to first base for the final out. The soundtrack fills with inspirational music and a narrator intones, "Monty Stratton has not won just a ballgame. He's won a greater victory. As he goes on pitching, winning, leading a rich, whole life, he stands as an inspiration to all of us, as living proof of what a man can do if he has the courage and determination to refuse to admit defeat." Over these words, Stratton lifts himself off the ground and strides off the field, where he is met by his jubilant teammates.

The Stratton Story, by the way, is not the only film in which James Stewart appears as a ballplayer. In *Strategic Air Command*, (1955, Paramount), he plays Dutch Holland, former B-29 commander and current star third baseman for the St. Louis Cardinals. During the past season, Holland drove in 152 runs, and has just signed a seventy-thousand-dollar contract. Unexpectedly, he is recalled for twenty-one months of active duty with the Strategic Air Command,

The Stratton Story: June Allyson as Ethel Stratton, James Stewart as Monty Stratton.

described as "the Air Force's global bombing outfit" and "the only thing keeping the peace. By staying combat-ready, we can prevent a war." At first, Holland is outraged. Even though he has already served his country, he is being asked to forfeit what may be his last productive years in baseball, as well as his fat salary and privacy with his new wife (June Allyson). Good citizen that he is, Holland comes to understand the necessity of SAC as America's safeguard against the commie menace. After completing his hitch, he even reenlists, passing up a return to baseball. "There are times when you're given certain responsibilities. You can't ignore them," he tells his wife. "There is a kind of war [going on]. We've got to stay ready to fight, without fighting. That's even tougher [than actually being in a war]." The film's purpose is to inform the public about SAC and urge the support of its mandate, even if it means that a baseball star must sacrifice his career to the service of his government.

(Stewart also starred on television in *Flashing Spikes* [1962, Alcoa Premiere], directed by John Ford, in which he played Slim Conway, ex-major leaguer banned from baseball for accepting a bribe. Also in the cast are Hall of Fame hurler Don Drysdale, playing a character named Gomer; Brooklyn–Los Angeles Dodgers' announcer Vin Scully, as an announcer; umpire

The Stratton Story: Frank Morgan as Barney Wile, Monty Stratton's mentor; James Stewart as Stratton; Jimmy Dykes (manager of the Chicago White Sox during Stratton's major-league tenure) as himself (left to right).

The Stratton Story: James Stewart as Monty Stratton, Cliff Clark as Southern All-Stars skipper Josh Higgins, Frank Morgan as Barney Wile (left to right).

Art Passarella, as an umpire; 1940s–'50s major-league infielder Vern Stephens, as a ballplayer; John Wayne's son, Pat; and the Duke himself, cast as a drill sergeant. Seven years earlier, Ford directed *Rookie of the Year* [1955, *Screen Directors Playhouse*]. This one featured Pat Wayne, Ward Bond, Vera Miles, and James Gleason, and John Wayne in a token appearance as a reporter named Mike.)

Woody Allen deftly parodies *The Stratton Story*, as well as the inherent hokiness of baseball biographies, in *Radio Days* (1987, Orion). The film is an affectionate reminiscence of growing up in the outer boroughs of New York City during the early 1940s, and an account of the impact of radio during this pretelevision age. In one vignette, the saga of Kirby Kyle is recalled by radio personality Bill Kern on his "Favorite Sports Legends" show. Kyle was "a lean southpaw from Tennessee who played for the old St. Louis Cardinals," according to Kern, as well as "a kid with a great future." One day, while hunting rabbit during the off-season, Kyle shot himself in the leg. It was amputated and, as Kern pronounces, "They said he could never pitch again." Kyle does indeed come back, and is shown on the mound with a peg leg. The following winter, another accident resulted in the loss of Kyle's arm. Fortunately, it wasn't the one he used for pitching, and there is Kyle back on the mound minus his right arm. While hunting duck during the

next off-season, the unfortunate moundsman's gun misfired, resulting in blindness. Even loss of eyesight did not deter the courageous Kirby Kyle, who continued his career garbed in dark glasses. "... He had instinct where to throw the ball," intones Kern. "Instinct—and heart." He concludes, "The following year, Kirby Kyle was run over by a truck and killed. The following season, he won eighteen games in the Big League in the Sky."

There is no such humor in *Eight Men Out* (1988, Orion), the one movie about baseball history that does not glorify its subjects. The ballplayers depicted are either greedy or naïve, or victims who do not make heroic, final-reel comebacks. The film is a typical work of its creator, John Sayles: a thoughtful, politically savvy film, produced independently of the major-studio assembly line, which transcends its subject matter to astutely comment on the time in which it is set. *Eight Men Out* is based on Eliot Asinof's chronicle of the infamous 1919 Black Sox scandal, with its scenario keying in on the various members of the Chicago White Sox who threw the World Series and rocked professional baseball.

The Sox are portrayed in ensemble style as a rowdy, hard-playing bunch, easily the best major-league team of their time. They are athletic heroes with diverse personalities and temperaments who are united in their love of dirtying their uniforms, and in their collective gullibility. Among them are Buck Weaver (John Cusack), a shortstop/third baseman who batted .296 in 1919 and .333 the following season, which was his last in the big time; outfielder Hap Felsch (Charlie Sheen), who compiled a .293 batting average in six major-league seasons; Eddie Cicotte (David Strathairn), wily veteran hurler who won twenty-eight games in 1917, twenty-nine in 1919, and 208 (while losing only 149) in fourteen major-league summers; and the legendary Joseph Jefferson "Shoeless Joe" Jackson (D.B. Sweeney), whose lifetime batting average of .356 is the third all-time highest. Ty Cobb described Jackson as "the finest natural hitter in the

Eight Men Out: D.B. Sweeney (left) as Shoeless Joe Jackson, with Charlie Sheen as Hap Felsch.

history of the game. He never figured anything out or studied anything with the scientific approach I used—he just swung." Babe Ruth even copied his batting stance.

As depicted by Sayles, the Black Sox are victimized as much by Charles "The Old Roman" Comiskey (Clifton James), the team's jowly, penny-pinching owner, as by underworld kingpin Arnold Rothstein (Michael Lerner) and the various two-bit gamblers and quick-money boys who scheme to throw the series. In this regard, the film—like Sayles's previous feature, *Matewan*, which chronicles a bitter coal miners' strike and its effect on a small West Virginia town—is an allegory of class exploitation and tainted innocence. Both films are based on fact, and both tell of owners exploiting workers in the years following World War I.

Comiskey is shown to be a cruel, petty capitalist. He had promised Eddie Cicotte a ten-thousand-dollar bonus if the pitcher won thirty games in 1919. Because Cicotte was racking up victories, Comiskey had him benched for two weeks. He missed five starts, and finished the season with twenty-nine victories. Twenty-nine does not equal thirty, so the player is out the ten grand. Comiskey brags to the media that his boys are an all-for-one, one-for-all lot. Yet, in fact, the blue-collar players resent Eddie Collins, a college boy; there is tension between Northern

and Southern teammates; and the players ride one another to the point of sadism. They are as different as any arbitrarily selected group of men. Chick Gandil (Michael Rooker) is a schemer who likes to play the smart angles. Hap Felsch is a lunkhead who relishes crashing into walls. Eddie Cicotte is a fading veteran with a family to feed, who knows that if he throws his arm out Comiskey wouldn't even pay his fare home. Shoeless Joe Jackson is an illiterate, easily coerced country boy. Buck Weaver is a hard-playing athlete who hates to lose, and who knows about the fix but decides not to participate.

While Comiskey and the reporters (whom he needs to help promote the Sox' public image) toast the team's success when the Sox cop the pennant, the players—the workers—are rewarded with flat champagne. Despite their celebrity, they are in the eyes of their boss just a bunch of lackeys who will win him pennants and humbly accept stale booze and broken promises. Had the owner not been such a "cheap bastard," the scenario argues, the ballplayers would not have been tempted by the fast buck into throwing the series. Sayles portrays even the worst of the Black Sox as victims of forces beyond their control, whose decision to fix the series results from exploitation combined with human weakness. "I always figured it was talent made a man big, you know . . . without us,

Eight Men Out: John Cusack as Buck Weaver, Michael Rooker as Chick Gandil, James Read as Lefty Williams, Perry Lang as Fred McMullin (top row, left to right); Don Harvey as Swede Risberg, Charlie Sheen as Hap Felsch, D.B. Sweeney as Shoeless Joe Jackson, David Strathairn as Eddie Cicotte (bottom row, left to right).

Eight Men Out: John Cusack as Buck Weaver, in the company of young admirers.

ized Shoeless Joe Jackson, Buck Weaver, and the rest were to be given their first dose of adult-world reality. When Shoeless Joe emerges from a courthouse where the game-fixing charges are being heard, one of them confronts him with the plea that has become a part of sports lore: "Say it ain't so, Joe."

As a result of the Black Sox scandal, Judge Kenesaw Mountain Landis (John Anderson) was named the first commissioner of baseball. Even though the accused were found innocent in court of committing any crime, Landis banned them from baseball for life. In 1939, Charles Comiskey was enshrined in the Baseball Hall of Fame. Despite his stats, Shoeless Joe Jackson, a simple man who knew only how to bash a baseball, has not been awarded his place in Cooperstown beside Ruth, Cobb, and Hornsby. History records him and the other Black Sox as bums, as the crooked lot who threw the World Series.

there ain't a ballgame," observes Eddie Cicotte, after the fix becomes public. "But look at who's holding the money, and look at who's facing a jail cell." Where are the gamblers? Where is Comiskey? Off in some back room, cutting up the profits.

Eight Men Out serves as a reminder that purity is an illusion, that innocence equals naïveté; in this regard, it makes for a stark contrast with *Field of Dreams*, whose scenario also employs the Black Sox. Back in 1919, America's Game literally was lily-white. Jackie Robinson was not to break baseball's color line for twenty-eight years; at one point, a black man cleaning up garbage wryly notes that the Sox are the "best white folks' team" he has ever seen. Even though baseball was played on real, green grass under unpolluted blue skies, those who ran the game were not above racism, penny-pinching, and corruption. Even the media are not blameless: Sayles casts himself as Ring Lardner, playing the sportswriter as a self-righteous snob who, from the beginning, exudes disdain for the players. In the end, the kids who idol-

The real 1919 Cincinnati Reds, the Black Sox's World Series opponents.

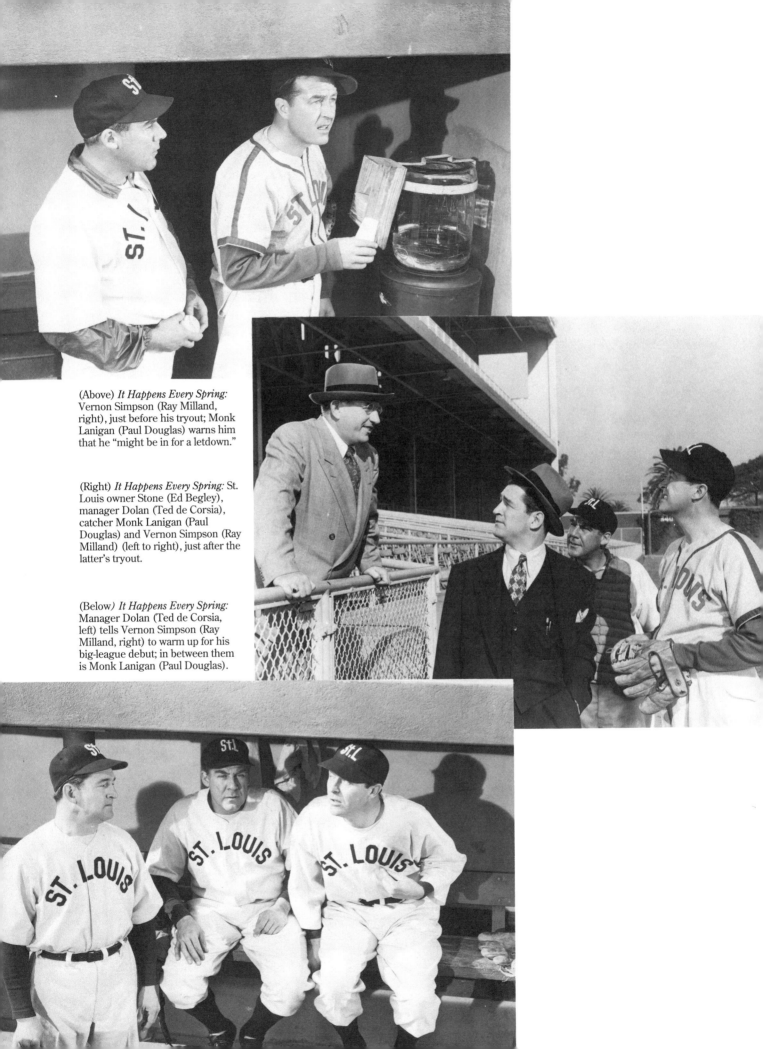

(Above) *It Happens Every Spring:* Vernon Simpson (Ray Milland, right), just before his tryout; Monk Lanigan (Paul Douglas) warns him that he "might be in for a letdown."

(Right) *It Happens Every Spring:* St. Louis owner Stone (Ed Begley), manager Dolan (Ted de Corsia), catcher Monk Lanigan (Paul Douglas) and Vernon Simpson (Ray Milland) (left to right), just after the latter's tryout.

(Below*) It Happens Every Spring:* Manager Dolan (Ted de Corsia, left) tells Vernon Simpson (Ray Milland, right) to warm up for his big-league debut; in between them is Monk Lanigan (Paul Douglas).

BASEBALL AND FANTASY

To the hardcore baseball fan, the idea of Anthony Perkins, Dan Dailey, or John Goodman playing major league ball may seem like science fiction. But baseball movies have depicted other types of fantasies, ones in which quirks of nature or otherworldly forces have an impact upon the "real" game, allowing the unlikeliest of ballplayers to star on the field or the lowliest of teams to confound the sports world by copping pennants.

It Happens Every Spring may feature the worst song in any baseball film: a gooey, cornball-sentimental title number, played over the opening credits. Nevertheless, the film remains one of the more successful baseball fantasies. Ray Milland stars as Vernon Simpson, shy and reserved, a "fine young man and brilliant scholar." Simpson is completing his doctorate at a university where he teaches chemistry courses and romances the daughter (Jean Peters) of the school president (Ray Collins), who is attempting to deemphasize athletics on campus. Simpson's one failing is his love of baseball. Every spring, at the start of the major-league season, this egghead becomes a stereotypically absentminded professor; while lecturing to a class, he happens to overhear a baseball game being broadcast and becomes humorously distracted. Simpson has been experimenting to create a substance that will repel insects from wood, the success of which will earn him enough money to wed his beloved. Some ballplaying kids knock a horsehide through the window of his lab, wrecking his work.

While cleaning up the mess, Simpson discovers that the errant ball, when dipped in what remains of his concoction, swerves away from or pops over the wood he had been using in his experiment. He realizes that, if the ball repels wood in the lab, it would repel wooden bats on a ballfield.

Simpson arrives for an unannounced tryout with the St. Louis ballclub, where he is derided by Stone (Ed Begley), the team's owner, and Dolan (Ted de Corsia), the manager. But he blows away the top of the batting order with his unhittable pitches, which mysteriously hop over the plate as they avoid the paths of swinging bats. "Musta been an optical illusion," remarks Monk Lanigan (Paul Douglas), who will become Simpson's catcher, roommate, and friend. Dolan adds, "He don't look like a pitcher. He don't throw like a pitcher," but Simpson soon is on his way to winning close to forty games and tossing a no-hitter. As he does not wish to offend his girl's father, he plays incognito under the name Kelly and refuses to have his photo taken to maintain his anonymity.

Newspapers ring out with such headlines as "King Kelly Bamboozles Brooklyn," and St. Louis makes it to the World Series against New York. Simpson gets the final out of the final game by snaring a vicious line drive, which fractures his hand and ends his baseball career. But Lanigan notes that Simpson enjoyed "a season like nobody ever had before." He thinks he cannot return to his girl and his job, but is unaware that everyone on campus knows the true identity of "Kelly." He is even named head of the

It Happens Every Spring: Monk Lanigan (Paul Douglas) strides to the pitcher's mound . . .

. . .and calms Vernon Simpson (Ray Milland).

school's new research lab.

It Happens Every Spring (whose original story is co-credited to University of Michigan registrar Shirley W. Smith) is filled with humorous gags, the best of which come at the expense of Lanigan. Simpson tells his roommate that a bottle filled with his invention is really hair tonic, which Lanigan promptly "borrows" to comic effect. He jams his finger, which the trainer sets with wooden splints; Simpson's pitches then elude not only the opponents' bats but the backstop, who can neither catch his pitches nor pick baseballs up after dropping them.

Zapped! (1982, Embassy) is a far-inferior, latter-day variation of *It Happens Every Spring.* Scott Baio stars as a high-school senior and scientific whiz kid. After an explosion in his lab, he develops telekinetic powers that allow him to make objects move at will. During a school baseball game, he causes balls hit by opponents to land in the gloves of his teammates, and enemy batters to haplessly swing through pitches. Guess what happens next? In the ninth inning, he uses his power to belt a pinch hit, game-winning homer.

In *It Happens Every Spring,* Paul Douglas is perfectly cast as Monk Lanigan; back in the early 1950s, he was fast becoming one of the movies' ablest comedic actors. The former professional football player and radio sportscaster followed his performance as

Lanigan with the lead role in *Angels in the Outfield* (1951, MGM), a fantasy about a bumbling baseball team which "could be any baseball team, in any league, in any town in America." Maybe so, but this club, major-league baseball's Pittsburgh Pirates, is mind-bogglingly inept. There are no Clementes, Stargells, or Waner brothers on its roster. These guys don't just lose: they lose big, by large and embarrassing margins, with plenty of errors on their side of the box score. In a typical game, in which they are on the short end of a 21–2 tally, three Bucs end up on one base during the same play.

The scenario of *Angels in the Outfield* details the manner in which the team is transformed from joke to champion. It highlights the reformation of Guffy McGovern (Douglas), the Pirates' gruff, profanity-spewing manager. A radio announcer (Keenan Wynn) who greets McGovern with a "How are things in seventh place?" is answered with a belt in the face. McGovern always is arguing and yelling and, off the field, always is alone. One day after a game, he is spoken to by a voice: an angel. It seems that the Angel Gabriel has taken a special interest in McGovern because someone has been praying for him. The voice promises the manager that if he "loves, and stops slugging, thy neighbor," the Pirates will begin to win. Perhaps they even might cop a pennant.

To prove his power, the voice tells McGovern to

90

Angels in the Outfield: Janet Leigh as Jennifer Paige, Paul Douglas as Guffy McGovern, Donna Corcoran as Bridget White (left to right).

Hellman, allows the hurler to pitch his soul out in the season's final, pennant-clinching contest against the New York Giants (who, interestingly, were the real National League champions of 1951).

Furthermore, an orphan with the appropriately sanitary name of Bridget White (played by cute little Donna Corcoran) attends a Pirates game and sees angels in the field, standing behind each Pirate—and even behind McGovern. Little Bridget, it seems, is the one who has been praying for the team "every night, and every morning ... and even during arith-

Angels in the Outfield: Guffy McGovern (Paul Douglas, lower right), scuffles with sarcastic radio announcer Fred Bayles (Keenan Wynn, bottom center).

Angels in the Outfield: Guffy McGovern (Paul Douglas, left) confers with Saul Hellman (Bruce Bennett).

watch for a miracle during the third inning of the following day's contest. Sure enough, the Bucs pull off some sparkling fielding plays, and hit like Murderers' Row. So McGovern starts behaving. He asks his players to dine with him, even begins reading Shakespeare—and the Pirates go on a ten-game winning streak. When he reverts to his old ways, the team loses. Later on, the voice tells McGovern that Saul Hellman (Bruce Bennett), a sixteen-year veteran pitcher on the decline, is fated to die by the following spring. The manager, who had been down on

metic." After being hit in the face during a game, McGovern tells the press that the angels are the cause of his team's success. Eventually, the Commissioner of Baseball (Lewis Stone) holds a hearing to determine McGovern's sanity. While a psychiatrist testifies against the manager, three clergymen claim that, by their religious teaching, they cannot deny the possible existence of angels: a victory of religion over rationalism, and a victory for McGovern.

Finally, there is the love interest: Jennifer Paige (Janet Leigh), a newspaper columnist whose specialty is "household hints," and who admittedly knows zilch

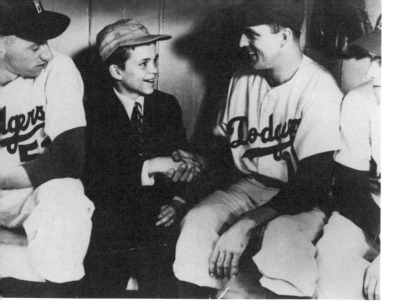

Roogie's Bump: Roogie (Robert Marriot) greets Brooklyn Dodger pitchers Carl Erskine (right) and Billy Loes (left).

Roogie's Bump: Roy Campanella, Billy Loes, Robert Marriot as Roogie, Russ Meyer (left to right).

about baseball. When the Pirates are stumbling, she is assigned by her paper to write about what is wrong with the team. She pens a piece damning McGovern; they meet, and the manager is anything but cordial. "Dogs have fleas," he tells her, ever so curtly. "Managers have sportswriters." You just know that, by the film's end, Guffy and Jennifer will be an item and Bridget White will have herself a pair of loving parents.

Despite its predictability, *Angels in the Outfield* is a pleasant, entertaining film. It is at its funniest when McGovern curses out his players, the umpires, and anyone else within earshot; this being 1951, when the Production Code ruled Hollywood and the contents of today's PG-rated films would be unthinkable in a movie, his words are cleverly masked in gibberish. There are some nice surprise cameos by Joe DiMaggio, Ty Cobb, Bing Crosby (then the Pirates' real-life part-owner), and Tin Pan Alley songwriter Harry Ruby (described as "America's number-one baseball fan"), who comment on McGovern's Angels. You even can find Barbara Billingsley, later to earn fame as the mom of Beaver and Wally Cleaver, cast in a bit as a hat-check girl.

In its presentation of ballplayer-spirits, *Angels in the Outfield* is a precursor to *Field of Dreams*. At the finale, McGovern wonders about the identities of the angels who were helping the Pirates. He is told that they included Lou Gehrig, Babe Ruth, Walter Johnson, Eddie Collins, and other deceased Hall of Famers: a "great group [and] great guys."

The plot formulas of *It Happens Every Spring* and *Angels in the Outfield* are united in *Roogie's Bump* (1954, Republic), featuring Robert Marriot as Remington "Roogie" Rigsby, a little boy who has just moved to Brooklyn. The youngster is excluded by the neighborhood kids from partaking in their ballgames. Because he feels bad for Roogie, and is in love with his grandmother, the ghost of Red O'Malley (William Harrigan), a deceased Brooklyn Dodgers' star hurler, appears before Roogie and provides him with a special bump on his arm that allows him to fire baseballs with the "speed of light." Soon, this "miracle kid with the super zoom ball" is playing for the Dodgers, and living out every young baseball fan's dream.

Roogie's Bump is not a very good movie. It is indifferently acted and poorly scripted, and the editing is especially inept; in one sequence, footage of Duke Snider grounding out is followed by that of him returning to the batter's box. The film's sole interest is in glimpsing real-life Brooklyn Dodgers Billy Loes, Carl Erskine, Russ Meyer, and, particularly, Roy Campanella in acting roles, as well as in noting the use of the name O'Malley. The owner of the Brooklyn Dodgers was, of course, Walter O'Malley; the character of Red O'Malley is nothing less than saintly, and even is patronizingly referred to as the "Great O'Malley." Within three years, however, real fans of Dem Bums were to wish for the demise of Walter O'Malley—but not for his canonization—after he

Rookie of the Year: Thomas Ian Nicholas as Henry Rowengartner.

Rookie of the Year: Henry (Thomas Ian Nicholas) clowns amid his grown-up teammates.

greedily abandoned the Borough of Churches for Los Angeles.

Rookie of the Year (1993, Twentieth Century-Fox) is a very unofficial remake of *Roogie's Bump*. It is the story of Henry Rowengartner (Thomas Ian Nicholas), a twelve-year-old Chicago Cubs' fanatic who is being raised by his single mom (Amy Morton). Unfortunately, Henry is so athletically inept that he is unable to catch an easy fly ball in a Little League game, and has become a laughingstock in his neighborhood. One day at school, while attempting to catch a ball thrown by one of his many tormentors, Henry slips, flies through the air, and fractures his arm. Upon its healing, he discovers that he now has a "super arm," and is able to effortlessly throw a ball at one-hundred-plus miles per hour.

As quickly as you can say Ernie Banks, Henry is signed by the Cubs and is sharing a locker room with his favorite ballplayers. With the help of Chet "Rocket" Steadman (Gary Busey), a once-brilliant hurler nearing the end of his career, Henry learns finesse and becomes the Cubbie's premier relief pitcher. The last-place ballclub (a team which, it is noted, hasn't won a pennant since 1945 or a World Series since 1908) zooms up in the standings, while Henry makes the cover of *Sports Illustrated* and stars in a Ray Charles–style Pepsi commercial. The villains of the story (Mrs. Rowengartner's power-crazed new boyfriend, and the team owner's money-hungry heir apparent) are easily exposed and eliminated. After

several sequences featuring Henry on the mound, dueling with various National League opponents, he slips and falls while on the field and about to pitch the Cubs into the World Series. As quickly as it arrived, the special power in his arm vanishes. But Henry uses various guises, including a hidden-ball trick and a "float" pitch tossed underhanded, to dispose of the final three opposing hitters, allowing the Cubs into the series.

Rookie of the Year, as *Roogie's Bump*, is every

Rookie of the Year: Aging hurler Chet Steadman (Gary Busey) advises young Henry (Thomas Ian Nicholas).

Rookie of the Year: Pitching coach Brickma (Daniel Stern) offers Henry (Thomas Ian Nicholas) some sage counsel.

Rookie of the Year: Henry (Thomas Ian Nicholas) celebrates with his teammates.

its intended audience: every Little Leaguer in America. It is fast paced, and appealingly silly: among the characters is Brickma (played by the film's director, Daniel Stern), the Cubs' pitching coach, an idiot who makes Gomer Pyle seem like Albert Einstein; the manager keeps comically mispronouncing Henry's surname, calling him "Gardenhoser" and "Runnermucker." There is a strong, loving bond between Henry and his mother (who, of course, is destined to dump her boyfriend for Chet Steadman, a nice guy and ideal father figure). Henry is an obedient son; upon being asked to join the Cubs, he responds, "Great, but I have to ask my mom first." And even before Henry loses the power in his arm, he decides to quit pro ball. After all, he is only twelve, and he does not want to miss out on the rest of his childhood.

The various baseball-related flaws in *Rookie of the Year* may be overlooked, given the spirit in which the film has been made. Among them: Henry does not practice with his new teammates before making his major-league debut; he may be a relief pitcher, but he always sits in the dugout rather than the bullpen and never warms up before entering a game; the Cubs beat the Mets to win the Division Championship and head straight to the World Series, rather than first facing the National League's other division champs. These oversights seem odd if only because of a sentiment expressed by the film's producers, which proves that they are not ignorant of the game. Among those they thank in the closing credits are "The Fans of Chicago Who Never Give Up."

Of baseball fantasies for adult audiences, one of the best is *Damn Yankees* (1958, Warner Bros.), a fiction about baseball, sex, and restored youth: a combination as appealing today as in 1955, when it opened on Broadway. The show, which ran on the Great White Way for 1,019 performances, is based on a book whose title was the dream of every New York Yankee–hater back in the 1950s: Douglass Wallop's *The Year the Yankees Lost the Pennant*.

Damn Yankees is the story of Joe Boyd (Robert Shafer), middle-aged and paunchy, an armchair player/manager/coach and rabid Washington Senators

baseball-loving boy's fantasy-come-true, never more so than when, after Henry's tryout, Cubs' manager Sal Martinella (Albert Hall) says to the twelve-year-old, "Hey, kid, how would you like to pitch for the Chicago Cubs?" But *Rookie of the Year* does differ from *Roogie's Bump* in that Henry's Cub teammates are not played by real major leaguers. (However, in one brief sequence, Henry is shown striking out Pedro Guerrero, Bobby Bonds, and Bobby Bonilla, who are billed in the credits as the Three Big Whiffers.) While no award-winner, *Rookie of the Year* is perfect fare for fan who is oblivious to the conversation of his sweet-tempered wife, Meg (Shannon Bolin). His Senators are mired in seventh place, their eternal position at season's end. "If we had one long ball hitter, just one ..." Boyd declares. "I'd sell my soul for one long ball hitter." Enter Mr. Applegate (Ray Walston), the Devil, nattily attired in dark suit, red tie, and conspicuous red socks. Applegate offers Boyd his wish, playing on his secret yearning to be a ballplayer. Boyd agrees, but only after forcing Applegate into accepting an escape clause that will allow him to return to his former life by midnight on September 24. Then—presto—Applegate transforms Joe Boyd into Joe Hardy (Tab Hunter), a strapping, twenty-two-year-old slugger destined to become his generation's Babe Ruth.

The Senators initially are depicted as a group of affable lunkheads. The first time they appear on screen, they are more concerned with insurance poli-

Damn Yankees: Gwen Verdon as Lola.

Damn Yankees: Tab Hunter as Joe Hardy.

cies and crossword puzzles than baseball strategy. Their attitudes change as Joe Hardy smashes dinger after dinger in his tryout, and then leads the revitalized Senators up the standings. Applegate, however, schemes to break the spirits of the Senators' fans by making the team lose the pennant to the Bronx Bombers on the final day of the season: September 25. He becomes incensed when Hardy, glum because he misses Meg, rents a room in her house. So he sends for a "real sexy baby" to distract him. She's Lola (Gwen Verdon), who is, in an understatement, "pretty good at making men forget their wives." Only Joe Hardy isn't any man: his soul is that of Joe Boyd, devoted (if not always attentive) husband. Lola and Joe instead become friends, "two lost souls on the highway of life." She eventually drugs her boss, allowing him to oversleep and miss most of the season's final game; the night before, Applegate had manipulated Hardy into letting the escape clause expire. After arriving at the ballpark for the contest's last moments, the fuming devil transforms Joe into his former self as he lunges for and makes a game-saving catch that allows the Senators the pennant. Joe Hardy disappears into nowhere, and Joe Boyd returns to Meg. He ignores the pleas of the snarling, grunting Applegate, who brands him a "wife-loving louse ... ya

95

Damn Yankees: Gloria Thorpe (Rae Allen) and Washington Senators sing and dance the praises of "Shoeless Joe from Hannibal, Mo."

thief, ya crook . . . " Joe Boyd has learned that there is more to life than being a hero. He is content with his identity as "a good, loyal, dumb, ordinary man," with a loving wife.

Gloria Thorpe (Rae Allen), one of the characters in *Damn Yankees*, is a rarity for the era: a female sports reporter. In the Yankee Stadium sequence in *Woman of the Year* (1942, MGM), a crusty, chauvinistic colleague of Sam Craig, played by Roscoe Karns, resents the presence of Tess Harding—a woman—in the press box. He complains that it is the worst scandal since the Black Sox; while his lines are comic in effect, his attitude is reflective of the status quo. But Gloria Thorpe's presence in *Damn Yankees* is no inspired, progressive blow for womens' rights; rather, she is a feminist's nightmare. Sure, she must deal with sexist abuse. Male character after male character advise her to "go home, get married, have children." Perhaps she should, given her personality. Gloria is sarcastic, and ever-suspicious. As Joe ads sock to the Senators, she pushes to get "the story on the kid." But she is not so much a dedicated, truth-seeking journalist as a gossip: Gloria is overeager to present evidence that Joe really is Shifty McCoy, banned from baseball for taking a bribe in

the Mexican League. She professes to love the Senators but, more than any male scribe, will eagerly destroy the team and its star player.

Three numbers from the stage show have been deleted from the screen version of *Damn Yankees*: "Near to You," a love ballad (which is replaced by the similar "There's Something About an Empty Chair"); "A Man Doesn't Know," a profoundly moving song that reflects on the feeling that lovers abuse love, and do not appreciate one another until after they have gone; and "The Game," a semi-risqué comical routine in which some of the ballplayers recall how their various sexual exploits are interrupted by thoughts of remaining true, pure, and in training.

Others remain, including the spirited "Heart," in which Russ Brown (playing Van Buren, the Washington manager) inspires his boys, telling them that the game is one-half skill and one-half "something else, something bigger"; "Six Months Out of Every Year," the eternal lament of the baseball fan's wife (Six months out of every year, I just might as well be made of stone because, when I'm with him, I'm alone); "Shoeless Joe from Hannibal, Mo.," sung by Rae Allen and danced by the ballplayers, with Bob Fosse's

Damn Yankees: Lola (Gwen Verdon) attempts to seduce Joe Hardy (Tab Hunter) with "Whatever Lola Wants."

96

Damn Yankees: Applegate (Ray Walston) chastises Lola (Gwen Verdon) for becoming a Joe Hardy booster.

expressive choreography incorporating pounding gloves, fielding grounders, tossing balls and sliding into bases with the dance steps; Gwen Verdon's show-stopping "A Little Brains—a Little Talent" and "Whatever Lola Wants," the latter performed while doing a striptease for Joe Hardy in the Senators' locker room; and Ray Walston's equally memorable "Those Were the Good Old Days," a grandly performed, vaudeville-style number in which Applegate boasts of his many devilish deeds.

Still, as a movie musical, *Damn Yankees* is no *Singin' in the Rain*. It is not very cinematic and, most annoyingly, it ends abruptly. *Damn Yankees* is a film in dire need of a rousing finale. But these are quibbles, given all of its entertainment value. The film does benefit from its grade-A cast, just about all of whom recreate their stage roles. One addition is Bob Fosse, replacing Eddie Phillips, who dances with Gwen Verdon (his offscreen mate) in the "Who's Got the Pain" number, performed at a benefit in Joe Hardy's honor. Besides Carol Haney, Verdon arguably is the best-ever interpreter of Fosse's distinctive choreography. It is no exaggeration to describe their pairing here as electric. Aside from Fosse, the chief newcomer is Tab Hunter, replacing Stephen Douglass as Hardy. Despite his reputation as a pretty-boy pinup who was later to parody himself in John Waters' *Polyester*, Hunter offers a likable performance. He does especially well dancing with Gwen Verdon and a chorus in the "Two Lost Souls" number, a night-club routine performed on the eve of the season's final game.

Finally, expect to hear the distinctive voice of Edith Bunker in *Damn Yankees*. Jean Stapleton employs it in her role as Meg's friend, Sister Miller. She is a delight as she gets all aflutter upon meeting Joe Hardy—*the* Joe Hardy—and, later, sings a couple of verses of "Heart." Footage of the real Washington Senators and New York Yankees is edited into the staging of the pennant-deciding game. Could that be Camilio Pascual on the mound for Washington? That must be Yogi Berra catching a foul popup. Indeed, Joe Hardy/Boyd's game-saving catch is off the bat of none other than Mickey Mantle.

Another baseball fantasy with a literary origin is *The Natural*, adapted from Bernard Malamud's first novel. Cinematically speaking, *The Natural* is a precursor to *Field of Dreams* as a fantasy ode to an idealized America and the idealized sport of baseball. It is a story of finding second chances and rediscovering true love, a magical tale in which honor and innocence triumph over greed and evil. The film opens with a slow-motion shot of a farmboy, Roy Hobbs, in an idyllic pasture, catching a ball hit by his father. He

Damn Yankees: Lola (Gwen Verdon) and Joe Hardy (Tab Hunter) as "Two Lost Souls on the Highway of Life."

and his dad are sharing the time-honored father-son ritual of baseball. The senior Hobbs instructs the boy in the game's fundamentals. "You've got a gift, Roy," he observes, after the youngster has thrown a perfect strike through the side of a chicken coop. "But it's not enough. You got to develop yourself." While Hobbs is shattered by his father's sudden death, he courts the girl-next-door and carves and sandpapers his own bat from the wood of a tree that was split by lightning. He names this model of perfection Wonderboy.

Hobbs (now played by Robert Redford) is called to Chicago for a tryout with the Cubs, and promises his girl Iris (Glenn Close) that he will "reach for the best that's in me." During a water stop made by his train, the Whammer (Joe Don Baker), a Babe Ruth clone, puts on a home run exhibition at a carnival. He agrees to bat against Hobbs, but the busher strikes out this reigning sultan of major-league

The Natural: Robert Redford as Roy Hobbs.

swat on three straight pitches. Hobbs's future seems secure but, as the scenario unfolds, his idealism is tested by a conglomeration of characters who are the personification of evil. The first is a mystery woman (Barbara Hershey), garbed in black, who exploits his youthful ardor, inexplicably shoots him, and then commits suicide. Sixteen years pass with Hobbs languishing in obscurity, separated from Iris, his confidence shot and his promise an unfulfilled dream. In 1939, as a middle-aged rookie, he finally makes the majors with the New York Knights, described by its blustery manager (Wilford Brimley) as a "last place, dead-to-the-neck-up" ballclub.

Hobbs's Ruthian home runs, belted with Wonderboy, propel the Knights on an upward spiral in the standings. With his first dinger, he literally knocks the cover off the ball; his last, hit just after he is diagnosed with a potentially fatal stomach ailment and with a different bat after cracking Wonderboy in two, crashes into the lights. As Hobbs circles the bases, he is rained on by a shower of oversized sparks. With this hit, the Knights win the pennant. But before Hobbs's rejuvenation is complete, he must defend himself against the machinations of the rest of the villains: a slimy sportswriter (Robert Duvall), who craves power and control and brags that he is bigger than the game or any of its players; a she-devil (Kim Basinger), whose seduction of Hobbs drains his power, sending the ballplayer into a slump, and who,

The Natural: Glenn Close as Iris.

symbolically, tells Hobbs over the phone that she is sitting in a white slip thinking of him but really is garbed in black; a judge (Robert Prosky), the Knights' sinister owner, who will forfeit his majority share if the team wins the pennant and so attempts to bribe and blackmail Hobbs into losing games; and a greedy gambler (Darren McGavin), who bets against Hobbs and the Knights.

Hobbs is reunited with Iris, who is mother to the teenage son of whose existence he has been unaware. "I believe we have two lives," she tells Hobbs, in the scenario's key lines. "The one we learn with, and the one we live with after that." At the finale, Hobbs and his own son play slow-motion catch in a sun-drenched field, with Iris looking on approvingly. He has learned that fame is transitory and love—pure, true love—is everlasting.

The Natural: Wilford Brimley as Pop Fisher, skipper of the New York Knights.

With such a moral, how could *The Natural* not be a crowd-pleasing film? Notwithstanding, the scenario's white/goodness vs. black/evil symbolism is simplistic and obvious, and the film is unfaithful to its source material. In Malamud's novel, the finale is downbeat, bitter. Hobbs does not learn from his experiences, let alone receive a second shot at happiness. *The Natural* will satisfy audiences who go to movies to live out fantasies. As a film adaptation of a great book or a look at the mythology of the American hero, it rings hollow.

Yet *The Natural* remains a profoundly important baseball movie. Before its release, films with heroes who jogged around basepaths were considered to be lethal at the box office. According to *Variety, The Natural* earned a respectable $25 million, a number that auguered well for the production of future baseball-related films.

Compared to *The Natural, Field of Dreams* is far more satisfying, and respectful of its literary roots. The film, adapted from W.P. Kinsella's superb novel, *Shoeless Joe,* is the *It's a Wonderful Life* of baseball movies: a wistful fantasy about love, dreams, and the timelessness of the game. The scenario deals with the Black Sox scandal from a wholly different perspective than that of *Eight Men Out.* Here, the defamed Chicago ballplayers are restored to their glory when their spirits come to play in an eternal, pastoral ballfield. The latter is constructed in the middle of an Iowa cornfield by farmer/dreamer/former sixties

flower child Ray Kinsella (Kevin Costner), upon hearing a divine voice instructing him that "If you build it, he will come."

"I'm thirty-six years old," Kinsella declares. "I have a wife, a child, and a mortgage, and I'm afraid of becoming my father." He had been alienated from his dad (who is long-deceased) since his teens, and had never forgiven the man for becoming old. "He must have had dreams, but he never did anything about 'em. . . . The man never did one spontaneous thing in all the years I knew him." So, after envisioning a ballfield rising out of his cornstalks and seeing the face of Shoeless Joe Jackson (Ray Liotta), Kinsella builds his ballfield. Soon he is visited by the spirit of Shoeless Joe, who tells him that "getting thrown out of baseball was like having part of me amputated." Jackson is joined by his teammates and, even later, by the likes of Smoky Joe Wood, Mel Ott, Gil Hodges. "Ty Cobb wanted to play," Jackson laughs, "But no one could stand the son-of-a-bitch when we were alive, so we told him to stick it."

Regarding the Black Sox, the scenario's point of view is that even if Jackson knew about the fix, he performed in the series at the top of his game. He batted .375 for the eight-game affair; among his twelve hits were three doubles and a homer. So his resurrection is warranted, and all of the Black Sox' sins become nonexistent as an idealized American innocence is recaptured. *Field of Dreams* is a story of baseball as religion, of the sport as a source of redemption.

99

Field of Dreams: Burt Lancaster (left) as Moonlight Graham, saves the life of little Karen Kinsella (Gaby Hoffman), in the arms of her father, Ray (Kevin Costner).

Kinsella's ballfield, with its deep green grass and pure blue sky hovering above, is nothing short of heaven. To Joe Jackson and his fellow ballplayers, finding it is like finding heaven.

Next, there is the character of Terence Mann (replacing J.D. Salinger, who is depicted in *Shoeless Joe*), played by James Earl Jones. Mann, a Pulitzer Prize–winning writer and father-figure to the left during the sixties, who had coined the phrase "Make love, not war," has become a bitter recluse. He, too, is rescued by Kinsella after the divine voice instructs the farmer to "ease his pain."

"The one constant through all the years, Ray, has been baseball," notes Mann. "Baseball has marked the time. This field, this game, is a part of our past, Ray. It reminds us of all that once was good, and that could be again." The characters in *Field of Dreams* fade in and out of time; Ray Kinsella, who was born in 1952, gets to pitch to Shoeless Joe Jackson, who died at age sixty-four in 1951. At the finale, Kinsella even gets to meet his dead father. Here, John Kinsella is not as Ray knew him, an old man who had been "worn down by life." He is a strapping young ballplayer, with his future in front of him. Ray can face his dad, and tell him what he was unable to as an angry young child of the sixties. The men shake hands. As they play catch—a rite of camaraderie shared by father and son—their differences melt away, and their relationship is completed.

In *Field of Dreams*, anything is possible. Back in 1922, Old Doc Graham (Burt Lancaster, in a lovely cameo) had played for the New York Giants in one game, without getting a turn at bat. He went on to study medicine, and settled into a quiet but productive

Field of Dreams: Ray Kinsella (Kevin Costner, right) comes face to face with his father, John (Dwier Brown).

Field of Dreams: Ray Liotta as Shoeless Joe Jackson.

Field of Dreams: Amy Madigan as Annie Kinsella, Kevin Costner as Ray Kinsella.

Field of Dreams: Burt Lancaster as Moonlight Graham.

life as the town doctor in Chisholm, Minnesota. Graham died in 1972, and Kinsella is transported back in time where he meets the old man, whose sip of coffee in the majors was "like coming this close to your dreams." Doc Graham's youth is restored. He is now Archie Graham, and he gets to play with Joe Jackson and the others, to stare down a major-league pitcher going into his wind-up. But young Archie fulfills his destiny by becoming old Doc Graham when little Karin Kinsella (Gaby Hoffman) falls out of the bleachers, and needs quick medical attention. The point, which is most meaningful in our celebrity-obsessed age, is that Graham need not have shined in the Show to have lived a full, useful life. "If I'd only gotten to be a doctor for five minutes," he says, "that would be a tragedy." By the way, there was a real Moonlight Graham. He was born Archibald Wright Graham in 1876 in Fayette, North Carolina, and passed away eighty-nine years later in Chisholm. In 1905, he played the outfield in one game for the New York Giants. His big-league stats: no at bats; no hits; no runs scored; no runs batted in.

A character as genuinely eloquent as Doc Graham might have added some spunk to *Mr. Destiny* (1990, Touchstone), a tired fantasy with an appealing premise. Prior to *Mr. Destiny*, Jim Belushi had the second lead in *About Last Night ...* (1986, Tri-Star), a romantic drama framed by softball games during succeeding summers in which the hero (Rob Lowe) and heroine (Demi Moore) first meet, and then become reacquainted after breaking up. In between, they attend a Chicago Cubs game that they watch not from Wrigley Field but from a nearby rooftop, where they can be alone. Here, Belushi is top-billed as Larry Burrows, an average guy with a wife (Linda Hamilton), a dog, and a house in the suburbs. Larry has had an exasperating day. His family and friends have seemingly forgotten that it is his thirty-fifth birthday. He has just been fired from his job with a sporting goods company. Now, his wreck of a car breaks down on a dark, desolate street. Larry expresses disillusionment over his ordinariness. "If I'd just have hit that goddamned ball," he complains, "my life would have turned out a whole hell of a lot better."

Twenty years before, on this very day, Larry played a decisive role in an all-state high school championship ballgame. There were two outs in the bottom of the ninth inning. A runner was leading off third base, and his team was down by a run. He was at bat. The count was three-and-two. The pitcher fired the

Before starring in *Mr. Destiny*, Jim Belushi played softball in *About Last Night*; he is pictured with Elizabeth Perkins.

ball. Larry swung … but just an instant too late, and his life was changed forever. For years, he has been obsessed with what his wife calls "that silly baseball game." "Why is it when you do something terrific, nine times out of ten you're all alone," Larry laments, "but when you screw up really big, the whole world is watching?"

Larry gets to relive this fortuitous moment, courtesy of a mysterious, magical bartender named Mike (Michael Caine), a character who could be the kid brother of Clarence, the angel in *It's a Wonderful Life*. Larry consumes one of Mike's concoctions and finds himself replaying that last at-bat. This time, he cracks a home run into the scoreboard and goes on to wed the prom queen and boss's daughter, rather than a working girl. He has become president of the company and lives in a mansion. While his life is different, is it any better? Larry must not be too happy in his marriage, because he has a mistress who is a vicious bitch. His parents are divorced. His best pal (Jon Lovitz) is a friendless, suicidal neurotic. A lot of people despise him. Instead of going bowling, he attends the opera. How boring. Larry realizes that he prefers his old hobby of collecting miniature sportscars to having a garageful of the real ones. More important, his hitting the homer prevented him from winning the girl he truly loves.

From a baseball standpoint, the idea behind the film is fascinating. What if Bobby Thomson had swung a split second later at Ralph Branca's pitch in that final 1951 playoff game between the Brooklyn Dodgers and New York Giants? What if any one of a hundred ballclubs had not sent down that young hurler or outfielder on the verge of making the team because he gave up a homer or swung an instant too late at a pitch in that last spring training game? Maybe that player would have meant the difference between a pennant and a second-place finish.

But *Mr. Destiny* is no *It's a Wonderful Life* or *Field of Dreams*. It is a stale, predictable retread, a movie that must have sounded far better in story conferences. However, its script does include one clever baseball line. Larry's father (Pat Corley), also employed at the sporting goods company, feels that a cutthroat executive (Hart Bochner) is trying to pass off some Japanese players as a championship ballteam from Osaka. "I talked to one of 'em," notes the elder Burrows. "He thinks Mickey Mantle is something over a mouse's fireplace."

Another all-time-great New York Yankee is portrayed in what may be the strangest of all baseball-related fantasies. There is nary a baseball diamond in *Insignificance* (1985, Island Alive), nor are there any idealistic depictions of ballplayers bashing heroic home runs. The film is an allegory about the meaning of fame, the persecution of intellectuals by anti-intellectuals, and the perils of atomic warfare. *Insignificance* remains very much a baseball film if only for its devastating, none-too-flattering characterization of one of the sport's immortals, Joe DiMaggio, played by Gary Busey and referred to only as "The Ballplayer."

The year is 1954, and "The Ballplayer" is married to "The Actress" (Theresa Russell), a blond movie star whom he watches shooting a movie scene over a Manhattan subway grating (just as DiMaggio's then-wife, Marilyn Monroe, did in *The Seven Year Itch*, a sequence whose filming the ballplayer reportedly observed). Like the real DiMaggio, he is bothered that his wife, whom he loves in a private way, is public property. It is mentioned that this athlete, who is now retired, once fashioned a fifty-six-game hitting streak. How many other major leaguers fashioned fifty-six-game hitting streaks?

Beyond this, the film serves as a fantasy portrait of both DiMaggio and the dynamics of the DiMaggio-

Joe DiMaggio.

Marilyn Monroe and Joe DiMaggio, the models for "The Actress" and "The Ballplayer" in *Insignificance.*

Monroe relationship. "The Ballplayer" is a dolt who cannot count past three because there are three bases on a ballfield. He suffers from a swelled ego: "Even my team …" he laments, "They'd rather stare at [my wife] than gab about old times. They treat her like a star or something." He proudly rattles off the names of all the bubble gum card companies who have printed his picture, including "Pinky's," "Tip Top Boys Best Baseball Tips" and "Hubbly Bubbly's Baseball Bites." To whom is he bragging? "The Professor" (Michael Emil), who is a double of Albert Einstein. So "The Actress" is right to tell him, "You're an idiot." Later on, he explains, "I am not stupid. I just enjoy giving the appearance of being stupid."

"The Ballplayer" laments that "The Actress" needs "a thousand people touching her all the time." Yet this is precisely what she despises. All of the people who stare at her make her lonely. This professional sex object with a troubled past actually is a bright, perceptive woman who is an emotional wreck because no one considers her for her intelligence. She seeks out "The Professor," to whom she is attracted because of his brilliant mind. He, in turn, is being persecuted by "The Senator" (Tony Curtis), a slimy Joseph McCarthy clone who lusts after a power that will be

guaranteed him by all the celebrities he is coercing into admitting they are subversives.

In addition to his cameo in *Angels in the Outfield,* the real Joe DiMaggio appears sweetly ill-at-ease in a comedy sketch with Henry Armetta in *Manhattan Merry-Go-Round* (1937, Republic), released during his sophomore year with the Yankees. DiMag is unable to explain himself to the character actor, who smothers the ballplayer with his patented, Italian-accented blathering. Joe auditions as a singer, and is embarrassingly off-key as he begins to croon, "Have you ever been in heaven …" The man will be no threat to Crosby. Armetta asks him, "You tenor, no? You basso, no …?" Joe D's response is simple: "I'm a center fielder." Armetta realizes the identity of the man in his presence. "Ah, DiMaggio," he says. Back in 1937, he may have been the only American not to instantly recognize the Yankee superstar.

Joe DiMaggio was more than a "center fielder." For his generation, he was an authentic, all-American

Marilyn Monroe waves to the crowd during a publicity appearance at Ebbets Field in the 1950s; note the billboard advertising Happy Felton and his Knot-Hole Gang TV show.

hero, a symbol of quiet dignity. But by the mid 1960s, the dawn of the Vietnam era, Simon and Garfunkel could ask, "Where have you gone, Joe DiMaggio?" in *The Graduate*, and answer their query by noting that "Joltin' Joe has left and gone away ..." By 1985, he could be portrayed as he is in *Insignificance*, which just may be the most cynical, unflattering depiction of a baseball player in any movie.

The final baseball fantasy is a sequence in *One Flew Over the Cuckoo's Nest* (1975, United Artists), the screen version of the Ken Kesey novel. Jack Nicholson plays R.P. McMurphy, a convict sent from a work farm to a psychiatric ward to be evaluated with regard to his sanity. The ward is lorded over by Nurse Ratched (Louise Fletcher), who refuses McMurphy's request for a work detail to be changed so that the patients can watch a televised World Series game. After McMurphy musters up sufficient support among the patients—"What's the matter with you guys? C'mon, be good Americans"—his request is nixed on a technicality. So he stares at the blank TV set and commences a radio-style description of an imaginary game in which Sandy Koufax kicks and fires to Bobby Richardson; the Yankee second sacker belts a double, and is followed in the batting order by Tom Tresh. Quickly, all of the men join McMurphy in watching the game, even if it is not a real one.

The nurse's authority is undermined, as it should be. Baseball, after all, is a game for *all* Americans. How dare she deny the men the ritual of enjoying the World Series.

"I'll be over tonight."

A First National Picture

FAVORITE FILMS Presents

TWO MUGS from BROOKLYN

WILLIAM BENDIX ★ MAX BAER in

with MARJORIE WOODWORTH JOE SAWYER

Directed by KURT NEUMANN
A HAL ROACH PRODUCTION

WILLIAM HAINES IN

"SLIDE KELLY SLIDE"

LISTEN to that roaring grand stand,
SPRINGTIME'S here, Oh boy!
BASEBALL, romance, love and laughter . . . .
REMEMBER William Haines in "Brown of Harvard"?
THAT was one glorious football picture!
AND now this happy, handsome star appears in
THE epic picture of the great National pastime
WITH lovely Sally O'Neil and — wow!
MIKE Donlin, Tony Lazzeri, and the
MEUSELS (Irish and Bob) themselves.
FOLLOW the crowd!

Slide Kelly Slide
with WILLIAM HAINES, SALLY O'NEIL, HARRY CAREY
An Edward Sedgwick Production
An original screen play by A. P. YOUNGER
Titles by JOE FARNHAM
Directed by EDWARD SEDGWICK

Metro-Goldwyn-Mayer

"More stars than there are in Heaven"

HAL ROACH presents

WILLIAM BENDIX · GRACE BRADLEY

TAXI, MISTER

JOE SAWYER · SHELDON LEONARD · JACK
NORTON · FRANK FAYLEN · CLYDE FILLMORE
JOE DEVLIN · IRIS ADRIAN

(Above) This ad for *Slide, Kelly, Slide* spotlights William Haines, popular leading man during the late-silent, early-talkie era, who was cast in the title role. Haines plays swaggering Jim Kelly, New York Yankees' ace pitcher and home run hitter, who constantly disobeys his manager. In short, he is a Babe Ruth caricature.

(Top Left) Anna Q. Nilsson and Babe Ruth lock eyes in *Babe Comes Home.* This 1927 comedy was the Bambino's second and last starring role in a feature, following *Headin' Home,* seven years earlier.

(Center and bottom left) William Bendix portrayed base-ball-loving Brooklynite Tim McGuerin in a trio of 1940s Hal Roach "streamliners": *Brooklyn Orchid, The McGuerins from Brooklyn* and *Taxi, Mister.* He proved to be more at home in a "Flatbush" uniform than as Babe Ruth in *The Babe Ruth Story.*

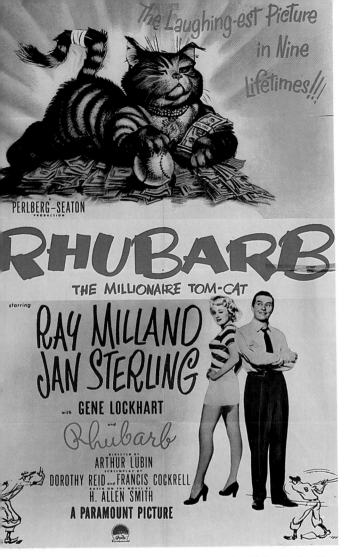

The Laughing-est Picture in Nine Lifetimes!!!

PERLBERG–SEATON PRODUCTION

RHUBARB
THE MILLIONAIRE TOM-CAT

starring

RAY MILLAND
JAN STERLING

with GENE LOCKHART

and *Rhubarb*

DIRECTED BY
ARTHUR LUBIN

SCREENPLAY BY
DOROTHY REID • FRANCIS COCKRELL

BASED ON THE NOVEL BY
H. ALLEN SMITH

A PARAMOUNT PICTURE

M·G·M PRESENTS A NEW AND WONDERFUL PICTURE FOR THE MILLIONS
WHO LOVED "THE STRATTON STORY"

ANGELS IN THE OUTFIELD

Starring

PAUL DOUGLAS
JANET LEIGH

with KEENAN WYNN
LEWIS STONE
SPRING BYINGTON
BRUCE BENNETT

Screen Play by DOROTHY KINGSLEY and GEORGE WELLS
Based on a Story by Richard Conlin
Produced and Directed by CLARENCE BROWN
A METRO-GOLDWYN-MAYER PICTURE

IT'S A PARADE OF PLEASURE FROM WARNER BROS!

"about face" TECHNICOLOR GORDON MacRAE · EDDIE BRAC

(Above) The focus of this poster for *Rhubarb* is the title feline, the Leo Durocher and Billy Martin of pets: a tough alley cat, who comes to inherit Brooklyn's major-league ballclub.

(Below) In *Kill the Umpire,* William Bendix plays Bill Johnson, a die-hard baseball fan forced into becoming "the lowest thing that can happen to a man": an umpire. He attempts to convince an umpire school operator (William Frawley) that he is too blind to attend classes. Frawley, of *I Love Lucy* fame, was cast in many baseball movies. His other credits include *Alibi Ike, It Happened in Flatbush, Whistling in Brooklyn, The Babe Ruth Story, Rhubarb,* and *Safe at Home!*

(Above Top) *Angels in the Outfield* features Janet Leigh as Jennifer Paige, "household hints" columnist-turned-sportswriter. Of course, by the finale, she and Pittsburgh Pirates manager Guffy McGovern (Paul Douglas) will be an item.

(Above Bottom) *About Face,* a musical remake of *Brother Rat,* features an almost identical sequence to one in the earlier film: ballplayer Boff Roberts (Eddie Bracken) being knocked out after he is conked on the head. At his side is Alice Wheatley/Mrs. Boff Roberts (Phyllis Kirk).

(Above Opposite Page) *Moonlight in Havana,* an obscure musical, toplines Allan Jones as ballplayer-singer Johnny Norton. Here, he takes aim before firing.

(Below Opposite Page) *Woman of the Year,* a non-baseball film, nonetheless features an all-time-great baseball sequence. Sportswriter Sam Craig (Spencer Tracy) takes baseball-illiterate newspaper columnist Tess Harding (Katharine Hepburn) to Yankee Stadium; his explanation of the rules of the game becomes a clever variation of Abbott and Costello's "Who's on First?" The comments of a loud-mouthed fan (Jack Carr), pictured directly behind Tracy, add to the humor. Ring Lardner, Jr. and Michael Kanin's screenplay earned an Academy Award.

COLUMBIA PICTURES presents
William BENDIX in
KILL THE UMPIRE

Moonlight In Havana

Spencer TRACY
Katharine HEPBURN
IN
WOMAN OF THE YEAR

A Metro-Goldwyn-Mayer PICTURE

"The Woman Of The Year" forgets her dignity at a baseball game!

FEAR STRIKES OUT

VISTAVISION

starring

ANTHONY KARL
PERKINS · MALDEN

Produced by Alan Pakula
Directed by Robert Mulligan
Screenplay by Ted Berkman and Raphael Blau
Based on a Story by James A. Piersall and Albert S. Hirzberg

A PARAMOUNT PICTURE

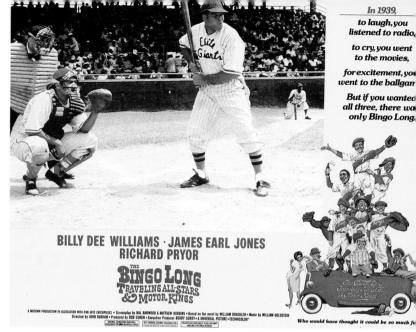

BILLY DEE WILLIAMS · JAMES EARL JONES
RICHARD PRYOR

THE
BINGO LONG
TRAVELING ALL-STARS
& MOTOR KINGS

A MOTOWN PRODUCTION IN ASSOCIATION WITH PAN ARTS ENTERPRISES • Screenplay by HAL BARWOOD & MATTHEW ROBBINS • Based on the novel by WILLIAM BRASHLER • Music by WILLIAM GOLDSTEIN
Directed by JOHN BADHAM • Produced by ROB COHEN • Executive Producer BERRY GORDY • A UNIVERSAL PICTURE • TECHNICOLOR®

Who would have thought it could be so much fun

Irate fathers of Little League baseball players tell manager Tom Ewell they want victories.

M-G-M
Presents "THE GREAT AMERICAN PASTIME"

Copyright © 1956 Loew's Incorporated   COUNTRY OF ORIGIN U.S.A.   6

(Above) In *Damn Yankees,* Lola (Gwen Verdon) really doesn't always get what she wants...

(Top Right) The artwork on this lobby card may have helped to sell *The Bingo Long Traveling All-Stars & Motor Kings,* but it trivializes the racism endured by black ballplayers of the pre–Jackie Robinson era.

(Center Right) In *The Great American Pastime,* a post-war comedy and *Bad News Bears* predecessor, suburbanite Bruce Hallerton (Tom Ewell) becomes manager of his son's Little League team, and must deal with the "win-at-all-costs" mentality of his charges' parents.

(Bottom Right) *Escapade in Japan,* another post-war feature, serves to heal the wounds between the United States and Japan. Here, a Japanese boy (Roger Nakagawa) and American lad (Jon Provost) symbolically are united by the American baseball cap worn by the former.

(Top Left) *Fear Strikes Out* chronicles the hows and whys of the mental breakdown of real-life ballplayer Jimmy Piersall (Anthony Perkins). This lobby card depicts Piersall's state of mind after he cracks up.

(Bottom Left) In *Big Leaguer,* Old Timer John B. "Hans" Lobert, ex-major league third baseman, runs a New York Giants' tryout camp. Here, Lobert (Edward G. Robinson, center) introduces Adam Polachuk (Jeff Richards), his number-one prospect, to his niece, Christy (Vera-Ellen).

The exciting adventures of two little
run-away boys in Japan!

ESCAPADE
in
JAPAN

FILMED IN
TECHNIRAMA® TECHNICOLOR®

ESCAPADE IN JAPAN (Color)   93 mins.
Teresa Wright, Cameron Mitchell, Jon Provost

A little boy, presumably lost in an airplane disaster, wanders across the length and breadth of Japan with a little Japanese boy in an effort to reach his parents. They had nothing in common save dirty faces and an unholy love of mischief. The exotic sights they saw, the strange friends they made, the fun they shared and the dangers they faced — all on the road to a happy ending! It's all here in a charming and thrillingly different motion picture! An Award-winning film that should be shown in every school and seen by every adult. A screen achievement that Hollywood can well be proud of!

TERESA WRIGHT · CAMERON MITCHELL · JON PROVOST · ROGER NAKAGAWA
PHILIP OBER · KUNIKO MIYAKE · Produced and Directed by ARTHUR LUBIN · WILLIAM DOZIER in Charge of Production

FILMED ENTIRELY
IN THE SELDOM-SEEN
CORNERS OF THE

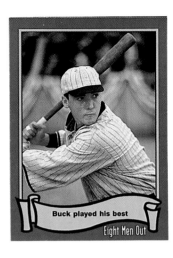

Buck played his best
Eight Men Out

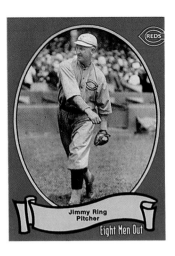

Jimmy Ring
Pitcher
Eight Men Out

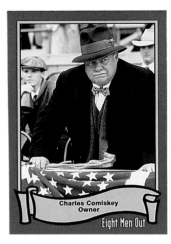

Charles Comiskey
Owner
Eight Men Out

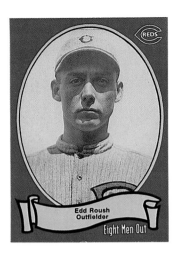

Edd Roush
Outfielder
Eight Men Out

(Above) As a portrayal of the infamous 1919 Black-Sox scandal, *Eight Men Out* is one baseball movie which does not romanticize its subject. Upon the film's release in 1988, Pacific Trading Cards marketed a series of baseball cards featuring the real-life principles (framed in ovals), along with the actors who played them and scenes from the film (framed in squares).

(Left) *Rookie of the Year* is the story of Henry Rowengartner (Thomas Ian Nicholas), a twelve-year-old who gets to realize every baseball-loving boy's dream: to pitch in the majors. Here he is, with his Chicago Cubs' teammates.

Schalk

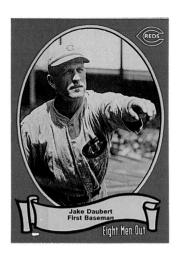

Jake Daubert
First Baseman

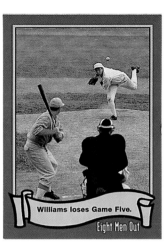

Williams loses Game Five.

Swede Risberg
Shortstop

Eddie Cicotte
29-7 In 1919

(Right) In *Talent for the Game,* Edward James Olmos stars as California Angels scout Virgil Sweet, who will trek to the bowels of the earth to check on a prospect. Lorraine Bracco plays his girlfriend; in a case of life imitating art, the pair (as Susan Sarandon and Tim Robbins, from *Bull Durham*) became romantically involved off screen, marrying in 1994.

(Below) Former minor league hurler Max Patkin, the "Clown Prince of Baseball," has gained fame for his expertise in comically bending his body into various unusual positions. Since 1951, he has been spending his summers entertaining at minor league ballparks. It is fitting, then, that Patkin makes a cameo appearance in *Bull Durham:* a story of life in the minors which is arguably the most knowing of all baseball movies. He is pictured here with Kevin Costner (left) and Susan Sarandon.

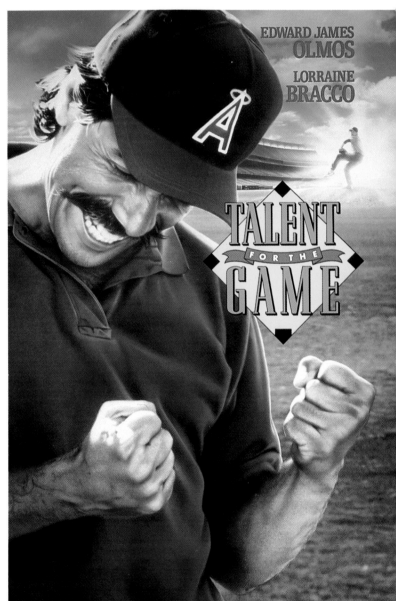

EDWARD JAMES
OLMOS

LORRAINE
BRACCO

TALENT
FOR THE
GAME

(Above) *The Bad News Bears,* an intelligent, immensely likable movie about Little League baseball, was followed by several far-inferior sequels and imitations. In *The Bad News Bears in Breaking Training,* Mike Leek (William Devane) replaces Morris Buttermaker (Walter Matthau) as the team's manager.

(Below) Despite the hype that "It's a whole new ball game!," *Here Come the Tigers i*s just another rip-off of *The Bad News Bears.*

AGING WARRIORS AND
HOT PROSPECTS

The main character in *Big Leaguer* (1953, MGM) is John B. "Hans" Lobert (Edward G. Robinson, a classy actor incapable of a stale performance), real-life major-league third baseman whose career lasted from 1903 to 1917, concluding in a three-year stint with the New York Giants. But the scenario does not chronicle Lobert's athletic feats. He is portrayed as a middle-aged man who runs a Giants' tryout camp in Melbourne, Florida, where eighteen-year-olds from across the country come to see if they have the stuff to earn professional contracts. Lobert's role is to evaluate these raw prospects, and prepare those fit to be signed by the Giants for the rigors of professional sports.

The film opens with an inspirational ode to the game and its great players and feats, with an example of the latter occurring "at the Polo Grounds a couple of years ago, when a young man named Bobby Thomson hit a ninth-inning home run that won the pennant, and every fan in America, for the New York Giants." Its scenario is the "story behind every

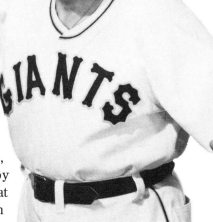

Big Leaguer: Edward G. Robinson as John B. "Hans" Lobert.

Bobby Thomson, every ninth-inning home run, every team like the Giants, and every Polo Grounds."

Among the hopefuls in Lobert's company are Bobby Bronson (Richard Jaeckel), a gutsy small-town hurler who fanned fourteen batters in a championship game and sleeps with a rubber ball in his hand; Tippy Mitchell (Bill Crandall), a shy first baseman whose father is a former big-league star; Julie Davis (William Campbell), a big city braggart and outfield prospect who masks his nervousness by acting tough and telling tall stories; Chuy Aguilar (Lalo Rios), a Cuban who is constantly practicing his English; and Adam Polachuk (Jeff Richards), the "sensitive loner," a strapping third baseman from Pennsylvania coal country to whom Lobert's niece Christy (Vera-Ellen) is attracted. By coming to the camp, Polachuk has defied his illiterate father, "a man who's never even heard of the Brooklyn Dodgers" and would prefer that the boy be studying law in college.

Who will be cut? Who will be signed? Will Lobert "boot one" by releasing a player who really has the ability to make it as a pro? As the camp opens,

Big Leaguer: Lobert (Edward G. Robinson) offers advice to strapping prospect Adam Polachuk (Jeff Richards).

mactic game, with the Giants behind 7–4 in the ninth inning, Carl Hubbell knowingly notes, "The game's now getting interesting": a comment that any baseball devotee will appreciate. Ultimately the film is an ode to the real "Hans" Lobert who, as Christy notes, is "as much a part of the Giants as the name itself."

The classic contrasting of wily elder statesman and young, raw rookie is found in *Bull Durham*, at once a tremendously entertaining film and arguably the most knowing of all baseball movies. Kevin Costner is perfectly cast as Crash Davis, a baseball sage who believes that there should be a constitutional amendment outlawing Astroturf and the designated hitter. Davis is an aging catcher for the Durham Bulls, a tenth-rate team in the low minor leagues. His Triple A contract has been bought by the Bulls, so that he may help mature one Ebby Calvin "Nuke" LaLoosh (Tim Robbins, who makes an ideal foil for Costner). LaLoosh is a rookie with "a million-dollar arm, but a five-cent head." He possesses a major-league fastball, but exhibits a wildness both on and off the field that he must learn to tame. In his first professional game,

Lobert observes, "This is the part I like best. ... Just before we open the Crackerjack box. Maybe there's a real diamond inside. Another Ott. Another Fitzsimmons. Another Hubbell." King Carl himself arrives on the scene to evaluate Lobert's prospects. It seems that a number of nonbaseball people in the Giants' front office have been pondering replacing Lobert. Finding a gem in this group will reaffirm the man's value to the franchise. That diamond might be Adam Polachuk, who belts a game-winning inside-the-park dinger at the finale, in a game between the Giants prospects and Dodgers rookies.

As baseball movies go, *Big Leaguer* rates above average as it details the rigamarole of the tryout camp, with fungos flying through the air that may or may not crash on the dreams of the young ballplayers. During the cli-

Big Leaguer: Lobert (Edward G. Robinson) is dusted off and almost beaned by pitcher Bobby Bronson.

LaLoosh strikes out eighteen, but also walks the same number. Four minutes before gametime, he is warming up not in the bullpen but in the clubhouse, making love to the sexy daughter of the local businessman who donated the stadium scoreboard.

Rounding out the trio of main characters is Annie Savoy (Susan Sarandon), a baseball groupie. "I believe in the church of baseball," she explains as the film opens, in a knowing monologue (which director-writer Ron Shelton has the good sense not to have spoken over a rendition of "Take Me Out to the Ball Game"). "I've tried all the major religions, and most of the minor ones. . . . I know things. For instance, there are 108 beads in a rosary, and there are 108 stitches in a baseball. When I learned that, I gave Jesus a chance. But it just didn't work out between us. The Lord laid too much guilt on me. . . . [But] you see, there's no guilt in baseball. And it's never boring. . . ." Each season, Annie selects one Bull to bed. Along with meeting this designated lover's sexual needs, she will read him Whitman, quote him Blake, and help him channel his energy into improving his game. "There's never been a ballplayer slept with me who didn't have the best year of his career," Annie continues. "Makin' love is like hittin' a baseball. You just gotta relax and concentrate. Besides, I'd never sleep with a player hitting less that .250, unless he had a lot of RBIs and was a great glove man up the middle. . . . 'Course, what I give them lasts a lifetime. What they give me lasts 142 games. Sometimes, it seems like a bad trade, but bad trades are a part of baseball. I mean, who can forget Frank Robinson for Milt Pappas, for god sakes!"

What follows is the story of two ballplayers with contrasting personalities, who are at opposite ends of the professional spectrum. The savvy but physically limited Davis is on his way down in a twelve-year career whose highlight was a cup of coffee in the big time; the dimwitted but physically gifted LaLoosh is on his way up in a career with Hall of Fame potential. Not to forget Annie, who in her own modest way is the consummate baseball fan.

Bull Durham is an astute ode to minor-league baseball, whose stars go unheralded. As the season begins, Davis has hit 227 homers; if he belts twenty more, he will be the all-time champ. As this is a minor-league mark, Annie notes upon his breaking the record that the accomplishment was not even cited in the *Sporting News*. Davis's obscurity is assured because he has spent only twenty-one days in the Show (where, he observes, "the ballparks are like cathedrals"). The scenario also includes many of the

Bull Durham: Annie Savoy (Susan Sarandon), and her Bulls. Crash Davis (Kevin Costner) is at top; Ebby Calvin "Nuke" LaLoosh (Tim Robbins) is at bottom.

rituals that are a special and integral part of baseball in the sticks: home-plate weddings; goofy gimmicks like the outfield mechanical bull that moos when hit by a batted ball; and corny promotions like "Eastern Seaboard Tobacco Growers City Council Little League Cash Drop Day."

Some of the film's most pointed sequences vividly illustrate the thoughts and strategies running through Davis's mind as he faces a rival pitcher, how he psyches himself up while trying to outpsyche the opponent. Baseball, after all, is as much mental as physical. Yet Davis knows that brains alone will not earn a ballplayer major-league stardom. Talent is what will do it: the kind of talent with which LaLoosh has been blessed. Near the end of *Bull Durham*, LaLoosh is called up to the majors when rosters are expanded to finish out the season. Davis tells the kid that he is sure to be roughed up by big-league hitters. "Don't worry about it. You be cocky and arrogant, even when you're getting beat," notes the veteran. "That's the secret. You've got to play this game with fear and arrogance."

The scenario may wax poetic about baseball, but it never ignores the bottom line of professional sports. Old Timers' Days aside, pro ball is a business, and the day-to-day decision-making in the game is devoid of sentiment. At one point, the Bulls' manager (Trey Wilson) must release a young player. The kid pleads for a second chance, remarking that he is in a slump. But the judgment already has been made, and the skipper only can offer sympathy. Despite Davis's success in "maturing" LaLoosh, all of his baseball sense will not prevent the Bulls from releasing him to make room for a younger backstop. There is a finality to this act. It serves as the last nail in the coffin that holds what remains of Davis's dream for baseball fame. While he heads for Asheville, where he has heard there might be an opening for a catcher—"You have to respect a ballplayer who's just trying to finish the season," Annie tells herself—Davis knows that his playing days are over. After hitting his record-breaking dinger at Asheville, he retires as an active player.

There may be a managerial opening the following season in Visalia. Like Annie's, Davis's true talent will be in teaching raw players, and remaining behind as they move up the professional ladder. But Davis will have a new dream: to someday manage in the majors.

Prior to *Bull Durham*, Ron Shelton co-scripted *Under Fire* (1983, Orion), a drama set in Nicaragua in 1979, just before the fall of the dictator Anastasio Somoza to the revolutionary Sandinista forces. In Nicaragua, as in so many Latin American countries where the populace is baseball-crazy, you will find photos of three icons adorning a wall in a house. One, of Somoza, is political. The next, of Jesus Christ, is religious. The third, of Hank Aaron, is baseball.

Photojournalist Russel Price (Nick Nolte) and radio reporter Claire (Joanna Cassidy) are covering the revolution. They come in contact with Pedro (Eloy Phil Casados), a bomb-throwing Sandinista who feels an affinity with Dennis Martinez, the Nicaraguan-born major-league pitcher. Pedro autographs a baseball and instructs Claire to give it to Martinez when she returns to the United States. With a grand gesture, he dons a cap of the Baltimore Orioles, which then was Martinez's team. Quickly, he hurls a grenade with pinpoint accuracy, just as his idol would burn in fastballs

Bull Durham: Crash Davis (Kevin Costner, right) attempts to psych out an opposing hitter.

to American League hitters. "Kid's got a hell of an arm," observes Price, who is told by Pedro that "Dennis Martinez, he is the best. He is from Nicaragua. He pitches major leagues. ... You see Dennis Martinez, you tell him that my curve ball is better, that I have good scroogie ... " Seconds later, Pedro is felled by a bullet.

Hub Kittle (Richard Masur), a political flack, is one of the secondary characters in *Under Fire*. He is named for a career minor league pitcher-skipper who began hurling in 1936 and managing in 1948. Kittle's last full season as a player was 1952, but he pitched occasionally until 1969! He finally made the majors, as a pitching coach for the Houston Astros between 1971 and 1975 and for the St. Louis Cardinals between 1981 and 1983.

With regard to baseball, Ron Shelton knows of what he speaks. He was a minor-league second baseman for five years, and he lived the life of all-night bus rides and ballpark promotions depicted in *Bull*

exists somewhere: the phenom, the kid who was born to be the next Mickey Mantle and, in Sweet's case, the player he could never be.

The scenario takes on a *Field of Dreams* quality when, by an Idaho wheatfield, Sweet discovers that potential Hall of Famer: Sammy Bodeen (Jeffrey Corbett), a raw, insecure farmboy with a one-hundred-plus-mph fastball. Predictably, at the finale, Bodeen will be on the mound for the Angels. Who will be his catcher? None other than Virgil Sweet in disguise, fulfilling his fantasy of at least making one appearance in the big time.

The character of Sweet is contrasted to the Angels' new owner (Terry Kinney), a smug young Steinbrenner who throws splashy parties for the media but has no understanding of the game. To him,

Bull Durham: Director-writer-former minor leaguer Ron Shelton (left), with Kevin Costner.

Durham. Shelton loves baseball, a game of "joy and verve and poetry." Annie's opening quote is bookended by her observation at the finale: "Walt Whitman once said, 'I see great things in baseball. It's our game. The American game. It will repair our losses and be a blessing to us.'" Then she quotes Casey Stengel: "You could look it up."

Bull Durham was followed by a pair of similar baseball dramas. In spite of its inherent hokiness, *Talent for the Game* (1991, Paramount) works as an unabashed feel-good entertainment and an insightful look at the business of baseball. Its primary appeal lies in the commanding performance of its star, Edward James Olmos. He plays Virgil Sweet, a California Angels scout. Sweet's playing career was cut short by injury; like Crash Davis, his dream of major-league glory went unfulfilled. Sweet is a dedicated baseball observer who will trek to the bowels of the earth to scout a prospect (if that prospect is a coal miner). His goal is to find what every scout knows

baseball—and Sammy Bodeen—are products to be marketed, like beer or bathroom tissue. To save money, he will cut what he perceives to be the fat from his operation: the type of baseball man like Sweet, who truly is at the heart of the game. In this regard, *Talent for the Game*, like *Big Leaguer*, is an ode to the obscure scout/coach/manager/teacher whose toiling for long, hard hours in obscurity does not diminish his dedication to baseball.

To its credit, *Talent for the Game* is a movie with a social conscience. Sweet's girlfriend (Lorraine Bracco) may have more education and a higher

Talent for the Game: Jeff Corbett (left) as Sammy Bodeen, Edward James Olmos as Virgil Sweet.

salary, but she loves the man for who he is and not for the size of his wallet. His old friend (Jamey Sheridan), an Angels front-office bureaucrat, offers the view that all might-have-beens spend their lives in the backs of buses drinking whiskey out of Dixie cups. This is a simplistic vision of the world as being divided into happy, wealthy "haves" and miserable "have-nots." It is a generalization that applies neither to Sweet nor to Doc Graham in *Field of Dreams.*

Why use a radar gun to clock a pitcher's speed if the device might eventually harm one's health? A scout who, as Sweet, really understands the game will instinctively know how fast those pitches are zipping toward the plate. Radar guns and computerized scouting reports can never replace the good baseball sense of a man like Virgil Sweet.

Pastime, as *Talent for the Game*, features a central character so likable (and so ingratiatingly played) that he transcends the clichés inherent in the storyline. The film resembles *Bull Durham* as an ode to baseball (at one point a professionally executed double play is compared to a poem), a depiction of life in the minors, and a portrait of a veteran career minor leaguer. Yet its scenario was written in 1973, fifteen years before *Bull Durham* came to movie theaters.

Roy Dean Bream (William Russ) is a forty-one-year old pitcher toiling for the Class D Tri City Steamers. The team's wimpy owner (Jeffrey Tambor) derisively calls him "Methuselah"; his

place on the Steamers' mound staff is secure only because of the kindness of his manager (Noble Willingham). Years before, Bream had pitched in one major-league game, in which he surrendered a grand-slam homer to Stan Musial that "musta traveled seven hundred feet." Now, he is six games away from tying Jack Quinn (who hurled for a number of big-league teams between 1909 and 1933, throwing his last pitch when he was fifty) for most professional baseball appearances by a pitcher. "Ain't gonna be on TV or nothin," he observes, of the feat, "but I'll know." After entering a game in relief and throwing a mile-wide wild pitch, allowing the winning run to score, it appears as if Bream will not be allowed to match Quinn.

The film is set during the summer of 1957, when baseball (like America) wasn't really integrated. Jackie Robinson may have broken the colorline in 1947, but no black ballplayer could be found on the roster of the Boston Red Sox until 1959, when infielder Pumpsie Green played in fifty games. The Steamers' new pitcher, a shy, well-mannered seventeen-year-old black kid named Tyrone Debray (Glenn Plummer, a Doc Gooden look-alike), is ignored by his teammates. Only Bream befriends him, offering the rookie pitching pointers and such fatherly advice as "You develop yourself right . . . who knows . . . It ain't the color. It's the smoke . . . " and "Just being in the game [is] what counts. And doing your best." When Debray doesn't look at him directly, Bream tells him,

Pastime: William Russ (left) as Roy Dean Bream, Glenn Plummer as Tyrone Debray.

"No reason to look at the ground for nobody."

In this regard, *Pastime* resembles so many 1950s Hollywood films, produced for white audiences, which feature heroic black and white characters. While no shuffling caricature, the black (usually played by Sidney Poitier) is a living saint who enjoys the charity of a fair-minded white, and who is fated to die at the hands of the racist heavy and become a martyr. *Pastime*, though, veers from this formula. After learning that he is to be released by the Steamers, Bream breaks into the ballpark and fires baseballs at home plate, trying to experience for one last time the competitive thrill of facing down a batter before a screaming crowd. Only there is no batter, and there is no crowd. Here, the film throws its audience a curve ball: Roy Dean Bream drops dead. Its title takes on a double meaning in that "Pastime" also means past time, or passed Roy Dean Bream's time.

Pastime is a film about might-have-beens. What might have been had Bream pitched those extra few games to tie Jack Quinn? What might have been had he been able to express his feelings and practice the advice he offers Debray, not hide his hurt behind his affable demeanor? What might have happened between Bream (who never married, because he was wedded to the game) and Inez Brice (Dierdre O'Connell), a pretty bartender who thinks he is a "real nice man" but doesn't get to know him before he dies? Bream's death does have a profound effect on Debray. He takes on the Steamers' resident redneck (Scott Plank), earning the respect of his teammates, and ages into a tough, competitive major leaguer. Surely, Bream's spirit lives within him.

Pastime also is of note for the ever-so-brief cameo appearances of Duke Snider, Don Newcombe, Ernie Banks, Bill Mazeroski, Harmon Killebrew and Bob Feller. It is fun to see if you can spot them.

Another similar baseball film whose scenario unspools during the now-ancient summer of 1957 is *Long Gone* (1987, HBO), an above average made-for-television baseball comedy-drama that is full of bite, grit, and good feelings. The story follows the plight of the Tampico Stogies, an inept minor-league team. Its manager and top pitcher, Stud Cantrell (William L. Petersen), is a career bush leaguer who almost-but-not-quite made the majors. He describes himself as "one of the all-time high-school phenoms. In my senior year there were so many big-league scouts on my daddy's front porch . . ." He signed with the St. Louis Cardinals, and rose in the team's minor-league system side-by-side with Stan Musial. Then World

Long Gone: William L. Petersen as Stud Cantrell, Virginia Madsen as Dixie Lee Boxx.

War II began. Cantrell enlisted in the marines and took shrapnel at Guadalcanal. Musial went on to the Baseball Hall of Fame. By 1946, Cantrell's chances for stardom were "down the tubes."

The Stogies are 12 and 23, and in last place. Cantrell is determined to acquire some first-rate players, and he signs Jamie Don Weeks (Dermot Mulroney), a naïve, eager-to-please second baseman who drinks milk, goes to church, and will lead the league in fielding percentage and assists; and Joe Louis Brown (Larry Riley), the "great colored hope," who will smash 37 homers and knock in 106 runs. The Stogies begin winning games and find themselves in a pennant race. Meanwhile, Cantrell becomes involved with a woman who is as persistent and crazy as he is: Dixie Lee Boxx (Virginia Madsen), an Alabama beauty queen.

Long Gone is a film about integrity, on and off the ballfield. The scenario favors the hardworking ballplayers over the greedy, fat-cat management: the Stogies' owners, who would rather sell their talented ballplayers for profit than win pennants; and the top brass of the rival Dotham Cardinals, who promise to hire Cantrell as manager for the following season if he assures them that the Stogies will lose the pennant. Cantrell is reminded that the Cards promote from within their organization, all the way to the "big city." Will Cantrell sell himself out to be back in the Cardinals' organization? Dixie Lee tells him that, if he does, he will be worse than any rich man: he will be white trash. Additionally, the Cards buy off Brown with a new car; Weeks gets the high-school girl with whom he has fallen in love pregnant, and he refuses to acknowledge his responsibility for her situation. All will work itself out by the finale, as this trio individually decides to do right by both their consciences and those who are depending upon them. They are rewarded by the last-second heroics that allow them victory in the league championship game.

Cantrell sums up what baseball should be like—and, metaphorically, what the world should be like—when he observes, "Baseball ain't nothin' but a little boys' game, played on some grass. It shouldn't matter who the pitcher's daddy is, or how much money he makes. It shouldn't matter what color a fella's skin is. You just go out there with a bat in your hands. You hit the ball. You run like hell. That's all."

Long Gone, like *Big Leaguer*, *Bull Durham*, *Talent for the Game*, and *Pastime*, is a film about an aging baseball warrior who links up with younger ballplayers. Some films, though, only focus on the fates of has-been jocks. Perhaps the ugliest of them all is Tenney, the character played by Lee Marvin in *Ship of Fools* (1965, Columbia). Tenney is an on-target cari-

Ship of Fools: Lee Marvin as Tenney.

cature of a lecherous, macho redneck. He is a never-was ex-ballplayer with a fondness for liquor, who attempts to exert his masculinity by acting out his lust for women. The sum of his miserable life is reflected in the scene in which he drunkenly attempts to illustrate for Glocken (Michael Dunn), a philosophizing dwarf, how his downfall in professional baseball resulted from his inability to "hit a curve ball on the outside corner."

As Virgil Sweet, Harry "The Wing" Willette (Alan Arkin), the protagonist of *Cooperstown* (1993, TNT), is a scout who knows the game so well that he does not need a radar gun to clock a young prospect's pitching speed. Otherwise, Sweet and Willette are as different as Babe Ruth and Fred Patek. From the late 1940s through early 1960s, with time off for military service in Korea, Willette was a solid pitcher on a not-so-solid ballclub, the Chicago Barons. Near the end of Willette's career, the Barons and Giants were tied for first place and facing each other with one game remaining in the season. Willette was on the mound for the Barons; this would be his sole shot at making it to the World Series. In the ninth inning, nursing a 1–0 lead, he surrendered a two-run homer to the Giants' Little Eddie McVee: the only dinger McVee ever hit in the majors. The gopher ball was "a bitter end to Willette's long season" and, for all intents and

Long Gone: Dermot Mulroney as Jamie Don Weeks, William L. Petersen as Stud Cantrell, Larry Riley as Joe Louis Brown (left to right).

purposes, a bitter end to the hurler's career.

For thirty years, Willette has been reliving the pitch in his mind. And for thirty years he has blamed this cruel loss on his longtime best friend and battery-mate, Raymond Maracle, a Mohawk Indian. The two had been pals ever since their days in the minors. Their relationship was cemented when Maracle was denied a room in a "whites only" hotel; the young catcher was forced to sleep on the team bus, where he was joined by Willette. However, during the season that climaxed in the Barons–Giants clash, Maracle had been traded to the Giants. Whenever he would throw a change-up, Willette's eye would twitch, and he was convinced that Maracle gave away his secret to McVee. So for all these years, Willette has not spoken to Maracle.

Willette learns that the Veterans Committee of the Baseball Hall of Fame has just voted Maracle into Cooperstown: the first Indian in the Hall since Chief Bender. The ex-hurler is bitter that he again has been passed over for the honor. Even though he has more career victories than ten pitchers already enshrined, Willette is considered a borderline candidate. "Every year for the rest of your life you wait," he says. Each year, "hope fades just a little bit more." If only he had played on a more successful ballclub. If only he had not "lost some of my best years to Korea." He remains hostile even upon learning that Maracle died of a heart attack the night before the announcement, and never even knew of his selection. So Willette hatches a scheme. If Maracle is getting in, he has decided, well then, so will he. He sets off in his car for Cooperstown, with the intention of erecting a mini-shrine to himself in the hall. Along the way, he retrieves his various trophies and mementos, which are scattered across the Eastern United States.

In Willette's company is the spirit of Raymond Maracle (who appears on screen in the person of Graham Greene). As a result of Maracle's "presence," Willette is forced to face various truths about himself and his career. He learns that Maracle did not inform McVee about the twitch. He learns that, even though they had not spoken for so long, Maracle still considered Willette his best friend. He breaks into the Hall of Fame during Maracle's induction ceremony, and he attempts to erect the shrine. But against his will, he becomes a part of the ceremony. In so doing, this faded, forgotten hero realizes that he, too, is being honored. Young fans recognize him and revere him. But most important of all, he has made his peace with Maracle.

Cooperstown: Harry "The Wing" Willette (Alan Arkin, left) vents his rage at the spirit of Raymond Maracle (Graham Greene).

Cooperstown is a story of the redemption of Harry Willette. And in this regard, it is seriously flawed. Willette may be boorish and opinionated, a self-involved grouch and, ultimately, a sad, broken-down shell of a man. Until the finale, most of the characters have never heard of him, or regard him with enmity. But in an instant, he is forgiven for his myriad sins. He is able to converse with, and come to an understanding with, a man who is no longer alive. His grandnephew and the granddaughter of the despised Little Eddie McVee have even become romantically involved.

But the film does offer some astute philosophical allusions to the game. "Baseball is completely zen," Willette tells the grandnephew. "Baseball is the ultimate test of patience, skill, and tactics. In it, momentum is equally balanced by faith." Willette speaks for the Ernie Bankses of the sport when he observes, "I was a meal ticket for a team that never made its way past breakfast." And McVee's granddaughter, a devoted fan, notes, "Baseball is the sport that's closest to

113

life because so much of it is composed of failure."

Trading Hearts (1988, Cineworld) is a film with a far more likable hero. It begins with a nice sequence, played over the opening credits, in which an aging Boston Red Sox hurler, Vinnie Iacona (Raul Julia), toils on a baseball mound. The time is—yet again—1957, the place is spring training, and Iacona is struggling to maintain his spot on the Bosox roster. He toys with the ball in his pitching hand, breathing in and urging himself to "keep it down, keep it down." He grunts as he hurls the ball toward home plate, at which point there is a solid crack of the bat. Iacona fondles the resin bag, wipes his face, and fires the next pitch. Crowd noise fills the soundtrack, along with a pair of sentences that tell the story of Vinnie Iacona: "You're a bum," and "You're all washed up."

Stealing Home: Mark Harmon as Billy Wyatt.

From then on, *Trading Hearts* spirals downhill as quickly as a Cleveland Indians nine plummets into last place. It is a bad film, with a bad script and a clichéd premise. The scenario asks the profound question: What happens to ex-ballplayers who seem headed down a road that will be strewn with boilermakers and empty beer bottles? Why, of course, they fall in love.

After surrendering thirteen hits, Iacona is informed by the Red Sox manager that he is being cut from the team. He may be young for a "human being," but in baseball years he is ancient. Once, he could "throw a hole through the wind." Now, as he wallows in self-pity, he keeps declaring that "this old soup bone . . . is worn, finished . . . I just can't pitch no more," adding that "It ain't my fault, but I'm a has-been now" and "I'm nobody. Nobody."

As Iacona learns of his release, the film cross-cuts to precocious, eleven-year-old Yvonne Rhonda Nottingham (Jenny Lewis) and her mother, Donna (Beverly D'Angelo), a semitalented singer who performs in two-bit gin mills before loutish drunks. They, too, are at a crossroads. Donna is jobless, and she must contend with the sexual advances of her sleazy manager and the attempt of her wealthy ex-husband to gain custody of Yvonne Rhonda.

Predictably, the only feeling Iacona and Donna share upon first meeting is hostility. However, he and Yvonne Rhonda become fast friends. She decides that she wants Iacona for her new father and sets about

manipulating him and her mom into marriage. Yvonne Rhonda is the type of kid who populates television sitcoms. She is wise beyond her years, and she knows more than her elders about what makes the human heart tick. A betting person would not lose a wager that, by the final reel, Iacona and Donna will be ecstatically in love, and the ex-pitcher will have learned how to be a "human being."

Beyond its opening sequence, the highlight of *Trading Hearts* is the presence of Hon. Edward I. Koch, former New York City mayor, in a bit role as a Florida tourist who has "seen herring on the Lower East Side" that is more alive than an alligator on the alligator farm that Iacona, Donna, and Yvonne Rhonda end up operating.

Stealing Home (1988, Warner Bros.) is another film featuring a hero in need of regaining his humanity. It is a likable if unmemorable allegory of baseball and fate, about how turns of events affect people's lives and how it is possible to recapture childhood dreams. Mark Harmon stars as Billy Wyatt, an ex-ballplayer in his late thirties who, as so many former or fading celluloid jocks, is as lost as lost could be. He is unshaven, disheveled, and "living in a motel with a cocktail waitress." The scenario is set into motion as he learns that his old, special friend, Katie Chandler (Jodie Foster), has committed suicide. She has been cremated, and in her will had directed that Wyatt be responsible for her ashes.

The Comeback Kid: John Ritter as Bubba Newman.

As Wyatt returns to his hometown, he remembers his friendship with Katie. When he was ten, she was almost sixteen: a reckless, fun-loving kid who was as much Wyatt's mentor as babysitter. Back then, he loved baseball, a game he shared with his father, Sam (John Shea). Katie presented Wyatt with a small, silver baseball on a chain, for him to wear around his neck. "When things get confused, and believe me, they will," she advised him, "this is to remind you that you're a ballplayer."

Wyatt next recalls his own teen years, as a ballplayer on the Carlton Academy nine. After breaking up a 1–1 tie by stealing home in the ninth inning, he was approached by Bud Scott (Ted Ross), top scout for his favorite team, the Philadelphia Phillies, who invited him to an instructional camp the following summer. "All I want to do is play in the majors," Wyatt told his dad. But his bad luck began after he removed Katie's gift, to give to a girl. His father was killed in a car crash, and he packed his bat, glove, and Phillies cap away in a trunk. "Promise me something," the all-knowing Katie advised him. "You're gonna call up

Bud Scott, and you're gonna start playing again. You're a ballplayer. That's who you are."

These were Katie's parting words to Wyatt, as their lives grew apart. Wyatt did play minor-league ball for the Phillies, but only halfheartedly. He and Mike Schmidt were considered the team's hot prospects, but Wyatt abruptly quit one day and disappeared. He never did see Katie again. She became a troubled woman, enduring a bad relationship with her parents and two failed marriages. Their lives only cross again after her death.

Upon arriving home, Wyatt and his childhood friend, Alan Appleby (Harold Ramis), don their old Carlton uniforms, get drunk, and gallivant around town like a pair of oversize teenagers. As Wyatt faces the responsibility of disposing of Katie's ashes in a manner most befitting the spirit of his friend, he recaptures his youthful zest for baseball and his identity as a jock. Conveniently, the girl to whom Wyatt had presented Katie's gift is now getting a divorce, and is free and willing to rekindle her love for him. Predictably, the film closes with Wyatt playing ball again. He smacks a triple in a tie game and steals home. He, his girl, and his best friend walk off into the horizon.

Billy Wyatt might have been one of the more contented players on the team depicted in *Million Dollar Infield* (1982, CBS), an introspective television movie about impending middle age and midlife crisis. The scenario focuses on a quartet of friends who are united by their love of baseball and their playing on a softball team, the Long Island Bucks. They are collectively sad because they have lost their youth and youthful dreams. They work at jobs they quietly despise, often for their fathers or fathers-in-law. They feel emasculated. They are stuck in predictable suburban life-styles. The trap into which they have fallen is symbolized by the logo on their team caps: a dollar sign.

"I feel like I have nothing to hold on to," observes one of them, Monte Miller (Rob Reiner). "I'm drifting in space. There's nothing to ground me. . . ." Miller loves sports and sports trivia; he realizes that he must do the kind of work he truly enjoys, so he

Chasing Dreams: Kevin Costner (left) is Ed, the older medical student brother of Gavin (David G. Brown).

quits his job and signs on as a reporter for a local newspaper. Miller may be taking a salary cut, but perhaps he will be able to feel some joy. Additionally, the scenario emphasizes the value of family and friendships. The Bucks may lose the season's final game when Miller pops out meekly, but he has learned that, after all, "it's only a game," and he takes his kids for ice cream.

Another effective, entertaining though familiar TV movie with a "there's more to life than baseball" theme is *The Comeback Kid* (1980, ABC), in which John Ritter stars as Bubba Newman, a character who may be charitably described as a clown in a baseball uniform. A pitcher for the minor-league San Jose Stallions, he finds himself getting tattooed, and booed, in a ballgame. Newman doesn't really care. Afterward, he will be able to drink, goof around with his buddies, and pick up some big-bosomed bimbo. His manager informs Newman that he is being sent down to Chattanooga, a city he saw while on his way up in his seven-year career. Poor Bubba Newman! He instigates a bar brawl, then bitterly crunches beer cans and pitches them on a sandlot ballfield. After this, he passes out drunk.

The Comeback Kid is the story of Newman's resurrection as a human being. He

becomes enamored of attractive, dedicated playground supervisor Megan Barrett (Susan Dey), whose track coach has just quit because of his inability to handle her kids. They are a well-scrubbed lot for a bunch of girls and boys who have been "abandoned or ignored, or just beaten down so much they already act like they don't care what happens in their lives ..." Newman covets the job solely because he is interested in Megan. He is reluctantly hired, but plans to make a comeback as a hitter and spends the money allocated for athletic equipment and uniforms on a hitting machine for his own use. He is re-signed by the Stallions and pinch-hits a double to win a game, but realizes that "I don't belong here ... I don't care about the game ... I just kept thinking I'm hanging on, and maybe it's time to let it go. See, I just want to connect with something in my life. ..." Newman had slowly been winning over his charges. With his new-found maturity comes reciprocated romantic affection from Megan.

A pair of innocuous baseball films, *Goodbye, Franklin High* (1978, Cal-Am) and *Chasing Dreams* (1982, Prism), focus solely on young, talented ballplayers who, as many seventeen- and eighteen-year-olds, "have too many questions and not enough answers."

Goodbye, Franklin High is the story of Will Armer (Lane Caudell), a star high-school pitcher.

Chasing Dreams: Parks, a baseball coach (John Fife, right), offers advice to Gavin (David G. Brown).

Chasing Dreams: David G. Brown as Gavin.

Should Armer accept an offer to try out for the California Angels? He could be a superstar, but he just as easily could be cut. Perhaps he should head off to Stanford, where he has been offered a full scholarship? Or he can join his best friend on a journey to Guatemala in search of youthful adventure. Armer also faces parental pressures. His father has a constant cough—he just might keel over and die any second—and his mother is having an affair.

Gavin Thompson (David G. Brown), the hero of *Chasing Dreams*, is an insecure farmboy who has recently graduated from high school and is attempting to "find himself." He discovers an ability to sock a baseball a mile, and is encouraged by his new girlfriend, a friendly coach, and his wheelchair-bound kid brother. His practical-minded father is unconcerned about his needs, and he pressures the boy to abandon

the sport and help out on the family farm.

Baseball may be a game, but if Gavin Thompson and Will Armer do not follow their dreams now, while they are young, they will never know just how good at baseball they might have been. In this regard, *Goodbye, Franklin High* and *Chasing Dreams* mean to be inspirational. Instead, both are corny and boring. They are the kind of films in which you can watch the first fifteen minutes, skip the middle part, and return for the finale without missing a plot thread.

Chasing Dreams is of interest solely for the presence of Kevin Costner, pre–*Bull Durham* and *Field of Dreams*, in the role of Thompson's older, medical-student brother. He appears at the beginning of the film, as he is going off to school, gives brother Gavin a pep talk, and is not seen again.

117

BASEBALL AND WOMEN

uring World War II, some of baseball's greatest stars exchanged their Yankee pinstripes or Dodger blue for GI khaki, and many minor leagues disbanded for the duration. To provide entertainment for those on the homefront as well as "make a buck while the boys are overseas," Chicago Cubs owner Phillip K. Wrigley initiated the formation of the All American Girls Professional Baseball League. The women who played in the league, which began in 1943 and remained in existence through 1954, did so during an era in which those of their sex were expected to remain in their homes and hometowns, changing diapers, scrubbing floors, and toiling over stoves.

The AAGPBL's first year of play is recreated in *A League of Their Own* (1992, Columbia), an entertaining, fictionalized history based on actual events in the lives of these little known, long forgotten women. The scenario is framed by a present-day reunion of surviving ballplayers, in their sixties and seventies, to honor an exhibit at the Baseball Hall of Fame commemorating the league. The two key characters are sisters. The elder, Dottie Hinson (Geena Davis), is a practical, self-assured woman who yearns for her husband's return from the war so that they can resume life on their chicken farm. Dottie has no sense of the importance of her playing in the league. Her sister, Kit Keller (Lori Petty), is constantly agitated because

A League of Their Own: (Left) Geena Davis as Dottie Hinson. (Right) Lori Petty as Kit Keller.

A League of Their Own: Madonna (standing) as Mae Mordabito; also pictured (left to right) are teammates Helen (Anne Elizabeth Ramsay) and Vivian (Sharon Szmidt), and chaperone Miss Cuthbert (Pauline Brailsford).

A League of Their Own: Tom Hanks, as manager Jimmy Dugan, hollers at one of his players (Bitty Schram, portraying Evelyn Gardner), causing her to cry.

A League of Their Own: The Rockford Peaches, played by Robin Knight, Renee Coleman, Rosie O'Donnell, Madonna, Bitty Schram, Anne Elizabeth Ramsay, Ann Cusack (top row, left to right) and Pauline Brailsford, Neezer Tarleton, Patti Pelton, Connie Pounds-Taylor, Kelli Simpkins, Megan Cavanagh, Geena Davis, Lori Petty, Freddie Simpson, Tracy Reiner, and Tom Hanks (bottom row, left to right).

Dottie is both prettier and the better athlete. Kit is bored with her rural life. Playing in the AAGPBL allows her a freedom that she otherwise would not enjoy. Among their teammates on the Rockford Peaches, one of four clubs in the league, are the sexually precocious Mae Mordabito (Madonna) and her buddy, Doris Murphy (Rosie O'Donnell). Their manager is Jimmy Dugan (Tom Hanks), an ex-major-league star and fall-down drunk, hired to helm the Peaches because he is "still a name." At first, Dugan is disdainful of his players. He forgets their names and passes entire games in an alcoholic haze. As the season progresses, he develops respect for the women. He coaches them, and berates them, as he would a team of males. Most of all, he has a deep professional respect for Dottie, the Peaches' catcher, leader, and star, who has earned the nickname "queen of diamonds."

As in real life, there is no feminist motivation behind the formation of the league by Walter Harvey (Garry Marshall), Phillip K. Wrigley's alter ego and the maker of Harvey Bars (rather than Wrigley's Chewing Gum). Prior to their first season, the players are sent to charm and beauty school to learn how to act like "ladies." Their uniforms, abbreviated dresses that reveal lots of leg, are unfit for sliding into bases or pivoting for the double play. Primarily, the women are expected to be sex objects. Marla Hooch (Megan Cavanagh), a frumpy, desperately shy lass who "has an eye like DiMaggio," is almost not signed by Scout Ernie Capadino (Jon Lovitz) because of her resemblance to General Omar Bradley. Once the season starts, the players are filmed by newsreel cameras powdering their noses after sliding into bases and knitting while on the bench. Despite these indignities, or the occasional fan who will deride them with chants of "Girls can't play ball," the Peaches practice hard and play capably and aggressively. They ignore their various sprained ankles and broken fingers, and are determined to win. As time passes, attendance at their games steadily increases (which allowed for the league's continuation after the war). They just miss winning the championship when Kit (who has been sold to the rival Racine Belles, the Peaches' opponents) crashes into home plate, jarring the ball out of Dottie's hand.

Happily, *A League of Their Own* does not preach about a woman's need for liberation. The film simply mirrors a woman's right to choose her own life-style, whether it be more traditional (as does Dottie, who returns to her farm at the end of the season upon her husband's arrival home from the war), or one that is different, which offers more possibilities (as does Kit). The scenario never dismisses the need for men in these womens' lives. One sequence records the heartbreak as a Peach learns that she has been widowed in the war. When Dottie's husband appears, they vow that they will hold each other for the rest of their lives. Yet the point is clear that women are capable of thinking for themselves, making decisions, and playing baseball, and that there is no need for a woman ever to be secondary to a man.

If *A League of Their Own* shows how women can,

and indeed did, play professional baseball in a league of their own, the point of *Blue Skies Again* (1983, Warner Bros.) is that a woman with the proper skills can play competitively and professionally *with* men, on a major-league level. The film's tone is set over the opening credits, in a dewy, surreal sequence in which a group of demure women in Victorian garb picnic on a lawn. Incongruously, they arise, produce a bat and don mitts, and commence tossing around and batting a baseball. Cut to Ft. Lauderdale Stadium, winter home of the Major League Denver Devils. Ballplayers are practicing on the field and Paula Fradkin (Robyn Barto) looks on admiringly from the empty stands,

Blue Skies Again: Harry Hamlin as Sandy Mendenhall.

with an I-can-do-this-as-well-as-they-can smile. A security guard informs Paula that the public is not allowed in the ballpark until noon. "Oh, I'm not the public," she responds. However, Paula is not cocky. She is a likable young woman who knows her baseball trivia as well as any sports-obsessed barfly. In this new era in which ballplayers are as concerned with agents, hold-outs, and no-trade clauses as with fielding, batting, and baserunning, all Paula wants is "to play second base for the Devils."

Liz West (Mimi Rogers), a ballplayers' agent, decides to support Paula not out of feminist inclination

Blue Skies Again: Robyn Barto as Paula Fradkin, incurring the ire of the Denver Devils as she is determined to make the team.

but because she could be "worth a fortune" in endorsements. West manipulates Dirk Miller (Kenneth McMillan), the Devils' manager, into allowing Paula a one-at-bat tryout. After bashing a line-drive, she gets a second pitch that brushes her off the plate. But she crashes the third delivery. And the fourth. And the fifth. In the field, she is quick. She makes all the plays, even the one in which the runner takes her out while she pivots at second base to complete the double play. Nonetheless most of the Devils consider her a freak. New team owner Sandy Mendenhall (Harry Hamlin), a bossy, smarmy yuppie who shamelessly bullies manager Miller, will not even consider her as a prospect, just because of her gender. During a second tryout, which Mendenhall allows because of his romantic interest in West, he directs the Devils to mercilessly taunt Paula into losing her concentration, swinging and missing at pitches, hitting meek pop-ups and grounders.

Paula questions her objectives, but she perseveres. To rankle his boss, Miller allows her a surprise pinch-hit at bat during the Devils' first preseason exhibition. She faces the Memphis Blues' star hurler, the notorious Chico "Brushback" Carrasco (Marcos Gonzales), hanging in against him and cracking a double down the third-

base line. Mendenhall, who has devised a "new look" for the Devils that includes sexy, dumb-blond ballgirls, is beseiged by the media and accepts credit for Paula's success. "Brushback," meanwhile, smiles at her approvingly. Not all ballplayers will be bothered by competition from a female.

While by no means a great film, *Blue Skies Again* is as insightful as any other baseball movie. At Paula's first tryout, a white ballplayer tells his black counterpart, "I can't see Mendenhall being the one to integrate base-ball." When the black man glares at him, the white man begins to sputter. "You know what I mean . . ." he says, and "integrate" is soon replaced by "interfeminate." Pre–Jackie Robinson, major-league ballplayers would have been equally incredulous at the thought of a Negro on the roster of the New York Yankees, Boston Braves, or St. Louis Browns. *Blue Skies Again* may be a baseball fairy tale, but it is not one in which angels inhabit outfields or devils transform middle-aged men into graceful Joe Hardys. It is a fairy tale which, one day, may indeed come true.

Blue Skies Again and *A League of Their Own* are not the initial Hollywood features depicting women on baseball diamonds. *Gracie at the Bat* (1937,

Girls Can Play: Jacqueline Wells (left) as Ann Casey, Rita Hayworth as Sue Collins.

122

Girls Can Play: Rita Hayworth (in catcher's gear) as ill-fated Sue Collins, George McKay as Sluggsy, Jacqueline Wells as Ann Casey.

Columbia) is a two-reel comedy that resembles the Ernest Lawrence Thayer poem in name only. Andy Clyde plays Pop, a former ballplayer of the Ty Cobb era who is called to Philadelphia to manage the Fillies, a girls' softball team. Predictably, he must contend with temperamental players who peruse romance magazines and powder their noses in the dugout. In the ninth inning of a tie game, his wife—who years before was known as "Fireball Gracie"—informs Pop that she is coming in to pitch. Gracie has the oddest wind-up, but she literally throws smoke at an opposing batter. Unlike the Mighty Casey, she belts the game-winning homer.

Despite the fact that the scenario portrays young women as athletes, *Girls Can Play* (1937, Columbia) is no ode to sexual equality. The "girls" of the title are cast primarily for their attractiveness, and the film is of note only for the presence of young Rita Hayworth, third-billed in the credits, then serving her apprenticeship as a Columbia B-film player.

Girls Can Play is the story of Foy Harris (John Gallaudet), a drugstore owner/ex-racketeer who organizes a girls' softball team as a front for selling watered-down liquor. Eventually, in a sequence that could be a replay from the baseball mystery *Death on the Diamond,* he murders his girlfriend, Sue Collins (Hayworth), because she "knows too much." Sue is the team's catcher and captain, and is poisoned on the ballfield. The athletic exploits of the women may be depicted: At one point, Sue belts a long double, and teammate Ann Casey (Jacqueline Wells, before she became Julie Bishop) is shown to be an ace hurler and home-run hitter. But next to the male characters, they are passive sex objects and victims. It is up to thick-witted reporter Jimmy Jones (Charles Quigley), who is supposedly in love with Ann, to uncover the culprit.

The film has less in common with *A League of Their Own* or *Blue Skies Again* than with *Squeeze Play* (1980, Troma), a loud, sloppy sexploitation comedy about a group of girls whose guys live for their softball team. The females, feeling neglected (and constantly exposing their cleavage), decide to form their own team and beat the boys at their own game.

Unfortunately, the manner in which women and sports are depicted on screen is more the rule in *Squeeze Play* and *Girls Can Play* than in *A League of Their Own* and *Blue Skies Again.*

Squeeze Play: Jim Harris as Wes, Jenni Hetrick as Samantha.

Death on the Diamond: Madge Evans as Frances, Robert Young (center) as Larry Kelly, David Landau as Pop Clark.

Death on the Diamond: Hogan (Nat Pendleton, left), the St. Louis Cards' catcher, has a comical love-hate relationship with O'Toole (Ted Healy), an umpire.

BASEBALL MYSTERIES
AND DRAMAS

n most baseball films, it is no mystery that the hero is destined to wallop a game-winning homer in the closing moments. Perhaps this explains why there are so few mysteries set on ballfields. Aside from the aforementioned *Girls Can Play*, there is *Death on the Diamond* (1934, MGM), an unconvincing thriller in which an unknown killer is knocking off the ballplayers who have transformed the St. Louis Cardinals, described at the start of the season as strictly a "tail end ballclub," into a pennant contender. The team's leading hitter (Joe Sauers, who later became Joe Sawyer) is shot through the heart while rounding third base after lashing a hit. A star pitcher (Robert Livingston) is strangled, and his corpse is stuffed into his locker. The catcher (Nat Pendleton) with a fondness for hot dogs is done in via some poisoned mustard. Could the killers be a pair of shifty ex-ballplayers, banned from the game for gambling, who have been hanging around the team? Perhaps the culprit is an emissary of Karnes (C. Henry Gordon), "one of the biggest gamblers in the country," who will lose close to a million dollars if the Cards cop the crown? Maybe he is a hired gun of the man who will gain financial control of the team from its manager, Pop Clark (David Landau), if the Cards finish anywhere in the standings below first place.

Robert Young stars as Larry Kelly, talented rookie pitcher up from the Texas League, who solves the riddle after noticing a shadowy figure in the Cards' dugout as he is set to toss a pitch in the game that will decide the pennant. Instead of throwing to home plate, he conks the culprit in the head. The villain is among the least obvious of all the characters: Patterson (DeWitt Jennings), the kindly old groundskeeper, an ex-ballplayer who reveals himself as a madman who covets Pop's job.

Among the film's more annoying contrivances: the players become increasingly edgy as teammate after teammate is murdered, yet Pop Clark barks at them to get on the field and play as if they are a bunch of shirkers. Of course, after his heroics in capturing the killer, Kelly wins the game, and the pennant, with an inside-the-park home run. *Death on the Diamond* is noteworthy only for the presence of Mickey Rooney, in a small role as a clubhouse boy, and for glimpses of Walter Brennan and Ward Bond in bit parts.

Play Ball (1925, Pathé) is an obvious name for a baseball movie. It is the title of a 1917 Pokes and Jabs comedy; a 1931 Aesop's Fables cartoon; a 1932 Terrytoons cartoon; a 1933 Willie Whopper cartoon; and a 1937 Terrytoons cartoon. This version is a ten-episode serial starring Allene Ray and Walter Miller, whom film historian and author Alan G. Barbour calls "the most famous serial team of the twenties," with a story attributed to John McGraw (but actually conjured up by Frank Leon Smith, the Pathé serial writer). The scenario details the plight of Jack Rollins (Miller), a senator's outcast son and New York Giants' rookie. He becomes involved with Doris Sutton (Ray), a rich man's daughter, and an exiled nobleman who is planning an insurrection in his native country. In the first three episodes alone, Rollins rescues Doris from

Play Ball: Walter Miller (third from left) as Jack Rollins.

Play Ball: Allene Ray as Doris Sutton, J. Barney Sherry as Thomas W. Sutton (both, front row center).

sharks, stops a quartet of runaway horses, and races a car against an express train. Rest assured that all will end happily, if only because of the title of episode number 10: "Home Plate Wedding."

Most of the action in *Play Ball* unspools away from the ballfield. "I didn't have to be told that Pathé wanted melodrama," wrote Frank Leon Smith, in a 1968 letter to *Films in Review,* "but how do you get life-&-death motives into a serial involving a ball team? You can't unless you keep your melodrama well away from the baseball diamond. . . . I've been criticized lately by film historians because the story's 'con-

trived.' Well, maybe one of these historians will try some day to evolve a film dramatizing a Big League team in action that is plausible and profitable. Maybe he will even try it with the Mets. I wish him luck."

The Adventures of Frank Merriwell (1936, Universal), a twelve-episode serial based on the Bert L. Standish stories, features Don Briggs in the title role. In the books, "Merry" attends Yale; on screen, he is a student at the fictional Fardale College. At the outset, he belts a grand slam homer to lead his school to a come-from-behind 4–3 victory, and then becomes involved with a "mysterious old ring that carries the secret to buried Spanish gold." He is hurled through raging rapids; battles a wildcat, a circus lion, and an octopus; and faces other perils while demonstrating his skills at boat rowing, during a track meet, and on the gridiron. The spirit of the serial is captured in the names of its chapters. The first and last are, respectively, "College Hero" and "The Winning Play." Those in between include "Death at the Crossroads," "Descending Doom," "Monster of the Deep," "Between Savage Foes," "Imprisoned in a Dungeon," and "The Crash in the Chasm."

In *Experiment in Terror* (1962, Columbia), a maniacal killer (Ross Martin) attempts to terrorize a bank teller (Lee Remick) into stealing $100,000, and a dedicated FBI agent (Glenn Ford) comes to her aid. The finale is set in San Francisco's Candlestick Park, where the Giants are battling the Los Angeles Dodgers. During the game, there are expressive close-ups of Dodger hurler Don Drysdale taking signs from his catcher, nodding, winding up, and pitching. The Giants' Harvey Kuenn is seen cracking a double; he is followed to the plate by Felipe Alou. The Dodgers' Wally Moon appears in close-up as he clutches a bat. He beats out an infield hit to shortstop Jose Pagan and announcer Vin Scully describes the ensuing rhubarb, the participants of which include Giant hurler Mike McCormick, catcher Ed Bailey, first baseman Willie McCovey, and second baseman Joe Amalfitano.

The game concludes, and the villain lurks behind a pillar as the fans file out of the ballpark. As he begins walking by the heroine's side, the hero and his fellow G-men close in for the capture. One pushes the heroine to safety, while the hero jumps on the villain. He escapes, rushes through the crowd, and makes his way onto the empty playing field. The hero shoots him, and he is sprawled across the pitcher's mound, where he wheezes and then dies.

To find another pure baseball mystery on a

The Adventures of Frank Merriwell: Donald Briggs as Frank Merriwell, flanked by Jean Rogers as Elsie Bellwood and John King as Bruce Browning.

movie screen, you have to go all the way to *Night Game* (1989, Trans World). The film opens with someone slashing to death a pretty blonde on a beach, near a Galveston, Texas, amusement park, bloodying her white dress. Her demise is the latest in a series of grisly murders of attractive women. With hard-boiled homicide cop Mike Seaver (Roy Scheider) on the case, you know that the culprit will be uncovered—but not before several other women meet similar fates.

What does all this have to do with baseball? Seaver, an ex-ballplayer, is not only a good cop but a Houston Astros fan. "If it's not the killer, it's baseball," complains his fiancée (Karen Young). "If it's not baseball, it's the killer." Even though there is a murderer on the loose, beautiful blondes keep mindlessly wandering off by themselves in this bubble-headed scenario, only to become bloody corpses. In the end, the fiancée finds herself in the killer's clutches and is rescued by Seaver via last-second heroics. This happens after the cop deduces that a killing occurs each time a certain Astro rookie hurler wins a night game at home. The culprit is a pitcher the club had released to make room for the newcomer. On the day he was let go, the bus he was riding in collided with a semi. His pitching hand was amputated and replaced by the hook that is the murder weapon.

Night Game qualifies as the first-ever baseball-slasher movie. Beyond this distinction, the sole inter-

esting moment is one in which Yogi Berra, then an Astros coach, is briefly seen in the Houston dugout. Thematically speaking, it has a predecessor of a sort in *Murder at the World Series* (1977, ABC), a by-the-numbers made-for-TV movie about a young ballplayer, angered after his rejection by the Astros, who masterminds a kidnapping scheme at the Astrodome during the World Series.

The first feature-length baseball films focusing more on melodrama than mystery date from the second decade of the century with *Right Off the Bat* and *One Touch of Nature*. Others followed during the 1920s, and you can bet that those that are strictly dramatic in tone feature villains conspiring to throw ballgames. In *Catch-as-Catch-Can* (1927, Lumas), William Fairbanks plays Reed Powers, a baseball manager accused of doing just that. He is in love with the sister of the real culprit, a pitcher (Larry Shannon). To protect the hurler, he stoically accepts blame but is destined to be exonerated and win the girl. Rockliffe Fellowes stars in *Trifling With Honor* (1923, Universal) as Bat Shugrue, an ex-con who earned the nickname "Gas-Pipe Kid," and whose resemblance to the Bambino ends with his other identity as the "Babe Ruth of the Pacific Coast League." Years before, Shugrue escaped to freedom during a trial. He comes in contact with his former sweetheart

Trifling With Honor: Rockliffe Fellowes as Bat Shugrue, Fritzi Ridgeway as Ida.

The Bush Leaguer: Monte Blue (right) as "Specs" White, with Clyde Cook as Skeeter McKinnon.

Warming Up: Tulliver (Richard Dix, second from right, in foreground) battles with McRae (Philo McCullough); holding the latter is Hippo (Roscoe Karns), the catcher.

Ida (Fritzi Ridgeway), who is now the stenographer typing his watered-down life story for a news service. Gamblers who know of Bat's past attempt to bribe him into throwing a game, but he refuses because he has come to appreciate his positive influence on young fans, and ends up pinch-hitting a game-winning round-tripper. In *Life's Greatest Game* (1924, FBO), Tom Santschi plays Jack Donovan, a hurler who refuses to throw a game. He is convinced by a vengeful gambler that his wife has been faithless and that he is not his son's real father. When he learns the truth, the wife and son supposedly have left for Europe. Only they have missed their ship, which ends up wrecked, and Donovan believes that they are lost at sea. Years later, the boy (Johnnie Walker) becomes a college pitching star, and joins the big-league team his dad is managing. To spite Donovan, whom he believes had abandoned his mother, young Jackie Donovan decides to throw a game, but good sportsmanship prevails at the end. According to *Variety,*

> The [boy] on meeting his father keeps his true identity hidden and finally at the precise minute of the crucial game for the world's champi-

onship between the Giants and the Yanks, the kid, though a rookie, is put in the box and saves the day by pitching a flawless inning, adding a heavy clout to cinch the world's championship, practically single-handed.

Two other 1920s dramas are more lighthearted in tone. Monte Blue stars as "Specs" White in *The Bush Leaguer* (1927, Warner Bros.). Specs is an Idaho garage owner and ace hurler who is called to the big leagues, where he suffers from "crowd fright" and

Warming Up: Richard Dix, as "Bee Line" Tulliver, tussles with an umpire.

128

falls for the heiress who owns his team (Leila Hyams). In a plot line similar to the one in Joe E. Brown's *Fireman, Save My Child* (1932, First National), he invents a gas pump and, noted *Variety,*

> While negotiating with some big business men for the marketing of his invention he forgets that he is supposed to be pitching his club to a victory in the game that clinches or loses the pennant. He arrives for [the] ninth inning, singlehanded snatching defeat from the visiting club.

In *Warming Up* (1928, Paramount), Richard Dix plays Bert "Bee Line" Tulliver, a small-town pitching star so named for his ability to control his tosses. Tulliver makes it to the major leagues but not before battling with McRae, his home-run-hitting soon-to-be ex-teammate and challenger for the hand of Mary Post (Jean Arthur), the club owner's daughter; their rivalry begins during spring training, when McRae fools Tulliver into thinking he has beaned a batter. Eventually Tulliver faces McRae in the World Series. Out of nervousness, the hurler walks his nemesis with the bases loaded, forcing in a run. He is removed from the game and doesn't return to the mound until the deciding contest. He again confronts McRae with the bases filled. With the encouragement of the girl he loves, "Bee Line" whiffs his adversary to win the championship.

Segue to the early 1940s, when the Brooklyn Dodgers were emerging from years of second-division ineptitude and rewarding their fans with championship baseball. In 1941, they battled to win their first National League title in twenty-one years (while, typically, losing four of five World Series games to the hated New York Yankees). At this time (as well as a decade later), the Dodgers (both real and fictional) and their legendary fanatical fans were featured in several Hollywood movies. *The Jackie Robinson Story* is the most consequential, but there were comedies such as *Whistling in Brooklyn* (1943, MGM) and childrens' fantasies such as *Roogie's Bump*. In the drama category, *It Happened in Flatbush* is an otherwise unmemorable film that does capture the flavor of baseball Ebbets Field–style, with the wear-your-emotions-on-your-sleeve enthusiasm of the Dodgers' faithful.

Lloyd Nolan stars as Frank Maguire, ex-Dodger who eight years before had made an error in a key game. He summarily left the

It Happened in Flatbush: Lloyd Nolan as Frank Maguire.

team, and has now been resurrected by the Dodgers' owner (Sara Allgood) as the team's skipper. Unfortunately, Maguire's benefactor dies and he must contend with her heirs, who view the game solely as a means of making money. He romances socialite Kathryn Baker (Carole Landis), in the hope that she will acquire major stock in the club. He deals with his lethargic players, who are unwilling to battle to win

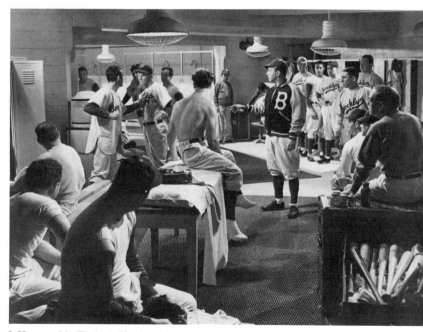

It Happened in Flatbush: Lloyd Nolan (center), as Frank Maguire, attempts to ease locker-room tensions.

Bang the Drum Slowly: Robert De Niro as Bruce Pearson.

Mammoths. Henry Wiggen (Michael Moriarty), the Mammoths' franchise player, is a glamour-boy star pitcher. He has just written a book, so everyone calls him "Author." Bruce Pearson (Robert De Niro), his roommate, is a backwoods boy and Vietnam veteran. He is a none-too-bright reserve catcher who might be described as the twenty-sixth man on a twenty-five-man roster. And he is terminally ill.

Wiggen, a kind and decent man, is determined to protect Pearson's secret for fear that the backstop will be dumped from the team. Before the season begins, he learns that the Mammoths' manager, Dutch Schnell (Vincent Gardenia), is planning to cut Pearson in favor of Piney Woods (Tom Ligon), a "wild, crazy" catcher who is "Dutch's good hope." Wiggen hasn't signed his contract, and is holding out for more money, but he agrees to compromise on a lesser amount if a clause is added "saying that I and Bruce Pearson will stay with the club together or else go together. Whatever happens to one must happen to the other. Traded. Sold. Whatever."

The pitcher evades the questions of Schnell, a hard-nosed veteran of the baseball wars, while Pearson for the first time in his career plays regularly and hits steadily. Eventually, Pearson's teammates learn of his illness and rally around him. The petty dif-

games. In the heat of the pennant race, the players get up a petition for Maguire's removal, but he refuses to quit. Instead, he rallies the team to a typical, predictable outcome in the season's crucial final game.

A year before appearing in *It Happened in Flatbush*, Lloyd Nolan starred (along with Robert Armstrong, cast as a sportwriter who constantly harasses Maguire) in a feature with a faint baseball theme: *Mr. Dynamite* (1941, Universal), a programmer in which Nolan plays Tommy N. Thornton, star major-league pitcher set to hurl in the World Series (for St. Louis, against Brooklyn), who becomes involved in murder and an international spy ring.

The single great baseball drama, as well as one of the best baseball movies of all time, is *Bang the Drum Slowly* (1973, Paramount), adapted by Mark Harris from his novel. This eloquent, heartbreaking story about the ebb and flow of a baseball season, and the ebb and flow of life, features a fresh, believable naturalism in its script, staging, and acting. The scenario highlights the bond between a pair of ballplayers on the same major-league team, the New York

Bang the Drum Slowly: Michael Moriarty (left) as Henry Wiggen, Robert De Niro as Bruce Pearson.

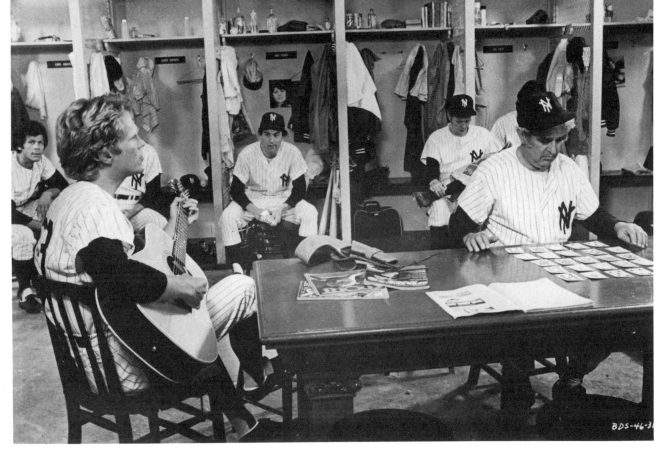

Bang the Drum Slowly: Piney Woods (Tim Ligon, with guitar) strums "Streets of Laredo"; Bruce Pearson (Robert De Niro) is at left center; Henry Wiggen (Michael Moriarty) reads a magazine; coach Joe Jaros (Phil Foster) plays solitaire.

ferences and ragging that have disrupted the team are replaced by a genuine camaraderie. Notes Wiggen, "It was a club, like it should have been all year. . . . " The Mammoths cop the pennant, but by then Pearson is too sick to continue playing. He returns home. Wiggen reports that the team succeeded in the play-offs, and won the World Series. He is last seen a couple of months later, in a Georgia cemetery, where he has just concluded his duties as one of Bruce Pearson's pallbearers.

Bang the Drum Slowly is crammed with bitter irony. After learning that he is to be sent to the minors in favor of Pearson, Piney Woods complains to Wiggen that "life is unfair," adding that he wishes someone on the roster would drop dead so a slot would open up for him. Later on, Pearson's father caustically notes that he cannot comprehend how his son can play so well yet be so sick.

The story is loaded with insight, as it offers a subtle but uncompromising condemnation of uncaring baseball executives who would have the players pay them to play ball; insensitive jocks who constantly rag one another over their ethnic or racial backgrounds, styles of dress, or whatever; and golddiggers like Katie (Ann Wedgworth), a tramp who wishes to

exploit the naïve Pearson by having him sign over to her his life insurance policy.

There is plenty of eloquence. In the film's first sequence, Wiggen and Pearson are seen jogging side by side, inside an empty ballpark. As the final out is recorded and the Mammoths win the pennant, the ballplayers are shown in slow motion celebrating on the field. By then, Pearson's illness is obvious. The gentlemanly Henry Wiggen retrieves his friend's fallen cap from the dust, and puts it back on Pearson's head.

And there is plenty of one-to-one humanity, the essence of which is found at the end of a heartbreaking sequence in which Pearson becomes ill during the night and requests of his roommate, "Hold on to me." Wiggen, meanwhile, keenly understands that there is more to life than power, money, and even baseball. At one point, he observes, "It's a ballgame, sir. You win 'em. You lose 'em."

Bang the Drum Slowly is a story of how fatal illness or accident can strike down the heartiest of young men, even a strapping athlete. There are more than a few Bruce Pearsons in real life: remember Harry Agganis, Ernie Davis, Ken Hubbs, Lyman Bostock, Hank Gathers, Thurman Munson—and Lou

Bang the Drum Slowly: Paul Newman (Henry Wiggen), George Peppard (Piney Woods) and Albert Salmi (Bruce Pearson), in the 1956 *U.S. Steel Hour* version (left to right).

Gehrig! A key to the film is the constant presence on the soundtrack of the song "Streets of Laredo." Soulful, mournful instrumental versions are heard at various intervals. At one point, it is sung in the locker-room by Piney Woods. Its lyric vividly captures the harshness of Bruce Pearson's fate: a young cowboy dies, and asks for gamblers to carry his coffin and for the drum to be banged slowly as he is hauled to the valley where he will be covered by sod.

The film is narrated by Wiggen, who bookends the scenario by observing near the opening, as he and Pearson are leaving the Mayo Clinic, that

> ... You're driving along with a man's been told he's dying, and yet everything keeps going on. I mean, it's been hard enough rooming with him when he was well. ... As a catcher, he was $1-million worth of promise worth two cents on delivery. Most people didn't know he was with the club. And, um, he was almost too dumb to play a joke on. And now he'd been played the biggest joke of all.

At the end, Wiggen is in the Georgia cemetery, at the conclusion of his friend's funeral. "There were no flowers from the club, and no person from the club," he notes. "They could have sent somebody. He [Pearson] wasn't a bad fellow. No worse than most, and probably better than some. And not a bad

ballplayer neither, when they gave him the chance, when they laid off him long enough.

"From here on in," Wiggen concludes, "I rag nobody."

Bang the Drum Slowly was originally produced on television in 1956, as a segment of *U.S. Steel Hour.* Paul Newman, then a young actor just about to earn celluloid superstardom, was cast as Henry Wiggen. Albert Salmi played Bruce Pearson, and George Peppard appeared as Piney Woods.

During the 1980s, a number of dramas, each with literary origins, featured telling baseball references and characters tainted by tragedy. *Birdy* (1984, Tri-Star), based on the novel by William Wharton, is the tale of two young men irreparably scarred by their service in Vietnam. Al Columbati (Nicolas Cage), whose face was disfigured in battle and has been reconstructed through plastic surgery, visits his pal Birdy (Matthew Modine), who is incarcerated in a psychiatric hospital. The latter has had a life-long fascination with birds; now, afflicted with severe combat fatigue, he has withdrawn into the fiction that he is a bird. As Columbati attempts to connect with Birdy, he remembers their youth in Philadelphia. The pair met when Birdy's mother balked at returning the baseballs Columbati and his pals would belt over her back fence.

The scenario of *Cannery Row* (1982, MGM), an adaption of John Steinbeck's "Cannery Row" and "Sweet Thursday," resembles *The Natural* in that it features a ballplayer-hero whose potential greatness is marred by disaster. Doc (Nick Nolte), a kindhearted marine biologist with a hidden past, is one of the inhabitants of Steinbeck's Cannery Row. According to Fauna (Audra Lindley), a madame-with-a-heart-of-gold, Doc "played some ball once." Eventually it is revealed that Doc's real name is Ed Daniels, who was known as "The Blur" when he pitched for the Philadelphia Athletics. "I had a couple of bad years ..." he tells Suzy (Debra Winger), a drifter-turned-trollop with whom he shares a hate-love relationship. Yet when he abandoned baseball, Doc was 21 and 10 with three weeks left in the season. "I threw a bad pitch," he finally admits.

> It hit a guy. It hit him in the head. At first I thought I'd killed him. He was in a coma for two weeks. He came out of it. But he was never the same after that. You know, I

yelled at him, but I don't think he ever saw the ball coming. My heart wasn't in [the game] anymore.

The player he beaned ended up in a mental hospital. Doc knew that he would not survive there, so he had the man released into his care. Doc looks after him, and no one knows that he is the most eccentric of Cannery Row's many down-and-outers. "I don't want to be around people who feel sorry for me because they're sure I could have been great," Doc tells Suzy. But in his modest way, Doc is a great man.

Ironweed (1987, Tri-Star), scripted by William Kennedy from his novel, stars Jack Nicholson as Francis Phelan, a middle-aged hobo surviving on the streets of Albany, New York, in 1938. Twenty-two years before, Phelan had accidently dropped his infant son. The baby died, resulting in a deep hurt within Phelan that he could not shake. So he abandoned his family, and hasn't been home since.

Phelan is a former major leaguer. After visiting the boy's grave, he calls on his wife, daughter, and son, and learns that he is a grandfather.

He is introduced to Danny (Ean Egas), a fourth-grader who responds, "You're the big leaguer. You played with the Washington Senators." Phelan's belongings are packed away in the attic, and among them are an ancient photo of his father and him on a ballteam, his old glove, and a baseball Ty Cobb autographed in 1911. "You see where Ty Cobb signed it," grandfather tells grandson. "Nineteen-eleven. The year he hit .420. He was a mean guy, Cobb. Come at me many times with his spikes up . . . " Phelan adds that Cobb was "better, and tougher, and meaner, and faster" than Babe Ruth, and he presents Danny with the ball. In so doing, he is passing a piece of baseball lore from one generation to another.

Harvey Keitel stars in *Bad Lieutenant* (1992, Aries Film Releasing) as a New York City cop and lapsed Catholic who is neck-deep in a world of violence and depravity. He has been on one-too-many murder scenes, and so religion and spirituality have become a sick joke. He is unpredictably violent: he is

Ironweed: Francis Phelan (Jack Nicholson) shares his memories with his grandson (Ean Egas).

a crack addict and a lush, a frequenter of prostitutes, a gambler who is betting and losing absurd amounts of money.

The Mets and Dodgers, division victors, are battling in a playoff for the right to represent the National League in the World Series. While the players' names (including the Dodgers' Darryl Strawberry, Brett Butler, and Orel Hershiser and the Mets' Bobby Bonilla, Howard Johnson, and Sid Fernandez) are real, the playoff is fictionalized. The Dodgers are ahead 3–0 in the best-of-seven series; a sports radio call-in show host observes, "There's no Ruth. There's no Gehrig and, goodness gracious, there's no Donn Clendenon."

The lieutenant is pleased with this development, because he has been betting heavily against the Mets. But to quote Yogi Berra, it ain't over 'til its over. Miraculously, the locals win four straight, and the cop will be unable to pay off his debt. In the film's final, jarring sequence, he is blown away by a hit man in broad daylight, as he sits in his car on a busy city street.

Bad Lieutenant is a story of innocence versus evil, and of how each exists side-by-side in our society. This is most evident when director Abel Ferrara cuts from the brutal raping of a nun to a shot of a little girl watching cartoons on TV. Similarly, the "pure" game of baseball is inexorably linked with the lieutenant's final, fatal undoing.

BASEBALL VAUDEVILLE
AND COMEDY

Of the scores of baseball songs, from George M. Cohan's "Take Your Girl to the Ball Game" and John Philip Sousa's "The National Game" through the compositions of Terry Cashman, no ditty has the enduring charm of Jack Norworth and Albert Von Tilzer's Tin Pan Alley perennial, "Take Me Out to the Ball Game," written in 1908. Its simple, unaffected lyrics, about a fan's idealized yearning to spend a day at a ballpark, reflect the lure of the game. *Take Me Out to the Ball Game* (1949, MGM) may not be the all-time best MGM musical, but as the song which is its inspiration, the film is irresistibly appealing for baseball fans.

The time is the turn-of-the-century, and Gene Kelly, Frank Sinatra, and Jules Munshin appear as Eddie O'Brien, Dennis Ryan, and Nat Goldberg, the "Three Musketeers of the bat and the ball," a Tinker-to-Evers-to-Chance–inspired double-play combination for the Wolves, baseball's world champions. O'Brien and Ryan are hoofers who spend the winter touring in vaudeville. They arrive in Sarasota for spring training to learn that the team has been willed to a new owner,

one K.C. Higgins, whom the players fear will be a meddlesome slavedriver. The Wolves assume that K.C. is a "he," and are shocked to discover that this "he" is beauteous Esther Williams (who almost immediately dons a bathing suit and frolics in the hotel swimming pool).

Ladies' man O'Brien tussles with K.C., so of course they will end up paired romantically. The shy, dreamy Ryan (who is portrayed by Sinatra as every bobby soxer's fantasy boyfriend) develops a crush on K.C., but is matched with his "right girl," a comically predatory female (Betty Garrett). There is a subplot, involving a conniving gambler (Edward Arnold) who meets his doom. The Wolves win another pennant. Everyone lives happily ever after.

Take Me Out to the Ball Game is loaded with energetic production numbers and song-and-dance routines. Not surprisingly, the first is the title song, done as a duet by Sinatra and Kelly. But for baseball fans, the musical highlight is the delightful comic song-and-dance routine, "O'Brien to Ryan to Goldberg," performed by Kelly, Sinatra, and Munshin. The trio sing about how they are a great double-play combination, and how they come through each time their opponents start a rally.

Almost twenty years before Gene Kelly and Frank Sinatra portrayed these ballplayer-vaudevillians, Gus Van and Joseph T. Schenck, real-life vaudeville headliners, played similar characters in *They Learned About Women* (1930, MGM), a melodious talkie filled with vintage songs, patter, and comic routines. Jerry

(Top opposite) *Take Me Out to the Ball Game:* Betty Garrett as Shirley Delwyn, Frank Sinatra as Dennis Ryan, Esther Williams as K.C. Higgins, Gene Kelly as Eddie O'Brien (left to right).

(Far left opposite) *Take Me Out to the Ball Game:* Frank Sinatra as Dennis Ryan.

(Left opposite) *Take Me Out to the Ball Game:* Esther Williams as K.C. Higgins.

Take Me Out to the Ball Game: Eddie O'Brien (Gene Kelly) reacts after he has been beaned, for his own good, by Dennis Ryan; he is surrounded by Wolves owner K.C. Higgins (Esther Williams), coach Slappy Burke (Tom Dugan), and a well-meaning doctor (Eddie Parkes).

Take Me Out to the Ball Game: Jules Munshin as Nat Goldberg.

Burke (Van), catcher for the Blue Sox, is first present-ed as an irresponsible funster who loves to drink and sing in the company of chorus girls; his partner, Jack Glennon (Schenck), the Sox' pitcher, is the depend-able one, insisting that Burke straighten himself out for the upcoming season. But Burke proves to be the more level-headed of the two. Glennon is set to wed Mary (Bessie Love), as nice a girl as there ever was. He naïvely allows Daisy (Mary Doran), who describes herself as a "lonely little girl in distress," to cloud his emotions and entrap him into marriage. Actually, Daisy is "so crooked they'll have to bury her in a trombone," and she succeeds in breaking up the boys' act, and their friendship. After she leaves Glennon for another, he tells Mary that "something went haywire and I forgot everything that mattered: Jerry, and you." In his absence, Mary and Burke have become engaged. Pal that he is, Burke realizes that Glennon and Mary belong together, so he gallantly steps aside.

The scenario is not devoid of baseball content. Upon returning to the Blue Sox, Glennon's yearning for Mary results in his slumping on the field. After Burke clears his romantic path, a revitalized Glennon comes in in relief in the deciding game of the World Series and extinguishes a rally by the opposing team, the Bears. "The old combination of Burke and

Take Me Out to the Ball Game: Eddie O'Brien (Gene Kelly) rallies the fans to his cause.

136

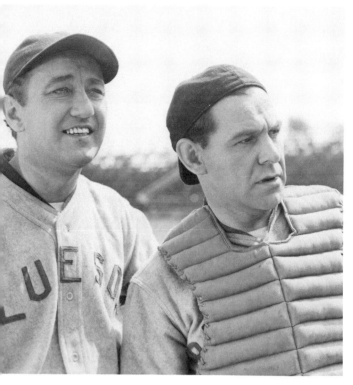

They Learned About Women: Joseph T. Schenck (left) as Jack Glennon, Gus Van as Jerry Burke.

They Learned About Women: Bessie Love as Mary, Joseph T. Schenck as Jack Glennon.

Glennon is working again," reports that famed radio sportscaster, Grahame McCracker, as the boys unite to win the game with typical ninth-inning heroics.

Benny Rubin, veteran vaudeville and burlesque comic, appears in a supporting role as a ballplayer in *They Learned About Women.* He is the star of *Hot Curves,* in which he is cast as Benny Goldberg, a double-talking Jewish train employee signed by the Pittsburgh ballclub because "he'll bring plenty of Jewish business through the gate in New York." Goldberg befriends Jim Dolan (Rex Lease), a highly touted rookie pitcher; links up romantically with Cookie (Pert Kelton), his zany female counterpart; and clashes with Slug (Paul Hurst), a bullying teammate. Eventually he comes to the aid of Dolan after the hurler is distracted by a golddigger (Natalie Moorhead) and forsakes his girlfriend, Elaine (Alice Day). At the finale, Goldberg singles and Dolan smacks an inside-the-park homer, spearheading a come-from-behind victory in the deciding World Series game.

The boys' manager (as well as Elaine's father) is named McGrew: supposedly, the story angle was culled from the real-life signing of

They Learned About Women: Jack Glennon (Joseph T. Schenck), leading off first base.

137

They Learned About Women: Blue Sox manager Brennan (Eddie Gribbon, center) chastises Jerry Burke (Gus Van). Jack Glennon (Joseph T. Schenck) is at far right; Sam (Benny Rubin) is at far left.

Andy Cohen, a Jewish infielder, by New York Giants' skipper John McGraw. Cohen lasted three seasons with the team.

Released in between the Rubin films and *Take Me Out to the Ball Game* is *Moonlight in Havana* (1942, Universal), a minor-league musical starring Allan Jones, then past his height as a celluloid actor-singer. He plays a ballplayer who can sing beautifully, but only when he is afflicted with a cold. His team is spending spring training in Havana, where his health constantly changes and he switches between ballplaying and singing in a nightclub.

The most famous of all baseball comedy-vaudeville numbers is the Bud Abbott and Lou Costello classic, *Who's on First?*, derived from several burlesque routines and shown each day at the Baseball Hall of Fame in Cooperstown, New York. Short versions pop up on the duo's television series, and they once performed it with Joe DiMaggio on the *Colgate Comedy Hour* TV show. However, the routine is presented most memorably in *The Naughty Nineties* (1945, Universal).

Lou Costello directed that the name of his birthplace, Paterson, New Jersey, be painted onto the backdrop. In 1992, thirty-three years after his death, a six-foot-high bronze statue of the comic, erected via privately raised donations, was unveiled in the city's Federici Park. Costello is garbed in a suit, but he

Hot Curves: Benny Rubin as Benny Goldberg.

Hot Curves: Benny Goldberg (Benny Rubin, center) cracks up Manager McGrew (John Ince, far left) and Slug (Paul Hurst), while eliciting sympathy from Cookie (Pert Kelton).

138

The Naughty Nineties: Bud Abbott (left) and Lou Costello perform *Who's on First?* "Paterson" was Costello's New Jersey hometown.

known as "Big Klu," was traded for Dee Fondy in 1957, and compiled a lifetime .298 batting average. Raymond can rattle off the entire Los Angeles Dodgers season schedule, as well as the team's pitching rotation.

After reciting *Who's on First?* for the upteenth time while on a cross-country odyssey, Raymond's younger brother Charlie (Tom Cruise) complains in frustration, "When you do it, you're not funny. You're the comedy team of Abbott and Abbott. . . . Ray, Ray, Ray, Ray, you're never gonna solve it . . . because it's not a riddle, man." Responds Raymond, "All I'm trying to find out is what's the guy's name on first base."

By the end of the trip, Charlie has developed a fondness for his long-lost sib-

Bud Abbott, in his wind-up, and Lou Costello, garbed in Boston Braves jerseys.

holds a baseball bat in his left hand, as he does while performing the routine.

Because he is the perfect straightman, Bud Abbott makes you believe the gibberish he is laying on Costello, the comic patsy, about the players on the Cooperstown ballclub: a first baseman, second baseman, third baseman, shortstop, pitcher, catcher, left fielder, and center fielder named, respectively, Who, What, I Don't Know, I Don't Care, Tomorrow, Today, Why, and Because. Costello grows increasingly flustered as he is overwhelmed by Abbott, whose nonsensical declarations keep adding up, layer upon layer. Primarily the routine works because of the pair's rapid-fire banter and immaculate comic timing. You need not be a baseball fan, or an Abbott and Costello aficionado, to love *Who's on First?*

The routine is paid homage to in *Rain Man* (1988, United Artists), in which Dustin Hoffman stars as Raymond Babbitt, an autistic savant who "has a problem communicating and learning. He can't even express himself, or probably even understand his emotions in a traditional way." What Raymond does understand is *Who's on First?*, which he recites, word for word, whenever he feels threatened. The room in the Cincinnati-based institution in which he lives is adorned with baseball cards, ballplayer photos, and sports pennants. He has memorized the data on the cards, and can tell you that Ted Kluszewski was ling. When they arrive in Los Angeles, he presents Raymond with a video of Abbott and Costello performing the routine.

Buster Keaton is another great comedian who incorporated baseball into his films, most famously in *College* and *The Cameraman* (1928, MGM). However, the closest the Great Stone Face came to making a "pure" baseball movie was the two-reel comedy *One Run Elmer* (1935, Educational), released when Keaton was past his zenith as a celluloid commodity. While *One Run Elmer* is a talking picture, most of its gags are visual. Buster plays a hapless gas station owner who practices ballplaying with his business rival. Elmer's pitches are promptly hit through the windows and walls of his rickety station. When it is his turn to bat, he misses the first pitch, which further destroys his building; he connects on the next toss, which smashes the window of a car whose owner will umpire the following day's game. Once that contest starts, the ball hits the arbiter in the face after catcher Elmer signals for a high pitch; Elmer comes to the

Buster Keaton, playing ball at the beach with wife Natalie Talmadge.

Buster Keaton, in a publicity still.

plate with an oversize bat; and the opposing pitcher puts chewing gum on the ball, which sticks to Elmer's club after he connects for what he thinks is a hit. The last of the ninth arrives, with Elmer's team behind by three runs. He bats with two outs and teammates leading off each base. Elmer has placed a bullet in a secret compartment in his bat, which pops when he hits the pitch. He rounds the bases and jump-slides into home plate, his feet landing on the catcher's chest and knocking him over. Elmer is safe. His team wins.

Baseball is only featured in a segment each of *College* and *The Cameraman*, with the first offering a comic takeoff on the basics of the game and the second featuring a poignant pantomime of every fan's fantasy heroics. Keaton stars in *College* as Ronald, the top scholar in his high-school class. At his graduation, after being presented with an "honor medal," he delivers a valedictory speech on the "Curse of Athletics." "The secret of getting a medal like mine is ... books not sports," Ronald proclaims. "The student who wastes his time on athletics rather than study shows only ignorance. ..." Of course, Ronald is not to be taken seriously, as he concludes his sermon by noting, "What have Ty Ruth and Babe Dempsey done for

ber up by swinging three bats at once, but only succeeds in conking himself in his noggin. He awkwardly steps up to the plate, only he is not the lead-off hitter. This player chases Ronald away, a bit that is repeated by the second batter. Finally, he does get to hit, but his stance is awkward; he faces away from home plate, and has to be corrected by the catcher. Eventually, Ronald is hit in the behind by the pitch. He leaps into the catcher's arms, toppling the backstop over. After taking first base, he attempts to steal second but promptly trips. The next batter pops up, but Ronald dashes around the bases, past the runners on base ahead of him. He somersaults into home plate, only to be informed by the umpire that "You forced two men out and you're out, too." So ends Ronald's baseball career.

The Cameraman is Keaton's first film for MGM after relinquishing his own studio and artistic control of his work. He plays Buster, a klutz who is a would-be newsreel photographer. At one point, he trudges out to Yankee Stadium with his camera to photograph the Yankees. Only, on that day, they are playing in St. Louis. What to do? He sets the camera down by the pitcher's mound and pantomimes a hurler about to go into his windup, acknowledging the sign from his catcher, attempting to pick off a runner, shifting his infielders and handling a double-play ball. Buster also

science?" None of this pleases the girl Ronald adores, Mary Haines (Anne Cornwall). "Anyone prefers an athlete to a weak-kneed teacher's pet," she declares. "When you change your mind about athletics, then I'll change my mind about you."

On to Clayton College. Ronald knows he will have to master sports in order to win Mary away from a rival, Jeff (Harold Goodwin), a jock who has graduated from high school after seven years. Ronald's suitcase is crammed with athletic equipment, as well as books on "How to Play Base Ball," "How to Play Football" and "How to Sprint." Nothing will help him. He appears at a ballfield and is told to play third base, which he mans garbed in catching attire: face mask, protector, and leg guards. The game begins, and a batter hits a ground ball that rolls between Ronald's legs. He avoids a line drive hit at him as if dodging a bullet. A runner tries to steal third base; Ronald misses the ball thrown by the catcher, and is knocked over by the sliding runner. Another grounder is hit to Ronald, which he picks up and holds helplessly. And so the sequence unfolds.

Ronald's team comes to bat. He tries to lim-

College: Buster Keaton, as Ronald. Baseball just isn't his sport.

The Cameraman: Buster Keaton, in the title role.

pantomimes a batter who is almost hit by a pitch, and who then smacks an inside-the-park home run. He slides head-first into home plate and waves his hat at the fans, who exist only in his mind.

Here, Keaton acts out every fan's dream of standing on the mound or in the batter's box of a major-league ballfield. While it may be the real Yankee Stadium, there are no teammates, no opposing players, no applauding throngs. It is just Buster, pantomiming the heroics that millions of boys, playing on sandlots, have imagined themselves performing.

Buster Keaton had a lifelong passion for baseball. Cast as the baseball coach in *College* is Sam Crawford, the Hall of Fame outfielder who played most of his career with the Detroit Tigers; Mike Donlin plays a Union general in *The General*, arguably Keaton's masterpiece. Writes Tom Dardis, in his biography *Keaton: The Man Who Wouldn't Lie Down,*

Harold Goodwin, the actor who appears as Keaton's nemesis in *College*, *The Cameraman*, and *One Run Elmer* and a close friend of the comic's for forty years, recalls that Buster gave a sort of exam for actors applying for work at the Keaton Studio. The exam consisted of only two questions: "Can you act?" and "Can you play baseball?" The passing score for a job was 50 percent, and nearly everyone passed. The Keaton Production Company was in fact an ever-ready baseball team, prepared to start a game on a moment's notice. That moment would often come whenever a production problem arose that seemed to defy immediate solution. Buster would officially declare that a game was in order. If someone had an inspiration halfway through it, the shooting would resume.

Aside from the humor in *College* and *The Cameraman*, you won't find a funnier silent baseball slapstick than *The Battling Orioles* (1924, Pathe). Neither will you find Cal Ripken, Jim Palmer, or Frank and Brooks Robinson cavorting in this knockabout, pie-in-your-eye comedy that is filled with cleverly staged chases, sight gags, pratfalls, and brawls. The Orioles depicted here are of another century. Back in 1874, they were a frisky, spirited bunch of "two-fisted, he-man baseball go-getters." But it is now 1924, and they "no longer roared—they snored." The Orioles have becomes doddering old stuffed shirts, content to pass their time at the stodgy National Club, where everyone—even the bellboy—is ancient, and where "it's against the law to laugh out loud."

Cut to Greenwood, a small town which is the home of Tommy Roosevelt Tucker (Glenn Tryon), a young barber whose dad was an Oriole. Tucker has a sweet young girlfriend, Hope Stanton (Blanche Mehaffey), who is taken to New York City by her shifty Uncle Sid and his pal, Jimmy the Mouse. Tucker follows her there, hired to work at the National Club and offer the elderly ballplayers "inspiration." His exuberance quickly rattles the establishment, whose drawing room ends up in shambles. However, the old codgers lose their grouches and sniffles, regain their youthful zest, and assist Tucker in rescuing his lady fair from the clutches of Sid and Jimmy.

142

The Battling Orioles is played as pure slapstick. The film opens with its sole baseball sequence, a flashback to the Orioles in their prime. In a typical gag, an Oriole runner desiring to steal a base ties string to the one he is on and drags it behind him so he won't be caught too far off it. Eventually, the contest degenerates into a full-scale brawl. The gags in the film are simple and unsubtle. At one juncture, Tucker sips some liquor in a bar, and his hat temporarily flies off his head. The scenario is sweetly illogical. Right in the middle of New York City, he and Hope literally and ever-so-conveniently run into each other. Our Gang fans are treated to a cameo appearance by Joe Cobb, Mickey Daniels, Jackie Condon, and Ernie "Sunshine Sammy" Morrison, who are seen watching Tommy's antics through his barbershop window as he fools with one of his customers.

Ladies' Day (1943, RKO-Radio) is an equally frenetic but far less successful comedy. Eddie Albert is appropriately ingenuous as Wacky Walters, ace pitcher for the Fighting Sox, who are battling for a pennant. Walters is a genial ladies' man whose on-field performance falters whenever he is involved with the opposite sex. His latest girlfriend, Pepita Zorita (Lupe Velez, who shrieks through the scenario), is a movie star traveling with the team to sell war bonds. "Why can't she leave us alone?" laments Hazel (wisecrack-

Ladies' Day: Lupe Velez as Pepita Zorita, Eddie Albert as Wacky Walters.

ing Patsy Kelly), wife of Hippo Jones (Max Baer, playing the stereotypical dumb jock), one of the Sox players. Hazel and her fellow baseball wives, in cahoots with their husbands, scheme to keep the pair apart so that Walters will keep hurling like an ace. Their goal is a World Series victory, and the extra money that will allow the women to buy a farm, open a steak

Ladies' Day: Max Baer (left) as Hippo Jones, Eddie Albert as Wacky Walters.

Ladies' Day: Max Baer and Patsy Kelly as Hippo and Hazel Jones.

143

Ladies' Day: The finale, with Cliff Clark as Dan, Max Baer as Hippo Jones, Eddie Albert as Wacky Walters, Lupe Velez as Pepita Zorita (bottom row, left to right); Patsy Kelly as Hazel Jones, Iris Adrian as Kitty, and Joan Barclay as Joan (top row, left to right).

house, or purchase a mink coat. They even kidnap Pepita, and then convince her that she has come down with a rare tropical rash. Inexplicably, at the finale, Walters is pitching poorly in Pepita's absence. Her arrival signals a change in his fortunes, and he hurls the Sox to a championship and happy ending.

(The May 4, 1941, edition of the *New York Daily Mirror* reported that Dizzy Dean "... will be offered the lead in 'Ladies Day,' the baseball comedy by sportswriter Bob Considine and the theatre man Edward Lillie. It's a comedy about the marital woes of a professional athlete.")

Eddie Albert had better material in his screen debut, *Brother Rat* (1938, Warner Bros.), in which he plays a role he created on Broadway: lovably bumbling Bing Edwards, Virginia Military Institute cadet who has secretly married his sweetheart. Edwards is VMI's star pitcher, who as the film opens is burning 'em in to his roommate and catcher (played by Ronald Reagan) during practice for the upcoming championship game against the Cavaliers. Edwards becomes distracted upon learning that he is to be a father. He opens the game by filling the bases, and then he surrenders a grand-slam homer. The fifth batter slams a

hard grounder at him. He doesn't duck, because he is thinking about his off-the-field situation, and gets conked in the head. "How can a fellow pitch when he's havin' a baby?" he laments. *Brother Rat* was followed by *Brother Rat and a Baby* (1940, Warner Bros.), whose scenario centers around underpaid high school coach Edwards' being a finalist for a job as VMI's varsity baseball coach, and was remade a decade later as a musical, *About Face* (1952, Warner Bros.), with Eddie Bracken in Albert's role. His character here is renamed Boff Roberts. A similarly distracted ballplayer can be found in the World War II comedy *The Horizontal Lieutenant* (1962, MGM). Jim Hutton plays Merle Wye, an accident-prone intelligence officer. While in Honolulu, he plays in an intraservice baseball game where he is hit by a foul ball and ends up as horizontal as Bing Edwards/Boff Roberts.

Another actor who appeared in multiple baseball movies is Ray Milland. He followed his starring role in *It Happens Every Spring* with *Rhubarb* (1951, Paramount), a slapstick in which he is upstaged by the title feline. Rhubarb is the Leo Durocher and Billy Martin of pets: a tough, spirited alley cat taken in by

Thaddeus J. Banner (Gene Lockhart), an eccentric millionaire whose only child, Myra (Elsie Holmes), is greedy and self-indulgent. The man believes that Rhubarb has more spunk than most humans; in fact, the cat's name is derived from the baseball term denoting argument and fight. Upon Banner's demise, Rhubarb finds itself its master's principal heir, inheriting $30 million and Brooklyn's major-league ballclub, an inept bunch known as the Loons.

Milland plays Eric Yeager, the team's press agent. He is designated as Rhubarb's guardian, an unpleasant task if only because his fiancée, Polly (Jan Sterling), appears to be allergic to cats. The ballplayers believe that toiling for a cat-owned team will make them laughingstocks. Yeager convinces them otherwise; Rhubarb becomes the club's good-luck charm, as well as a fan favorite, and the Brooklynites—rechristened the Rhubarbs—begin winning ballgames.

Trouble comes when Myra sues her father's estate, claiming that the real Rhubarb is dead, a falsehood later exposed in court. Then a ring of gamblers, who have bet against the team in the World Series, "catnap" Rhubarb. The feline is eventually tracked down by Yeager in time to set the team back on its winning ways.

Primarily the humor in *Rhubarb* is derived from the cat's involvement with Eric and Polly, and the Brooklyn players. While playing St. Louis during the season, Brooklyn batters who pet Rhubarb as they head to home plate promptly bash base hit after base hit. Dud Logan (Henry Slate), an ornery Loon, sticks his tongue out at his "boss" and is rewarded by comically tripping over a row of bats lined up by the dugout.

Logan grounds to third base; Rhubarb runs onto the field to chase the ball and is followed by a boxer, the St. Louis mascot. The animals reach the ball at the same time as two infielders, who trip over one another. In the confusion, a Brooklyn runner scores and the ball ends up in left field. The outfielder hurls the ball wildly toward home plate. It arrives just after the dog and cat scamper across the plate, but before two more Brooklyn runners score. The last one barely eludes the catcher's tag. The umpire decrees the hit a foul ball; before returning to the batter's box, a now-converted Logan pets Rhubarb—and belts the first pitch he sees for a long home run.

Brother Rat: Ronald Reagan as Dan Crawford, Wayne Morris as Billy Randolph, Eddie Albert as Bing Edwards (left to right).

The Horizontal Lieutenant: Jim Hutton, as Merle Wye, under the bench.

Featured in *Rhubarb* is an otherwise forgettable song whose title does symbolize the manner in which diehard Brooklynites felt about their borough during the era of Reese, Robinson and the Duke of Flatbush: "It's a Privilege to Live in Brooklyn."

Rhubarb: Players for St. Louis, the Loons' rivals, and their canine companion. Billy Wayne, pictured directly behind the dog, plays the team's manager.

Rhubarb: The title feline and its team; young Leonard Nimoy is the player to the left of the cat.

Rhubarb is the story of a fictional Brooklyn team. But the real Brooklyn Dodgers are featured in *Whistling in Brooklyn*. This zany comedy is one in a three-film series featuring Red Skelton as Wally

Benton, a popular radio sleuth known as "the Fox," who finds himself involved in off-the-air murder and mayhem. Someone has been killing various seemingly unrelated individuals, and sending untraceable notes, signed "Constant Reader," to the *Brooklyn Standard.* Benton becomes the prime suspect. He is chased into Brooklyn and eventually arrives at Ebbets Field, where the Dodgers are playing an exhibition with the Battling Beavers. A police inspector (Henry O'Neill), who has been targeted for death, is set to throw out the first pitch.

Benton makes his way through the bowels of the ballpark and sneaks into the Beavers' locker room. He dons a uniform, only to realize that all the Battling Beavers sport long beards. What to do? Benton conks on the head and ties up the Beavers' star pitcher, who has arrived after his teammates have left for the field. He snips off the hurler's beard and attaches it to his own face. This being a farce, everyone from the Beavers' manager on down takes Benton for the pitcher. As he attempts to warn the inspector that the killer is at his side, Benton's pitches hit the first three Dodger batters, Billy Herman, Arky Vaughan, and Ducky Medwick. Dolph Camilli, number four in the line-up, pops up to Benton, who catches the ball in his beard. Then Benton is seen batting, and the pitches thrown at him manage to first unbutton his shirt and then undo his pants.

The Dodgers appearing in *Whistling in Brooklyn* are not all players. What would such a film be without Leo "the Lip" Durocher, then the Bums' manager (and occasional player), who gets to argue with both Benton and an umpire?

The baseball sequence in *Whistling in Brooklyn* was reworked forty-five years later at the finale of *The Naked Gun: From the Files of Police Squad!* (1988, Paramount). The setting is a contest between the California Angels and Seattle Mariners, battling for the American League Western Division lead. Bumbling Lt. Frank Drebin (Leslie Nielsen) is trying to thwart an assassination attempt on the Queen of England, who is attending the game.

The play-by-play announcers are Curt Gowdy and Jim Palmer ... and Tim McCarver, Dick Vitale, Mel Allen, Dick Enberg, and Dr. Joyce Brothers. Drebin gets on the ballfield by knocking out and impersonating the opera star who is scheduled to sing the National Anthem. Not only is the lieutenant's voice off-key, but halfway through he begins blowing, and soon forgetting, the words. He then knocks out, and replaces, the home plate umpire.

The gags that follow are comic exaggerations of the sport's idiosyncrasies. Before the game begins, the players partake in an orgy of spitting and crotch-scratching, and are joined in the former by their wives in the stands. Jay Johnstone (an outfielder who recently had concluded a twenty-year major-league stint) is the Mariners' lead-off hitter. He and the Angels' catcher are frisked by Drebin, as if they are being measured for suits. As the game progresses, the lieutenant overtheatrically calls strikes, at one point breaking into a Michael Jackson–inspired dance routine. A pitcher whom Drebin thinks is doctoring the ball has on his person a large piece of sandpaper, a strange-looking drill, and a jar of Vaseline. Drebin cleans home plate with a dustbuster, and opens a bat with a cork to see if it is hollow. Players and managers slap themselves silly doing high-fives and giving signals.

The assassin proves to be Mr. Humility himself, Reggie Jackson, who eventually struts like a zombie in a Grade B horror film as he stalks across the field, uttering "I-must-kill-the-Queen." Additionally, before the game, the fans are entertained by the airing on the gigantic Angelvision screen of "some of those unusual moments in baseball over the years": players diving into the stands or crashing into each other while trying to nab batted balls. Interspersed with authentic clips are ones of an infielder hit by a car as he signals for a pop-up; a baserunner mauled by a

Whistling in Brooklyn: Red Skelton (right), as Wally Benton, clowning on the set.

tiger while sliding into second base; and an outfielder decapitated as he leaps for a ball sailing over the fence. After the latter, Mel Allen adds a hearty "How 'bout that!"

This sequence is a grand slam homer when compared with a film whose plot is entirely devoted to baseball: *Brewster's Millions,* filmed six times prior to

Whistling in Brooklyn: Wally Benton (Red Skelton) will be unable to impersonate a Battling Beaver without a beard; Dewey Robinson is second from right.

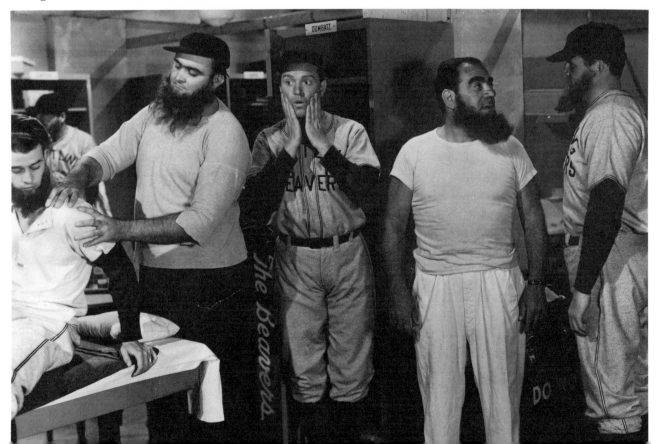

The World War II–era Brooklyn Dodgers, who are featured in *Whistling in Brooklyn*; manager Leo Durocher, who is his usual argumentative self in the film (and between 1947 and 1960 was wed to Laraine Day), is fifth from the left in the bottom row.

Whistling in Brooklyn: Wally Benton (Red Skelton) in his comical at-bat.

this tepid reworking of the story, placing it within a baseball framework. The first version was released in 1914, and it was remade in 1921 with Fatty Arbuckle; in 1926 (as *Miss Brewster's Millions*) with Bebe Daniels, Warner Baxter and Ford Sterling; in 1935 with Jack Buchanan and Lili Damita; in 1945 with Dennis O'Keefe and Eddie "Rochester" Anderson; and in 1961 (as *Three on a Spree*) with Jack Watling.

Richard Pryor stars as Montgomery Brewster, veteran of fifteen professional seasons, "a relief pitcher in the minor leagues of life." Brewster's highest yearly salary has not exceeded eleven thousand dollars, and he has never had a credit card. He toils for the Hackensack Bulls, and is ever hopeful that next year will be his year to make the majors. Just as the Bulls manager (Jerry Orbach) releases him and his catcher and best pal, Spike Nolan (John Candy), Brewster learns of the death of his great-uncle, Rupert Horn (Hume Cronyn). Horn was one of the richest men in America, and Brewster is his sole living relative. He has willed $300 million to the ballplayer, but on one condition: Brewster must spend $30 million in thirty days, without accumulating any assets, and must not tell a soul about the arrangement. If he succeeds, he'll receive the $300 million. If he fails, he walks away with nothing.

Brewster sponsors a three-inning exhibition game in which the Bulls are pitted against the New York Yankees. He will be the minor-league club's starting pitcher, and he is convinced that the media coverage will boost his chances for a major-league contract. Amid a whirlwind of activity surrounding Brewster's various schemes to spend the $30 million, the game begins. Several snazzy fielding plays and Nolan's insulting a batter to destroy his concentration keep the Yankees scoreless. But in the third inning, the pitcher surrenders a grand slam homer and is sent to the showers. He retires from baseball, but does at least get to pitch against the Yankees. Brewster is a decent, well-meaning fellow, and the beautiful auditor (Lonette McKee) with whom he falls in love is a woman with character and values. But *Brewster's Millions* is a perfect film for the money-mad mid-1980s, in that its ultimate point is that money *does* buy happiness.

Brewster's Millions features one clever baseball bit, which satirizes life in the minor leagues. Railroad tracks run across the outfield of the Bulls' ballpark, and each time a train passes through the umpire must halt the game.

Joining *Brewster's Millions* in the lower rung of baseball comedies is *Major League*, a silly, decidedly minor-league farce. It is the story of how a purposefully awful Cleveland Indians ballclub outsmarts its

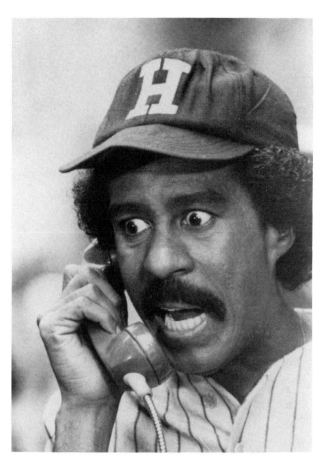

Brewster's Millions: Richard Pryor as Montgomery Brewster.

Brewster's Millions: Richard Pryor (left) as Montgomery Brewster, John Candy as Spike Nolan.

Brewster's Millions: Jerry Orbach as Charlie, manager of the Hackensack Bulls.

149

Brewster's Millions: Lonette McKee as Angela Drake,
Richard Pryor as Montgomery Brewster.

shrewish new owner and wins the American League pennant. In real life, the Indians last won the World Series in 1948. Six years later they were the American League's best, only to be swept in the series by the New York Giants. Since then ... nothing. No player-managers like Lou Boudreau. No pitching staffs anchored by Early Wynn, Mike Garcia, Bob Lemon, and Bob Feller. No teammates with the sock of Larry Doby, Ken Keltner, Joe Gordon, Jim Hegan, Al Rosen. No pennants. No glory. Nothing but losing streaks, losing seasons, last-place finishes.

As the film opens, the team's owner has just died and his snooty ex-showgirl wife, Rachel Phelps (Margaret Whitton), has taken over the ballclub. Rachel "never liked Cleveland much." The city of Miami has promised her a new stadium, a mansion in Boca Raton, and membership in the Palm Beach Polo and Country Club, so she is set to move the franchise. The only catch: the Indians have a lease for their stadium with the city of Cleveland, which can be broken only if attendance falls below 800,000. This is sure to happen, Phelps figures, if she assembles the worst possible team, one guaranteed to insure her last

Major League: Dennis Haysbert, Andy Romano, James Gammon, Steve Yeager, Chelcie Ross, Wesley Snipes (top row, left to right); Corbin Bernsen, Charlie Sheen, Tom Berenger (bottom row, left to right).

place, and few fannies in the ballpark seats.

She hires a new manager (James Gammon) who is a career minor leaguer. She invites to spring training a menagerie of has-beens and never-weres: hungover, broken-down Jake Taylor (Tom Berenger), an ex-All-Star catcher who is "just a guy trying to put his life back together"; Rickie Vaughan (Charlie Sheen), a hot-tempered jailbird whose last league was the California Penal, and whose ninety-seven-mile-per-hour pitches usually land in the stands; Roger Dorn (Corbin Bernsen), a good-hit, no-field third baseman who is more concerned with his investment portfolio than with diving for ground balls; outfielder Willie Mays Hayes (Wesley Snipes), who "runs like Mays, but hits like shit"; veteran pitcher Steve Harris (Chelcie Ross), a Jesus freak who doctors his baseballs with mucus; and first baseman Pedro Serrano (Dennis Haysbert), a black man who thinks voodoo will put life into his bat.

Predictably the Indians start off the season horribly. Predictably the players realize Rachel Phelps's scheme, and they come together as a team. Predictably they start winning games, and they finish the season in a first-place tie with the dreaded New

The Odd Couple: Walter Matthau as Oscar Madison.

York Yankees. Predictably all of the key players contribute to the victory in a one-game playoff. Predictably Jake Taylor wins back his reluctant ex-wife (Rene Russo).

Major League is a barely funny film. Its best moments are when Bob Uecker, playing the Indians' radio announcer, offers his inimitable Ueckerisms. He greets his audience with "a big wahoo welcome," and dubs the team's fans "featherheads." At its worst, Pedro Serrano's obsession with voodoo is unabashedly racist. A running gag about Japanese groundskeepers who keep describing the Indians as "shitty" in Japanese (with English subtitles) verges on caricature. It is a smug, head-in-the-sand view of Orientals, at a time when Americans were not only driving Japanese-made cars and dining in Japanese restaurants but selling their real estate and corporations to Japanese firms.

Trivia note: Sheen's character earns the nickname "Wild Thing," a moniker that caught on with several real-life major-league relievers.

Baseball, among other sports, is featured

Major League: Rachel Phelps (Margaret Whitton) disrupts the locker room. Seated at left is Willie Mays Hayes (Wesley Snipes); seated at right is Rickie Vaughn (Charlie Sheen).

The Odd Couple: Oscar Madison (Walter Matthau, right) and Felix Ungar (Jack Lemmon); the latter is more at home tossing teacups than baseballs.

in abundance in the comedies of Neil Simon. Oscar Madison, slob-extraordinaire and one half of *The Odd Couple* (1968, Paramount), is "one of the highest paid sportswriters in the East." Madison (Walter Matthau, who played the role on stage) is forever garbed in a New York Mets' cap, and his apartment is decorated with photos of Stan Musial, Yogi Berra, and various long-forgotten Mets of the pre–Tom Seaver era. In one sequence, he covers a game at Shea Stadium. The Mets are a run up on the Pittsburgh Pirates, who have loaded the bases with Bill Mazeroski coming to bat. "That's the ballgame," predicts a fellow scribe (Heywood Hale Broun, in a cameo), not expecting the Mets to hold such a slim lead. "What's the matter, you never heard of a triple play?" is Madison's response. The writer's new roommate and nemesis, neurotic Felix Ungar (Jack Lemmon), phones with an "emergency": he tells Madison not to eat any frankfurters because he's making franks and beans for dinner. At that moment, Maz smacks into a game-ending triple play. "Greatest fielding play I ever saw . . . [and] you missed it," yells Broun, to Madison's consternation. Reportedly, Hall of Famer Roberto Clemente was scheduled to be at bat during the gag, but declined the indignity.

Like Oscar Madison, George Schneider

(James Caan), Simon's alter-ego in *Chapter Two* (1979, Columbia), is a writer. He may not cover the Yankees or Mets, but he and his press agent brother (Joe Bologna) play softball in Central Park in the Broadway Show League. George is an avid sports fan, and the scenario features references to Yankee games and baseball cards. In *Max Dugan Returns* (1983, Twentieth Century-Fox), Matthew Broderick plays fifteen-year-old Michael McPhee, a good-field/no-hit first baseman. His grandfather, Max Dugan (Jason Robards), a terminally ill con man who abandoned Michael's mother when she was nine years old, arrives one day and belatedly attempts to be the ideal parent and grandparent. Charlie Lau, batting coach for the Chicago White Sox, magically appears, courtesy of Dugan's pocketbook, to teach the boy his "philosophy of hitting." "If you don't have the right philosophy," Lau observes, "you're not going to hit your weight." He works with McPhee on "stance and balance," and on becoming "positive and aggressive." This results in the kid hitting a game-winning home run, with Lau looking on.

Brighton Beach Memoirs (1987, Universal) is the story of Eugene Jerome (Jonathan Silverman), a young teenager suffering the pangs of puberty in 1937 Brooklyn. Eugene is obsessed with sex . . . and base-

Max Dugan Returns: Matthew Broderick (left) as Michael McPhee, Charlie Lau as himself.

152

The Slugger's Wife: Michael O'Keefe as Darryl Palmer.

The Slugger's Wife: Martin Ritt (right) as Burly De Vito, Cleavant Derricks as Manny Alvarado.

ball. The first shot of his room starts with a New York Yankees team photo on his wall. In his initial dialogue, he recites the play-by-play of a Yankees-Giants World Series in which Red Ruffing fires away at Jo-Jo Moore, and plays at being the Yankee right-hander. "I hate my name, Eugene Morris Jerome," he announces. "How am I ever gonna play for the Yankees with a name like that? You have to be a Joe, or a Tony, or a Frankie. All the best Yankees are Italian." When he grows up, Eugene hopes to become a writer of books, plays, or movies "if things don't work out with the Yanks . . ."

The Slugger's Wife (1985, Columbia) is Simon's most obvious baseball project, if only because it is completely set within a world of ballplayers. Unfortunately, this is not one of the writer's more successful works. Michael O'Keefe stars as Darryl Palmer, slugging right fielder for the Atlanta Braves, a brash, carefree ladies' man who falls in love at first sight with

The Slugger's Wife: Michael O'Keefe as Darryl Palmer, Randy Quaid as Moose Granger, Cleavant Derricks as Manny Alvarado (left to right).

153

That Touch of Mink: Mickey Mantle, Doris Day as Cathy Timberlake, Cary Grant as Philip Shayne, Roger Maris (left to right).

Debby (Rebecca De Mornay), a cute singer. He ardently woos and wins her, and they marry. Palmer is an overgrown child who expects Debby to abandon her career, cheer him on at every home game, and follow him across America on road trips. When she is around, he confidently bashes home run after home run, and finds himself pursuing Roger Maris's season record of sixty-one dingers. Debby feels smothered by Palmer's behavior. She is an independent, career-minded woman who will not walk behind any man. So she leaves him. He slumps, but learns not to be so dependent upon her. As the film concludes, it is clear that they will soon be reconciled.

There is one inventive scene in *The Slugger's Wife*. Palmer and Debby are in bed, and she writhes in ecstasy as he uses her body to explain to her base locations and the various types of pitches. Otherwise, the film is pedestrian and boring. If *The Odd Couple* is a solid hit, *Chapter Two* and *Max Dugan Returns* are respectable batted balls and *Brighton Beach Memoirs* earns an intentional pass based on its stage origin,

The Slugger's Wife is a whiff on three straight pitches.

Comic baseball bits have been included in dozens of other films. Here are a few choice samples.

In the climactic sequence of *A Night at the Opera* (1935, MGM), the Marx Brothers set about wrecking poor Sig Rumann's theater. At one juncture, the orchestra bursts into a waltz arrangement of "Take Me Out to the Ball Game," the sheet music of which the boys have placed on the musicians' music stands. Harpo and Chico have been hiding in the orchestra pit. The former dons a baseball mitt and begins an impromptu game of catch with his brother. As Chico winds up in imitation of a pitcher, Harpo grabs a violin that he employs as a bat and promptly swings at the ball. Not to be outdone, Groucho appears in the opera hall hawking fresh roasted peanuts.

In *That Touch of Mink* (1962, Universal), Doris Day plays Cathy Timberlake, an unemployed

154

"computing machine" operator from Upper Sandusky who has come to New York where she rides the subways and dines in the Automat. Cary Grant is Philip Shayne, a wealthy mover, shaker, and jet-setter who only knows from limousines and private planes, and delivers speeches at the United Nations that even the Russians applaud. Cathy is an apple-pie type who used to sing in the church choir. Her father is a druggist. Her mother is a schoolteacher. Her brother is an eagle scout. And she is a baseball fan. What does a pretty girl do in Upper Sandusky after the sun sets, Shayne wants to know? "Baseball," Cathy responds. "I went to a lot of baseball games. ... The Cougars won the pennant in 'fifty-eight." New York has a local team of its own: the Yankees. So the pair head for Yankee Stadium where, during the game, they sit in the dugout with three players named Mantle, Maris, and Berra. Cathy Timberlake, all-American baseball fan, loudly protests umpire Art Passarella's strike call. Her abrasiveness results in the Yankee trio's expulsion from the contest.

In his first appearance in *The Family Jewels* (1965, Paramount), Jerry Lewis is garbed schizophrenically in a Los Angeles Dodgers cap and San Francisco Giants jersey. While retrieving a ball hit through the opening in a fence, he comically intrudes on some robbers set to loot a bank truck. In *The Geisha Boy* (1958, Paramount),

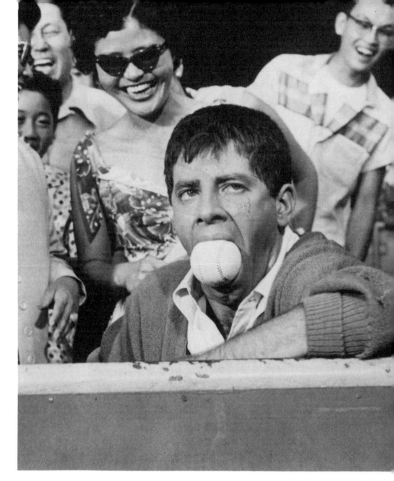

The Geisha Boy: The Great Wooley (Jerry Lewis) is the recipient of one of the Great Ichiyama's "famous Nipponese sideways curveballs."

Lewis plays the Great Wooley, an out-of-work magician touring Japan with the USO. The Great Ichiyama (Ryuzo Demura), an oversize, brainless jock who is "one of Japan's greatest baseball heroes," erroneously thinks the magician is romancing his intended (Nobu Atsumi McCarthy). The magician is chased by the athlete into a bathhouse. Ichiyama dives into a pool, and the entire street is flooded. Later, during an exhibition game between Tonichi, Ichiyama's team, and the Los Angeles Dodgers, Wooley introduces the Americans—Pee Wee Reese, Charlie Neal, Jim Gilliam, Gil Hodges, Gino Cimoli, Carl Furillo, Duke Snider, Carl Erskine, Johnny Roseboro— and it is wonderful to see them all in brief color clips. Wooley mercilessly razzes Ichiyama; the fired-up ballplayer, who is an outstanding pitcher but not much of a batter, first smacks a hit and, when the Dodgers come to bat, tosses his "famous Nipponese sideways curveball" at Hodges.

The Family Jewels: Jerry Lewis as Willard Woodward, innocently foiling a robbery.

155

The pitch avoids the first baseman's bat like one of Vernon Simpson's tosses in *It Happens Every Spring*, and lands in Wooley's mouth.

Ferris Bueller (Matthew Broderick), hero of the teen comedy *Ferris Bueller's Day Off* (1986, Paramount), cons most of the world into thinking he is deathly ill so that he can skip school. He is joined by his girl and best friend at Wrigley Field, and he nabs a foul ball just when he should be slogging through gym class. Ferris is almost but not quite observed on a TV monitor by the hapless school dean. Later on, he uses the ball to silence one of the cleverly devised contraptions that have enabled him to fool his parents.

In *Funny Farm* (1988, Warner Bros.), Chevy Chase plays a New York sportswriter who, as Oscar Madison, often wears a Mets cap. With his wife (Madolyn Smith), he forsakes the rigors of city life for what he assumes will be the peace and friendliness of the idyllic rural town of Redbud. "This move is for keeps," he tells his coworkers. "That's what Billy Martin said," one of them quips. Sure enough, country life is an endless nightmare of bugs, snakes, and obnoxious neighbors. At one point, the writer attends a softball game, in which the dense, demented rurals are so involved that they remain oblivious to the fact that the catcher has seemingly dropped dead.

The Dream Team (1989, Universal) is the story of four lunatics (played by Michael Keaton, Christopher Lloyd, Peter Boyle, and Stephen Furst), incarcerated in a psychiatric hospital, who set off with their therapist on a field trip to Yankee Stadium. This is a boring movie, which asks the viewer to laugh at the mentally disturbed. But the doctor (Dennis Boutsikaris), as he requests permission for the outing, insightfully notes, "I want to give them the opportunity to taste a hot dog at Yankee Stadium . . . to hear the crowd roar when Mattingly hits one out."

In *Woman of the Year*, Tess Harding and Sam Craig do attend that ballgame at Yankee Stadium. He explains the rules of the game, and their resulting repartee is a clever variation of "Who's on First?" Tess's reactions are logical responses to Craig's describing the difference between a strike and an out and how an umpire can call a strike if the pitcher puts the ball across the plate but the batter doesn't swing. Her hat blocks the view of a gloriously loud fan sitting behind her (Jack Carr), which becomes a running gag throughout the sequence. By the ninth inning, this "number-two dame in the country, right next to Mrs. Roosevelt" is rooting at a decibel that rivals the blowhard's, and the two have become pals. Plus, Craig is calling her Tessie, and she is calling him Sammy.

A similar transformation occurs in *The Talk of the Town* (1942, Columbia), released almost seven months after *Woman of the Year* (and also directed by George Stevens). Ronald Colman plays Michael Lightcap, a stuffy, by-the-book law professor who is set to be a Supreme Court nominee.

Funny Farm: Chevy Chase and Madolyn Smith as Andy and Elizabeth Farmer.

Woman of the Year: Sam Craig (Spencer Tracy) takes Tess Harding (Katharine Hepburn) out to a ballgame. The loud fan (Jack Carr) is directly behind Tracy and Hepburn.

Bros.) and the convict comedy *Up the River* (1930, Fox). The former is a disappointment, despite a topnotch cast headed by Edward G. Robinson, Jane Wyman, Broderick Crawford, and Anthony Quinn. The latter is a far more enjoyable yarn, as well as the feature debut of Spencer Tracy. He and Warren Hymer play St. Louis and Dannemora Dan, comical escaped cons. At the finale, they break back *into* jail so that, in typical baseball-movie fashion, they can assist their "alma mater" in winning a game against a rival reformatory.

Before he is fit for such a lofty position, he must be humanized, and baseball will help do the trick. After attending a ballgame, Lightcap observes, "A great thing, this baseball. It gets the legal cobwebs out of the brain."

Prison baseball games are incorporated into the gangster spoof *Larceny, Inc.* (1942, Warner

But for sheer silliness, no film can top *Schoolday Love* (1929, Educational), a comedy short in which a group of monkeys indulge in a game of "snappy baseball." Via editing, they pitch balls and swing bats just like their human counterparts. The umpire, a mutt, is outfitted with a pair of signs, marked *S* for strike and *B* for ball.

JOE E. BROWN
AND RING LARDNER

Ring Lardner, along with Grantland Rice, were America's most famous sportswriters during the heyday of Babe Ruth. Previously, during the dead-ball era, Lardner had spent a half-dozen years covering the Chicago Cubs and White Sox. His role as a sportswriter during the Black Sox scandal is tellingly portrayed by John Sayles in *Eight Men Out*. In his many fictional works, he satirically celebrates the boyishness, awkwardness, and vanity of ballplayers. Lardner's athletes are, in all their glory, far less than heroic. They are no idealized Frank Merriwells, but instead are all-too-human and flawed.

In "The Lardners: My Family Remembered," Ring Lardner, Jr. notes, "One way to make some extra money was to write for the movies, and as early as 1916 [my father] contracted to write twelve baseball shorts for two hundred and fifty dollars each." The arrangement was with Universal-Jewel; the films were based on Lardner's "Busher's Letters," featuring a character named Jack Keefe, a naïve but narcissistic, self-indulgent hurler from the Central League who pens letters to Al Blanchard, a hometown pal, after his purchase by the White Sox. The "letters" were initially published in the *Saturday Evening Post,* and later reprinted in three volumes. The first, titled *You Know Me Al*, was the name of the film series. Among the

individual titles are *The Busher Breaks In, The Busher Comes Back, The Busher Abroad,* and *The Home Run Smash.*

The New Klondike, based on a Lardner story, features typical Lardner athletes. The hero is Tom Kelly (Thomas Meighan), "popular pitcher of the New York team" and the previous year's World Series star, and the setting is the club's Beach Haven, Florida, spring training site. Dave Cooley (J.W. Johnston), Kelly's manager, who is in cahoots with a crooked land developer, sees the ballplayer as a threat to his power and, disregarding the wishes of the team owner, tells him he has been cut from the squad. Kelly unknowingly becomes a pawn in the scheme, in which his former teammates invest their money. Soon, the ballplayers are more concerned with real estate than spring training. They are unaware that the land they have purchased is no "Eden-by-the-sea," but rather a worthless swamp.

Movies like this are fated to have makeshift happy endings, so the swamp proves to be coveted by another realtor who wishes to convert it into a Venetian canal. Cooley is deposed, and his place is taken by Kelly. The ballplayer wins the girl with whom he has become smitten: wealthy Evelyn Curtis (Lila Lee), who with her grandmother is innocently embroiled in the controversy. Primarily the scenario is a cautionary (and despite its literary roots, convoluted) tale of the 1920s Florida land boom.

The New Klondike is of note for two reasons. In most baseball films, the gambler is an outsider, but

(Left) *Alibi Ike:* "Ike" (Joe E. Brown), just up from Sauk Center, impresses the Chicago Cubs catcher (Roscoe Karns).

159

Eight Men Out: John Sayles (center), cast as Ring Lardner, with Studs Terkel (right) as fellow Chicago scribe Hugh Fullerton.

ly describes his athletic abilities. Plus, he is constantly making excuses.

The veteran ballplayers humor Farrell by playing pranks on him. He becomes romantically involved with his manager's sister-in-law (Olivia de Havilland). Gamblers attempt to bribe him into throwing the game that will land the Cubs in the "World Serious" (Farrell's name for the World Series). Eventually he is kidnapped, but he escapes in time to smack a game-winning inside-the-park home run, diving over the catcher, who comes out to block the plate. He and his girl have a spat but are reunited at the finale.

Brown starred in Lardner's *Elmer the Great* (1933, First National) on stage as well as screen; however, Walter Huston initiated the role on Broadway in 1928, in a play coauthored by Lardner and George M. Cohan, and the character was portrayed on celluloid

here he is the manager of the World Champions. Like the worst of the Black Sox, he is a greedy soul with treachery in his heart. Cooley, as Connie Mack, may never wear a uniform, but he is no distinguished baseball pioneer. Instead, his lack of baseball garb makes him an outsider to the sport. Lest we forget that he is a villain, his face is adorned with a mustache. Second, there is the haircut of Bing Allen (Paul Kelly), the "local Babe Ruth" of Tom Kelly's home town, who joins the veteran on his Florida trip and serves as his second banana. Allen's head is shaved to the skin all around its sides, but is unshorn on top. He looks like a refugee from *House Party.*

Another typical Lardner concoction is *Alibi Ike* (1935, Warner Bros.), played by Joe E. Brown in the last of the comedian's three baseball movies. Ike may know how to hit, but is unable to field, take instructions, or relate to others. In fact, a player with a reputation for complaining was to come to be labeled an "Alibi Ike."

Brown is cast as Frank X. Farrell, fire-balling right-handed rookie pitcher who comes to the Chicago Cubs from Sauk Center, a small town. Farrell is a comical character with a silly, exaggerated pitching motion, and he first appears on-screen by crashing his car through an outfield wall. However, Farrell is as brash and overconfident as he is talented. After throwing blazing strikes, he observes that he is not even trying, that he has not even warmed up. He utters such lines as "I don't never brag," and then immodest-

The New Klondike: Thomas Meighan as Tom Kelly, Lila Lee as Evelyn Curtis.

first by Jack Oakie in *Fast Company* (1929, Paramount) and later by Bert Wheeler in a football setting in *The Cowboy Quarterback.* The Elmer Kane of *Fast Company,* the first talkie baseball film, is a small-town rube who falls for Evelyn Corey (Evelyn Brent), a flighty actress, and makes the major leagues. He slumps upon learning that he has been conned into thinking she cares for him; she discovers she really loves him, allowing him to recover in time

Alibi Ike: In or out of uniform, "Ike" (Joe E. Brown) proves an enigma to Cap (William Frawley), his manager.

to perform the usual World Series heroics. Kane is described in *Variety* as

> a character that carries reality, a blend of sap, boundless naïveté, a horse's appetite for food, and a heart that's a melon size. And with it all not a trace of smart aleck. It's

thoroughly human. Elmer wins the sympathies while remaining Elmer and not going through one of those complete overnight last-minute changes of nature by which Mr. Haines [in *Slide, Kelly, Slide*] makes himself companionable and lovable in the end.

Alibi Ike: Roscoe Karns as Carey, William Frawley as Cap, Joe E. Brown as "Ike" (left to right).

Fast Company: Gwen Lee as Rosie La Clerq, Jack Oakie as Elmer Kane.

161

Elmer the Great: Elmer (Joe E. Brown, center) attempts to convince his manager (Preston Foster, right) and team owner (Berton Churchill, left) that he is not a cheat.

Despite differences in the scenarios of *Elmer the Great* and *Alibi Ike*—Elmer Kane is a home run hitter rather than pitcher, and he comes with a small-town Indiana girlfriend (Patricia Ellis)—Brown's Elmer is a virtual clone of his Ike. His major-league team is the Chicago Cubs. He is a "sassy and ignorant" braggart and rube, whose personality is contrasted to a new paint job: "fresh and all wet." He alienates his teammates, who make him the butt of their humor. He leads the Cubs to the summit of the standings. He refuses to be bought by gamblers. He fights and

Elmer the Great: Elmer (Joe E. Brown, center) and High-Hips Healy (Frank McHugh, second from right, up front) break training and do some innocent but ill-fated gambling.

makes up with his girl. He thwarts a sneaky Yankee pitcher's attempts to cheat by making it appear that he is hurling a ball when he really isn't. He wins the deciding game of the World Series with an inside-the-park homer. And he, too, refers to the World Series as the "World Serious."

In his autobiography, *Laughter Is a Wonderful Thing,* Brown wrote,

> The character of Elmer in *Elmer the Great*, as originally conceived by Ring Lardner, was based on big Ed Walsh of Meriden, Connecticut. Walsh was a member of the old Chicago White Sox when they were called the Hitless Wonders because they dominated the American League for so many years. This was the period when Ring Lardner was known as a good baseball reporter and nothing more. Traveling, dining, and card playing with the noble athletes gave Lardner a great slant on their off-the-diamond characters. He discovered that even the greatest heroes had their human moments, and he made a special close study of Big Ed Walsh . . .
>
> Elmer the Great was—well, to put it mildly, he was rather sold on himself. Like Dizzy Dean, he would blandly announce that he'd knock the potatoes out of the other team, and then would make good his bragging by striding out onto the diamond and doing exactly what he had predicted.

Joe E. Brown's initial baseball feature was *Fireman, Save My Child*, which may not be based on a Ring Lardner work but which establishes the formula replayed in *Elmer the Great* and *Alibi Ike*. He is cast as "Smokey" Joe Grant, a small-town fireman with a shy, sweet girlfriend, Sally (Evalyn Knapp). Grant's pitching prowess earns him a spot with the St. Louis Cardinals. "Shucks, baseball don't mean nothin' to me," he says. As real-life Hall of Fame hurler Rube Waddell, he would rather be chasing fire trucks. In fact, he has even perfected an invention, a fire extinguisher bomb that, he tells one and all, "lets loose chemicals that'll smother the blaze like a wet blanket." As he anxiously waits to see a businessman who may take an option on his invention, Grant forgets that he is to pitch in the final game of the World Series.

As in the Charles Ray films, the scenario of *Fireman, Save My Child* trumpets rural American life

Fireman, Save My Child: Joe E. Brown as Joe Grant, Rosedale's favorite son.

Fireman, Save My Child: Joe Grant (Joe E. Brown) demonstrates his invention for his girlfriend, Sally (Evalyn Knapp).

and values over the ways of the Big City. Back in his hometown of Rosedale, Kansas, Grant is a hero. Kids fawn over him, and his teammates and opponents patiently await his return if he is called away during a game to fight a fire. But in St. Louis, his manager (Guy Kibbee) is forever gruff and growling, and his teammates ride him for his country values. Grant innocently starts up a friendly conversation with a woman, who automatically assumes he is a masher. June (Lillian Bond), a golddigger, hoodwinks him, taking all his money. "It must be *too* exciting to live in a small town," she snootily observes. But Sally loves him for who he is, not for his money. Despite his various distractions, he manages to perform the requisite heroics at the finale, leading the Cards to victory against the New York Yankees in the World Series.

BASEBALL AND KIDS

The Bad News Bears may be the most famous group of ragtag kids to bat, field, and slide on a celluloid ballfield. But by far, they were not the first. Take, for instance, the two reeler *Shut Out in the 9th* (1917, Edison), in which one Jimmy Beal, a lad of about twelve or thirteen, and his pal Spike Matthews laugh at the town sheriff after being ordered to cease their game of catch. They chide one of their contemporaries, a "sissy" who wouldn't know a baseball bat from a tennis racket. Jimmy and Spike play for the Greenpoint Giants. After their team loses a spirited game to their rivals from Johnsville, the boys discover puberty and compete for the affection of a pretty young miss from the Big City. In the end, they realize that "the guy what said 'a pretty face hides many a false heart, was right.'"

Most of the sports-related "Our Gang" and "Little Rascals" one- and two-reel comedies featured the kids on football fields or in boxing rings. One of their rare appearances with bat and ball is in *Giants vs. Yanks* (1923, Pathé), and even here baseball is depicted only in passing. The kids play for the Giants; their game is put on hold as various players scheme to avoid completing household chores. They arrive at the field and the contest begins, but the kids soon are involved with a litter of puppies and other shenanigans. Baseball is the starting point in *1-2-3 Go!* (1941,

MGM), in which Mickey Gubitosi (who grew up to be Robert Blake) chases a fly ball into a street, is hit by a car, and finds himself hospitalized; and in *Rover's Big Chance* (1942, MGM), in which the title pooch plays second base in a ballgame.

Homerun Hawkins, filmed in Milwaukee, is one of the oddest baseball films of the silent era, if not all time. Seckatary Hawkins is the star of a kids' team scheduled to play the Pelhams in a championship fray. The scenario is standard fare: Sec and and his pals chase a thief who's robbed a filling station and stashed the loot in their dugout; and they seek a bat that will be guaranteed to help them win the game. However, *Homerun Hawkins* is crammed with pitches that have nothing to do with baseballs. Local merchants sponsored the film's production: prominently displayed throughout are various products and emporiums, among them Gridley Ice Cream, the E.M. Jordan Buick Company, and Schusters Department Store, where the boys purchase the "Schuster Home Run Special" that Sec will use to smack the game-winning round tripper.

Generally, during the Depression and World War II, the focus of films featuring youngsters and baseball was on their elders. A typical example: *I'll Fix It* (1934, Columbia), the story of an unscrupulous but likable town boss (Jack Holt). His kid brother is chosen to captain the school baseball team, but is disqualified because of poor schoolwork. The elder sibling thinks he can easily "fix it" for the kid, but must tangle with a no-nonsense teacher (Mona Barrie). The sport

Giants vs. Yanks: Mickey Daniels (left), Joe Cobb.

plays small but important roles in films like *Black Legion* (1936, Warner Bros.) and *Remember the Day* (1941, Twentieth Century-Fox), in which boys who love baseball serve as symbols of Americanism. Then there is *Mr. Winkle Goes to War* (1944, Columbia), the story of an overaged, henpecked bank employee (Edward G. Robinson) who finds himself drafted into the military. He shares a close relationship with a boy, Barry (Ted Donaldson), the only character who admires poor Mr. Winkle. You know Barry is a good kid the instant he appears on screen, because he's carrying a baseball glove and wearing a baseball cap and jersey. (Coincidentally, another middle-aged draftee, who lost his kid brother at Wake Island, is anxious to "squeeze himself a Jap." He is played by Robert Armstrong, and named Joe Tinker, as in Tinker-to-Evers-to-Chance.)

The Kid From Cleveland: Rusty Tamblyn as Johnny Barrows, with Cleveland Indians' hurlers Satchel Paige, Bob Feller, Steve Gromek (left to right).

Swell-Head: Dickie Moore as Billy, dwarfed by "real" ballplayers. Generally, kids in pre–World War II baseball features were depicted in relation to adults.

166

It wasn't until the postwar era that movies about boys, girls, and baseball began to proliferate on screen. In addition to *Angels in the Outfield* and *Roogie's Bump*, there is *Boys' Ranch* (1946, MGM), a minor, formula entry about a ballplayer (James Craig) who becomes involved in establishing a ranch where troubled teens can learn sportsmanship and honesty. More intriguing (if only for its cast) is *The Kid from Cleveland*, in which Rusty (later known as Russ) Tamblyn stars as Johnny Barrows, a misunderstood youth who finds a mentor in a kindhearted sports announcer, Mike Jackson (George Brent).

Johnny's alienation stems from his lack of rapport with his stepfather. But he loves baseball, and in particular the Cleveland Indians. Here is where *The Kid from Cleveland* becomes essential viewing for baseball fans. About thirty Indians, the 1948 World Series champs, portray the "godfathers" recruited by Jackson to help Johnny. Among the ballplayers cast are Gene Bearden, Steve Gromek, Mickey Vernon, Ken Keltner, Ray Boone, Dale Mitchell, Larry Doby, Bob Kennedy, Jim Hegan, Joe Gordon, and Hall of Famers Tris Speaker, Hank Greenberg, Lou Boudreau, Bob Feller, Satchel Paige, and Bob Lemon.

Lest we forget the Indians' owner, Bill Veeck. Given his legendary flair for theatrics, it is no surprise that *Variety* reported that Veeck "shapes up surprisingly well as a thespian." While there is newsreel footage of the ballplayers in action, and sequences in which they warm up, their primarily function in the film is as actors. In this regard, they were no competition for Clark Gable, Gary Cooper, and Humphrey

Bogart (or even George Brent). In "Everything Baseball," James Mote quotes Boudreau, then the Indians' player-manager, on *The Kid From Cleveland*: "I would like to buy every print of the film and burn it. Boy, that picture was a dog." Added Veeck, "I have one unwritten law at home that I adhere to: I never allow my kids to mention or see that abortion."

A far more satisfying "kid" movie is *The Kid From Left Field*, an offbeat, entertaining example of Hollywood hokum. Dan Dailey, who the year before had played Dizzy Dean in *The Pride of St. Louis*, stars as Larry "Pop" Cooper, a widowed ex-jock and Bisons star who hawks peanuts at the team's ballpark. The Bisons are consistently inept—only 123 fans are on hand to watch the team lose yet another game—and Larry is the only person who understands how poor managerial decisions are wrecking the club. He lives with Christy (Billy Chapin), his cloyingly cute nine-year-old son, in a dreary one-room apartment crammed with baseball memorabilia, including a

The Kid From Cleveland: Rusty Tamblyn as Johnny Barrows, dining with a trio of Indians.

photo of Cooper with Babe Ruth. "They don't pay no attention to me no more," he tells his son. "I'm just another has-been."

After Cooper is fired by the head concessionaire, Christy attempts to plead his case to Whacker (Ray

The Cleveland Indians, around the time of *The Kid From Cleveland*. Team owner Bill Veeck, who is prominently featured in the film, is the bald man in the first row.

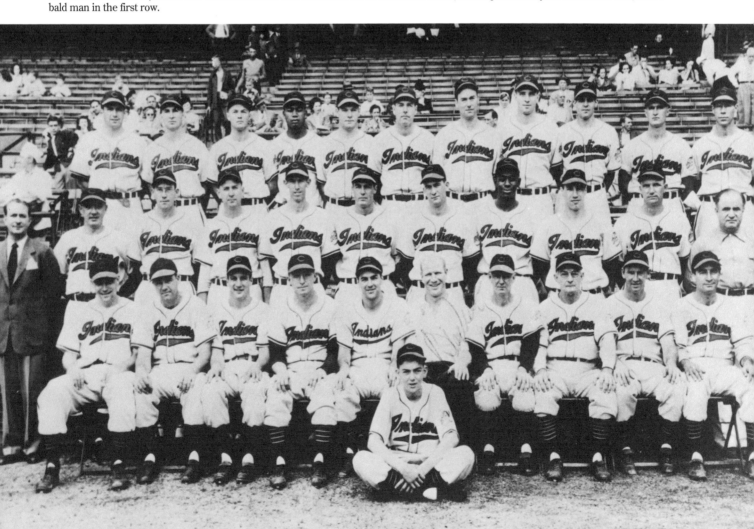

Collins), the Bisons' owner. The result: Cooper is reinstated and, over the protests of Lorant (Richard Egan), the team's manager, Christy becomes the club batboy. Soon, this little boy in an oversize baseball suit is feeding Larry's batting tips to Pete Haines (Lloyd Bridges), a slumping Bison.

Haines starts hitting again. His teammates consider Christy a lucky charm. The youngster begins passing them plays, devised by his dad. The Bisons go on a winning streak, and move up in the standings. In a critical situation, Christy advises a Bison (John Berardino) to disobey Lorant and lay down an unorthodox bunt. The play works, the winning run scores, and Whacker lauds Lorant for devising the "most brilliant piece of baseball strategy I've ever seen."

Lorant learns that Christy was responsible for the play. He

The Kid From Left Field: Dan Dailey as Larry Cooper.

tells the boy that his father was a "swell-head," because he was banished from baseball for belting a fan. "You're just like him," Lorant claims. "No good. And now you're through, just like he is." After the Christy-less Bisons are routed, a committee of players tells Whacker the truth. "Son," the owner asks, "how would you like to run my ballclub?" Complications arise when a truant officer orders Christy to school; he survives this crisis, but eventually collapses with viral pneumonia and reveals that his dad is the true Bisons' strategist. Cooper is hired as the team's skipper. Pete Haines, who at thirty-six has become slow-footed and has been rejecting the advice of his fiancée (Anne Bancroft) to retire, becomes a Bison coach.

The Kid From Left Field was remade a quarter century later as a TV movie. The scenario is almost

The Kid From Left Field: Dan Dailey as Larry Cooper, Anne Bancroft as Marian, Billy Chapin as Christy, Lloyd Bridges as Pete Haines (left to right).

The Kid From Left Field: The Bisons are anxious for Christy (Billy Chapin) to feed them playing tips.

The Kid From Left Field: Whacker (Ray Collins, left) lauds manager Lorant (Richard Egan) for baseball strategy really devised by Larry Cooper (Dan Dailey, in vendor's uniform).

The Kid From Left Field: Christy (Billy Chapin) gets to live out every young baseball fan's dream, from warming up with professionals to tussling with an umpire (played by real-life ump John "Beans" Reardon, pictured with Lloyd Bridges).

identical, except that the fictional Bisons are replaced by a real major-league team, the San Diego Padres; and Christy is now a precocious, pint-size child-man of eleven called J.R. (shortened from Jackie Robinson), and played by Gary Coleman.

The film is most interesting for its casting of Tab "Joe Hardy" Hunter as the heavy: Bill

The Kid From Left Field: Lloyd Bridges (sliding) as Pete Haines.

Lorant, the Padres' thick-witted manager. At its best, this *Kid From Left Field* is pleasantly antiseptic, in spite of its canned music score which, when not being

The Kid From Left Field: Gary Collins as Pete Sloane, Gary Coleman as J.R. Cooper, Tab Hunter as Bill Lorant (left to right), in the made-for-television remake.

cutesy, telegraphs the characters' emotions.

Kids are neither potential juvenile delinquents nor big-league skippers in *The Great American Pastime* (1956, MGM). They are Little Leaguers, and the film serves as a predecessor to *The Bad News Bears* (1976, Paramount) as a satire of American suburbia. Tom Ewell stars as Bruce Hallerton, a lawyer who wants to bond with his son (Rudy Lee) and chooses to manage the Panthers, the lad's Little League team. But he cannot imagine what he will be facing. His players are incompetent. Their parents pressure him not only to win games but to favor each individual boy, and he misconstrues the motives of a widow (Ann Miller) who desires that Hallerton allow her son to pitch. This agitates his wife (Anne Francis), who hates baseball but learns how to keep score in order to defuse the situation.

Competitively speaking, the Panthers are kittens. As a result, Hallerton is not the most popular man in town. Actually, he is a stereotypically inept suburban husband-father. But his essential decency prevails, and he becomes the hero as he leads his boys to the league title.

The Great American Pastime, unlike *The Bad News Bears*, is strictly a formula comedy with one major distinction: the presence on the Panthers of sev-

The Great American Pastime: Tom Ewell as Bruce Hallerton, dealing with chaos and complaints (from Judson Pratt).

The Great American Pastime: Will a real Panther somehow motivate the Little League Panthers?

eral black players, an unusual but refreshing touch for a film released in 1956.

Not all celluloid suburban dads were as accommodating as Bruce Hallerton. *Boys' Night Out* (1962, MGM) is a tepid comedy about four Greenwich, Connecticut, males—one is a bachelor and the rest are married—who rent a Manhattan apartment that they plan to outfit with a blonde who will keep company with each one on separate nights of the week. They "hire" a woman (Kim Novak) who, unbeknownst to them, is a sociology student completing a thesis on "Adolescent Sexual Fantasies in the Adult Suburban Male."

What does this have to do with baseball? Little League is a ritual of suburban America from which the married men envision escaping. But each one lacks the guts to frolic with Novak. They return to Greenwich, and the routine of life with their monotonous mates and distasteful ballplaying children. Predictably they're joined by the bachelor, who weds their fantasy sex object.

Released two months prior to *Boys' Night Out* is the camp classic of baseball movies: *Safe at Home!* (1962, Columbia), a harmless kiddie film that is great nostalgia for New York Yankee buffs if only because they will see the M & M boys, Mickey Mantle and Roger Maris, in their prime. Maris had just whacked sixty-one home runs, besting Babe Ruth's single season record. Mantle had smacked fifty-four round-trippers, and for almost a decade had been a fixture in Yankee Stadium. Now the fun part: as in *The Kid From Cleveland* (a film that lacks the geniality of *Safe at Home!*), these real-life heroes not only shag flies and smash fastballs but are called upon to act.

Bryan Russell plays Hutch

171

The Great American Pastime: Bruce Hallerton (Tom Ewell) is none too happy as he leads his boys in calisthenics.

Lawton, a motherless ten-year-old. He has moved with his father, Ken (Don Collier), to Palms, Florida, where the elder Lawton is struggling to pay off his charter boat. Hutch is baseball crazy, and has made a

Boys' Night Out: Suburbanites Tony Randall, Howard Morris, James Garner, and Howard Duff (left to right) would rather be elsewhere than dealing with Little League.

Little League team. Henry, a snooty banker's son, chides Hutch because Mr. Lawton is too busy working to watch the boys practice. Hutch is intimidated. He responds that not only does his dad know more about baseball than any other dad, but that he is best pals with the players from the greatest baseball team, the New York Yankees. Especially Mickey Mantle and Roger Maris. Why, Ken Lawton even is "Roger Maris's best friend in the whole South."

Hutch gets caught in his lie when pressured to produce Mantle and Maris at the league dinner. What will the boy do? "I'm gonna go see 'em," he tells his pal Mike Torres (not the same Mike Torrez who pitched for the Yankees in 1977). "That's what I'm gonna do. I'm gonna ask 'em to help. They just gotta say yes." Hutch heads off to Fort Lauderdale, the Yankees' spring training base, hidden in the back of Mike's father's fish truck. Once there, he sneaks into Mantle's hotel room and Ft. Lauderdale Stadium; showers in the same stall used by the Yankees, and falls asleep in the team locker room while wearing Maris's jersey as a nightshirt and using Mantle's as a blanket; and tangles with irascible Yankee coach Bill Turner (William Frawley, turning up in yet another baseball movie, in his final screen role). Eventually Hutch learns that it is not good to tell lies, no matter what the circumstances. His dad realizes that Hutch is still a child, in need of attention and understanding. Hutch and his teammates get to share a special day

Safe at Home!: Bryan Russell as Hutch Lawton.

with the Yankees in Fort Lauderdale.

Mantle and (especially) Maris may be stiffs as actors, but who cares! They *are* Mickey Mantle and Roger Maris, clean-cut all-American heroes. Plus, they are not the only Yankees in *Safe at Home!* During a training sequence, the names Phil and Tom are discernible among the chatter. Could they be Linz and Tresh? When someone says "Pepi," you know that he is referring to Joe Pepitone. (The film is set fifteen years after Jackie Robinson broke the major-league color line, yet it is fascinating to note the lack of black players on the Yankees.) Whitey Ford recites a bit of dialogue: "Hey Rog, Mickey. Houk wants to see you right away." Ralph Houk, the recent successor to Casey Stengel as Yankee skipper, has several lines: "Hey, Bill, can I see you for a minute. ... What's that youngster doing on the bench? ... Keep on running. Run harder than that ..." As would any all-American ten-year-old boy back in 1962, Hutch fantasizes that he is a Yankee outfielder, making spectacular catches and cracking base hits to thunderous applause. And he constantly sighs, "Mickey Mantle ... Roger Maris ... Gosh ... Gee ...."

As you might guess, the script for *Safe at Home!* was not penned by F. Scott Fitzgerald.

The Great American Pastime and *Safe at Home!* may have preceded *The*

Safe at Home!: Bill Turner (William Frawley, left), with a worried Ken Lawton (Don Collier, second from right) and Joanna Price (Patricia Barry).

Bad News Bears as chronicles of Little League baseball. But the latter has come to define this type of baseball movie. The film is immensely likable and intelligent, and its success spawned several far-inferior sequels and imitations as well as a short-lived television series.

Old pro Walter Matthau offers a crackerjack performance as Morris Buttermaker, a former minor-league pitcher employed as a swimming-pool cleaner, whose favorite pastime is guzzling beer. Buttermaker is paid by a local politician to manage a newly formed Little League team, the Bears, whose members are a conglomeration of out-of-shape goofballs and loud-mouths. They're epitomized by Engelberg (Gary Lee Cavagnaro), the fat catcher, who stuffs himself with candy while practicing and gets chocolate all over the ball. Buttermaker initially amuses his charges with stories of how he struck out Ted Williams twice in a long-ago spring training game. Rather than teaching them baseball fundamentals, he shows them how to mix martinis and help him clean his pools. When he does attempt to teach, he falls down drunk on the pitcher's mound.

The Bears are humiliated in their first game,

The Bad News Bears: Amanda Whurlitzer (Tatum O'Neal) and Morris Buttermaker (Walter Matthau) are constantly in conflict.

which is called off in the first inning with them on the short end of a 16–0 score. The kids confront Buttermaker with the fact that he is nothing but a drunken wash-out. Roy Turner (Vic Morrow), coach of the Yankees, the best team in the league, advises him to disband the Bears. But Buttermaker will not give in. He tells his charges, "This quitting thing, it's a hard habit to break once you start." He begins coaching seriously and instilling spirit into the Bears. He reminds them that they will be playing the Athletics in the next game and that means one thing: Bad News for the Athletics!

Buttermaker recruits Amanda Whurlitzer (Tatum O'Neal), his ex-girlfriend's daughter, who is almost twelve and an ace pitcher. The team's final addition is Kelly Leak (Jackie Earle Haley), a Moped-riding, cigarette-smoking punk who is "the best athlete in the area." The Bears begin winning games, and they face the Yankees for the championship. Buttermaker gets caught up in a win-at-all-cost men-

174

ter of Amanda Whurlitzer, *The Bad News Bears* shows how a girl can play ball as well as a boy. Kelly Leak becomes humanized, realizing that being a loner is indeed a lonely life. The various other players, from Timmy Lupus on down, learn about friendship, teamwork, and self-assertiveness.

Even more tellingly, the film offers a reminder that the purpose of Little League is to have fun. All the kids should be allowed to participate, not just the most athletically gifted. Little League, after all, is for the kids, not their parents or coaches. This point is succinctly expressed during the championship game, when Roy Turner cruelly berates his pitcher, who also happens to be his son, even smacking the boy when he doesn't throw exactly as instructed. In retaliation, the boy holds on to a ball he fields, allowing the Bears' batter to circle the bases. He strides to his father, drops the ball at his feet, and walks off with his mother.

The Bears do not cop the championship, and that is what makes the film so appealing. The Bears are flawed, are destined to come in second no matter

The Bad News Bears: Amanda Whurlitzer (Tatum O'Neal) winds and fires.

tality when he orders Kelly to cover for the rest of the Bears on defense. But in the final inning he sends the subs onto the field, the kids who haven't played all season. In an inferior film, the Bears would beat the Yankees anyway. In *The Bad News Bears*, they fall short—but have gained in the process. A Yankee patronizingly tells the Bears, "We still don't think you're all that good a baseball team, (but) you got guts." Timmy Lupus (Quinn Smith), the smallest, shyest Bear, whom other, bigger kids have abused throughout the story, responds with a valiant, defiant "Wait til next year."

The Bad News Bears succeeds primarily because of Bill Lancaster's genuinely funny, perceptive script, and the talents of Matthau and a hand-picked supporting cast. The kids spout four-letter words, which back in 1976 was a departure from the G-rated dialogue spoken for decades by celluloid moppets. This nod to realism is not included solely for effect, just as the film is more than a mindless entertainment. In the charac-

Team photos from (Left-top to bottom) *The Bad News Bears* (with proud manager Walter Matthau, holding Tatum O'Neal's hand), *The Bad News Bears in Breaking Training* (with new manager William Devane), and *The Bad News Bears Go to Japan.*

how hard they try. They are human, and they triumph not because they win the game but because they try, they have spirit, they take no guff from those born with silver baseball bats in their hands.

The film was followed by *The Bad News Bears in Breaking Training* (1977, Paramount), in which it *is* next year. The Bears, billed as the "California Champs" (even though they were losers in the previous film), are supposed to travel to Houston to play their Texas equivalents in the Astrodome. They are lacking a coach and pitcher, because Walter Matthau and Tatum O'Neal have (smartly) not returned for the sequel. Kelly Leak (still played by Jackie Earle Haley) produces a stolen van. The kids lie to their parents that they have a coach, and head off to Texas with Kelly at the wheel. Once in Houston, Kelly looks up his father, Mike (William Devane), whom he has not seen in eight years. Mike tutors the Bears and Kelly's friend Carmen Ronzonni (Jimmy Baio), a wild-armed pitcher who has joined the team. At the finale, Mike and Kelly are reconciled, and the Bears earn the come-from-behind victory that sets up a second sequel, *The Bad News Bears Go to Japan* (1978, Paramount).

. . . Breaking Training is at best boring, and at worst sexist and racist. In the original, Amanda Whurlitzer's presence and athletic ability are refreshing nods to fair play. The Bears accept her as a teammate who can help them win ballgames. Here, if Amanda were to appear, the boys probably would maul her because they have become moronic chauvinists-in-training. While driving to Texas, they attempt to pick up a nubile hitchhiker who flees in terror after seeing them. They avidly devour copies of *Playboy*. They whistle at an attractive girl in the company of their opponents.

Ahmed Abdul Rahim (Erin Blunt), the Bears' token black player, is obsessed with a fear of getting busted and ending up in the "joint": a "concern" that a nonthinking white American would expect from a black American. While heading to Texas, the Bears take on a team of American Indians. After losing, one of the Bears observes, "Looks like we've been scalped," a comment that is witless and exasperatingly racist. The Indians remain behind, to play in their garbage-strewn lot, while the Bears continue on to glory in the Astrodome.

Finally, *The Bad News Bears in Breaking Training* is a beer commercial disguised as a movie, ironic for a film whose primary audience is preteens. There are several unabashed plugs for Budweiser and Anheiser-Busch. Once in Houston, the Bears are housed by the company free of charge. Thus, Anheiser-Busch is portrayed as a corporate Santa Claus, but there is no acknowledgment of the reams of free publicity such a generous act would earn. Then again, *The Bad New Bears in Breaking Training* is the kind of film that tells its young viewers that it is okay to lie to your parents, just so long as you win the game.

Sequel Number Two, *The Bad News Bears Go to Japan*, is not so much about the Bears as about their new "promoter," Marvin Lazar (Tony Curtis), a down-and-out show biz hustler. Lazar brings the boys across the Pacific to play the Japanese Junior Baseball Champions, a journey that he hopes to exploit. The scenario focuses on Lazar's various money-making schemes, and his tug-of-war relationship with the Japanese coach (Tomosaburo Wakayama).

With the exception of Kelly Leak (still played by Jackie Earle Haley) and his interest in the opposite sex, Engelberg (now played by Jeffrey Louis Starr) and his interest in food, and the addition of cute little Mustapha Rahim (Scoody Thornton), Ahmed Abdul Rahim's kid brother, the Bears barely have individual personalities. Kelly, however, is no longer a junior James Dean. He has been sanitized, completely transformed into a charming young man who sweetly romances a pretty Japanese girl (Hatsune Ishihara).

By the finale, Lazar learns what the Bears already know: that it is not nice to be a manipulator, a peddler of commercialized, homogenized sporting events. Youngsters should play baseball just for fun. Plus, the sport transcends national barriers in that it can be shared by Americans and Japanese. While the message is worthy, the film is barely funny, and mostly boring (despite a script by Bill Lancaster and an earnest performance by Curtis, playing an aged, polyester-suited variation of Sidney Falco, the New York press agent he depicted so memorably twenty-one years before in *Sweet Smell of Success*).

The Bad News Bears in Breaking Training: The Bears scare off a hitchhiker.

The Bad News Bears served as inspiration for *Here Come the Tigers* (1978, American International), also known as *Manny's Orphans*, a terminally moronic alleged comedy. The film opens with a veteran small-town cop/Little League coach losing his sanity after the season's first practice. He calls his new players "pea-brained losers," and it is up to a coworker, Eddie

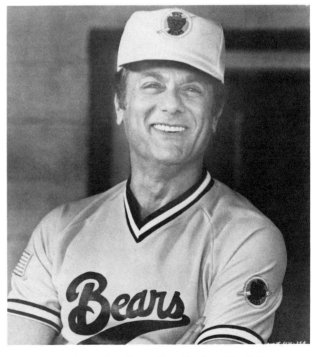

The Bad News Bears Go to Japan: Tony Curtis as Marvin Lazar.

Here Come the Tigers: Catcher and umpire collide.

Here Come the Tigers: Philip Scuder as Danny Mayfield.

Here Come the Tigers: "Ballbuster" Rivera (Xavier Rodrigo), after belting the game-winning hit.

Burke (Richard Lincoln), to replace him. Burke's charges are a brawling, inept bunch. A typical player is a pint-size Public Enemy Number One named Francis Xavier "Ballbuster" Rivera, who refers to baseball uniforms as "fag threads."

Only in the movies could such a bunch eventually be battling for the championship, pulling off an unassisted triple play and coming from behind for the victory, with a reformed "Ballbuster" busting the winning hit. In *The Bad News Bears*, the first part of this fantasy works because of the talents of the actors and

178

creators. Not so in *Here Come the Tigers*.

Characters like "Ballbuster"—foul-mouthed terrors whose dialogue, unlike that in *The Bad News Bears*, is written solely for shock value—have unfortunately remained constant in movies. A typical example: the title brat in *Problem Child* (1990, Universal), a crass, crude comedy about a devilish orphan named Junior (Michael Oliver). Junior is adopted by a Mr. Nice Guy, Ben Healy (John Ritter), who coaches Little League, and his bitchy wife Flo (Amy Yasbeck). Healy sends Junior up to bat during a game. After hitting the ball, the boy bashes the opposing players with the bat as he rounds the bases. As he approaches home plate, Junior smashes the catcher in his private parts and starts yelling "Touchdown! Touchdown!"

Thematically and critically, *Tiger Town* (1983, The Disney Channel) is a throwback to *The Kid From Left Field*, with a tinge of *Angels in the Outfield*–style faith. This television movie tells of a young, diehard Detroit Tigers fan, his favorite ballplayer, and how the pair are spiritually united in their mutual desire to bring their team a pennant. Alex (Justin Henry) is a grade-schooler whose father (Ron McLarty), a laid-off factory worker, tells him one morning, "If you believe in something with all your heart, you can make it happen. Don't ever stop believing. ... That's all a person's got." When Alex returns home from school, he learns that his beloved dad has died.

Here Come the Tigers: A team photo.

The ballplayer is Billy Young (Roy Scheider), Big Number 6, the Tigers' veteran right fielder, who is "one of baseball's true greats, and the oldest Tiger of them all." Young is concluding a career in which he has amassed almost four hundred home runs, earned nine Gold Gloves, and compiled a .309 batting average. He is a fictionalized Ernie Banks in that he is one of the game's great gentlemen, but has never played in a World Series. His team, unlike the real Detroit Tigers, has for decades held a monopoly on last place.

Young has been slumping badly of late. Alex attends a Tigers game and prays hard, "concentrating" with all his heart. As a result, Young smacks a long, game-winning home run. Each time Alex prays, his ballplayer hits successfully, resulting in the Tigers winning games and edging up in the standings. The catch is that Alex must be at the ballpark for his system to work. At the finale, the Tigers are battling the Baltimore Orioles in the pennant-deciding game. Some school bullies delay the boy's arrival at Tiger Stadium until the ninth inning, just in time for his hero to belt a game-winning, pennant-winning inside-the-park home run.

Tiger Town may be formulaic, but its "Ya Gotta Believe" message and depiction of a warmhearted father-son relationship, existing within a cruel, inhospitable world and transcending the former's death, cannot be faulted.

A number of recent films featuring young

ballplayers symbolically link baseball to issues of significance that transcend the game. *The Chosen* (1982, Twentieth Century-Fox), a fine adaptation of Chaim Potok's novel, and *Alan & Naomi* (1991, Triton Pictures), a well-meaning but stagey drama, are set in Brooklyn during the 1940s; at the beginning of each, ethnic teenagers are depicted playing ball. While in each case the sport serves as a means to set the story in motion, its presence also illustrates each boy's assimilation into the American mainstream.

Amazing Grace and Chuck (1987, Tri-Star) is a Capraesque story whose good intentions are obscured by its unsuccessful execution. It is the saga of twelve-year-old Chuck Murdock (Joshua Zuehlke), an all-American boy, the type of kid every parent would be proud to have as a son. Chuck is a strike-out artist on his Livingston, Montana, Little League team. His consciousness is awakened to the perils of nuclear war after visiting a missile base. In his youthful naïveté, he cannot under-

Problem Child: Junior (Michael Oliver, left) menaces a fellow Little Leaguer (Cody Beard).

stand the rationale for the existence of nuclear warheads. "Can't play ... I'm not sick. I just can't play," he tells his coach before a game. "Can't play because there are nuclear weapons."

Amazing Grace Smith (Alex English), a Boston

Tiger Town: Roy Scheider as Billy Young.

© Walt Disney Productions

Tiger Town: Justin Henry (left) as Alex, Roy Scheider as Billy Young.

Tiger Town: Detroit Tigers skipper Sparky Anderson (right) plays himself; at left is the film's director-writer, Alan Shapiro.

Celtics basketball star, quits his team in support of Chuck. "He gave up what he did best for this ideal," Amazing Grace tells the press. "I am giving up basketball until there are no more nuclear weapons." Chuck and Amazing Grace are joined by other professional athletes. Chuck's action, originally an act of solitary inspiration, has international repercussions. The film concludes with the United States and USSR agreeing to eliminate all nuclear weapons. Chuck returns to the pitcher's mound, to hurl in front of the United States President (Gregory Peck), the Soviet Premier, and the international media.

Big (1988, Warner Bros.), an affectionate comedy, celebrates ballplaying and collecting baseball cards, rituals that children should experience even if their desire to become instant adults could be fulfilled. Thirteen-year-old Josh Baskin (David Moscow) is an average American kid who, like millions of his peers, whizzes down the street on his bike and recites a monologue about how the fans are cheering while the New York Yankees star pitcher—himself, of course—arrives on the mound from the bullpen. In a playground, he becomes Yank hurler Rick Reuschel tossing pitches to his friend Billy (Jared Rushton) in a game of stickball. Josh returns to reality as his pal belts the ball a city mile and yells, triumphantly, "Goodbye, Mr. Spaldeen." Next, the boys examine a pack of freshly opened baseball cards with Josh noting, "Got it. Need it. Need it. Got it."

A carnival wishing machine transforms Josh into a big person (played by Tom Hanks). He now can go to the real Yankee Stadium, as well as earn money and enjoy the company of a girlfriend. Upon visiting his hometown and watching a couple of kids playing ball, one hitting fungoes to the other, Josh realizes that he has missed out on completing his childhood. He decides to return to his former physical state. "Before I met you, I was in Little League," are his first words to his girl (Elizabeth Perkins) as he tries to explain the situation. After the re-transformation, the film ends with Josh and Billy strolling down the street talking about . . . stickball.

Parenthood (1989, Universal), an exceptional comedy, opens at a ballgame. The teams already have played four innings when a father arrives with his son. It is their yearly birthday outing and, as always, Dad departs after paying an usher to watch the boy. This sequence is unfolding in the

Amazing Grace and Chuck: Alex English (left) as Amazing Grace, Joshua Zuehlke as Chuck.

memory of Gil (Steve Martin), a happily married father of three, whose childhood experiences have taught him to be an attentive parent.

Gil takes his kids to ballgames out of love rather than obligation. He coaches his eldest child, Kevin (Jasen Fisher), in Little League. Only Kevin is a hypersensitive boy, and an inept athlete. Gil sends Kevin in to play second base at a key point in a game; only the kid muffs a popup, which allows the tying and winning runs to score. The result is humiliation for Kevin, and heartbreak for Gil. Later on, of course, Kevin makes a game-saving catch. Observes Gil, "Isn't that demented? A grown man's happiness depends upon whether a nine-year-old catches a popup."

Hook (1991, Tri-Star) is as lifeless and overproduced as *Parenthood* is knowing and special. Robin Williams stars as Peter Banning, a corporate bigshot who is too busy to attend his son Jack's Little League game. He orders an underling to show up ahead of him and tape what he misses. Jack (Charlie Korsmo), distraught

Amazing Grace and Chuck: Chuck Murdock (Joshua Zuehlke) tells his dad (William L. Petersen) why he is forsaking Little League.

The Sandlot: The Junior Boys of Summer, played by Patrick Renna, Victor DiMattia, Shane Obedzinski, Mike Vitar, Marty York, Tom Guiry, Chauncey Leopardi (foreground), Grant Gelt, and Brandon Adams (left to right).

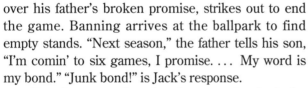

Amazing Grace and Chuck: Chuck (Joshua Zuehlke), with the President of the United States (Gregory Peck).

over his father's broken promise, strikes out to end the game. Banning arrives at the ballpark to find empty stands. "Next season," the father tells his son, "I'm comin' to six games, I promise. . . . My word is my bond." "Junk bond!" is Jack's response.

Banning, an orphan, has forgotten that he is the real Peter Pan. He was taken in as a child by Granny Wendy (Maggie Smith), who found him foster parents. While visiting Wendy in England, Jack (who is forever garbed in a baseball jersey, and carrying around a ball and glove) and his sister Moira (Carolyn Goodall) are kidnapped by Captain Hook (Dustin Hoffman). As "Take Me Out to the Ball Game" is played on a calliope, Hook's cohorts join Jack in the most bizarre baseball game. "This is for all the games your daddy missed," declares Hook, attempting to sway Jack against his father. "Hook would never miss your games, son." As Banning recalls his life as Peter Pan and rescues Jack and Moira, he remembers how to be a kid. The point is that grown-ups must remain in touch with the child within themselves, and see life as a great adventure.

The message in *Hook* and *Parenthood* is that adults should relish parenthood. The joy of having babies is far more rewarding than making money and obtaining power, and the essence of a father-son relationship is coaching Little League, or at least cheering your kid from the bleachers.

Among movies that focus solely on sports, *The Sandlot* is by far the best kids' baseball film since *The Bad News Bears*. However, its pint-size heroes are not inept Little Leaguers but rather a band of boys who play by themselves on a makeshift field and have honed themselves into a unit. They are crackerjack mini-professionals who take pride in their collective ability to whip the ball around the infield and slide into bases.

The scenario is structured as a reminiscence, with an offscreen voice making appropriate observations. The time is the summer of 1962, and that narrator is Scotty Smalls (played on screen by Tom Guiry), a shy, athletically inept fifth-grader and self-described "egghead" who has just moved into a suburban California community with his mother and new stepfather. As the story progresses, young Scotty is initiated into the group and becomes bonded with the boys as they share in various misadventures.

Finally, *The Sandlot* is the saga of how the boys'

leader and best player, Benny Rodriguez (Mike Vitar), becomes a local legend. To begin with, Benny is special. "Baseball was the only thing he cared about," observes Scotty. Even when it was too hot for a game, and the boys would rather cool off at the local swimming pool and ogle the sexy lifeguard, Benny would rather play ball. One day Benny belts a ball so hard that he knocks off its covering. As this is the kids' last horsehide, the eager-to-please Scotty "borrows" his step-dad's prized memento: a ball autographed by Babe Ruth. Scotty promptly whacks it over a fence, on the other side of which resides a junkyard dog whom the boys have come to believe is a fearsome, over-size beast, a "giant gorilla-dog thing."

"Whatever goes over that fence stays there," Scotty has been told. But this special ball must be retrieved. Benny's legendary status—one that transcends the major-league career he is destined to go on to enjoy as Benny "the Jet" Rodriguez—is secured upon his going over the fence to fetch the ball, and his going one-on-one with the animal. This leads to a meeting with the dog's reclusive owner: the elderly, blind Mr. Mertle (James Earl Jones), an ex-ballplayer from the era of Ruth and Gehrig. "Baseball was life, and I was real good at it," Mertle tells the boys. "Real good." He has collected a treasure chest of baseball memorabilia, and he trades

The Sandlot: Benny (Mike Vitar, left) and Scotty (Tom Guiry) are mesmerized by Mr. Mertle (James Earl Jones) and his baseball memorabilia.

a ball signed by the entire 1927 New York Yankees for the now filthy, chewed-up autographed one.

The scenario of *The Sandlot* nicely captures the essence of American boyhood as it depicts the playing of baseball as a sacred rite of youth. At first, the boys regard Scotty with disdain because he "throws like a sissy." But once he catches his first ball, however awkwardly, he immediately is accepted by his peers and officially becomes a part of the group.

The boys' love of baseball is simple and pure.

The Sandlot: Mike Vitar as Benny Rodriguez.

The Sandlot: Tom Guiry as Scotty Smalls.

183

Their games are unencumbered by the presence of adults as coaches and umpires. They are a team, and their loyalty and shared experience transcends what goes on on the playing field. Still, the sandlot in which they play is a special place: a "baseball kingdom" in which the boys are scruffy princes and heirs to the memory of Babe Ruth, who is constantly described with awe as the Great Bambino, the Sultan of Swat.

In *The Sandlot*, baseball is equated with patriotism. Benny Rodriguez's full name is Benjamin Franklin Rodriguez; in a lovely sequence, the boys get to play the summer's sole night game on the Fourth of July, under the glare of fireworks, with Ray Charles's version of "God Bless America" on the soundtrack.

While not a Babe Ruth biography, the film poignantly attests to the power and longevity of the Ruthian legend. Unlike the warts-and-all depiction of Ruth in *The Babe* and *Babe Ruth*, the Bambino is seen through the perceptions of adoring, baseball-mad American boys. "People say he was less than a god, but more than a man," Benny says of the ballplayer, who comes alive to him one night in a dream. The Babe (Art La Fleur) inspires Benny to take the appropriate action needed to retrieve the autographed ball. "Heroes get remembered, but legends never die," the Babe knowingly tells the boy. Benny's retrieving the ball surely will make him a legend.

The Sandlot is not without flaws and omissions. Thelonious Mertle (a character who is an ancient version of Jones's Leon in *Bingo Long . . .*) is shown to be a contemporary of Babe Ruth—he even is shown in a photograph standing between Ruth and Lou Gehrig—yet there is no reference to the fact that major-league baseball in the Bambino's day was for whites only. Perhaps Mertle, as other Negro Leaguers, barnstormed with major leaguers during the off-season, but this is never made clear.

And the film is not without its stereotypes: the team's catcher, Hamilton "Ham" Porter (Patrick Renna), is a roly-poly lad who loves to eat. But *The Sandlot* succeeds as a heartfelt ode to boyhood and baseball.

BASEBALL ABROAD

I n *A Foreign Affair* (1948, Paramount), a postwar black comedy set amid the devastation of Berlin, the military has organized youth clubs for German kids in the American zone. A congressional committee on tour comes upon a rubble-strewn lot in which some boys are immersed in a spirited baseball game. Explains colonel Millard Mitchell, "Those weren't ordinary youngsters when we came in. They were mean old men. . . . We had to kick the goose step out of them and cure them of blind obedience, and teach them to beef with the referee. If they feel like stealing, make sure it's second base." Disputing an umpire's call, then, is a sacred American rite, a symbolic exercise of freedom of speech that would be disallowed under fascist rule. The colonel adds, "One [German] family has already christened their kid DiMaggio Schultz. That's when I started believing we'd really won the war."

Baseball, like bluejeans, rock 'n' roll, and other liberating aspects of American culture, has been exported across the globe from Latin America to Japan. To some, this may be shameless cultural imperialism. But baseball has not been thrust upon the world. Its popularity is guaranteed because of the sport's inherent appeal. People can identify with and enjoy the basics of baseball, whether they are playing the game themselves or watching it from the stands of Yankee Stadium in The Bronx or Gehrig Stadium in Yokohama.

Baseball was embraced by the Japanese long

Indiana Jones and the Temple of Doom: Ke Huy Quan as Short Round.

before World War II. American All-Star teams visited the country in 1913, 1922, 1931, 1932, and 1934. Babe Ruth was as well known in the Land of the Rising Sun as any Japanese celebrity; during World War II, Japanese soldiers harassed their American counterparts with cries of "To hell with Babe Ruth" and "Babe Ruth is a . . . " Reports Dan Schlossberg, in *The Baseball Catalog,*

185

In December 1941, Dr. Alexander Paul, a missionary in China, was subjected to a search by Japanese soldiers. In his home, they spotted copies of *The Sporting News.* "Baseball!" they shouted, then argued how to divide the captured newspapers. At Guadalcanal, PFC John Mooney, Jr., of Worcester, Massachusetts, recalled taking a prisoner who asked, in plain English, "Who won the World Series?"

The popularity of baseball in the Orient is acknowledged by Steven Spielberg in *Indiana Jones and the Temple of Doom* (1984, Paramount), a prequel to *Raiders of the Lost Ark.* The year is 1935, and intrepid archaeologist Indiana Jones (Harrison Ford) is joined in his cliffhanging exploits by Short Round (Ke Huy Huan), a trusty, pint-size sidekick garbed in a vintage New York Giants cap.

If, during wartime, Hollywood depicted the Japanese as heartless, sadistic swine, postwar films featured a more conciliatory tone with baseball serving as a bond between the two cultures. These films feature the plight of children, who are symbols of future relations between the nations. The sport is worked into the scenario of *Three Stripes in the Sun,*

Three Stripes in the Sun: Aldo Ray (right) as Hugh O'Reilly, warming up before battling the Japanese with balls and gloves, rather than guns and grenades.

MacArthur's Children: Masako Natsume as Komako.

the based-on-fact story of Hugh O'Reilly (Aldo Ray), a Bronx-born, Japan-hating GI survivor of Pearl Harbor. O'Reilly comes to the country in 1949, as a member of the occupying American army, and is humanized after observing the appalling conditions of Japanese orphans and romancing Yuko (Mitsuko Kimura), a pretty military interpreter. In order to procure money to build an orphanage, he stages a baseball game between American and Japanese teams. This is a sure-fire fundraiser because, as Yuko correctly observes, "Everyone likes baseball." The proceeds total six thousand dollars but, interestingly, the Americans lose the game. *Escapade in Japan* (1957, Universal) is the tale of two mischievous little boys, one American (Jon Provost) and the other Japanese (Roger Nakagawa), who befriend one another and share adventures as they search throughout Japan for the former's parents. Their relationship transcends cultural barriers and is symbolically linked by the New York Yankees baseball cap worn by the Asian lad. In *The*

lation is *Boys' Baseball Team of Setouchi*. The setting is a small island in the Inland Sea, and the scenario depicts the changes undergone by its populace upon the Japanese surrender to the Americans on August 15, 1945, ending World War II. As the story opens, schoolchildren are ordered to "erase all references of the Imperial Shrine." "Japan lost the war," one boy tells another. "We no longer have a country." This proves not quite true because, later on, Komako (Masako Natsume), their teacher, tells her class that their country may be occupied by American troops but "our spirit will never be occupied." Japan will continue to exist, but as a nonmilitaristic nation. One of the symbols of this pacification is the reintroduction into Japanese society of baseball.

As Komako remembers her husband, who has been missing in the war and is presumed dead, she picks up his old baseball glove: a memento of their peaceful prewar life. One evening, the husband arrives on the island. He is minus a leg and walks on crutches. He asks the boys to give his wife a battered baseball. "Show it to Komako," he says. "She'll understand. She'll know and she'll come." The ball is the companion of the glove. On it is written HIGH SCHOOL CHAMPIONSHIP—1937.

Komako later suggests that her class form a

Geisha Boy, the Great Wooley's antics cause Mitsuo (Robert Kazuyoshi Hirano), a little orphan, to laugh for the first time since his parents' death. The boy decides that the magician is his "honorable father," and the American becomes Mitsuo's surrogate dad as he dines on Japanese food, wears kimonos, and practices Japanese customs. Plus, there's a spark of romance between Wooley and Mitsuo's aunt (rather than the American WAC played by Suzanne Pleshette). The humanistic nature of *Three Stripes in the Sun, Escapade in Japan,* and *The Geisha Boy* was an element of many American movies for decades, and is one of the key components of *The Bad News Bears Go to Japan.*

A similar tone is one aspect of the Japanese-made *MacArthur's Children* (1985, Orion Classics). The film's original title is *Setouchi shonen yakyu dan*, whose English trans-

Gung Ho: Michael Keaton (left) as Hunt Stevenson, George Wendt as Buster.

Chuck Connors's notoriety as a ballplayer-turned-actor is exploited in *Sakura Killers*, a 1986 low-budget actioner in which he appeared.

baseball team. They go about making homemade balls, gloves and bats, practicing their hitting and fielding, and deciding upon a team name. The Giants and Senators are mentioned as possibilities, before the kids settle on Tigers: Kosaka Tigers. Here, most succinctly, does baseball represent a return to peace, to normalcy. A game that evolved in America can again be played by Japanese children. They will wear baseball whites, rather than military greens. They will jog while training to play ball, not while training to kill. Their weapons are bats and balls, not guns and grenades. Near the finale, the Tigers take on a team of American soldiers in a "Japan-U.S. All-Star baseball game": a contest which, symbolically, is played to a draw. Komako tells her husband, "All you think about [are] flowers and baseball," and *MacArthur's Children* is a film about a country looking toward its future.

Other Japanese features that detail the experience of postwar Japan and that feature baseball motifs are *I'll Buy You* (1956, Shochiku, originally titled *Anata Kaimasu*), an expose of a ruthless scout, deter-

mined to sign a high-school prospect, who upsets the young man's relationships with his family and girlfriend; *One-Legged Ace* (1971, Daiei, *Kata Ashi No Ace*), an Asian version of *The Stratton Story*, about a heroic amputee ballplayer; and *A Boy Called Third Base* (1978, Gentosha/ATG, *Sado*), the story of an aimless eighteen-year-old boy in a reform school, who's called "Third Base" because of his love of baseball. Then there is the Korean-made *Just the Beginning* (1977, Yung Bang Films), a *Bad News Bears* clone about an ex-baseball star who coaches a group of losers to the championship. Perhaps the most revealing is *The Ceremony* (1971, Shibata, *Gishiki*), which tells of a young boy, born in Japanese-occupied Manchuria during World War II, who grows up in Japan, becomes a ballplayer, and then abandons the game. "Baseball games punctuate Masuo's youth," notes Joan Mellen, in *The Waves at Genji's Door: Japan Through Its Cinema,* "symbolic of the Westernization and so-called 'democratization' of Japan."

By the 1980s, Japan's expanded world economic dominance, coupled with increased ownership of American companies by Japanese firms, resulted in a cooling of relations between the nations. In *Gung Ho* (1986, Paramount), a Japanese automobile manufacturer purchases and reopens a plant in a depressed blue-collar Midwestern town. Inevitably the Japanese managers and American workers clash in a softball game. The Japanese are garbed in New York Yankees–style pinstripes. They warm up ritualistically, with a patterned set of exercises, and employ strategy during the game. The Americans, meanwhile, wear T-shirts and jeans. They warm up raucously and are disorganized on the field, responding with frustration to their opponents' expertise.

With the winning runs on base, Hunt Stevenson (Michael Keaton) hits a high infield pop-up. One of the runners, an overweight hothead played by George Wendt, purposely barrels into the infielder set to make the catch. The ball falls safely and the Americans win, but it is a tainted, bitter victory. While *Gung Ho* ends on a conciliatory note, with the point made that Americans and Japanese share a common humanity and have much to learn from one another, the real-life tension between the two nations was to spiral upon the recession of the early 1990s.

The issues in *Gung Ho* are further explored in *Mr. Baseball* (1991, Universal), starring Tom Selleck as a veteran American ballplayer continuing his career in Japan. The film's production was a source of

Mr. Baseball: Tom Selleck (above) as Jack Elliot, and Ken Takakura (below) as Uchiyama.

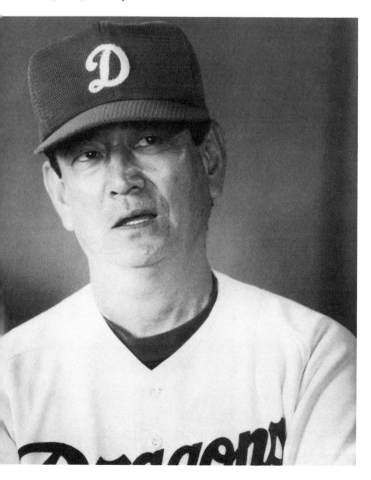

controversy. In an article written by Steven R. Weisman and published in the November 20, 1991, *New York Times,* it was reported that

> When Universal Pictures first agreed to make "Mr. Baseball," it was intended to be a broad comedy about a genial but boorish baseball player who, after being let go by the New York Yankees, joins a team in Japan and clashes head-on with Japan's devotion to martial spirit, group harmony, saving face, grueling workouts and love-hate feelings for foreigners. Then last year the Matsushita Electric Industrial Company acquired MCA, Inc., the owner of Universal. Now the film is a more complex romantic tale of an athlete coming to terms with himself and Japan. ... [The film is] the first test of the Japanese promise to leave creative control in Hollywood. The people involved with "Mr. Baseball" say all changes were carried out by Americans to make the movie funnier and more sophisticated and to make the characters more compelling, not to cater to Matsushita. They deny that any self-censorship was involved. But the script, rewritten this year, now turns more completely on the idea of the Selleck character, Jack Elliot, accepting Japanese ways before he can succeed. ... In addition, at least two jokes about World War II from earlier scripts have been eliminated. ... Balancing these changes, the script has deepened the complexity of the characters of the American's Japanese love interest (Aya Takanashi) and team manager (Ken Takakura). ...

Thomas Pollock, Universal Pictures chairman, and Keiya Toyonaga, Matsushita's senior managing director, went on to declare that the latter company had no involvement in any script alterations.

Mr. Baseball, released more than ten months after the *Times* report, is the story of Elliot, an aging Yankee first sacker who may have been the World Series Most Valuable Player four years before, but the previous season hit a paltry .235. His superiors are displeased with his penchant for boozing, sleeping with bimbos, and giving unsuspecting rookies hotfoots. A newcomer at his position (Frank Thomas, the real-life Chicago White Sox superstar), described by management as "the real thing," is burning up the

Mr. Baseball: Jack Elliot (Tom Selleck, center) conflicts with his manager, Uchiyama (Ken Takakura, right).

grapefruit league. Before Elliot can say sayonara, his contract is sold "not to Canada, not to Cleveland," but to the Chunichi Dragons, a Japanese baseball team.

Elliot deeply resents his fate. He tells the Japanese press that he has come to the Orient because of his "yen" to play there, adding that Japan is filled with "lots of little people walking and talking very fast." He stubbornly refuses to accept Japanese customs or follow the team's exercise regimen. He continues his American habit of spitting on the field, which in Japan is considered a disgrace to his uniform. He continually disobeys the orders of Uchiyama, his manager, and will not "work together in harmony" with his teammates.

Hiroko, the "love interest" and Uchiyama's daughter, is unlike the traditional Japanese woman in that she's determinedly independent-minded. "I'm a big girl," she declares at one point. "I can do what I want." Before they become romantically involved, Hiroko feeds Elliot bits of advice about her country. "Japan takes the best from all over the world and makes it her own," she proclaims. And she tells him what he must do to fit in. "Sometimes, acceptance and cooperation are strengths," she says. "It is not enough just to show up. You must accept, and welcome, and try . . ."

The American is not beloved by the Japanese. His teammates take an immediate dislike to him; upon meeting him, one even extends his first name to "Jackass." Predictably, Elliot begins slumping badly, with his temper tantrums resulting in his being fined

and eventually suspended. Even Max "Hammer" Dubois (Dennis Haysbert), an American teammate, labels Elliot a "hot-shot."

The ballplayer's fortunes change when be begins accepting Hiroko's counsel and respecting Uchiyama's authority. He commences a grueling exercise regimen, apologizes—in Japanese—to his teammates, and soon is vying to break a record for hitting home runs in consecutive games, a mark set by Uchiyama in his playing days. The now humble Elliot sacrifices his chance at the record to lay down a bunt that wins the Dragons the pennant. His reward is a shot with the Detroit Tigers the following spring. He now gives rookies advice, rather than hotfoots.

To add depth to *Mr. Baseball* (as well as make it more palatable to American audiences), Uchiyama is depicted as a cold-hearted martinet who barks orders at his players as if they are wearing GI fatigues rather than baseball jerseys. After striking out, a Dragon is slapped by Uchiyama while still on the field, and the athlete is expected to accept the abuse. Even when Elliot plays well, the manager criticizes him for having "a hole in his swing." When the American argues an umpire's call, the Japanese tells him to shut up and stop embarrassing the team. Furthermore, Uchiyama resents his daughter's independent streak. He represents an "old Japan" while she personifies the "new Japan," a modern nation of spirit and independence.

Uchiyama comes to accept Hiroko, as well as to loosen up on the ballfield; baseball, after all, is just a game, and not a war. He learns that you don't lose face if you argue what you think is an umpire's bad call.

But while there is no motivation for Elliot's behavior except his own immaturity, Uchiyama is given an excuse for his attitude. His bosses wanted to import a different player. Now, the manager may be fired because Elliot is his choice, his responsibility, and the player's failure reflects on his decision-making ability.

As a comedy, *Mr. Baseball* offers few laughs; however, the baseball sequences are well-directed. You really feel the impact of a pitcher letting go with a pitch, a ball sailing off a bat, and a runner sliding into a base. More important, the film is an allegory about why Japan has surpassed America as a force in the world economy, offering the Eastern sensibility as a solution for America's ills. Jack Elliot is a symbol of the Japanese view of Americans as lazy and unwilling to change with a changing world. He and the other "ugly Americans" playing abroad are collectively cynical as they attempt to cope with their situation. They joke about Japanese cuisine; Elliot even rudely insists on smoking while riding on a train, ignoring the discomfort of his fellow passengers. It is just this sort of attitude that has caused America's economic decline. Elliot can only succeed when he abandons his intolerance. Hiroko's advice to him serves as Japan's advice to America; once the ballplayer learns to "accept," he becomes a better man and wins the love of his life. He and Hiroko (and, symbolically, America and Japan) have a future together because, as Hiroko notes, "Jack and Hiroko accept one another."

The premise of *Mr. Baseball* is reworked in the television movie *The Comrades of Summer* (1992, HBO). Only the locale has been changed. *Comrades of Summer* is a byproduct of world events during the early 1990s, when the Soviet Union was dissolved, the Berlin Wall came tumbling down, and America won the Cold War. The film is the antithesis of all those 1950s and 1960s espionage dramas in which stalwart American agents were pitted against deadly KGB operatives whose bosses were played by Oscar Homolka. Its scenario is as much about the ideological triumph of capitalism over communism as the joy of sport. It reveals how the East is ripe for the great game of baseball and the glories of consumerism American-style.

The hero is Sparky Smith (Joe Mantegna), player-manager and, according to media hype, "spark plug" of the Seattle Mariners. Smith personifies the modern athlete-entrepreneur. As the National Anthem

The Comrades of Summer: Joe Mantegna as Sparky Smith.

blasts over the loudspeaker before a Mariners game, he is elsewhere in the stadium taping a quickie car commercial. He kicks up his heels during the shoot, trips, and ruptures a ligament in his ankle, and his playing career is ended. Just as Smith tells journalists that at least he is still the Mariners' skipper, word comes that he has been fired by the team owner (Michael Lerner), with whom he has been constantly, loudly feuding.

Smith is broke, and unemployable because of his "bad name with management." Baseball is to be a medal sport at the 1992 Olympics, and a less-than-enthusiastic Smith is hired to coach the Russian Olympic team. His players are masters of hockey, handball, the shotput, and the hundred-meter dash, but on a ballfield they are little more than Bad News Bolsheviks. The practice field is a dump, and the equipment is beat up. Despite these obstacles, better balls and gloves are acquired on the black market and, under Smith's tutelage, the players improve.

In his absence, the Mariners become "the hottest team in baseball" and win the World Series. The Russians arrive in America to play a five-game exhibition; just a few years before, who would have believed that an American movie would be fashioned to compel the viewer to root for the Russians against the home teams? In a nod to realism, the Russians are handily beaten by the New York Yankees, Boston Red Sox, Kansas City Royals, and Toronto Blue Jays. In the finale, they go up against Smith's former club. Before the game, he notes, "There's always a chance. This isn't a science. It's a game. . . . There is a chance." The Russians play with gusto and, while the Mariners win, it is only by a run. A radio announcer declares, "The Russians have come of age in the American game of baseball." The happy ending is poured on as the Mariners' owner compliments Smith, even though the day before he had chided his ex-employee.

One of the points of *The Comrades of Summer* is that a free marketplace beats dealing in the black market or waiting on breadlines, and this is irrefutable. But the film is a feature-length television commercial in that it is loaded with images of name-brand prod-ucts, from Bekins moving vans to Budweiser to Jif peanut butter, which intrude on the narrative. When Smith appears in a Coca-Cola commercial, there is even a Coke ad within the film.

The Russians in *The Comrades of Summer* remain textbook stereotypes. There is the pretty but businesslike Sports Ministry official (Natalya Negoda), who thaws under Smith's romantic attention; the close-minded, bureaucratic holdover from the bad old days (Mark Rolston), a coach who stubbornly insists on instructing the ballplayers out of a manual; and the ballplayers' mothers, each a pudgy, matronly clone of the next. The film chauvinistically depicts how American culture (as opposed to politics) is far superior to anything Russian. This is expressed in the character of Andrei (Ian Tracey), initially the sole skilled Russian ballplayer. He once lived in America, and insists on forsaking his own name to be called Andy. Later on, he wears a New York Yankees cap. After beating a Cuban (translate: still communist) team, the Russians join not in a chorus of their own ethnic hymn but in that old standby of baseball movies, "Take Me Out to the Ball Game."

THE FAN

Over the decades, a cross-section of entertainers have been loyal, vocal baseball aficionadoes. Among them are Buster Keaton, G.M. "Broncho Billy" Anderson, George M. Cohan, Ethel Barrymore, Tallulah Bankhead, and Pearl Bailey; more contemporary fans include Tom Hanks, Donald Sutherland, Glenn Close, and Bill Murray. Singing cowboy Gene Autry is the longtime owner of the California Angels. Bob Hope, Bing Crosby, and Danny Kaye each held shares in, respectively, the Cleveland Indians, Pittsburgh Pirates, and Seattle Mariners. Spike Lee and Tom Selleck are recognized for wearing baseball caps of their favorite teams, the Brooklyn Dodgers and Detroit Tigers. According to the Associated Press, Michael Keaton "returned to his hometown [of Pittsburgh] for a premiere of *Batman Returns*, but ducked out early to [head] for Three Rivers Stadium, where he saw his favorite baseball team, the Pittsburgh Pirates, lose 4–0 to the Montreal Expos." "I wanted to be a baseball player—shortstop or second base," Billy Crystal told *People* magazine. What happened? During a 1966 game, in which he played second base for Marshall University, "There was a runner on first, a slow ground ball to short— and I knew I was going to get dumped going for the double play. Then *boom*! The runner hit me, and I went flying in the air. As I was coming down, I saw this big sign on the ballpark fence that said, AUDITIONS TODAY."

Of all movie-actor/baseball fans, Joe E. Brown

Gene Autry, ex-singing cowboy and owner of the California Angels.

was perhaps the most knowledgeable. "I have always loved baseball more than any other sport," the comic wrote in his autobiography. "Looking back upon my long love affair with sports and especially baseball is one of the happiest things I do." Not only was Brown a great fan, and friend to some of his era's celebrated baseball personalities (including Lou Gehrig, Tris Speaker, and Connie Mack), but he was an active participant in the sport. As a young man, Brown played minor-league ball. "Actually, I was once offered a contract to play with the New York Yankees," he remembered.

> I didn't accept it because it came at a time when I was beginning to get a foothold on Broadway, and weighing together my future in the two careers, I figured my best chance for success would be the stage. Nevertheless, I did don a Yankee uniform and spent several weeks working out with the team . . .

The comic further recalled,

> My contract with Warner Brothers . . . was probably one of the most unusual ever signed in Hollywood. One of the clauses it contained was one that said Warners must

In recent years, the increased popularity of baseball-related paraphernalia among the general public has translated onto the screen. In *Jacknife*, Megs (Robert De Niro), a Vietnam veteran who is neither past, present, nor future major leaguer, dons a Boston Red Sox cap.

> supply me with a baseball team. It was they who first suggested calling it Joe E. Brown's All-Stars—probably because they thought it would never amount to much. Buster Keaton had a team about the same time, and it was comprised of stage hands and extras, legitimate studio employees. Not mine. I went out and hired professional athletes and some of them were experienced ballplayers . . .

Brown was a collector of sports trophies. "I started the collection with the autographed baseball used in the 1906 World Series," he noted.

> It bears the signatures of Ed Walsh and Three-Fingered Brown . . . there are the shoes that Tris Speaker wore in the 1920 series, gloves belonging to Herb Pennock, Chief Bender, Mickey Cochrane, and Roger Bresnahan; Paul Waner's bat the year he won the National League bat crown, and Babe Ruth's bat the year he hit sixty homers; and Dizzy Dean's uniform from the 1934 Series . . .

Brown had Lou Gehrig's first baseman's glove,

Tom Selleck as Tom Selleck, photographed while taking batting practice with the Baltimore Orioles.

194

which he described as "another trophy among my most cherished."

During the 1930s, Brown and Tris Speaker were part-owners of the minor league Kansas City Blues. In 1953, Brown was a pregame and postgame announcer for the New York Yankees. He was president of Pony League baseball, a boys' sports network for thirteen- and fourteen-year-olds. His son, Joe L. Brown, grew up to become general manager of the Pittsburgh Pirates.

Joe E. Brown's identification with baseball is acknowledged in *Buddy's Bearcats* (1934, Warner Bros.), a Looney Tunes cartoon featuring a caricature of the comic, who announces a game between Buddy's Bearcats and the Battling Bruisers. In his *New York Times* obituary, it was noted, "Mr. Brown loved baseball and developed several routines, including one of a young pitcher harried by batters, umpires and base runners. He used it on the stage, in the movies and on television."

The earliest celluloid shorts featuring baseball devotees predate *Buddy's Bearcats*. In *How the Office Boy Saw the Ball Game* (1906, Edison), the title character maneuvers to duck out of work for an afternoon at the ballpark, only to discover his boss occupying the adjoining seat. *How Jones Saw the Baseball Game* (1907, Lubin) features a similar storyline. In *Baseball, That's All!* (1910, Melies), a fan lies to his boss so that he can attend a game. *Baseball Bug* (1911, Thanhouser) is the story of a clerk who fantasizes that

he's a pitching star. Mr. and Mrs. Sidney Drew are featured in *His First Game* (1917, Metro), in which he takes her to a ballgame at New York's Polo Grounds. Also featured is New York Yankee first sacker Wally Pipp. *Take Me Out to the Ball Game* (1910, Essanay), written and directed by G.M. "Broncho Billy" Anderson, the movies' first cowboy hero, tells of a baseball nut who manages to forget his wife at the ballpark.

Variety describes *The Baseball Fan* (1908, Essanay), also made by Anderson, as

> timely and well worked out. A rabid fan springs the "important business" thing on his wife, hiking to the ball park to see the White Sox wallop the benighted Highlanders [who later were to become the New York Yankees]. After hanging on the back platform—an excellent replica of Chicago's traction service—he arrives at Comiskey's ball-yard to find the S.R.O. sign. He peeks through a knot hole and is chased by one of the finest; he climbs a telegraph pole and falls in a tub of water; he finally gets a foul ball which passports him in. He quarrels with a neighbor, probably a Cub fan, and is hit by a foul tip. A pickpocket purloins his carfare, and the fan walks home, where wifey awaits the issue with a meat axe.

Whew!

Baseball caps have become de rigueur attire for film makers on the sets of their movies. In *The Big Picture*, a motion-picture-industry satire, a young director (Kevin Bacon, left) wears a requisite cap, this one representing the Philadelphia Phillies. He is shown establishing a shot with his cinematographer (Michael McKean).

For decades, movie and television actors have been posed playing baseball for publicity purposes. This charming still features Don Knotts (right) and Ron Howard, regulars on *The Andy Griffith Show* during the 1960s.

Fans were featured in one- and two-reelers of the sound era. Pompous bureaucrats masquerading as baseball loyalists are chided in *Opening Day* (1938, MGM), starring humorist Robert Benchley as the treasurer of the city of Sneeversport. He offers a long-winded speech while preparing to throw out the first pitch commemorating the opening of the town's new ballpark and the season's initial ballgame. The fans begin clamoring for the contest to begin, and the ballplayers play patty-cake and toss paper airplanes.

The Heckler (1940, Columbia) is one of the best-ever baseball-related talkie shorts. Charley Chase, a brilliant, often overlooked comic, plays the title character, a boorish booster who disrupts the quiet decorum of a tennis match by annoying his fellow fans and heckling one of the players into blowing the contest. He then razzes "one of the outstanding baseball players of all time ... that slugging left-fielder of the Green Sox, Ole Margarine (Bruce Bennett)," who is

on hand to present a trophy, and is scheduled to play the following day in the World Series. At the ball-game, the heckler continues his obnoxious behavior. Typically, he rips a bandage off another fan's neck to patch a leak in his inflatable seat cushion, and he cheers so loudly that he showers those sitting near him with soda. He continues mercilessly riding Ole, who summarily strikes out and muffs an easy fly ball. A pair of gamblers approach the boor, ordering him to keep heckling Ole during the next game. That night, Ole and the Sox manager sneak into his room, where he's even bashing the Sox in his sleep, and put ice cubes on his chest. In the morning, his voice is too hoarse for him to heckle effectively. As Ole comes to the plate with the score tied in the ninth inning, the gamblers pull a gun on the heckler, who's terrified into yelling loudly. This time, the ballplayer belts a home run.

The Heckler was remade almost shot-by-shot as *Mr. Noisy* (1946, Columbia), featuring the Three Stooges' Shemp Howard. Both films are reworkings of *The Loud Mouth* (1932, Paramount), starring Matt McHugh. Here, boxing replaces tennis at the outset; the title character heckles a ballplayer named Swat Butler; and Franklyn Pangborn is on hand as Freddie, Swat's Ping-Pong-playing rival for the affection of the ballplayer's girlfriend.

Among all the actors who've played fans, the one who embodies the soul of the baseball zealot is, ironically, William Bendix, whose role in baseball movies extends beyond his characterization of Babe Ruth. During World War II, one of the character types found in a typical military unit in a typical Hollywood war movie was the energetic Brooklynite: a lovable "woiking"-class Flatbush Joe who would blab on and on about Dem Bums, the Dodgers, while bullets from the guns of the heinous "Japs" and "Krauts" zipped by overhead. Weren't our boys in uniform battling Hitler, Tojo, and Mussolini to preserve baseball as much as mom's apple pie and the red, white, and blue? This character, the most celebrated of all celluloid Brooklyn Dodger fans, was played most memorably by Bendix.

In the ads for *Guadalcanal Diary* (1943, Twentieth Century-Fox), Bendix's character (named Taxi Potts, a Brooklyn cabbie turned marine) is described as follows: "All he wanted was to be back in Brooklyn watching them beautiful bums!" At one point in the scenario, he exclaims, "I'm no hero. I'm just a guy." The actor portrayed a baseball-loving guy from Brooklyn, in Brooklyn, in a trio of Hal Roach

Joe E. Brown stretches to make a put-out in *Alibi Ike*.

"streamliners": films with lengths between that of a short and feature, to be added to programs with long main features or for movie houses that normally would not run double features. Their titles are *Brooklyn Orchid* (1942, United Artists); *The McGuerins from Brooklyn*, also known as *Two Mugs from Brooklyn* (1943, United Artists); and *Taxi, Mister* (1943, United Artists). They chronicle the misadventures of Tim McGuerin (Bendix) and Eddie Corbett (Joe Sawyer), a pair of rough-hewn but likable co-owners of a Brooklyn taxi company.

The McGuerins from Brooklyn may have been advertised as a comedy in which Bendix and Sawyer "... Bat Out Laughs Like the Dodgers Bat Out Runs," but baseball is most prevalent in *Taxi, Mister*. The scenario, told in flashback, recounts how McGuerin and Corbett built up their taxi company, and how the former met his wife Sadie (Grace Bradley), who predates Trixie (wife of Ed) Norton of television's *The Honeymooners* as a fictional burlesque queen wed to a blue-collar Brooklynite. McGuerin is a pitcher on a sandlot baseball team; Corbett is the catcher; their nine is named for one of the most famous Brooklyn neighborhoods, Flatbush. Glorio (Sheldon Leonard),

a mobster, plots to do in McGuerin during a game. The pitcher's ability to throw a wicked curveball allows him to knock out the villain, in a sequence

The Heckler: Charley Chase (center), in the title role, loses his voice after passing the night with ice cubes on his chest.

William Bendix, playing ball with daughter Stephanie during the 1950s.

which ends in a free-for-all.

Two years after so ingloriously impersonating Babe Ruth, Bendix was perfectly cast in *Kill the Umpire* (1950, Columbia), a film whose theme might have been a song included in *I Wonder Who's Kissing Her Now*, a biography of 1890s songwriter-entertainer Joseph E. Howard: "The Umpire Is a Most Unhappy Man." Bendix plays Bill Johnson: ex-ballplayer, loud-mouth, and die-hard fan. Johnson resides with his family in St. Petersburg. He cannot keep a job because he is always sneaking off to spring-training games, where he constantly disputes arbiters' calls. His voice wafts above the crowd as he thoughtlessly yells his favorite refrain: "Kill the Umpire." After he gets fired yet again, Johnson's ever-flustered wife (Una Merkel) is about to leave him when her father (Ray Collins), a retired major-league umpire, suggests that his son-in-law take up the profession. This way, his workplace will be a ballpark, and he can be paid for seeing all the games he desires.

"Trying to make an umpire out of me, that's the lowest thing that can happen to a man," protests an indignant Johnson. But faced with his wife's departure, he agrees to be enrolled in an umpire school

operated by his father-in-law's old friend (William Frawley). Johnson does all he can to be expelled, but comes to understand the importance of the umpire after observing some kids playing ball on a sandlot. He completes the course and becomes an ump in the Texas Interstate League, where baseball enthusiasts are lynch mobs who will almost literally kill an umpire if they disagree with his call. Now, Bill Johnson learns how it feels to be the object of indiscriminate abuse. Yet he has become an efficient, proud professional who cannot be bribed by gamblers. There is an extended, frantically paced chase-sequence finale, in which a determined Johnson avoids a horde of angry fans and gun-toting thugs, and arrives at the ballpark to fulfill his professional duties.

Bendix and his comic antics are the entire show here. As Bill Johnson, baseball zealot, rushes onto the field to go one-on-one with an ump, he raises his beer bottle to smack his adversary but only succeeds in pouring brew on his own head. He demolishes the English language, pronouncing "ostracized" as "ostrichized." In the film's funniest sequence, he dons glasses upon his arrival at the school and acts the part of a blind man.

Ultimately, *Kill the Umpire* satirizes the no-win fate of the umpire. If he calls a close pitch thrown to a home-team hitter a ball, the fans will ignore him and praise the hitter's batting eye. If he calls the pitch a strike, he will surely be called every name from ass to zombie.

William Bendix as Chester A. Riley in *The Life of Riley*, pictured with Lanny Rees (playing his son).

Kill the Umpire: Bill Johnson (William Bendix) will go to all extremes to flunk out of umpire school.

Baseball boosters of all ages, sizes, sexes and temperaments have been depicted in features as diverse as *Kill the Umpire, Safe at Home!,* and *Bull Durham.* Other than being comically boorish, a fan's zeal for the game occasionally may supplant his good judgment, resulting in dire consequences. In *Twelve Angry Men* (1957, United Artists), a happy-go-lucky, baseball-mad salesman (Jack Warden) sits on a jury. He's so anxious to get to a game that he fails to thoughtfully examine the evidence regarding the guilt or innocence of the accused, neglecting his responsibilities as a citizen. But most baseball nuts are like Bill Johnson, Hutch Lawton, and Annie Savoy, each a model fan. They are joined by characters found in four other films: a pair of comedies, produced sixty years apart; a romantic comedy; and a made-for-television movie.

The latter is *Aunt Mary* (1979, CBS), the warm-hearted account of "Aunt Mary" Dobkin (Jean Stapleton), a die-hard fan whose involvement with baseball transcends rooting for her home team. Mary is a Baltimore spinster who lives on welfare, and she comes to coach a sandlot baseball team. The film opens with a title: "This is a true story. It's about a woman named Mary Dobkin, a bunch of kids, and baseball." The time is the 1950s, and the St. Louis Browns recently have relocated to Baltimore. Mary, garbed in an Orioles cap, listens intently to the radio as her team plays—and, typically, loses to—the New

York Yankees. Some of the neighborhood kids are talking about starting up a baseball team. Billy (K.C. Martel) is the young grandson of Mary's neighbor, Mr. Strassberg (Martin Balsam). He and the others think it would be great to have Aunt Mary as coach.

In contrast to Mary, Strassberg is a complainer. "What's to like . . . mediocrity flourishes [today]," he says. "They haven't made a good picture since *Meet John Doe.*" Even baseball has changed. "All [the Orioles] are interested in today," according to Strassberg, "is [a] big fat paycheck." (This was back when Clint Courtney and Chuck Diering were on the team. How might Strassberg respond to Cal Ripken, and to $6-million-a-year contracts to star players in the 1990s?)

Strassberg doubts that Mary can mold "juvenile delinquents" into a ball team. But he is eventually won over by the lady, who is an optimist in a world of negativity. She sees coaching as a way of saying thanks to God for getting her out of a hospital bed. She urges her charges to work hard in school and eliminate profanity from their vocabulary. "It's the way you play the game that earns the other peoples' respect," she tells her team (called the Dobkin Dynamites). Mary must practice the positive thinking she preaches when her leg is amputated. She no longer wants to coach. "I never thought you'd be a quitter," says the toughest of

Twelve Angry Men: Juror number 7 (Jack Warden, rear, with hat), a die-hard baseball fan, is quick to affirm a defendant's guilt because he is eager to attend a game.

199

Speedy: Harold Lloyd (left) as Harold Swift, with Babe Ruth.

her kids. "I'm so tired of being a loser," Mary complains to her doctor. But she lightens up after meeting Andy, a fellow Orioles fan, a young boy who's lost his right arm. "You can do anything you want to do if you want to hard enough," she advises him. "You just never give up. Hands are overrated, just like legs." She implores her doctor to design a baseball glove for kids like Andy. Soon, Aunt Mary is back coaching.

"You have to earn the right, just like any new player," she tells a black kid who'd like to play for the Dobkin Dynamites. Yet Mary is the first to defend him when the parents of some of her players remove their kids from the team. Mary receives obscene phone calls. A brick is thrown through her window. Strangers chide her for being a "nigger lover." Yet she perseveres, and endures.

Aunt Mary, like so many movies of its type, is about sassy slum kids who steal candy bars and hot dogs (and are as authentic as a 1949 Mickey Mantle baseball card); with a bit of caring and straightforward advice, they're transformed into upright citizens. But her story is refreshingly feminist as it shows how the unlikeliest of women can do a "man's job," and function in her own modest way as an activist.

Primarily, *Aunt Mary* mirrors the idealism of baseball. "Being an Oriole is being better than president, if you ask me," says Mary Dobkin, consummate baseball fan. "Baseball is what this country's all about . . . because they're both based on the rules of fair play. They both give the little guy a chance. There's room for everybody on a baseball team, no matter where they come from."

In *Sleepless in Seattle* (1993, Tri-Star), baseball is a byword for romance, a loving family, and bliss. As the film opens, Sam Baldwin (Tom Hanks), a Chicago architect, is devastated: his wife has just died of cancer. As Sam mourns the loss of his beloved, there is a split-second flashback to a memory from a happier time: he, his late wife, and their young son, Jonah (Ross Malinger), are posed in front of Wrigley Field.

Meanwhile, Annie Reed (Meg Ryan), a Baltimore newspaper reporter, has just become engaged. At a family dinner during which the union is announced, her fiancé (Bill Pullman) quotes Lou Gehrig: "Today I am the happiest man on the face of the earth."

But Sam and Annie are fated to fall in love. How do we know this? Why, Annie knows baseball and, even though she and Sam have never met, it is noted that both think that Brooks Robinson is the greatest third baseman, ever. Surely, Annie will be a better match for Sam than Victoria (Barbara Garrick), a woman he begins dating. How do we know this? When Jonah asks Victoria, "Do you like baseball," her response is less than enthusiastic.

Baseball even is on the periphery of the film. In the office of Annie's editor (Rosie O'Donnell), there is a life-size cardboard blow-up of James Dean—garbed in a Brooklyn Dodgers jersey.

Aunt Mary: Jean Stapleton, as Mary Dobkin.

Harold Lloyd plays a classic baseball fan in *Speedy*, in which he is cast as a man-child who, if he were alive today, would have amassed millions of baseball cards—not for investment, but for joy.

Back in 1917, over a decade before the film's release, Lloyd was just another screen comedian whose trademark character, Lonesome Luke, was modeled after Chaplin's Little Tramp. Both Lloyd and his producer-director, Hal Roach, had grown tired of Luke. So Roach created a new screen persona for his star, one that was a daring break from the convention of having a comic appear with fake mustache, grotesque makeup and absurd clothes. These were replaced by average clothes, to be worn by an average-looking guy who would be funny, or find himself in comic situations. Integral to Lloyd's new screen persona were the horn-rimmed glasses that were to become his trademark. The comic first wore them in a baseball short, *Over the Fence* (1917, Pathe), in which he and Snub Pollard play a pair of oafish tailors who come upon tickets to a ballgame, where they become involved in various shenanigans.

By the time he starred in *Speedy*, Lloyd had become one of the silent cinema's premier comedians. He plays Harold Swift, also known as "Speedy," an irresponsible dreamer who, according to his girlfriend, Jane Dillon (Ann Christy), "gets plenty of jobs—but he'll never keep one while his mind is full of baseball." Indeed, "the only thing Speedy required of his employers is that their store be within phoning distance of Yankee Stadium."

Much of the scenario concerns Jane's grandfather, Pop Dillon (Bert Woodruff), who operates the last horse-drawn trolley franchise in New York City, and what happens when Speedy uncovers a scheme to sabotage Pop's business. But baseball remains a major component of the film, as Speedy's obsession with the game is cleverly incorporated into the scenario. His latest gig is as soda jerk, and he does not serve his customers because he is too busy on the phone getting updates on the Yankees–White Sox game. Then, an order is placed for an orangeade; Speedy dons a baseball glove, and a coworker pitches him the oranges. He updates the kitchen help on the Yanks–Sox score by creating a mock scoreboard in a glass case. Speedy turns the doughnuts into zeros, the crullers into ones, and broken pretzels into threes.

In *Speedy*, all of New York is baseball-crazy. A crowd of men gather by a storefront to learn the latest ballscores. Speedy perches himself atop a cab, so that he might see above the crowd, and he barely man-

City Slickers: Billy Crystal as Mitch Robbins.

ages to land safely on the street when the taxi pulls off. Speedy's next job is taxi driver, and he reads in the newspaper that Babe Ruth will be spending the noon hour at the City Orphan Asylum, "giving signed baseballs to his young admirers." Speedy is parked across the street, so he heads over to get a glance at the Babe. The ballplayer, who is surrounded by screaming, adoring fans, must rush off to Yankee Stadium, and he calls for Speedy's cab. The ecstatic fan gives the Babe the ride of his life as he swerves in and out of traffic, just missing other cars and pedestrians as he gushes, "Gee, Babe, you've done more for baseball than cheese did for Switzerland" and "Gosh, Babe—this is the proudest moment of my life." The Bambino becomes increasingly flustered at Speedy's ineptitude. "If I ever want to commit suicide I'll call you," is all the Babe can say at the end of the ride.

Lloyd hasn't finished using Ruth as a comic prop. Speedy is invited by the ballplayer into Yankee Stadium to watch the game, and looks on as the Babe

201

smashes a homer. He's overcome with excitement and smacks the head of the fan sitting in front of him, who happens to be his boss. Speedy's new job proves to be a one-day stint.

Even though there is nary a ballfield in *City Slickers* (1991, Columbia), the film features richly conceived characters who are identifiable to every statistic-spewing baseball nut. Like *A League of Their Own*, *Parenthood*, and *Gung Ho*, *City Slickers* is knowingly scripted by Lowell Ganz and Babaloo Mandel. And as the film opens, Mitch (Billy Crystal), a vacationing radio-ad salesman/average American male, runs with the bulls in Pamplona garbed in a New York Mets jersey and cap. On the airplane home, he observes, "Baseball fantasy camp, until Phil [his friend, a grocery store manager, played by Daniel Stern] threw up on Willie Mays, was fabulous. . . . I'll never forget Willie's face. 'Say Hey, that's lunch on me.'"

Mitch and Phil are joined by a third friend, Ed (Bruno Kirby, replaying his role in *Million Dollar Infield* as a baseball-lover/womanizer, approaching middle age, who realizes that all he needs is one special woman). Ed owns a sporting-goods store; his surname is Furillo (as in Carl). Together, this trio spend their next vacation on a cattle drive. Before heading out, Mitch tries on various Western-style hats. None looks right. Finally, he chooses to don his trusty Mets cap.

While on the drive, Phil and Ed argue the merits of Roberto Clemente versus Henry Aaron as their generation's greatest left fielder. The one woman in the group (Helen Slater) says she does not understand how men can memorize baseball trivia obsessively, how they can respond in unison when arbitrarily asked who played third base for the Pittsburgh Pirates in 1960. (The answer is Don Hoak.) She does not dislike baseball, she claims, but it is not "real life." Real life is "relationships—are they working out, are they not." Ed speaks for the walking baseball encyclopedias of the world when he responds, "If that were as interesting as baseball, they'd have cards for it and sell it with gum." Phil forever disproves her statement when he chimes in, "I guess it is childish but, uh, when I was about eighteen and my dad and I couldn't communicate about anything at all, we would talk about baseball. That was real."

Several minutes later, Phil asks Mitch to recall the best day of his life (excluding when his kids were born). Mitch's response: when he was seven years old, and his father took him to Yankee Stadium for his first live ballgame. The stadium seemed huge. The grass was green. The dirt was brown. All of this was a revelation to a kid who had only seen baseball on a black-and-white TV set. Mitch's dad taught him how to keep score. "And Mickey hit one out. Good day," he concludes.

Later on, still out in the wilderness, the three friends explore some long-dormant youthful feelings as they indulge in a scraggly ballgame. As kids so often do, they employ the names (and take on the identities of) real ballplayers. In this brief, eloquent shot, Bob Turley is again a Yankee right-hander, zinging in fastballs to Yogi behind the plate.

Lastly, after his pals rescue Mitch from drowning, he says, "Nice catch. It was like Mays in the 'fifty-four World Series." In the spirit of the film, Phil and Ed can only chime in, "Vic Wertz."

FILMOGRAPHY

THEATRICAL FEATURES

RIGHT OFF THE BAT

(1915) Arrow Film Corp. All Feature Booking Agency B&W 5 reels *Director:* Hugh Reticker. *Writer:* Albert S. LeVino. *Cinematographers:* Henry Bredeson, C.W. Van Ranst. *Cast:* Mike Donlin (Himself), John J. McGraw (Himself), Claire Mersereau (Viola Bradley), Rita Ross Donlin (Lucy), Roy Hauck (Young Mike Donlin), Henry Grady (His Father), Fan Bourke (His Mother), Doris Farrington (Little Viola Bradley), George Henry (Hiram Bradley), Mabel Wright (Mrs. Hiram Bradley).

CASEY AT THE BAT

(1916) Fine Arts Film Co. Triangle Film Corp. B&W 5 reels *Director:* Lloyd Ingraham. *Writer:* William Everett Wing, inspired by the poem "Casey at the Bat," by Ernest L. Thayer. *Cast:* DeWolf Hopper (Casey), Kate Toncray (His Sister), May Garcia (Her Daughter), Carl Stockdale (Hicks), William H. Brown (Judge Blodgett), Marguerite Marsh (His Daughter), Frank Bennett (Her Sweetheart), Robert Lawler (The Politician), Bert Hadley (Casey's Brother-in-law), Hal Wilson (The Doctor), Frank Hughes (Casey's Admirer).

SOMEWHERE IN GEORGIA

(1916) Sunbeam Motion Picture Corp. B&W 6 reels *Director:* George Ridgwell. *Writer:* L. Case Russell, based on a story by Grantland Rice. *Cinematographer:* Walter Arthur. *Cast:* Ty Cobb, Elsie MacLeod, Will Corbett, Harry Fisher, Eddie Boulden, Ned Burton.

THE PINCH HITTER

(1917) New York Motion Picture Corp. Triangle Distributing Corp. B&W 5 reels *Director:* Victor L. Schertzinger. *Story:* C. Gardner Sullivan. *Cinematographer:* Paul Eagler. Supervised by Thomas H. Ince. *Cast:* Charles Ray (Joel Parker), Sylvia Bremer (Abbie Nettleton), Joseph J. Dowling (Obediah Parker), Jerome Storm (Jimmie Slater), Darrel Foss (Alexis Thompson), Louis Durham (Coach Nolan).

ONE TOUCH OF NATURE

(1917) Thomas A. Edison, Inc. K-E-S-E Service B&W 5 reels *Director:* Edward H. Griffith. Based on a short story by Peter B. Kyne in the *Saturday Evening Post. Cinematographer:* Charles Gilson. *Cast:* John Drew Bennett (William Vandervoort "Battling Bill" Cosgrove), Viola Cain (Leonora O'Brien), John J. McGraw (Himself), George Henry (E.P. Cosgrove), Helen Strickland (Mrs. Cosgrove), Edward O'Connor (Shamus O'Brien).

THE BUSHER

(1919) Thomas H. Ince Corp. Famous Players-Lasky Corp. B&W 5 reels *Director:* Jerome Storm. *Scenario:* R. Cecil Smith, based on a story by Earle Snell. *Cinematographer:* Chester Lyons. *Supervisor:* Thomas H. Ince. *Cast:* Charles Ray (Ben Harding), Colleen Moore (Mazie Palmer), Jack (John) Gilbert (Jim Blair), Jay Morley (Billy Palmer), Otto Hoffman (Deacon Nasby).

HEADIN' HOME

(1920) Kessel & Baumann Yankee Photo Corp. B&W 5 reels *Director:* Lawrence Windom. *Writer:* Arthur "Bugs" Baer, based on a story by Earle Brown. *Producer:* William A. Shea. *Supervisor:* R.A. Walsh. *Cast:* Babe Ruth (Babe), Ruth Taylor (Mildred Tobin), William Sheer (Harry Knight), Margaret Seddon (Babe's Mother), Frances Victory (Pigtails), James A. Marcus (Cyrus Tobin).

AS THE WORLD ROLLS ON

(1921) Andlauer Productions Elk Photo Plays B&W 7 reels *Cinematographer:* W.A. Andlauer. *Cast:* Jack Johnson, Blanche Thompson.

Shoeless Joe Jackson.

TRIFLING WITH HONOR

(1923) Universal Pictures B&W 8 reels *Director:* Harry A. Pollard. *Writers:* Frank Beresford, Raymond L. Schrock, based on the story "His Good Name" by William Slavens McNutt, published in *Collier's. Cinematographer:* Jack Brown. *Cast:* Rockliffe Fellowes (The Gas-Pipe Kid/Bat Shugrue), Fritzi Ridgeway (Ida), Buddy Messinger (Jimmy), Hayden Stevenson (Kelsey Lewis).

HIT AND RUN

(1924) Universal Pictures B&W 6 reels *Director:* Edward Sedgwick. *Writers:* Edward Sedgwick, Raymond L. Schrock. *Cinematographer:* Virgil Miller. *Cast:* Hoot Gibson (Swat Anderson), Marion Harlan (Joan McCarthy), Cyril Ring (George Collins), Harold Goodwin (Tex Adams), Mike Donlin (Red McCarthy), DeWitt Jennings (Joe Burns), William A. Steele (The Gopher).

LIFE'S GREATEST GAME

(1924) Emory Johnson Productions Film Booking Offices of America B&W 8 reels *Director-Producer:* Emory Johnson. *Writer:* Emilie Johnson. *Cinematographer:* Paul Perry *Cast:* Tom Santschi (Jack Donovan), Johnnie Walker (Jack Donovan, Jr.), Jane Thomas (Mary Donovan), Dave Kirby (Mike Moran), Gertrude Olmstead (Nora Malone).

THE BATTLING ORIOLES

(1924) Hal E. Roach Studios Pathé Exchange B&W 6 reels *Directors:* Ted Wilde, Fred Guiol. *Writer:* Hal Roach. *Producer:* Hal Roach. *Cinematographers:* Fred Jackman, George Stevens. *Cast:* Glenn Tryon (Tommy Roosevelt Tucker), Blanche Mehaffey (Hope Stanton), John T. Prince (Cappy Wolfe), Noah Young (Sid Stanton), Sam Lufkin (Jimmy the Mouse), Robert Page (Inspector Joslin), Joe Cobb, Mickey Daniels, Jackie Condon, Ernie "Sunshine Sammy" Morrison (Our Gang Kids).

PLAY BALL

(1925) Pathé Exchange B&W 10 chapter serial (2 reels each) *Director:* Spencer G. Bennet. *Writer:* Frank Leon Smith, based on stories suggested by John J. McGraw. *Cast:* Allene Ray (Doris Sutton), Walter Miller (Jack Rollins), J. Barney Sherry (Thomas W. Sutton), Harry Semels (Count Segundo), Mary Milnor (Maybelle Pratt), Wally Oettel (Rutger Farnsworth), Franklyn Hanna (Senator Hornell), John McGraw and the New York Giants (Themselves).

THE PINCH HITTER

(1925) Associated Exhibitors B&W 7 reels *Director:* Joseph Henabery. *Story:* C. Gardner Sullivan. *Cinematographer:* Jules Cronjager. *Cast:* Glenn Hunter (Joel Martin), Constance Bennett (Abby Nettleton), Jack Drumier (Obediah Parker), Reginald Sheffield (Alexis Thompson), Antrim Short (Jimmy Slater), George Cline (Coach Nolan).

THE NEW KLONDIKE

(1926) Famous Players-Lasky Paramount Pictures B&W 8 reels *Director:* Lewis Milestone. *Screenplay:* Thomas J. Geraghty, J. Clarkson Miller, based on a story by Ring Lardner. *Cinematographer:* Alvin Wyckoff. *Cast:* Thomas Meighan (Tom Kelly), Lila Lee (Evelyn Lane), Paul Kelly (Bing Allen), Hallie Manning (Flamingo Applegate), Robert Craig (Morgan West), George De Carlton (Owen), J.W. Johnston (Dave Cooley), Brenda Lane (Peggy DeVoe).

YOUNG APRIL

(1926) DeMille Pictures Producers Distributing Corp. B&W 7 reels *Director:* Donald Crisp. *Writers:* Jeanie Macpherson, Douglas Doty, from a novel by Egerton Castle. *Cinematographer:* Peverell Marley. *Cast:* Joseph Schildkraut (Prince Caryl), Rudolph Schildkraut (King Stefan), Bessie Love (Victoria), Bryant Washburn (Prince Michael).

OUT OF THE WEST

(1926) R-C Pictures Film Booking Offices of America B&W 5 reels *Director:* Robert De Lacy. *Continuity:* Wydham Gittens. *Story:* Fredrick Arthur Mindlin. *Cinematographer:* John Leezer. *Cast:* Tom Tyler (Tom Hanley), Bernice Welch (Bernice O'Connor), Ethan Laidlaw (Bide Goodrich), Alfred Henston (John O'Connor), Frankie Darro (Frankie), Gertrude Claire (Grannie Hanley).

SLIDE, KELLY, SLIDE

(1927) Metro-Goldwyn-Mayer B&W 8 reels *Director:* Edward Sedgwick. *Writer:* A.P. Younger. *Titles:* Joe Farnham. *Cinematographer:* Henry Sharp. *Editor:* Frank Sullivan. *Technical adviser:* Mike Donlin. *Cast:* William Haines (Jim Kelly), Sally O'Neil (Mary Munson), Harry Carey (Tom Munson), Karl Dane (Swede Hansen), Junior Coghlan (Mickey Martin), Warner Richmond (Cliff Macklin), Paul Kelly (Dillon), Guinn "Big Boy" Williams (McLean), Mike Donlin (Himself), Bob Meusel (Himself), Irish Meusel (Himself), Tony Lazzeri (Himself), Edward Brophy (Joe).

CASEY AT THE BAT

(1927) Famous Players-Lasky Paramount Pictures B&W 6 reels *Director:* Monte Brice. *Writer:* Jules Furthman. *Adaptation:* Brice, Reginald Morris, from "Ernest L. Thayer's Immortal Poem." *Titles:* Sam Hellman, Grant Clarke. *Producer:* Hector Turnbull. *Cinematographer:* Barney McGill. *Cast:* Wallace Beery (Casey), Ford Sterling (O'Dowd), ZaSu Pitts (Camille), Sterling Holloway (Elmer Putnam), Spec O'Donnell (Spec), Iris Stuart (Trixie), Sidney Jarvis (John McTague).

THE BABE COMES HOME

(1927) First National Pictures B&W 6 reels *Director:* Ted Wilde. *Writer:* Louis Stevens, based on the story "Said With Soap," by Gerald Beaumont, published in *Redbook. Producer:* Wid Gunning. *Cinematographer:* Karl Struss. *Cast:* Babe Ruth (Babe Dugan), Anna Q. Nilsson (Vernie), Louise Fazenda (Laundry Girl), Ethel Shannon (Georgia), Arthur Stone (Laundry Driver), Lou Archer (Peewee), Tom McGuire (Angel Team Manager), Mickey Bennett (Mascot).

CATCH-AS-CATCH-CAN

(1927) Gotham Productions Lumas Film Corporation B&W 5 reels *Director:* Charles Hutchinson. *Writer:* L.V. Jefferson, based on his story. *Cinematographer:* James Brown. *Cast:* William Fairbanks (Reed Powers), Jack Richardson (George Bascom), Rose Blossom (Lucille Bascom), Larry Shannon (Phil Bascom).

THE BUSH LEAGUER

(1927) Warner Bros. B&W 7 reels *Director:* Howard Bretherton. *Writer:* Harvey Gates, based on a story by Charles Gordon Saxton. *Cinematographer:* Norbert Brodin. *Cast:* Monte Blue (Buchanan "Specs" White), Clyde Cook (Skeeter McKinnon), Leila Hyams (Alice Hobbs), William Demarest (John Gilroy), Richard Tucker (Wallace Ramsey), Bud Marshall (Stetson), Tom Dempsey (The Parson), Wilfred North (Stokes), William Wilson (Lefty Murphy).

COLLEGE

(1927) Buster Keaton Productions United Artists B&W 6 reels *Director:* James W. Horne. *Writers:* Carl Harbaugh, Bryan Foy, based on their story. *Cinematographers:* Dev Jennings, Bert Haines. *Editor:* J.S. Kell. *Technical adviser:* Fred Gabourie. *Cast:* Buster Keaton (Ronald), Anne Cornwall (Mary Haines), Flora Bramley (Mary's Friend), Harold Goodwin (Jeff Brown), Buddy Mason (Jeff's Friend), Grant Withers (Jeff's Friend), Snitz Edwards (Dean Edwards), Carl Harbaugh (Crew Coach), Sam Crawford (Baseball Coach), Florence Turner (Ronald's Mother), University of Southern California Baseball Team (Themselves).

SPEEDY

(1928) Harold Lloyd Corp. Paramount Famous Lasky Corp. B&W 8 reels *Director:* Ted Wilde. *Story:* John Grey, Lex Neal, Howard

Emmett Rogers, Jay Howe. *Titles:* Albert De Mond. *Cinematographer:* Walter Lundin. *Cast:* Harold Lloyd (Harold "Speedy" Swift), Ann Christy (Jane Dillon), Bert Woodruff (Pop Dillon), Brooks Benedict (Steven Carter), Babe Ruth (Himself).

WARMING UP

(1928) Paramount Famous Lasky Corp. B&W 8 reels *Director-Producer:* Fred Newmeyer. *Writer:* Ray Harris, based on a story by Sam Mintz. *Titles:* George Marion. *Cinematographer:* Edward Cronjager. *Editor:* Otto Lovering. *Cast:* Richard Dix (Bert "Bee Line" Tulliver), Jean Arthur (Mary Post), Claude King (Mr. Post), Philo McCullough (McRae), Wade Boteler (Doyle), Billy Kent Schaefer (Edsel), Roscoe Karns (Hippo), James Dugan (Brill), Mike Donlin (The Veteran).

Slide, Kelly, Slide: Jim Kelly (William Haines) romances Mary Munson (Sally O'Neil).

THE CAMERAMAN

(1928) Metro-Goldwyn-Mayer B&W 8 reels *Director:* Edward Sedgwick. *Writer:* Richard Schayer, based on a story by Clyde Bruckman, Lew Lipton. *Titles:* Joe Farnham. *Producer:* Buster Keaton. *Cinematographers:* Elgin Lessley, Reggie Lanning. *Editor:* Hugh Wynn. *Technical adviser:* Fred Gabourie. *Cast:* Buster Keaton (Buster), Marceline Day (Sally), Harry Gribbon (Cop), Harold Goodwin (Stagg), Sidney Bracey (Editor).

FAST COMPANY

(1929) Paramount Famous Lasky Corp. B&W 8 reels *Director:* A. Edward Sutherland. *Writers:* Florence Ryerson, Patrick Kearney, Walton Butterfield, based on the play *Elmer the Great,* by Ring Lardner, George M. Cohan. *Dialogue:* Joseph L. Mankiewicz. *Cinematographer:* Edward Cronjager. *Editor:* Jane Loring. *Cast:* Jack Oakie (Elmer Kane), Evelyn Brent (Evelyn Corey), Skeets Gallagher (Bert Wade), Sam Hardy (Dave Walker), Arthur

Casey at the Bat: Wallace Beery as Casey, Sterling Holloway as Elmer Putnam, Ford Sterling as O'Dowd (left to right).

Housman (Barney Barlow), Gwen Lee (Rosie La Clerq), Chester Conklin (C. of C. President), E.H. Calvert (Platt), Eugenie Besserer (Mrs. Kane), Bert Rome (Hank Gordon), Irish Meusel (Himself), Arnold "Jigger" Statz (Himself).

THEY LEARNED ABOUT WOMEN

(1930) Metro-Goldwyn-Mayer B&W   11 reels *Directors:* Jack Conway, Sam Wood. *Scenario:* Sarah Y. Mason. *Dialogue:* Arthur "Bugs" Baer. Based on a story by A.P. Younger. *Cinematographer:* Leonard Smith. *Editor:* James McKay. *Words and music:* Jack Yellen, Milton Ager. *Cast:* Joseph T. Schenck (Jack Glennon), Gus Van (Jerry Burke), Bessie Love (Mary), Mary Doran (Daisy), J.C. Nugent (Stafford), Benny Rubin (Sam), Tom Dugan (Tim), Eddie Gribbon (Brennan), Francis X. Bushman, Jr. (Haskins).

HOT CURVES

(1930) Tiffany Productions B&W   9 reels *Director:* Norman Taurog. *Writer:* Earle Snell, based on a story by A.P. Younger, Frank Mortimer. *Dialogue:* Frank Mortimer, Benny Rubin. *Cinematographer:* Max Dupont. *Editor:* Clarence Kolster. *Cast:* Benny Rubin (Benny Goldberg), Rex Lease (Jim Dolan), Alice Day (Elaine McGrew), Pert Kelton (Cookie), John Ince (Manager McGrew), Mary Carr (Grandma Dolan), Mike Donlin (The Scout), Natalie Moorhead (Mazie), Paul Hurst (Slug).

UP THE RIVER

(1930) Fox B&W   92 minutes *Director:* John Ford. *Writer:* Maurine Watkins. *Cinematographer:* Joseph August. *Editor:* Frank E. Hull. Music: Joseph McCarthy, James E. Hanley. *Cast:* Spencer Tracy (St. Louis), Warren Hymer (Dannemora Dan), Humphrey Bogart (Steve), Claire Luce (Judy), William Collier, Sr. (Pop).

FIREMAN, SAVE MY CHILD

(1932) First National and Vitaphone B&W   67 minutes *Director:* Lloyd Bacon. *Writers:* Ray Enright, Robert Lord, Arthur Caesar, based on their story. *Cinematographer:* Sol Polito. Editor: George Marks. *Cast:* Joe E. Brown (Joe Grant), Evalyn Knapp (Sally Toby), Lillian Bond (June Farnum), George Meeker (Stevens), Guy Kibbee (Pop), George Ernest (The Mascot), Ben Hendricks, Jr. (Larkin), Virginia Sale (Miss Gallop), Frank Shellenback (The Pitcher), Richard Carle (Dan Toby), Louis Robinson (Trainer).

MADISON SQUARE GARDEN

(1932) Paramount Pictures B&W   70 minutes *Director:* Harry Joe Brown. Writers: P.J. Wolfson, Allen Rivkin, from a story by Thomas Burtis. *Producer:* Charles R. Rogers. *Cinematographer:* Henry Sharp. *Cast:* Jack Oakie (Eddie Burke), Marian Nixon (Bee), Thomas Meighan (Carley), William Boyd (Sloane), Zasu Pitts (Florrie), Lew Cody (Roarke), William Collier, Sr. (Doc Williams), Mike Donlin, Jack Johnson, Tom Sharkey, Tod Sloan, Billy Papke, Stanislaus Zybyszko, Damon Runyon, Jack Lait, Grantland Rice, Westbrook Pegler, Paul Gallico (Themselves).

ELMER THE GREAT

(1933) First National and Vitaphone B&W   74 minutes *Director:* Mervyn LeRoy. *Writer:* Tom Geraghty, based on the play by Ring Lardner, George M. Cohan. *Cinematographer:* Arthur Todd. *Editor:* Thomas Pratt. *Cast:* Joe E. Brown (Elmer Kane), Patricia Ellis (Nellie Poole), Frank McHugh (High-Hips Healy), Claire Dodd (Evelyn), Preston S. Foster (Dave Walker), Russell Hopton (Whitey), Sterling Holloway (Nick Kane), Emma Dunn (Mrs. Kane), Berton Churchill (The Colonel).

DEATH ON THE DIAMOND

(1934) Metro-Goldwyn Mayer B&W   69 minutes *Director:* Edward Sedgwick. *Writers:* Harvey Thew, Joe Sherman, Ralph Spence, based on the novel by Cortland Fitzsimmons. *Producer:* Lucien Hubbard. *Cinematographer:* Milton Krasner. *Editor:* Frank Sullivan. *Technical adviser:* Pat Flaherty. *Cast:* Robert Young (Larry Kelly), Madge Evans (Frances Clark), Nat Pendleton (Truck Hogan), Ted Healy (O'Toole), C. Henry Gordon (Karnes), Paul Kelly (Jimmie), David Landau (Pop Clark), DeWitt Jennings (Patterson), Edward Brophy (Grogan), Willard Robertson (Cato), Mickey Rooney (Mickey), Robert Livingston (Higgins), Joe Sauers (later Sawyer) (Spencer), James Ellison (Sherman), Pat Flaherty (Pat), Francis X. Bushman, Jr. (Sam Briscow), Franklyn Farnum (Fan), Jack Norton (Gambler), Walter Brennan (Hot Dog Vendor), Ward Bond (Cop).

I'LL FIX IT

(1934) Columbia Pictures B&W   68 minutes *Director:* Roy William Neill. *Writers:* Ethel Hill, Dorothy Howell, based on a story by Leonard Spiegelgass. *Cinematographer:* Benjamin Cline. *Cast:* Jack Holt (Bill Grimes), Mona Barrie (Anne Barry), Winnie Lightner (Elizabeth), Jimmy Butler (Bobby), Edward Brophy (Tilly).

SWELL-HEAD

(1935) Columbia Pictures B&W   62 minutes *Director:* Ben Stoloff. *Writer:* William Jacobs, based on a story by Gerald Beaumont. *Producer:* Bryan Foy. *Cinematographer:* Joseph A. Valentine. *Editor:* Arthur Hilton. *Cast:* Wallace Ford (Terry McCall), Dickie Moore (Billy Malone), Barbara Kent (Mary Malone), J. Farrell MacDonald

(Umpire), Marion Byron (Bessie), Sammy Cohen (Casey Cohen), Frank Moran (The Rube), Mike Donlin (Brick Baldwin).

ALIBI IKE

(1935) Warner Bros. and Vitaphone B&W 73 minutes *Director:* Ray Enright. *Writer:* William Wister Haines, based on a story by Ring Lardner published in the *Saturday Evening Post. Producer:* Edward Chodorov. *Cinematographer:* Arthur Todd. Editor: Thomas Pratt. *Cast:* Joe E. Brown (Frank X. Farrell), Olivia de Havilland (Dolly Stevens), Roscoe Karns (Carey), William Frawley (Cap), Joseph King (Owner), Ruth Donnelly (Bess), Paul Harvey (Crawford), Eddie Shubert (Jack Mack).

A NIGHT AT THE OPERA

(1935) Metro-Goldwyn-Mayer B&W 93 minutes *Director:* Sam Wood. *Writers:* George S. Kaufman, Morrie Ryskind, from a story by James Kevin McGuinness. *Producer:* Irving G. Thalberg. *Cinematographer:* Merritt B. Gerstad. Editor: William Levanway. Music: Herbert Stothart. *Cast:* Groucho Marx (Otis B. Driftwood), Harpo Marx (Tomasso), Chico Marx (Fiorello), Margaret Dumont (Mrs. Claypool), Sig Rumann (Herman Gottlieb), Kitty Carlisle (Rosa), Allan Jones (Ricardo), Walter Woolf King (Lasspari).

THE ADVENTURES OF FRANK MERRIWELL

(1936) Universal Pictures B&W 12-chapter serial (2 reels each) *Director:* Cliff Smith. *Writers:* George Plympton, Maurice Geraghty, Ella O'Neill, Basil Dickey, based on the stories of Burt L. Standish (Gilbert Patten). *Producer:* Henry MacRae. *Cinematographers:* Richard Fryer, John Hickson, E.T. Estabrook. *Cast:* Don Briggs (Frank Merriwell), Jean Rogers (Elsie Bellwood), John King (Bruce Browning), Carla Laemmle (Carla Rogers), Sumner Getchell (Harry Rattleton), Wallace Reid, Jr. (Wallace Reed), House Peters, Jr. (House Peters), Allan Hersholt (Allan Hersholt), Bryant Washburn, Jr. (Bryant Washburn), Carlyle Blackwell, Jr. (Carlyle Blackwell), Peter Gowland (Peter Gowland), Edward Arnold, Jr. (Edward Arnold), Herschel Mayall, Jr. (Herschel Mayall), Dickie Jones (Jimmy McLaw), Bentley Hewett (Daggett).

BLACK LEGION

(1936) Warner Bros. B&W 80 minutes *Director:* Archie L. Mayo. *Writers:* Abem Finkel, William Wister Haines, based on a story by Robert Lord. *Cinematographer:* George Barnes. *Editor:* Owen Marks. *Cast:* Humphrey Bogart (Frank Taylor), Dick Foran (Ed Jackson), Erin O'Brien-Moore (Ruth Taylor), Ann Sheridan (Betty Grogan), Helen Flint (Pearl Danvers), Joe Sawyer (Cliff Moore), Clifford Soubier (Mike Grogan), Dickie Jones (Buddy Taylor), Henry Brandon (Joe Dombrowski).

GIRLS CAN PLAY

(1937) Columbia Pictures B&W 6 reels *Director-Writer:* Lambert Hillyer, based on the story "Miss Casey at the Bat" by Albert De Mond. *Producer:* Ralph Cohn. *Cinematographer:* Lucien Ballard. *Cast:* Jacqueline Wells (later Julie Bishop) (Ann Casey), Charles Quigley (Jimmy Jones), Rita Hayworth (Sue Collins), John Gallaudet (Foy Harris), George McKay (Sluggy), Gene Morgan (Pete), Patricia Farr (Peanuts), Guinn Williams (Lieutenant Flannigan), Joseph Crehan (Brophy).

MANHATTAN MERRY-GO-ROUND

(1937) Republic Pictures B&W 82 minutes *Director:* Charles F. Riesner. *Writer-Producer:* Harry Sauber, based on a story by Frank Hummert. *Cinematographer:* Jack Marta. *Editors:* Murray Seldeen, Ernest Nims. *Cast:* Phil Regan (Jerry Hart), Leo Carillo (Gordoni), Ann Dvorak (Ann Rogers), James Gleason (Danny the Duck), Henry Armetta (Spadoni), Joe DiMaggio (Himself).

RAWHIDE

(1938) Principal Productions, Inc. Twentieth Century-Fox B&W 60 minutes *Director:* Ray Taylor. *Writers:* Dan Jarrett, Jack Natteford, based on a story by Jarrett. *Producer:* Sol Lesser. *Cinematographer:* Allen Q. Thompson. *Editor:* Robert Crandall. *Cast:* Smith Ballew (Larry Kimball), Lou Gehrig (Himself), Evalyn Knapp (Peggy Gehrig), Arthur Loft (Ed Saunders), Carl Stockdale (Bascomb), Si Jenks (Pop Mason), Cy Kendall (Sheriff Kale), Lafe McKee (McDonnell), Dick Curtis (Butch).

BROTHER RAT

(1938) Warner Bros. B&W 90 minutes *Director:* William Keighley. Producer: Robert Lord. *Writers:* Richard Macaulay, Jerry Wald, from the play by John Monks, Jr., F. Fred Finklehoffe. *Cinematographer:* Ernest Haller. *Editor:* William Holmes. Music: Leo F. Forbstein. *Cast:* Priscilla Lane (Joyce Winfree), Wayne Morris (Billy Randolph), Johnnie Davis (A. Furman Townsend, Jr.), Jane Bryan (Kate Rice), Eddie Albert (Bing Edwards), Ronald

John McGraw.

It Happened in Flatbush: Carole Landis as Kathryn Baker, Lloyd Nolan (center) as Frank Maguire, James Burke as Shaunnessy.

Reagan (Dan Crawford), Jane Wyman (Claire Adams), Henry O'Neill (Colonel Ramm).

BROTHER RAT AND A BABY

(1940) Warner Bros. B&W 87 minutes *Director:* Ray Enright. *Producer:* Robert Lord. *Writers:* Richard Macaulay, Jerry Wald, from an original story by John Monks, Jr., Fred Finklehoffe. *Cinematographer:* Charles Rosher. *Editor:* Clarence Kolster. *Music:* Leo F. Forbstein. *Cast:* Eddie Albert (Bing Edwards), Wayne Morris (Billy Randolph), Priscilla Lane (Joyce Winfree), Jane Wyman (Claire Ramm), Ronald Reagan (Dan Crawford), Jane Bryan (Kate), Henry O'Neill (Colonel Ramm).

MR. DYNAMITE

(1941) Universal Pictures B&W 63 minutes *Director:* John Rawlins. *Writer:* Stanley Crea Rubin. *Producer:* Marshall Grant. *Cinematographer:* John Boyle. *Editor:* Ted Kent. *Music:* Charles Previn. *Cast:* Lloyd Nolan (Tommy N. Thornton), Irene Hervey (Vicki Martin), J. Carroll Naish (Professor), Robert Armstrong (Paul), Ann Gillis (Joey), Elisabeth Risdon (Achilles), Shemp Howard (Abdullah).

· MEET JOHN DOE

(1941) Warner Bros. B&W 129 minutes *Director-Producer:* Frank Capra. *Writer:* Robert Riskin, from a story by Richard Connell, Robert Presnell. *Cinematographer:* George Barnes. *Editor:* Daniel Mandell. *Music:* Dmitri Tiomkin. *Technical adviser:* Pat Flaherty. *Cast:* Gary Cooper (Long John Willoughby/John Doe), Barbara Stanwyck (Ann Mitchell), Edward Arnold (D.B. Norton), Walter Brennan (The Colonel), Spring Byington (Mrs. Mitchell), James Gleason (Connell), Gene Lockhart (Mayor Lovett), Rod LaRocque (Ted Sheldon), Irving Bacon (Beany), Regis Toomey (Bert

Hansen), Warren Hymer (Angelface), Sterling Holloway (Dan), Pat Flaherty (Mike).

REMEMBER THE DAY

(1941) Twentieth Century-Fox B&W 85 minutes *Director:* Henry King. *Writers:* Tess Slesinger, Frank Davis, Allan Scott, based on a play by Philo Higley, Philip Dunning. *Producer:* William Perlberg. *Cinematographer:* George Barnes. *Editor:* Barbara McLean. *Music:* Alfred Newman. *Cast:* Claudette Colbert (Nora Trinell), John Payne (Dan Hopkins), John Shepperd (later Shepperd Strudwick) (Dewey Roberts), Ann Todd (Kate Hill), Douglas Croft (Young Dewey Roberts).

WOMAN OF THE YEAR

(1942) Metro-Goldwyn Mayer B&W 112 minutes *Director:* George Stevens. *Writers:* Ring Lardner, Jr., Michael Kanin. *Producer:* Joseph L. Mankiewicz. *Cinematographer:* Joseph Ruttenberg. *Editor:* Frank Sullivan. Music: Franz Waxman. *Cast:* Spencer Tracy (Sam Craig), Katharine Hepburn (Tess Harding), Fay Bainter (Ellen Whitcomb), Reginald Owen (Clayton), Minor Watson (William J. Harding), William Bendix (Pinkie Peters), Jack Carr (Baseball Fan).

LARCENY, INC.

(1942) Warner Bros. B&W 94 minutes *Director:* Lloyd Bacon. *Writers:* Everett Freeman, Edwin Gilbert, based on the play *The Night Before Christmas* by Laura and S.J. Perelman. *Producers:* Jack Saper, Jerry Wald. *Cinematographer:* Tony Gaudio. *Editor:* Ralph Dawson. *Music:* Adolph Deutsch. *Cast:* Edward G. Robinson (Pressure Maxwell), Jane Wyman (Denny Costello), Broderick Crawford (Jug Martin), Jack Carson (Jeff Randolph), Barbara Jo Allen (Mademoiselle Gloria), Anthony Quinn (Leo Dexter), Edward Brophy (Weepy Davis), Harry Davenport (Homer Bigelow), John Qualen (Sam Bachrach), Jackie C. Gleason (Hobart).

IT HAPPENED IN FLATBUSH

(1942) Twentieth Century-Fox B&W 80 minutes *Director:* Ray McCarey. *Writers:* Harold Buchman, Lee Loeb. *Producer:* Walter Morosco. *Cinematographer:* Charles Clarke. *Editor:* J. Watson Webb. *Music:* Emil Newman. *Cast:* Lloyd Nolan (Frank Maguire), Carole Landis (Kathryn Baker), Sara Allgood (Mrs. McAvoy), William Frawley (Sam Sloan), Robert Armstrong (Danny Mitchell), Jane Darwell (Mrs. Maguire), George Holmes (Roy Anderson), Scotty Beckett (Squint), Joseph Allen, Jr. (Walter Rogers), James Burke (Shaunnessy), Roger Imhof (Maguire), Matt McHugh (O'Doul), LeRoy Mason (Scott), Pat Flaherty (O'Hara), Dael Van Sickel (Stevenson).

THE PRIDE OF THE YANKEES

(1942) The Samuel Goldwyn Company RKO-Radio B&W 128 minutes *Director:* Sam Wood. *Writers:* Jo Swerling, Herman J. Mankiewicz, based on a story by Paul Gallico. *Producer:* Samuel Goldwyn. *Cinematographer:* Rudolph Mate. *Editor:* Daniel Mandell. *Music:* Leigh Harline. *Cast:* Gary Cooper (Lou Gehrig), Teresa Wright (Eleanor Twitchell Gehrig), Walter Brennan (Sam Blake), Dan Duryea (Hank Hanneman), Babe Ruth (Himself), Elsa Jansen (Mom Gehrig), Ludwig Stossel (Pop Gehrig), Virginia Gilmore (Myra), Bill Dickey (Himself), Ernie Adams (Miller Huggins), Pierre Watkin (Mr. Twitchell), Harry Harvey (Joe McCarthy), Bob

Meusel (Himself), Mark Koenig (Himself), Bill Stern (Himself), Addison Richards (Coach), Hardie Albright (Van Tuyl), Douglas Croft (Young Lou Gehrig), Veloz & Yolanda, Ray Noble and His Orchestra, Frank Faylen (Third Base Coach), Bernard Zanville (later Dane Clark) (Fraternity Brother).

THE TALK OF THE TOWN

(1942) Columbia Pictures B&W   116 minutes *Director-Producer:* George Stevens. *Writers:* Sidney Buchman, Irwin Shaw, from a story by Sidney Harmon. *Adaptation:* Dale Van Every. *Cinematographer:* Ted Tetzlaff. *Editor:* Otto Meyer. *Music:* Frederick Hollander. *Cast:* Cary Grant (Leopold Dilg), Jean Arthur (Nora Shelley), Ronald Colman (Michael Lightcap), Edgar Buchanan (Yates), Glenda Farrell (Regina Bush), Charles Dingle (Andrew Holmes), Emma Dunn (Mrs. Shelley), Rex Ingram (Tilney).

TAXI, MISTER

(1942) Hal Roach Studios United Artists B&W   49 minutes *Director:* Kurt Neumann. *Writers:* Earle Snell, Clarence Marke. *Producer:* Fred Guiol. *Cinematographer:* Robert Pittack. *Editor:* Richard Currier. *Music:* Edward Ward. *Cast:* William Bendix (Tim McGuerin), Grace Bradley (Sadie McGuerin), Joe Sawyer (Eddie Corbett), Sheldon Leonard (Glorio), Joe Devlin (Stretch), Jack Norton (Van Nostrum), Frank Faylen (Slick), Mike Mazurki (Joe).

MOONLIGHT IN HAVANA

(1942) Universal Pictures B&W   63 minutes *Director:* Anthony Mann. *Writer:* Oscar Brodney. *Producer:* Bernard W. Burton. *Cinematographer:* Charles Van Enger. *Editor:* Russell Schoengarth. *Songs:* Dave Franklin. *Cast:* Allan Jones (Johnny Norton), Jane Frazee (Gloria Jackson), Marjorie Lord (Patsy Clark), William Frawley (Barney Crane), Don Terry (Eddie Daniels), Sergio Orta (Martinez), Wade Boteler (Joe Clark), Hugh O'Connell (Charlie), Jack Norton (George), Tom Dugan (Doc), Horton Dance Group, Jivin' Jacks and Jills, Grace & Nico.

LADIES' DAY

(1943) RKO-Radio B&W   62 minutes *Director:* Leslie Goodwins. *Writers:* Charles E. Roberts, Dane Lussier, based on the play by Robert Considine, Edward Clark Lilley, Bertrand Robinson. *Producer:* Bert Gilroy. *Cinematographer:* Jack Mackenzie. *Editor:* Harry Marker. *Music:* Roy Webb. *Cast:* Lupe Velez (Pepita Zorita), Eddie Albert (Wacky Walters), Patsy Kelly (Hazel Jones), Max Baer (Hippo Jones), Jerome Cowan (Updike), Iris Adrian (Kitty), Joan Barclay (Joan), Cliff Clark (Dan), Carmen Morales (Marianna), George Cleveland (Doc), Jack Briggs (Marty), Russ Clark (Smokey), Nedrick Young (Tony), Eddie Dees (Spike).

HITLER'S CHILDREN

(1943) RKO-Radio B&W   80 minutes *Director:* Edward Dmytryk. *Writer:* Emmett Lavery, based on the novel *Education for Death*, by Gregor Ziemer. *Producer:* Edward A. Golden. *Cinematographer:* Russell Metty. *Editor:* Joseph Noriega. *Music:* Roy Webb. *Cast:* Tim Holt (Karl Bruner), Bonita Granville (Anna Muller), Kent Smith (Professor Nichols), Otto Kruger (Colonel Henkel), H.B. Warner (The Bishop).

WHISTLING IN BROOKLYN

(1943) Metro-Goldwyn-Mayer B&W   87 minutes *Director:* S. Sylvan Simon. *Writer:* Nat Perrin. *Producer:* George Haight. *Cinematographer:* Leslie White. *Editor:* Ben Lewis. *Music:* George Bassman. *Cast:* Red Skelton (Wally Benton), Ann Rutherford (Carol Lambert), Jean Rogers (Jean Pringle), Rags Ragland (Chester), Ray Collins (Grover Kendall), Henry O'Neill (Inspector Holcomb), William Frawley (Detective Ramsey), Sam Levene (Creeper), Arthur Space (Detective MacKenzie), Robert Emmet O'Connor (Detective Finnegan), Tom Dillon (Beavers Manager), The Brooklyn Dodgers (Themselves).

The Babe Ruth Story: Note the "fans" painted onto the backdrop in this production still.

GUADALCANAL DIARY

(1943) Twentieth Century-Fox B&W   90 minutes *Director:* Lewis Seiler. *Writer:* Lamar Trotti. *Adaptation:* Jerry Cady, based on the book by Richard Tregaskis. *Producer:* Bryan Foy. *Cinematographer:* Charles Clarks. *Editor:* Fred Allen. *Music:* Emil Newman. *Cast:* Preston Foster (Father Donnelly), Lloyd Nolan (Hook Malone), William Bendix (Taxi Potts), Richard Conte (Captain Davis), Anthony Quinn (Soose), Richard Jaeckel (Private Johnny Anderson).

MR. WINKLE GOES TO WAR

(1944) Columbia Pictures B&W   80 minutes *Director:* Alfred E. Green. *Writers:* Waldo Salt, George Corey, Louis Solomon, based on a novel by Theodore Pratt. *Producer:* Jack Moss. *Cinematographer:* Joseph Walker. *Editor:* Richard Fantl. *Music:* Carmen Dragon, Paul Sawtell. *Cast:* Edward G. Robinson (Wilbert

Winkle), Ruth Warrick (Amy Winkle), Ted Donaldson (Barry), Bob Haymes (Jack Pettigrew), Richard Lane (Sergeant "Alphabet"), Robert Armstrong (Joe Tinker), Richard Gaines (Ralph Westcott).

THE NAUGHTY NINETIES

(1945) Universal Pictures B&W 76 minutes *Director:* Jean Yarbrough. *Writers:* Edmund L. Hartmann, John Grant, Edmund Joseph, Hal Fimberg. *Producers:* Hartmann, Grant. *Cinematographer:* George Robinson. *Editor:* Arthur Hilton. *Music:* Edgar Fairchild. *Cast:* Bud Abbott (Dexter), Lou Costello (Sebastian), Alan Curtis (Crawford), Rita Johnson (Bonita), Henry Travers (Captain Sam), Lois Collier (Caroline), Joe Sawyer (Bailey), Jack Norton (Drunk).

Two Mugs From Brooklyn.

210

DEADLINE AT DAWN

(1946) RKO-Radio B&W 83 minutes *Director:* Harold Clurman. *Writer:* Clifford Odets, based on a novel by William Irish (Cornell Woolrich). *Producer:* Adrian Scott. *Cinematographer:* Nicholas Musuraca. *Editor:* Roland Gross. *Music:* Hans Eisler. *Cast:* Susan Hayward (June), Paul Lukas (Gus), Bill Williams (Alex), Joseph Calleia (Bartelli), Osa Massen (Helen Robinson), Lola Lane (Edna Bartelli), Jerome Cowan (Lester Brady), Marvin Miller (Sleepy Parsons), Joe Sawyer (Babe Dooley).

MAKE MINE MUSIC

(1946) Walt Disney Productions RKO-Radio Color 75 minutes *Director of "Casey at the Bat" Sequence:* Clyde Geronimi. *Production Supervisor:* Joe Grant. *Cast:* Jerry Colonna.

BOYS' RANCH

(1946) Metro-Goldwyn-Mayer B&W 97 minutes *Director:* Roy Rowland. *Writer:* William Ludwig, based on his story. *Producer:* Robert Sisk. *Cinematographer:* Charles Salerno, Jr. *Editor:* Ralph E. Winters. *Music:* Nathaniel Shilkret. *Cast:* Jackie "Butch" Jenkins (Butch), James Craig (Dan Walker), Skippy Homeier (Skippy), Dorothy Patrick (Susan Walker), Ray Collins (David Banton), Darryl Hickman (Hank), Sharon McManus (Mary Walker).

THE BEST YEARS OF OUR LIVES

(1946) RKO-Radio B&W 172 minutes *Director:* William Wyler. *Writer:* Robert E. Sherwood, based on the novel *Glory for Me*, by MacKinlay Kantor. *Producer:* Samuel Goldwyn. *Cinematographer:* Gregg Toland. *Editor:* Daniel Mandell. *Music:* Hugo Friedhofer. *Cast:* Myrna Loy (Millie Stephenson), Fredric March (Al Stephenson), Dana Andrews (Fred Derry), Teresa Wright (Peggy Stephenson), Virginia Mayo (Marie Derry), Cathy O'Donnell (Wilma Cameron), Hoagy Carmichael (Butch Engle), Harold Russell (Homer Parrish).

THE BABE RUTH STORY

(1948) Allied Artists B&W 106 minutes *Director-Producer:* Roy Del Ruth. *Writers:* Bob Considine, George Callahan, adapted from *The Babe Ruth Story*, by Babe Ruth as told to Bob Considine and serialized in the *Saturday Evening Post. Cinematographer:* Philip Tannura. *Editor:* Richard Heermance. *Music:* Edward Ward. *Technical adviser:* Pat Flaherty. *Cast:* William Bendix (Babe Ruth), Claire Trevor (Claire Ruth), Charles Bickford (Brother Matthias), Sam Levene (Phil Conrad), William Frawley (Jack Dunn), Gertrude Niesen (Night Club Singer), Fred Lightner (Miller Huggins), Stanley Clements (Western Union Boy), Bobby Ellis (Babe Ruth as a Boy), Lloyd Gough (Balton), Matt Briggs (Col. Ruppert), Paul Cavanagh (Dr. Menzies), Pat Flaherty (Bill Carrigan), Mark Koenig (Himself), Richard Lane (Coach), Tony Taylor (The Kid), Harry Wismer (Sports Announcer), Mel Allen (Sports Announcer), H.V. Kaltenborn (News Announcer), Knox Manning (Announcer).

A FOREIGN AFFAIR

(1948) Paramount Pictures B&W 115 minutes *Director:* Billy Wilder. *Writers:* Wilder, Charles Brackett, Richard L. Breen. *Adaptation:* Robert Harari, based on a story by David Shaw. *Cinematographer:* Charles B. Lang, Jr. *Editor:* Doane Harrison. *Music:* Frederick Hollander. *Cast:* Jean Arthur (Phoebe Frost), John Lund (John Pringle), Marlene Dietrich (Erika Von Schluetow), Millard Mitchell (Colonel Rufus J. Plummer).

TAKE ME OUT TO THE BALL GAME

(1949) Metro-Goldwyn-Mayer Color 93 minutes *Director:* Busby Berkeley. *Writers:* Harry Tugend, George Wells, based on a story by Gene Kelly, Stanley Donen. *Producer:* Arthur Freed. *Cinematographer:* George Folsey. *Editor:* Blanche Sewell. *Music and Lyrics:* Betty Comden, Adolph Green, Roger Edens. *Cast:* Frank Sinatra (Dennis Ryan), Esther Williams (K.C. Higgins), Gene Kelly (Eddie O'Brien), Betty Garrett (Shirley Delwyn), Edward Arnold (Joe Lorgan), Jules Munshin (Nat Goldberg), Richard Lane (Michael Gilhuly), Tom Dugan (Slappy Burke), Murray Alper (Zalinka), William Graff (Nick Donford).

THE STRATTON STORY

(1949) Metro-Goldwyn-Mayer B&W 106 minutes *Director:* Sam Wood. *Writers:* Douglas Morrow, Guy Trosper, based on a story by Trosper. *Producer:* Jack Cummings. *Cinematographer:* Harold Rosson. *Editor:* Ben Lewis. *Technical adviser:* Monty Stratton. *Cast:* James Stewart (Monty Stratton), June Allyson (Ethel), Frank Morgan (Barney Wile), Agnes Moorehead (Ma Stratton), Bill Williams (Eddie Dibson), Bruce Cowling (Ted Lyons), Cliff Clark (Josh Higgins), Mary Lawrence (Dot), Dean White (Luke Appling), Robert Gist (Earnie), Gene Beardon (Himself), Jimmy Dykes (Himself), Mervyn "Spec" Shea (Himself), Bill Dickey (Himself).

IT HAPPENS EVERY SPRING

(1949) Twentieth Century-Fox B&W 87 minutes *Director:* Lloyd Bacon. *Writer:* Valentine Davies, based on a story by Davies, Shirley W. Smith. *Producer:* William Perlberg. *Cinematographer:* Joe MacDonald. *Editor:* Bruce Pierce. *Music:* Leigh Harline. *Cast:* Ray Milland (Vernon Simpson), Jean Peters (Deborah Greenleaf), Paul Douglas (Monk Lanigan), Ed Begley (Stone), Ted de Corsia (Dolan), Ray Collins (Dr. Greenleaf), Jessie Royce Landis (Mrs. Greenleaf), Alan Hale, Jr. (Schmidt), Bill Murphy (Isbell), Edward Keane (Bell), Gene Evans (Mueller), Al Eben (Parker), Debra Paget (Alice).

THE KID FROM CLEVELAND

(1949) Republic Pictures B&W 89 minutes *Director:* Herbert Kline. *Writer:* John Bright, based on a story by Bright, Kline. *Producer:* Walter Colmes. *Cinematographer:* Jack Marta. *Editor:* Jason H. Bernie. *Music:* Nathan Scott. *Cast:* George Brent (Mike Jackson), Lynn Bari (Katherine Jackson), Rusty Tamblyn (Johnny Barrows), Tommy Cook (Dan Hudson), Ann Doran (Emily Novak), Louis Jean Heydt (Carl Novak), K. Elmo Lowe (Dave Joyce), John Berardino (Mac), Bill Veeck (Himself), The Cleveland Indians (Themselves), Bill Summers (Umpire), Bill Grieve (Umpire), Franklin Lewis (Sportswriter), Gordon Cobbledock (Sportswriter), Ed MacAuley (Sportwriter).

KILL THE UMPIRE

(1950) Columbia Pictures B&W 78 minutes *Director:* Lloyd Bacon. *Writer:* Frank Tashlin. *Producer:* John Beck. *Cinematographer:* Charles Lawton, Jr. *Editor:* Charles Nelson. *Music:* Heinz Roemheld. *Cast:* William Bendix (Bill Johnson), Una Merkel (Betty Johnson), Ray Collins (Jonah Evans), William Frawley (Jimmy O'Brien), Gloria Henry (Lucy), Richard Taylor (Bob Landon), Connie Marshall (Susan), Tom D'Andrea (Roscoe Snooker), Luther Crockett (Sam Austin), Jeff York (Panhandle Jones), Glenn Thompson (Lanky), Robert Wilke (Cactus), Jim Bannon (Dusty), Alan Hale, Jr. (Harry Shay).

Ladies' Day: Manager Dan (Cliff Clark) lectures Wacky Walters (Eddie Albert).

THE JACKIE ROBINSON STORY

(1950) Jewell Pictures Corp. Eagle-Lion Films B&W 77 minutes *Director:* Alfred E. Green. *Writers:* Lawrence Taylor, Arthur Mann. *Producer:* Mort Briskin. *Cinematographer:* Ernest Laszlo. *Editor:* Arthur H. Nadel. *Music:* Herschel Burke Gilbert. *Cast:* Jackie Robinson (Himself), Ruby Dee (Rachel Robinson), Minor Watson (Branch Rickey), Louise Beavers (Mrs. Robinson), Richard Lane (Clay Hopper), Harry Shannon (Charlie), Ben Lessy (Shorty), Bill Spaulding (Himself), Joel Fluellen (Mack Robinson), Billy Wayne (Clyde Sukeforth), Bernie Hamilton (Ernie), Kenny Washington (Tigers Manager), Pat Flaherty (Karpen), Larry McGrath (Umpire), Emmett Smith (Catcher), Howard Louis MacNeely (Jackie as a Boy)

SUNSET BOULEVARD

(1950) Paramount Pictures B&W 110 minutes *Director:* Billy Wilder. *Writers:* Wilder, Charles Brackett, D.M. Marshman, Jr. *Producer:* Brackett. *Cinematographer:* John F. Seitz. *Editor:* Arthur Schmidt. *Music:* Franz Waxman. *Cast:* William Holden (Joe Gillis), Gloria Swanson (Norma Desmond), Erich Von Stroheim (Max Von Mayerling), Nancy Olson (Betty Schaefer), Fred Clark (Sheldrake), Lloyd Gough (Morino), Jack Webb (Artie Green), Cecil B. DeMille, Hedda Hopper, Buster Keaton, Anna Q. Nilsson, H.B. Warner (Themselves).

ANGELS IN THE OUTFIELD

(1951) Metro-Goldwyn-Mayer B&W 99 minutes *Director-Producer:* Clarence Brown. *Writers:* Dorothy Kingsley, George Wells, based on a story by Richard Conlin. *Cinematographer:* Paul C. Vogel. *Editor:* Robert J. Kern. *Music:* Daniele Amfitheatrof. *Cast:* Paul Douglas (Guffy McGovern), Janet Leigh (Jennifer

In *The Winning Team*, the mate (Doris Day, left) and mother (Dorothy Adams) of Grover Cleveland Alexander (Ronald Reagan) are at his side after a discouraging medical diagnosis.

Paige), Donna Corcoran (Bridget White), Keenan Wynn (Fred Bayles), Lewis Stone (Arnold P. Hapgood), Spring Byington (Sister Edwitha), Bruce Bennett (Saul Hellman), Marvin Kaplan (Timothy Durney), Ellen Corby (Sister Veronica), Jeff Richards (Dave Rothberg), John Gallaudet (Reynolds), King Donovan (McGee), Don Haggerty (Ronson), Paul Salata (Tony Minelli), Fred Graham (Chunk), John McKee (Bill Baxter), Joe DiMaggio, Bing Crosby, Ty Cobb, Harry Ruby (Themselves).

RHUBARB

(1951) Paramount Pictures B&W   94 minutes *Director:* Arthur Lubin. *Writers:* Dorothy Reid, Frances Cockrell, based on the novel by H. Allen Smith. *Producers:* William Perlberg, George Seaton. *Cinematographer:* Lionel Lindon. *Editor:* Alma Macrorie. *Music:* Van Cleave. *Cast:* Ray Milland (Eric Yeager), Jan Sterling (Polly), Gene Lockhart (Thaddeus J. Banner), Elsie Holmes (Myna Banner), Taylor Holmes (P. Duncan Munk), William Frawley (Len Sickles), Willard Waterman (Orlando Dill), Henry Slate (Dud Logan), James Hayward (Doom), Anthony Redecki (First Ballplayer), Leonard Nimoy (Second Ballplayer), James J. Griffith (Oggie Meadows), Donald MacBride (Pheeny), Hal K. Dawson (Mr. Fisher), Strother Martin (Shorty McGirk), Billy Wayne (St. Louis Manager).

THE PRIDE OF ST. LOUIS

(1952) Twentieth Century-Fox B&W   93 minutes *Director:* Harmon Jones. *Writer:* Herman Mankiewicz, based on a story by Guy Trosper. *Producer:* Jules Schermer. *Cinematographer:* Leo Tover. *Editor:* Robert Simpson. *Music:* Arthur Lange. *Cast:* Dan Dailey (Dizzy Dean), Joanne Dru (Patricia Nash Dean), Richard

Hylton (Johnny Kendall), Richard Crenna (Paul Dean), Hugh Sanders (Horst), James Brown (Moose), Leo T. Cleary (Manager Ed Monroe), Kenny Williams (Castleman), John McKee (Delaney), Stuart Randall (Frankie Frisch), Chet Huntley (Baseball Announcer).

ABOUT FACE

(1952) Warner Bros. Color   93 minutes *Director:* Roy Del Ruth. *Writer:* Peter Milne, from the play *Brother Rat*, by John Monks, Jr., Fred Finklehoffe. *Producer:* William Jacobs. *Cinematographer:* Bert Glennon. *Editor:* Thomas Reilly. *Music:* Charles Tobias, Peter De Rose. *Cast:* Gordon MacRae (Tony Williams), Eddie Bracken (Boff Roberts), Dick Wesson (Dave Crouse), Virginia Gibson (Betty Long), Phyllis Kirk (Alice Wheatley), Aileen Stanley, Jr. (Lorna Carter), Joel Grey (Bender).

THE WINNING TEAM

(1952) Warner Bros. B&W   98 minutes *Director:* Lewis Seiler. *Writers:* Ted Sherdeman, Seeleg Lester, Merwin Gerard, based on a story by Lester and Gerard. *Producer:* Bryan Foy. *Cinematographer:* Sid Hickox. *Editor:* Alan Crosland, Jr. *Music:* David Buttolph. *Technical advisers:* Mrs. Grover Cleveland Alexander, Arnold "Jigger" Statz, Gerry Priddy. Cast: Doris Day (Aimee), Ronald Reagan (Grover Cleveland Alexander), Frank Lovejoy (Rogers Hornsby), Eve Miller (Margaret), James Millican (Bill Killifer), Rusty Tamblyn (Willie Alexander), Gordon Jones (Glasheen), Hugh Sanders (McCarthy), Frank Ferguson (Sam Arrants), Walter Baldwin (Pa Alexander), Dorothy Adams (Ma Alexander), Fred Millican (A Catcher), Pat Flaherty (Bill Klem), Billy Wayne (Red Dooin), Bob Lemon, Gerry Priddy, Peanuts Lowrey, George (Catfish) Metkovich, Irving (Irv) Noren, Hank Sauer, Al Zarilla, Gene Mauch (The Big Leaguers).

BIG LEAGUER

(1953) Metro-Goldwyn-Mayer B&W   70 minutes *Director:* Robert Aldrich. *Writer:* Herbert Baker, based on a story by John McNulty, Louis Morheim. *Producer:* Matthew Rapf. *Cinematographer:* William Mellor. *Editor:* Ben Lewis. *Technical adviser:* John B. "Hans" Lobert. *Cast:* Edward G. Robinson (John B. "Hans" Lobert), Vera-Ellen (Christy), Jeff Richards (Adam Polachuk), Richard Jaeckel (Bobby Bronson), William Campbell (Julie Davis), Carl Hubbell (Himself), Paul Langton (Brian McLennan), Lalo Rios (Chuy Aguilar), Bill Crandall (Tippy Mitchell), Frank Ferguson (Wally Mitchell), John McKee (Dale Alexander), Mario Siletti (Mr. Polachuk), Al Campanis (Himself), Bob Tricolor (Himself), Tony Ravish (Himself).

THE KID FROM LEFT FIELD

(1953) Twentieth Century-Fox B&W   80 minutes *Director:* Harmon Jones. *Writer:* Jack Sher. *Producer:* Leonard Goldstein. *Cinematographer:* Harry Jackson. *Editor:* William Reynolds. *Music:* Lionel Newman. *Cast:* Dan Dailey (Larry "Pop" Cooper), Anne Bancroft (Marian), Billy Chapin (Christy), Lloyd Bridges (Pete Haines), Ray Collins (Whacker), Richard Egan (Billy Lorant), Bob Hopkins (Bobo Noonan), Alex Gerry (J.R. Johnson), Walter Sande (Barnes), Fess Parker (McDougal), John Berardino (Hank Dreiser), John "Beans" Reardon (Umpire).

ROOGIE'S BUMP

(1954) Republic Pictures B&W 71 minutes *Director:* Harold Young. *Writers:* Jack Hanley, Dan Totheroh, from a story by Frank Warren, Joyce Selznick. *Producers:* John Bash, Elizabeth Dickensen. *Cinematographer:* Burgi J. Contner. *Music:* Lehman Engel. *Cast:* Robert Marriot (Remington "Roogie" Rigsby), Ruth Warrick (Mrs. Rigsby), Olive Blackeney (Mrs. Andrews), Robert Simon (Boxi), William Harrigan (Red O'Malley), David Winters (Andy), Michael Mann (Benji), Archie Robbins (P.A. Riker), Louise Troy (Kate), Guy Rennie (Danny Doowinkle), Tedd Lawrence (Sports Announcer/Narrator), Michael Keene (Barney Davis), Roy Campanella, Billy Loes, Carl Erskine, Russ Meyer (Themselves).

STRATEGIC AIR COMMAND

(1955) Paramount Pictures Color 110 minutes *Director:* Anthony Mann. *Writers:* Valentine Davies, Bierne Lay, Jr., based on a story by Lay. *Producer:* Samuel J. Briskin. *Cinematographer:* William Daniels. *Editor:* Eda Warren. *Music:* Victor Young. *Cast:* James Stewart (Robert "Dutch" Holland), June Allyson (Sally Holland), Frank Lovejoy (General Ennis C. Hawkes), Barry Sullivan (Rocky Samford), Alex Nicol (Ike Knowland), Bruce Bennett (General Espy), Jay C. Flippen (Doyle), Henry Morgan (Bible).

THREE STRIPES IN THE SUN

(1955) Columbia Pictures B&W 93 minutes *Director-Writer:* Richard Murphy. *Adaptation:* Albert Duffy, based on E.J. Kahn's *New Yorker* article "The Gentle Wolfhound." *Producer:* Fred Kohlmar. *Cinematographer:* Burnett Guffey. *Editor:* Charles Nelson. *Music:* George Duning. *Technical adviser:* Hugh O'Reilly. *Cast:* Aldo Ray (Hugh O'Reilly), Phil Carey (Colonel), Dick York (Cpl. Neeby Muhlendorf), Mitsuko Kimura (Yuko), Chuck Connors (Idaho), Camille Janclaire (Sister Genevieve), Henry Okawa (Father Yoshida).

I'LL BUY YOU

(1956) Shochiku B&W 113 minutes *Director:* Masaki Kobayashi. *Writer:* Zenzo Matsuyama, based on the novel by Minoru Ono. *Cinematographer:* Yuharu Atsuta. *Music:* Chuji Kinoshita. *Cast:* Keiji Sata, Keiko Kishi, Minoru Oki, Yunosuke Ito, Mitsuko Mito.

THE GREAT AMERICAN PASTIME

(1956) Metro-Goldwyn-Mayer B&W 89 minutes *Director:* Herman Hoffman. *Writer:* Nathaniel Benchley. *Producer:* Henry Berman. *Cinematographer:* Arthur E. Arling. *Editor:* Gene Ruggiero. *Music:* Jeff Alexander. *Cast:* Tom Ewell (Bruce Hallerton), Anne Francis (Betty Hallerton), Ann Miller (Doris Patterson), Dean Jones (Buck Rivers), Rudy Lee (Dennis Hallerton), Judson Pratt (Ed Ryder), Raymond Bailey (George Carruthers), Raymond Winston (Man Mountain O'Keefe).

FEAR STRIKES OUT

(1957) Paramount Pictures B&W 100 minutes *Director:* Robert Mulligan. *Writers:* Ted Berkman, Raphael Blau, based on a story by James A. Piersall, Albert S. Hirshberg. *Producer:* Alan Pakula. *Cinematographer:* Haskell Boggs. *Editor:* Aaron Stell. *Music:* Elmer Bernstein. *Technical adviser:* Thomas E. "Pep" Lee. *Cast:* Anthony Perkins (Jim Piersall), Karl Malden (John Piersall), Norma Moore (Mary Teevan Piersall), Adam Williams (Dr. Brown), Perry Wilson (Mrs. John Piersall), Peter J. Votrian (Young Jim Piersall), Bart Burns (Joe Cronin).

The Great American Pastime: Tom Ewell as Bruce Hallerton, lecturing his charges; at center, behind the ballplayers, is Dean Jones.

12 ANGRY MEN

(1957) Orion-Nova Production United Artists B&W 95 minutes *Director:* Sidney Lumet. *Screenplay:* Reginald Rose, based on his television play. *Producers:* Rose, Henry Fonda. *Cinematographer:* Boris Kaufman. *Editor:* Carl Lerner. *Music:* Kenyon Hopkins. *Cast:* Henry Fonda (Juror #8), Lee J. Cobb (Juror #3), Ed Begley (Juror #10), E.G. Marshall (Juror #4), Jack Warden (Juror #7), Martin Balsam (Juror #1), John Fiedler (Juror #2), Jack Klugman (Juror #5), Edward Binns (Juror #6), Joseph Sweeney (Juror #9), George Voskovec (Juror #11), Robert Webber (Juror #12).

ESCAPADE IN JAPAN

(1957) Universal Pictures Color 90 minutes *Director:* Arthur Lubin. *Writer:* Winston Miller. *Cinematographer:* William Snyder. *Editor:* Otto Ludwig. *Music:* Max Steiner. *Cast:* Teresa Wright (Mary Saunders), Cameron Mitchell (Dick Saunders), Jon Provost (Tony Saunders), Roger Nakagawa (Jiko), Philip Ober (Lt. Col. Hargrave), Kuniko Miyake (Michiko), Susumu Fujita (Kei Tanaka), Clint Eastwood (Dumbo).

DAMN YANKEES

(1958) Warner Bros. Color 110 minutes *Directors-Producers:* George Abbott, Stanley Donen. *Writer:* George Abbott, based on the musical play by Abbott, Douglass Wallop (which is based on Wallop's book *The Year the Yankees Lost the Pennant*). *Cinematographer:* Harold Lipstein. *Editor:* Frank Bracht. *Music and Lyrics:* Richard Adler, Jerry Ross. *Dances and musical numbers*

A GRAND SLAM!

FUN AND LAUGHTER WITH THE GREATEST GUYS IN BASEBALL ...and the luckiest kid in the world!

MICKEY MANTLE   ROGER MARIS

SAFE at HOME!

co-starring
WILLIAM FRAWLEY · PATRICIA BARRY · DON COLLIER
with BRYAN RUSSELL · Screenplay by ROBERT DILLON
(The Luckiest Kid in the World) · Based on a story by TOM NAUD and STEVE RITCH
Produced by TOM NAUD · Directed by WALTER DONIGER
A NAUD-HAMILBURG Production · A COLUMBIA PICTURES RELEASE

Where every young New York Yankees fan would liked to have been during the early 1960s: right between Mickey Mantle and Roger Maris.

staged by Bob Fosse. *Cast:* Tab Hunter (Joe Hardy), Gwen Verdon (Lola), Ray Walston (Mr. Applegate), Russ Brown (Van Buren), Shannon Bolin (Meg Boyd), Nathaniel Frey (Smokey), Jimmie Komack (Rocky), Rae Allen (Gloria Thorpe), Robert Shafer (Joe Boyd), Jean Stapleton (Sister Miller), Albert Linville (Vernon), Bob Fosse (Dancer).

THE GEISHA BOY

(1958) Paramount Pictures Color   95 minutes *Director-Writer:* Frank Tashlin. Based on a story by Rudy Makoul. *Producer:* Jerry Lewis. *Cinematographer:* Haskell Boggs. *Editor:* Alma Macrorie. *Music:* Walter Scharf. *Cast:* Jerry Lewis (Gilbert Wooley), Marie McDonald (Lola Livingston), Sessue Hayakawa (Father), Barton MacLane (Major Ridgley), Suzanne Pleshette (Beatty Pearson), Nobu Atsumi McCarthy (Kimi Sikita), Robert Kazuyoshi Hirano (Mitsuo Watanabe), Ryuzo Demura (The Great Ichiyama), The Los Angeles Dodgers (Themselves).

SAFE AT HOME!

(1962) Naud-Hamilburg Productions Columbia Pictures B&W 83 minutes *Director:* Walter Doniger. *Writer:* Robert Dillon, based on a story by Tom Naud, Steven Ritch. *Producer:* Naud. *Cinematographer:* Irving Lippman. *Editor:* Frank P. Keller. *Music:* Van Alexander. *Cast:* Mickey Mantle (Himself), Roger Maris (Himself), William Frawley (Bill Turner), Patricia Barry (Johanna Price), Don Collier (Ken Lawton), Bryan Russell (Hutch Lawton), Eugene Iglesias (Mr. Torres), Flip Mark (Henry), Scott Lane (Mike Torres), Ralph Houk (Himself), Whitey Ford (Himself), Fred A. Schwab (Coach Benton).

EXPERIMENT IN TERROR

(1962) Geoffrey-Kate Productions Columbia Pictures B&W   123 minutes *Director-Producer:* Blake Edwards. *Writers:* The Gordons. *Cinematographer:* Philip Lathrop. *Editor:* Patrick McCormack. *Music:* Henry Mancini. *Cast:* Glenn Ford (John Ripley), Lee Remick (Kelly Sherwood), Stefanie Powers (Toby Sherwood), Ross Martin (Red Lynch), Roy Poole (Brad), Ned Glass (Popcorn).

THE HORIZONTAL LIEUTENANT

(1962) Euterpe, Inc. Metro-Goldwyn-Mayer Color   90 minutes *Director:* Richard Thorpe. *Writer:* George Wells, based on the novel *The Bottletop Affair,* by Gordon Cotler. *Producer:* Joe Pasternak. *Cinematographer:* Robert Bronner. *Editor:* Richard Farrell. *Music:* George Stoll. *Cast:* Jim Hutton (Merle Wye), Paula Prentiss (Molly Blue), Jack Carter (William Monck), Jim Backus (Jerry Hammerslag), Charles McGraw (Charles Korotny), Miyoshi Umeki (Akiko), Yoshido Yoda (Roy Tada), Marty Ingels (Buckles).

THAT TOUCH OF MINK

(1962) Granley Company-Arwin Productions-Nob Hill Productions Universal-International Color   99 minutes *Director:* Delbert Mann. *Writers:* Stanley Shapiro, Nate Monaster. *Producers:* Shapiro, Martin Melcher. *Cinematographer:* Russell Metty. *Editor:* Ted Kent. *Music:* George Duning. *Cast:* Cary Grant (Philip Shayne), Doris Day (Cathy Timberlake), Gig Young (Roger), Audrey Meadows (Connie), Alan Hewitt (Dr. Gruber), John Astin (Beasley), Mickey Mantle, Roger Maris, Yogi Berra (Themselves, New York Yankees), Art Passarella (Umpire).

BOYS' NIGHT OUT

(1962) Filmways, Inc./Kimco Pictures/Embassy Pictures Metro-Goldwyn-Mayer Color   114 minutes *Director:* Michael Gordon. *Writer/Adaptation:* Ira Wallach/Marion Hargrove, from a story by Arne Sultan, Marvin Worth. *Producer:* Martin Ransohoff. *Cinematographer:* Arthur E. Arling. *Editor:* Tom McAdoo. *Music:* Frank DeVol. *Cast:* Kim Novak (Cathy), James Garner (Fred Williams), Tony Randall (George Drayton), Howard Duff (Doug Jackson), Janet Blair (Marge Drayton), Patti Page (Joanne McIllenny), Jessie Royce Landis (Ethel Williams), Oscar Homolka (Dr. Prokosch), Howard Morris (Howard McIllenny), Anne Jeffreys (Toni Jackson), Zsa Zsa Gabor (Girlfriend), Fred Clark (Mr. Bohannon), William Bendix (Slattery), Jim Backus (Peter Bowers).

THE FAMILY JEWELS

(1965) York Pictures Paramount Pictures Color   100 minutes *Director-Producer:* Jerry Lewis. *Writers:* Lewis, Bill Richmond. *Cinematographer:* W. Wallace Kelley. *Editor:* John Woodcock.

Bang the Drum Slowly: Robert De Niro, Tom Signorelli, Danny Aiello, Vincent Gardenia, Pierrino Mascarino, Dell Bethel, Andy Jarrell, Michael Moriarty (left to right).

Music: Pete King. *Cast:* Jerry Lewis (Willard/Everett/James/Eddie/Julius/"Bugs"/Skylock), Sebastian Cabot (Dr. Matson), Donna Butterworth (Donna Peyton).

SHIP OF FOOLS

(1965) Columbia Pictures B&W   149 minutes *Director-Producer:* Stanley Kramer. *Writer:* Abby Mann, based on the novel by Katherine Anne Porter. *Cinematographer:* Ernest Laszlo. *Editor:* Robert C. Jones. *Music:* Ernest Gold. *Cast:* Vivien Leigh (Mary Treadwell), Simone Signoret (La Condesa), Jose Ferrer (Rieber), Lee Marvin (Tenny), Oskar Werner (Dr. Schumann), Elizabeth Ashley (Jenny), George Segal (David), Michael Dunn (Glocken).

THE ODD COUPLE

(1968) Paramount Pictures Color   105 minutes *Director:* Gene Saks. *Writer:* Neil Simon, based on his play. *Producer:* Howard W. Koch. *Cinematographer:* Robert Hauser. *Editor:* Frank Bracht. *Music:* Neal Hefti. *Cast:* Jack Lemmon (Felix Ungar), Walter Matthau (Oscar Madison), John Fiedler (Vinnie), Herbert Edelman (Murray), David Sheiner (Roy), Larry Haines (Speed), Monica Evans (Cecily), Carole Shelley (Gwendolyn), Heywood Hale Broun (Sportswriter).

THE CEREMONY

(1971) Sozosha-Atg Shibata Org. Color   122 minutes *Director:* Nagisa Oshima. *Writers:* Oshima, Tsutomu Tamura, Mamoru Sasaki. *Cinematographer:* Toichiro Narushima. *Editor:* Keichiro Uracka. *Cast:* Kenzo Kawarazaki (Masuo), Atsuko Kaku (Ritsuko), Atsuo Nakamura (Terumichi), Aiko Koyama (Setsuko), Kei Sato (Kazuomi), Kiyoshi Tsuchiya (Tadashi).

ONE-LEGGED ACE

(1971) Katsu Productions Daiei Color   100 minutes *Director:* Kazuo Ikehiro. *Writer:* Masato Ide.

BANG THE DRUM SLOWLY

(1973) Paramount Pictures Color   97 minutes   PG *Director:* John Hancock. *Writer:* Mark Harris, based on his novel. *Producers:* Maurice and Lois Rosenfield. *Cinematographer:* Richard Shore. *Editor:* Richard Marks. *Music:* Stephen Lawrence. *Cast:* Michael Moriarty (Henry Wiggen), Robert De Niro (Bruce Pearson), Vincent Gardenia (Dutch Schnell), Phil Foster (Joe Jaros), Ann Wedgeworth (Katie), Patrick McVey (Mr. Pearson), Tom Ligon (Piney Woods), Heather MacRae (Holly Wiggen), Selma Diamond (Tootsie), Barbara Babcock (Team Owner), Maurice Rosenfield (Team Owner), Andy Jarrell (Ugly Jones), Marshall Efron (Bradley Lord), Barton Heyman (Red Traphagen), Donny Burks (Perry), Hector Elias (Diego), Tom Signorelli (Goose Williams), James Donahue (Canada Smith), Nicolas Surovy (Aleck Olson), Danny Aiello (Horse), Hector Troy (George), Tony Major (Jonah), Pierrino Mascarino (Sid Goldman), Dell Bethel (Third Base Coach).

ONE FLEW OVER THE CUCKOO'S NEST

(1975) Fantasy Films United Artists Color   133 minutes   R *Director:* Milos Forman. *Writers:* Lawrence Hauben, Bo Goldman, from the novel by Ken Kesey. Producers: Saul Zaentz, Michael Douglas. *Cinematographer:* Haskell Wexler. *Supervising Editor:* Richard Chew. *Editors:* Lynzee Klingman, Sheldon Kahn. *Music:* Jack Nitzsche. *Cast:* Jack Nicholson (R.P. McMurphy), Louise Fletcher (Nurse Ratched), William Redfield (Harding), Will Sampson (Chief Bromden), Brad Dourif (Billy Bibbit), Danny De Vito (Martini), Christopher Lloyd (Taber).

THE BAD NEWS BEARS

(1976) Paramount Pictures Color   102 minutes   PG *Director:* Michael Ritchie. *Writer:* Bill Lancaster. *Producer:* Stanley R. Jaffe. *Cinematographer:* John A. Alonzo. *Editor:* Richard A. Harris. *Music:* Jerry Fielding. *Cast:* Walter Matthau (Morris Buttermaker), Tatum O'Neal (Amanda Whurlitzer), Vic Morrow (Roy Turner), Joyce Van Patten (Cleveland), Ben Piazza (Bob Whitewood), Jackie Earle

215

The Natural: Robert Redford as Roy Hobbs.

Haley (Kelly Leak), Alfred W. Lutter (Ogilvie), Chris Barnes (Tanner Boyle), Erin Blunt (Ahmad Abdul Rahim), Gary Lee Cavagnaro (Mike Engelberg), Jaime Escobedo (Jose Agilar), Scott Firestone (Regi Tower), George Gonzales (Miguel Agilar), Brett Marx (Jimmie Feldman), David Pollock (Rudi Stein), Quinn Smith (Timmy Lupus), David Stambaugh (Toby Whitewood), Brandon Cruz (Joey Turner).

THE BINGO LONG TRAVELING ALL-STARS & MOTOR KINGS

(1976) Motown Production/Pan Arts Enterprises Universal Pictures Color   110 minutes   PG *Director:* Jon Badham. *Writers:* Hal Barwood, Matthew Robbins, based on the novel by William Brashler. *Producer:* Rob Cohen. *Cinematographer:* Bill Butler. *Editor:* David Rawlins. *Music:* William Goldstein. *Cast:* Billy Dee Williams (Bingo Long), James Earl Jones (Leon Carter), Richard Pryor (Charlie Snow), Stan Shaw (Esquire Joe Calloway), Ted Ross (Sallison Potter), Rico Dawson (Willie Lee), Sam "Birmingham" Briston (Louis), Jophery Brown (Champ Chambers), Leon Wagner (Fat Sam), Tony Burton (Isaac), John McCurry (Walter Murchman), DeWayne Jessie (Rainbow), Mabel King (Bertha), Sam Laws (Henry), Alvin Childress (Horace), Ken Force (Honey), Carl Gordon (Mack), Ahna Capri (The Prostitute), Joel Fluellen (Mr. Holland), Jester Hairston (Furry Taylor), Emmett Ashford (Umpire).

THE BAD NEWS BEARS IN BREAKING TRAINING

(1977) Paramount Pictures Color   100 minutes   PG *Director:* Michael Pressman. *Writer:* Paul Brickman, based on characters created by Bill Lancaster. *Producer:* Leonard Goldberg. *Cinematographer:* Fred Koenekamp. *Editor:* John W. Wheeler. *Music:* Craig Safan. *Cast:* William Devane (Mike Leak), Clifton James (Sy Orlansky), Jackie Earle Haley (Kelly Leak), Jimmy Baio (Carmen Ronzonni), Chris Barnes (Tanner Boyle), Erin Blunt (Ahmad Abdul Rahim), Jaime Escobedo (Jose Agilar), George Gonzales (Miguel Agilar), Alfred W. Lutter (Ogilvie), Brett Marx (Jimmie Feldman), David Pollock (Rudi Stein), Quinn Smith (Timmy Lupus), David Stambaugh (Toby Whitewood), Jeffrey Louis Starr (Mike Engelberg), Lane Smith (Officer Mackie), Dolph Sweet (Manning), Pat Corley (Morris), Bob Watson, Enos Cabell, Roger Metzger, J.R. Richard, Joe Ferguson, Ken Forsch, Cesar Cedeno, Bill Virdon (Houston Astros).

JUST THE BEGINNING

(1977) Yung Bang Films Color   105 minutes   *Director:* Jung In Yup. *Writer:* Suh Yoon Sung. *Producer:* Choi Chun Ji. *Cinematographer:* Paing Jung Moon. *Editor:* Chang Kil Sang. *Music:* Jung Soung Jo. *Cast:* Jin Yoo Young (Whan Tai), Ha Myoung Jung (Coach Cha), Kang Ju Hee (Hae-Sook), Doh Kum Bong (Mrs. Lee), Han Se Hun (Segun).

HERE COME THE TIGERS

(1978) Filmways Pictures American International Color   90 minutes   PG *Director:* Sean S. Cunningham. *Writer:* Arch McCoy. *Producers:* Cunningham, Stephen Miner. *Cinematographer:* Barry Abrams. *Editor:* Miner. *Music:* Harry Manfredini. *Cast:* Richard Lincoln (Eddie Burke), James Zvanut (Burt Honneger), Samantha Grey (Betty Burke), William Caldwell (Kreeger), Manny Lieberman (Feliz the Umpire), Fred Lincoln (Aesop), Xavier Rodrigo (Buster Rivera), Terry Vance (Mrs. Mayfield), Kathy Bell (Patty O'Malley), Noel John Cunningham (Noel "Peanuts" Cady), Sean P. Griffin (Art "The Fart" Bullfinch), Max McClellan (Mike "The Bod" Karpel), Kevin Moore ("Eaglescout" Terwilliger), Lance Norwood (Ralphy Parks), Ted Oyama (Umeld Siddaharo), Michael Pastore (Roger "Fingers" Ross), Philip Scuder (Danny Mayfield), David Schmalholz (Fritz "Bionic Mouth" Curtis), Nancy Willis (Sharon Dixon), Andy Weeks ("Scoop" Maxwell), Todd Weeks (Timmy Deutsch).

THE BAD NEWS BEARS GO TO JAPAN

(1978) Paramount Pictures Color   91 minutes   PG *Director:* John Berry. *Writer:* Bill Lancaster. *Producers:* Lancaster, Michael Ritchie. *Cinematographers:* Jean Polito, Kozo Okazaki. *Editor:* Richard A. Harris. *Music:* Paul Chihara. *Cast:* Tony Curtis (Marvin Lazar), Jackie Earle Haley (Kelly Leak), Tomosaburo Wakayama (Coach Shimizu), Hatsune Ishihara (Arika), George Wyner (Network Director), Lonny Chapman (Louis the Gambler), Matthew Douglas Anton (E.R.W. Tillyard III), Erin Blunt (Ahmad Abdul Rahim), George Gonzales (Miguel Agilar), Brett Marx (Jimmie Feldman), David Pollock (Rudi Stein), David Stambaugh (Toby Whitewood), Jeffrey Louis Starr (Mike Engelberg), Scoody Thornton (Mustapha Rahim).

GOODBYE, FRANKLIN HIGH

(1978) Cal-Am Productions Color   94 minutes   PG *Director-Producer:* Mike MacFarland. *Writer:* Stu Krieger. *Cinematographer:*

Dean Cundey. *Editor:* Peter Parasheles. *Music:* Lane Caudell. *Cast:* Lane Caudell (Will Armer), Julie Adams (Janice Armer), William Windom (Clifford Armer), Darby Hinton (Mark Jeffries), Ann Dusenberry (Sharon Browne), Ron Lombard (Gregg), Stu Krieger (Kurt)

A BOY CALLED THIRD BASE

(1978) Gentosha and ATG Color   102 minutes *Director:* Yoichi Higashi. *Writer:* Shuji Terayama, based on the novel *Kugatsu no Machi* [*September Town*], by Haku Kenju. *Producer:* Katsuhiro Maeda. *Cinematographer:* Koichi Kawakami. *Editor:* Keiko Ichihara. *Music:* Michi Tanaka. *Cast:* Toshiyuki Nagashima (Third Base), Tsuguaki Yoshida (II-B), Aiko Morishita (Newspaper Club), Akiko Shikata (Tennis).

CHAPTER TWO

(1979) Rastar Columbia Pictures Color   103 minutes   PG *Director:* Robert Moore. *Writer:* Neil Simon, based on his play. *Producer:* Ray Stark. *Cinematographer:* David M. Walsh. *Editor:* Michael E. Stevenson. *Music:* Marvin Hamlisch. *Cast:* James Caan (George Schneider), Marsha Mason (Jennie MacLaine), Joseph Bologna (Leo Schneider), Valerie Harper (Faye Medwick).

SQUEEZE PLAY

(1980) Troma Color   92 minutes   R   *Director:* Samuel Weil. *Writers:* Haim Pekelis, Charles Kaufman. *Producers:* Lloyd Kaufman, Samuel Weil. *Cinematography:* Kaufman. *Editor:* George T. Norris. *Cast:* Jim Harris (Wes), Jenni Hetrick (Samantha), Rick Gitlin (Fred), Helen Campitelli (Jamie), Rick Hahn (Tom), Al Corley (Buddy), Melissa Michaels (Mary Lou).

IT'S MY TURN

(1980) Rastar Columbia Pictures Color   91 minutes   R *Director:* Claudia Weill. *Writer:* Eleanor Bergstein. *Producer:* Martin Elfand. *Cinematographer:* Bill Butler. *Editors:* Byron Brandt, Marjorie Fowler, James Coblenz. *Music:* Patrick Williams. *Cast:* Jill Clayburgh (Kate Gunzinger), Michael Douglas (Ben Lewin), Charles Grodin (Homer), Beverly Garland (Emma), Steven Hill (Jacob).

THE CHOSEN

(1982) Twentieth Century-Fox Color   108 minutes   PG *Director:* Jeremy Paul Kagan. *Writer:* Edwin Gordon, based on the novel by Chaim Potok. *Producers:* Edie and Ely Landau. *Cinematographer:* Arthur Ornitz. *Editor:* David Garfield. *Music:* Elmer Bernstein. *Cast:* Maximilian Schell (David Malter), Rod Steiger (Reb Saunders), Robby Benson (Danny Saunders), Barry Miller (Reuven Malter), Hildy Brooks (Mrs. Saunders), Val Avery (Baseball Coach).

CANNERY ROW

(1982) Metro-Goldwyn-Mayer Color   120 minutes   PG *Director-Writer:* David Ward. Based on John Steinbeck's *Cannery Row* and *Sweet Thursday.* *Producer:* Michael Phillips. *Cinematographer:* Sven Nykvist. *Editor:* David Bretherton. *Music:* Jack Nitzsche. *Cast:* Nick Nolte (Doc), Debra Winger (Suzy), Audra Lindley (Fauna), Frank McRae (Hazel), M. Emmet Walsh (Mack), Sunshine Parker (The Seer), John Huston (Narrator).

In *Death on the Diamond*, pitcher Larry Kelly (Robert Young) is diverted by the film's love interest (played by Madge Evans).

ZAPPED!

(1982) Embassy Pictures Color   96 minutes   R *Director:* Robert J. Rosenthal. *Writers:* Rosenthal, Bruce Rubin. *Producer:* Jeffrey D. Apple. *Cinematographer:* Daniel Pearl. *Editor:* Robert Ferretti. *Music:* Charles Fox. *Cast:* Scott Baio (Barney Springboro), Willie Aames (Peyton), Heather Thomas (Jane Mitchell), Robert Mandan (Walter Johnson), Felice Schachter (Bernadette), Scatman Crothers (Dexter Jones), Roger Bowen (Mr. Springboro), Marya Small (Mrs. Springboro).

CHASING DREAMS

(1982) Nascent Productions Prism Entertainment Corp. Color   96 minutes   PG *Directors:* Therese Conte, Sean Roche. *Writer:* David G. Brown. *Producers:* Therese Conte, David G. Brown. *Cinematographer:* Connie Holt. *Editors:* Jerry Weldon, Robert Sinese. *Music:* Gregory Conte. *Cast:* David G. Brown (Gavin), John Fife (Parks), Jim Shane (Father), Matthew Clark (Ben), Kevin Costner (Ed), Lisa Kingston (Sue), Claudia Carroll (Mother), Don Margolin (Coach Stevens).

MAX DUGAN RETURNS

(1983) Twentieth Century-Fox Color   98 minutes   PG *Director:* Herbert Ross. *Writer:* Neil Simon. *Producers:* Ross, Simon.

Warming Up: Jean Arthur as Mary Post, Richard Dix as "Bee Line" Tulliver.

Cinematographer: David M. Walsh. *Editor:* Richard Marks. *Music:* David Shire. *Cast:* Marsha Mason (Nora McPhee), Jason Robards (Max Dugan), Donald Sutherland (Brian Costello), Matthew Broderick (Michael McPhee), Dody Goodman (Mrs. Litke), Sal Viscuso (Coach Roy), Panchito Gomez (Luis), Charlie Lau (Himself).

ZELIG

(1983) Jack Rollins-Charles H. Joffe Production Orion Pictures/ Warner Bros. Color/B&W 79 minutes PG *Director-Writer:* Woody Allen. *Producer:* Robert Greenhut. *Cinematographer:* Gordon Willis. *Editor:* Susan E. Morse. *Music:* Dick Hyman. *Cast:* Woody Allen (Leonard Zelig), Mia Farrow (Dr. Fletcher), Susan Sontag, Irving Howe, Saul Bellow, Bricktop, Bruno Bettelheim, John Morton Blum (Interviewees).

BLUE SKIES AGAIN

(1983) Lantana Production Warner Bros. Color 96 minutes PG *Director:* Richard Michaels. *Writer:* Kevin Sellers. Producers: Arlene Sellers, Alex Winitsky. *Cinematographer:* Don McAlpine. *Editor:* Danford B. Greene. *Music:* John Kander. *Baseball Commentary:* Jerry Coleman. *Cast:* Harry Hamlin (Sandy Mendenhall), Mimi Rogers (Liz West), Robyn Barto (Paula Fradkin), Kenneth McMillan (Dirk Miller), Dana Elcar (Lou Goff), Cilk Cozart (Alvin "Wallstreet" Chandler), Andy Garcia (Ken Lagomarsino), Joey Gian (Calvin Berry), Doug Moeller (Carroll Brezski), Ray Negron (Jerry Washburn), Tommy Lane (Roy Williams), Rooney Kerwin (Mike Ross), Marcos Gonzales (Chico "Brushback" Carrasco).

UNDER FIRE

(1983) Lion's Gate Film Orion Pictures Color 128 minutes R *Director:* Roger Spottiswoode. *Writers:* Ron Shelton, Clayton Frohman, from a story by Frohman. *Producer:* Jonathan Taplin. *Cinematographer:* John Alcott. *Editor:* Mark Conte. *Music:* Jerry Goldsmith. *Cast:* Nick Nolte (Russel Price), Gene Hackman (Alex Grazier), Joanna Cassidy (Claire), Jean-Louis Trintignant (Jazy), Richard Masur (Hub Kittle), Ed Harris (Oates), Rene Enriquez (Somoza), Eloy Phil Casados (Pedro).

THE NATURAL

(1984) Tri-Star-Delphi II Tri-Star Pictures Color 134 minutes PG *Director:* Barry Levinson. *Writers:* Roger Towne, Phil Dusenberry, based on the novel by Bernard Malamud. *Producer:* Mark Johnson. *Cinematographer:* Caleb Deschanel. *Editor:* Stu Linder. *Music:* Randy Newman. *Cast:* Robert Redford (Roy Hobbs), Robert Duvall (Max Mercy), Glenn Close (Iris Gaines), Kim Basinger (Memo Paris), Wilford Brimley (Pop Fisher), Barbara Hershey (Harriet Bird), Robert Prosky (The Judge), Richard Farnsworth (Red Blow), Darren McGavin (Gus), Joe Don Baker (The Whammer), Michael Madsen (Bump Bailey), Sibbi Sisti (Pirates Manager).

INDIANA JONES AND THE TEMPLE OF DOOM

(1984) Lucasfilm Ltd. Paramount Pictures Color 118 minutes PG *Director:* Steven Spielberg. *Writers:* Willard Huyck, Gloria Katz, based on a story by George Lucas. *Producer:* Robert Watts. *Cinematographer:* Douglas Slocombe. *Editor:* Michael Kahn. *Music:* John Williams. *Cast:* Harrison Ford (Indiana Jones), Kate Capshaw (Willie Scott), Ke Huy Quan (Short Round), Amrish Puri (Mola Ram), Roshan Seth (Chatter Lal), Philip Stone (Captain Blumburtt), Dan Aykroyd (Weber).

A SOLDIER'S STORY

(1984) Columbia Pictures Color 102 minutes PG *Director:* Norman Jewison. *Writer:* Charles Fuller, based on his play *A Soldier's Play.* *Producers:* Jewison, Ronald L. Schwary, Patrick L. Palmer. *Cinematographer:* Russell Boyd. *Editors:* Mark Warner, Caroline Biggerstaff. *Music:* Herbie Hancock. *Cast:* Howard E. Rollins, Jr. (Davenport), Adolph Caesar (Waters), Art Evans (Wilkie), David Alan Grier (Cobb), David Harris (Smalls), Dennis Lipscomb (Taylor), Larry Riley (C.J. Memphis), Robert Townsend (Ellis), Denzel Washington (Peterson), William Allen Young (Henson), Patti LaBelle (Big Mary).

PROTOCOL

(1984) Warner Bros. Color 96 minutes PG *Director:* Herbert Ross. *Writer:* Buck Henry, based on a story by Charles Shyer, Nancy Meyers, Harvey Miller. *Producer:* Anthea Sylbert. *Cinematographer:* William A. Fraker. *Editor:* Paul Hirsch. *Music:* Basil Poledouris. *Cast:* Goldie Hawn (Sunny Davis), Chris Sarandon (Michael Ransome), Richard Romanus (Emir), Andre Gregory (Nawaf Al Kabeer), Gail Strickland (Mrs. St. John), Cliff De Young (Hilley), Keith Szarabajka (Crowe), Ed Begley, Jr. (Hassler), Kenneth Mars (Lou), Kenneth McMillan (Senator Norris), Jean Smart (Ella).

BIRDY

(1984) Tri-Star/Delphi III Tri-Star Color 120 minutes R *Director:* Alan Parker. *Writers:* Sandy Kroopf, Jack Behr, based on the novel by William Wharton. *Producer:* Alan Marshall. *Cinematographer:* Michael Seresin. *Editor:* Gerry Hambling. *Music:* Peter Gabriel. *Cast:* Matthew Modine (Birdy), Nicolas Cage (Al Columbato), John Harkins (Dr. Weiss), Sandy Baron (Mr. Columbato), Karen Young (Hannah Rourke), Bruno Kirby (Rinaldi), Nancy Fish (Mrs. Prevost), George Buck (Birdy's Father), Dolores Sager (Birdy's Mother).

MACARTHUR'S CHILDREN

(1985) Orion Classics Color   115 minutes   PG *Director:* Masahiro Shinoda. *Writer:* Tsutomu Tamura, based on the novel by Yu Aku. *Producers:* You-Bo-Kai, Yu Aku, Masato Hara. *Cinematographer:* Kazuo Miyagawa. *Editor:* Sachiko Yamaji. *Music:* Shinichiro Ikebe. *Cast:* Takaya Yamuchi (Ryuta), Yoshiyuki Omuri (Saburo), Shiori Sakura (Mume), Masako Natsume (Komako), Shuji Otaki (Tadao), Shuji Otako (The Policeman), Jiro Kawarazaki (Nakai), Juzo Itami (The Captain), Hiromi Go (Masao), Shima Iwashita (Tome).

THE SLUGGER'S WIFE

(1985) Rastar Columbia Pictures Color   105 minutes   PG-13 *Director:* Hal Ashby. *Writer:* Neil Simon. *Producer:* Ray Stark. *Cinematographer:* Caleb Deschanel. *Editors:* George C. Villasenor, Don Brochu. *Music:* Patrick Williams. *Cast:* Michael O'Keefe (Darryl Palmer), Rebecca De Mornay (Debby Palmer), Martin Ritt (Burly De Vito), Randy Quaid (Moose Granger), Cleavant Derricks (Manny Alvarado), Lisa Langlois (Aline Cooper), Loudon Wainwright III (Gary), Georgann Johnson (Marie De Vito), Danny Tucker (Coach O'Brien), Lynn Whitfield (Tina Alvarado), Mark Fidrych (Himself), Al Hrobosky (Himself), Ted Turner (Himself), Pete Van Wieren (Sports Narrator), Ernie Johnson (Sports Narrator), Skip Caray (Sportscaster), Nick Charles (Sportscaster).

BREWSTER'S MILLIONS

(1985) Universal Pictures Color   97 minutes   PG *Director:* Walter Hill. *Writers:* Herschel Weingrod, Timothy Harris, based on the novel by George Barr McCutcheon. *Producers:* Lawrence Gordon, Joel Silver. *Cinematographer:* Ric Waite. *Editors:* Freeman Davies, Michael Ripps. *Music:* Ry Cooder. *Cast:* Richard Pryor (Montgomery Brewster), John Candy (Spike Nolan), Lonette McKee (Angela Drake), Stephen Collins (Warren Cox), Jerry Orbach (Charley Pegler), Pat Hingle (Edward Roundfield), Tovah Feldshuh (Marilyn), Hume Cronyn (Rupert Horn), Joe Grifasi (J.B. Donaldo), Rick Moranis (Morty King).

INSIGNIFICANCE

(1985) Zenith Productions Island Alive Color   105 minutes   R *Director:* Nicolas Roeg. *Writer:* Terry Johnson, based on his play. *Producer:* Jeremy Thomas. *Cinematographer:* Peter Hannan. *Editor:* Tony Lawson. *Music:* Stanley Myers. *Cast:* Gary Busey ("The Ballplayer"), Michael Emil ("The Professor"), Theresa Russell ("The Actress"), Will Sampson ("The Indian"), Tony Curtis ("The Senator").

GUNG HO

(1986) Paramount Pictures Color   111 minutes   PG-13 *Director:* Ron Howard. *Writers:* Lowell Ganz, Babaloo Mandel, from a story by Edwin Blum, Ganz, Mandel. *Producers:* Tony Ganz, Deborah Blum. *Cinematographer:* Don Peterman. *Editors:* Daniel Hanley, Michael Hill. *Music:* Thomas Newman. *Cast:* Michael Keaton (Hunt Stevenson), Gedde Watanabe (Kazihiro), George Wendt (Buster),

Hot Curves: Benny Rubin as Benny Goldberg, Pert Kelton as Cookie.

Mimi Rogers (Audrey), John Turturro (Willie), Soh Yamamura (Mr. Sakamoto), Sab Shimono (Saito), Rick Overton (Googie), Jihmi Kennedy (Junior), Clint Howard (Paul).

FERRIS BUELLER'S DAY OFF

(1986) Paramount Pictures Color   103 minutes   PG-13 *Director-Writer:* John Hughes. *Producers:* Hughes, Tom Jacobson. *Cinematographer:* Tak Fujimoto. *Editor:* Paul Hirsch. *Music:* Ira Newborn. *Cast:* Matthew Broderick (Ferris Bueller), Alan Ruck (Cameron Frye), Mia Sara (Sloane Paterson), Jeffrey Jones (Ed Rooney), Jennifer Grey (Jeanie), Cindy Pickett (Katie), Lyman Ward (Tom), Charlie Sheen (Boy in Police Station).

ABOUT LAST NIGHT . . .

(1986) Tri-Star Pictures Color   113 minutes   R *Director:* Edward Zwick. *Writers:* Tim Kazurinsky, Denise DeClue, based on the play *Sexual Perversity in Chicago*, by David Mamet. *Producers:* Jason Brett, Stuart Oken. *Cinematographer:* Andrew Dintenfass. *Editor:* Harry Keramidas. *Music:* Miles Goodman. *Cast:* Rob Lowe (Danny), Demi Moore (Debbie), James Belushi (Bernie), Elizabeth Perkins (Joan), George DiCenzo (Flavio).

BRIGHTON BEACH MEMOIRS

(1987) Rastar Universal Pictures Color   110 minutes   PG-13 *Director:* Gene Saks. *Writer:* Neil Simon, based on his play. *Producer:* Ray Stark. *Cinematographer:* John Bailey. *Editor:* Carol Littleton. *Music:* Michael Small. *Cast:* Blythe Danner (Kate), Bob Dishy (Jack), Jonathan Silverman (Eugene), Brian Drillinger

(Stanley), Stacey Glick (Laurie), Judith Ivey (Blanche), Lisa Waltz (Nora), Steven Hill (Mr. Stroheim).

RADIO DAYS

(1987) Jack Rollins-Charles H. Joffe Production Orion Pictures Color 85 minutes PG *Director-Writer:* Woody Allen. *Producer:* Robert Greenhut. *Cinematographer:* Carlo Di Palma. *Editor:* Susan E. Morse. *Cast:* Mia Farrow (Sally White), Jeff Daniels (Biff Baxter), Julie Kavner (Mother), Michael Tucker (Father), Dianne Wiest (Bea), Seth Green (Joe), Diane Keaton (New Year's Singer), Brian Mannain (Kirby Kyle), Guy Le Bow (Bill Kern), Woody Allen (Narrator).

Hot Curves: Paul Hurst (left) as Slug, Benny Rubin as Benny Goldberg.

AMAZING GRACE AND CHUCK

(1987) Turnstar Production Tri-Star Pictures/Rastar Color 115 minutes PG *Director:* Mike Newell. *Writer-Producer:* David Field. *Cinematographer:* Robert Elswit. *Editor:* Peter Hollywood. *Music:* Elmer Bernstein. *Cast:* Gregory Peck (President), William L. Petersen (Russell Murdock), Joshua Zuehlke (Chuck Murdock), Alex English (Amazing Grace Smith), Frances Conroy (Pamela), Jamie Lee Curtis (Lynn Taylor).

IRONWEED

(1987) Taft Entertainment Pictures Tri-Star Pictures Color 144 minutes R *Director:* Hector Babenco. *Writer:* William Kennedy, based on his novel. *Producers:* Keith Barish, Marcia Nasatir. *Cinematographer:* Lauro Escorel. *Editor:* Anne Goursaud. *Music:* John Morris. *Cast:* Jack Nicholson (Francis Phelan), Meryl Streep

(Helen), Carroll Baker (Annie Phelan), Michael O'Keefe (Billy), Diane Venora (Peg), Fred Gwynne (Oscar Reo), Margaret Whitton (Katrina), Tom Waits (Rudy), Jake Dengel (Pee Wee), Nathan Lane (Harold Allen), James Gammon (Reverend Chester), Ean Egas (Danny).

FUNNY FARM

(1988) Cornelius-Pan-Arts Production Warner Bros. Color 101 minutes *Director:* George Roy Hill. *Writer:* Jeffrey Boam, based on a book by Jay Cronley. *Producer:* Robert L. Crawford. *Cinematographer:* Miroslav Ondricek. *Editor:* Alan Heim. *Music:* Elmer Bernstein. *Cast:* Chevy Chase (Andy Farmer), Madolyn Smith (Elizabeth), Joseph Maher (Michael Sinclair), Jack Gilpin (Bud Culbertson).

BIG

(1988) Gracie Films Production Twentieth Century-Fox Color 102 minutes PG *Director:* Penny Marshall. *Writers:* Gary Ross, Anne Spielberg. *Producers:* James L. Brooks, Robert Greenhut. *Cinematographer:* Barry Sonnenfeld. *Editor:* Barry Malkin. *Music:* Howard Shore. *Cast:* Tom Hanks (Josh Baskin), Elizabeth Perkins (Susan), Robert Loggia (MacMillan), John Heard (Paul), Jared Rushton (Billy), David Moscow (Young Josh), Jon Lovitz (Scotty), Mercedes Ruehl (Mrs. Baskin).

BULL DURHAM

(1988) Mount Company Orion Pictures Color 115 minutes R *Director-Writer:* Ron Shelton. *Producers:* Thom Mount, Mark Burg. *Cinematographer:* Bobby Byrne. *Editors:* Robert Leighton, Adam Weiss. *Music:* Michael Convertino. *Cast:* Kevin Costner (Crash Davis), Susan Sarandon (Annie Savoy), Tim Robbins (Ebby Calvin "Nuke" LaLoosh), Trey Wilson (Skip), Robert Wuhl (Larry), William O'Leary (Jimmy), David Neidorf (Bobby), Danny Gans (Deke), Tom Silardi (Tony), Jenny Robertson (Millie), Rick Marzan (Jose), Lloyd Williams (Mickey), Max Patkin (Himself).

STEALING HOME

(1988) Mount Company Warner Bros. Color 98 minutes PG-13 *Directors-Writers:* Steven Kampmann, Will Aldis. *Producers:* Thom Mount, Hank Moonjean. *Cinematographer:* Bobby Byrne. *Editor:* Antony Gibbs. *Music:* David Foster. *Cast:* Mark Harmon (Billy Wyatt), Jodie Foster (Katie Chandler), Blair Brown (Ginny Wyatt), Jonathan Silverman (Teenage Alan Appleby), Harold Ramis (Alan Appleby), William McNamara (Teenage Billy Wyatt), Richard Jenkins (Hank Chandler), John Shea (Sam Wyatt), Christine Jones (Grace Chandler), Beth Broderick (Neighbor), Jane Bruckner (Sheryl), Ted Ross (Bud Scott), Thacher Goodwin (Young Billy Wyatt).

EIGHT MEN OUT

(1988) Orion Pictures Color 115 minutes PG *Director-Writer:* John Sayles. Based on the book by Eliot Asinof. *Producers:* Sarah Pillsbury, Midge Sanford. *Cinematographer:* Robert Richardson. *Editor:* John Tintori. *Music:* Mason Daring. *Cast:* John Cusack (Buck Weaver), David Strathairn (Eddie Cicotte), D.B. Sweeney (Shoeless Joe Jackson), Michael Rooker (Chick Gandil), Charlie Sheen (Hap Felsch), Don Harvey (Swede Risberg), Perry Lang (Fred Mullin), James Read (Lefty Williams), John Mahoney (Kid Gleason), John Sayles (Ring Lardner), Studs Terkel (Hugh Fullerton), Clifton James (Charles Comiskey), Michael Lerner

(Arnold Rothstein), Christopher Lloyd (Sleepy Bill Burns), Gordon Clapp (Ray Schalk), Jace Alexander (Dickie Kerr), Bill Irwin (Eddie Collins), Richard Edson (Billy Maharg), Kevin Tighe (Sport Sullivan), Michael Mantell (Abe Attell), John Anderson (Kenesaw Mountain Landis), Eliot Asinof (Heydler), Clyde Bassett (Ban Johnson).

NAKED GUN: FROM THE FILES OF POLICE SQUAD

(1988) Paramount Pictures Color 85 minutes PG-13 *Director:* David Zucker. *Writers:* David Zucker, Jim Abrahams, Jerry Zucker, Pat Proft. *Producer:* Robert K. Weiss. *Cinematographer:* Robert Stevens. *Editor:* Michael Jablow. *Music:* Ira Newborn. *Cast:* Leslie Nielsen (Frank Drebin), George Kennedy (Ed Hocken), Priscilla Presley (Jane Spencer), Ricardo Montalban (Vincent Ludwig), O.J. Simpson (Nordberg), Nancy Marchand (Mayor), John Houseman (Driving Instructor), Jeannette Charles (Queen Elizabeth II), Reggie Jackson (Angel Right Fielder), Lawrence Tierney (Angel Manager), Jay Johnstone (Seattle First Up), Hank Robinson, Joe West (Umpires), Curt Gowdy, Jim Palmer, Tim McCarver, Dick Vitale, Mel Allen, Dick Enberg, Dr. Joyce Brothers (Play-by-Play Announcers).

RAIN MAN

(1988) Guber-Peters Company United Artists Color 140 minutes R *Director:* Barry Levinson. *Writers:* Ronald Bass, Barry Morrow. *Producer:* Mark Johnson. *Cinematographer:* John Seale. *Editor:* Stu Linder. *Music:* Hans Zimmer. *Cast:* Dustin Hoffman (Raymond Babbitt), Tom Cruise (Charlie Babbitt), Valeria Golino (Susanna), Jerry Molen (Dr. Bruner).

TRADING HEARTS

(1988) The Vista Organization Cineworld Enterprises/IVE Color 88 minutes PG *Director:* Neil Leifer. *Writer:* Frank DeFord. *Producer:* Josi W. Konski. *Cinematographer:* Karen Grossman. *Editor:* Rick Shaine. *Music:* Stanley Myers. *Cast:* Raul Julia (Vinnie Iacona), Beverly D'Angelo (Donna Nottingham), Jenny Lewis (Yvonne Rhonda Nottingham), Parris Buckner (Robert Nottingham), Frank DeFord (Bartender #2), Hon. Ed Koch (Tourist Husband).

MAJOR LEAGUE

(1989) Morgan Creek/Mirage Production Paramount Pictures Color 106 minutes R *Director-Writer:* David Ward. *Producers:* Chris Chesser, Irby Smith. *Cinematographer:* Reynaldo Villalobos. *Editor:* Dennis M. Hill. *Music:* James Newton Howard. *Technical consultant:* Steve Yeager. *Cast:* Tom Berenger (Jake Taylor), Charlie Sheen (Rickie Vaughn), Corbin Bernsen (Roger Dorn), Margaret Whitton (Rachel Phelps), James Gammon (Lou Brown), Rene Russo (Lynn Westland), Bob Uecker (Harry Doyle), Charles Cyphers (Charlie Donovan), Wesley Snipes (Willie Mays Hayes), Dennis Haysbert (Pedro Cerrano), Andy Romano (Pepper Leach), Steve Yeager (Duke Temple), Pete Vuckovich (Haywood), Chelcie Ross (Steve Harris), Stacey Carroll (Suzanne Dorn).

THE DREAM TEAM

(1989) Imagine Entertainment Universal Pictures Color 113 minutes PG-13 *Director:* Howard Zieff. *Writers:* Jon Connolly, David Loucka. *Producer:* Christopher W. Knight. *Cinematographer:* Adam Hollander. *Editor:* Timothy O'Meara. *Music:* David McHugh. *Cast:* Michael Keaton (Billy Caulfield), Christopher Lloyd (Henry

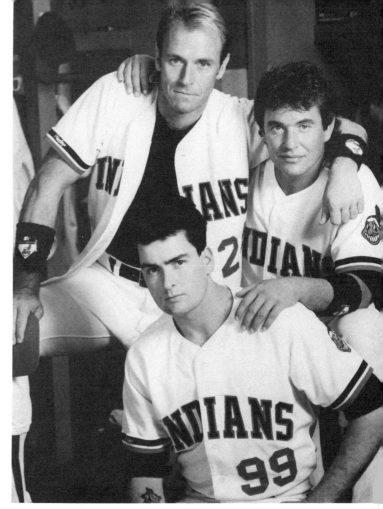

Major League: Corbin Bernsen (top) as Roger Dorn, Charlie Sheen (bottom) as Rickie Vaughn, Tom Berenger as Jake Taylor.

Sikorsky), Peter Boyle (Jack McDermott), Stephen Furst (Albert Ianuzzi), Dennis Boutsikaris (Dr. Weitzman), Lorraine Bracco (Riley), Milo O'Shea (Dr. Newald), Philip Bosco (O'Malley).

FIELD OF DREAMS

(1989) Gordon Company Production Universal Pictures Color 107 minutes PG *Director-Writer:* Phil Alden Robinson. Based on the novel *Shoeless Joe,* by W.P. Kinsella. *Producers:* Lawrence and Charles Gordon. *Cinematographer:* John Lindley. *Editor:* Ian Crafford. *Music:* James Horner. *Cast:* Kevin Costner (Ray Kinsella), Amy Madigan (Annie Kinsella), Gaby Hoffman (Karin Kinsella), James Earl Jones (Terence Mann), Timothy Busfield (Mark), Ray Liotta (Shoeless Joe Jackson), Burt Lancaster (Doc Graham), Dwier Brown (John Kinsella), Frank Whaley (Archie Graham), Michael Milhoan (Buck Weaver), Steve Eastin (Eddie Cicotte), Charles Hoyes (Swede Risberg), Art LaFleur (Chick Gandil).

PARENTHOOD

(1989) Imagine Entertainment Universal Pictures Color 124 minutes PG-13 *Director:* Ron Howard. *Writers:* Lowell Ganz, Babaloo Mandel, based on a story by Ganz, Mandel, Howard. *Producer:* Brian Grazer. *Cinematographer:* Donald McAlpine. *Editors:* Michael Hill, Daniel Hanley. *Music:* Randy Newman. *Cast:* Steve Martin (Gil), Tom Hulce (Larry), Rick Moranis (Nathan), Martha Plimpton (Julie), Keanu Reeves (Tod), Jason Robards (Frank), Mary

Bang the Drum Slowly: Robert De Niro as Bruce Pearson.

Steenburgen (Karen), Dianne Wiest (Helen), Harley Kozak (Susan), Dennis Dugan (David Brodsky), Leaf Phoenix (Garry), Jasen Fisher (Kevin).

NIGHT GAME

(1989) Epic Productions Trans World Entertainment Color 95 minutes R *Director:* Peter Masterson. *Writers:* Spencer Eastman, Anthony Palmer, based on a story by Eastman. *Producer:* George Litto. *Cinematographer:* Fred Murphy. *Editor:* Robert Barrere. *Music:* Pino Donaggio. *Baseball adviser:* Norm Miller. *Cast:* Roy Scheider (Mike Seaver), Karen Young (Roxy), Richard Bradford (Nelson), Paul Gleason (Broussard), Carlin Glynn (Alma), Lane Smith (Lamar), Anthony Palmer (Mendoza), Rex Linn (Epps), Alex Garcia (Sil Baretto).

PROBLEM CHILD

(1990) Imagine Entertainment Universal Pictures Color 81 minutes PG *Director:* Dennis Dugan. *Writers:* Scott Alexander, Larry Karazewski. *Producer:* Robert Simonds. *Cinematographer:* Peter Lyons Collister. *Editors:* Daniel Hanley, Michael Hill. *Music:* Miles Goodman. *Cast:* John Ritter (Ben Healy), Michael Oliver (Junior), Jack Warden (Big Ben), Amy Yasbeck (Flo), Gilbert Gottfried (Mr. Peabody), Michael Richards (Martin Beck).

MR. DESTINY

(1990) Laurence Mark Productions Touchstone Pictures Color 110 minutes PG-13 *Director:* James Orr. *Writers-Producers:* James Orr, Jim Cruickshank. *Cinematographer:* Alex Thomson. *Editor:* Michael R. Muller. *Music:* David Newman. *Cast:* James Belushi (Larry Burrows), Linda Hamilton (Ellen Burrows), Michael Caine (Mike), Jon Lovitz (Metzler), Hart Bochner (Niles Pender), Rene Russo (Cindy Jo), Bill McCutcheon (Leo Hansen), Pat Corley (Harry Burrows), Courteney Cox (Jewel Jagger), Kathy Ireland (Gina), Jay O. Sanders (Jackie Earle), Maury Chaykin (Guzelman).

PASTIME

(1991) Bullpen Ltd./Open Road Productions Miramax Color 95 minutes PG *Director:* Robin B. Armstrong. *Writer:* D.M. Eyre, Jr. *Producers:* Armstrong, Eric Tynan Young. *Cinematographer:* Tom Richmond. *Editor:* Mark Westmore. *Music:* Lee Holdridge. *Technical advisers:* Geoff Zahn, Joey Banks. *Cast:* William Russ (Roy Dean Bream), Glenn Plummer (Tyrone Debray), Noble Willingham (Clyde Bigby), Jeffrey Tambor (Peter Laporte), Scott Plank (Randy Keever), Dierdre O'Connell (Inez Brice), Reed Rudy (Spicer), Pat O'Bryan (Walsh), Charles Tyner (Arnold), Peter Murnik (Simmons), Ricky Paull Goldin (Hahn), John Jones (Colbeck), Duke Snider, Don Newcombe, Ernie Banks, Bill Mazeroski, Harmon Killebrew, Bob Feller (Bit Roles).

CITY SLICKERS

(1991) Castle Rock Entertainment/Nelson Entertainment/A Face Production Columbia Pictures Color 112 minutes PG-13 *Director:* Ron Underwood. *Writers:* Lowell Ganz, Babaloo Mandel. *Producer:* Irby Smith. *Cinematographer:* Dean Semler. *Editor:* O. Nicholas Brown. *Music:* Mark Shaiman. *Cast:* Billy Crystal (Mitch Robbins), Daniel Stern (Phil Berquist), Bruno Kirby (Ed Furillo), Patricia Wettig (Barbara Robbins), Helen Slater (Bonnie Rayburn), Jack Palance (Curly), Noble Willingham (Clay Stone), Tracey Walter (Cookie), Josh Mostel (Barry Shalowitz), David Paymer (Ira Shalowitz), Bill Henderson (Ben Jessup), Jeffrey Tambor (Lou).

TALENT FOR THE GAME

(1991) Paramount Pictures Color 91 minutes PG *Director:* Robert M. Young. *Writers:* David Himmelstein, Tom Donnelly, Larry Ferguson. *Producer:* Martin Elfand. *Cinematographer:* Curtis Clark. *Editor:* Arthur Coburn. *Music:* David Newman. *Cast:* Edward James Olmos (Virgil Sweet), Lorraine Bracco (Bobbie Henderson), Jeffrey Corbett (Sammy Bodeen), Jamey Sheridan (Tim Weaver), Terry Kinney (Gil Lawrence), Thomas Ryan (Paul), Felton Perry (Fred), Tom Bower (Reverend Bodeen), Janet Carroll (Rachel Bodeen), Bobby Tolan, Derrel Thomas, Lenny Randle, Todd Cruz, John D'Aquisto, Phil Lombardi, Lee Lacy, Rudy Law, Steve Ontiveros (Ballplayers).

HOOK

(1991) Amblin Entertainment Tri-Star Pictures Color 144 minutes PG *Director:* Steven Spielberg. *Writers:* Jim V. Hart, Malia Scotch Marmo, from a story by Hart, Nick Castle. *Producers:* Kathleen Kennedy, Frank Marshall, Gerald R. Molen. *Cinematographer:* Dean Cundey. *Editor:* Michael Kahn. *Music:* John Williams. *Cast:* Dustin Hoffman (Capt. Hook), Robin Williams (Peter Banning/Peter Pan), Julia Roberts (Tinkerbell), Bob Hoskins (Smee), Maggie Smith (Granny Wendy), Charlie Korsmo (Jack), Carolyn Goodall (Moira), Phil Collins (Inspector), Glenn Close (Pirate), David Crosby (Pirate).

ALAN & NAOMI

(1992) Leucadia Film Corp./Maltese Companies Triton Pictures Color 96 minutes PG *Director:* Sterling VanWagenen. *Writer:* Jordan Horowitz, based on a novel by Myron Levoy. *Producers:* David Anderson, Mark Balsam. *Cinematographer:* Paul Ryan. *Editor:* Cari Coughlin. *Music:* Dick Hyman. *Cast:* Lukas Haas (Alan Silverman), Michael Gross (Sol Silverman), Amy Aquino (Ruth Silverman), Zohra Lampert (Mrs. Liebman), Kevin Connolly (Shaun Kelly), Vanessa Zaoui (Naomi Kirschenbaum).

THE BABE

(1992) Waterhorse/Finnegan-Pinchuk Universal Pictures Color 113 minutes PG *Director:* Arthur Hiller. *Writer/Producer:* John Fusco. *Cinematographer:* Haskell Wexler. *Editor:* Robert C. Jones. *Music:* Elmer Bernstein. *Cast:* John Goodman (Babe Ruth), Kelly McGillis (Claire Ruth), Trini Alvarado (Helen Ruth), Bruce Boxleitner (Jumpin' Joe Dugan), Peter Donat (Harry Frazee), James Cromwell (Brother Mathias), J.C. Quinn (Jack Dunn), Joe Ragno (Miller Huggins), Richard Tyson (Guy Bush), Ralph Marrero (Ping), Bob Swan (George Ruth, Sr.), Bernard Kates (Colonel Ruppert), Michael McGrady (Lou Gehrig), Stephen Caffery (Johnny Sylvester, age thirty), W. Earl Brown (Herb Pennock), Thom C. Simmons (McKechnie), Rick Reardon (Ernie Shore), Randy Steinmeyer (Ty Cobb), Andy Voils (Young George Herman Ruth).

A LEAGUE OF THEIR OWN

(1992) Parkway Production Columbia Pictures Color 124 minutes PG *Director:* Penny Marshall. *Writers:* Lowell Ganz, Babaloo Mandel, based on a story by Kim Wilson, Kelly Candaele. *Producers:* Robert Greenhut, Elliot Abbott. *Cinematographer:* Miroslav Ondricek. *Editor:* George Bowers. *Music:* Hans Zimmer. *Cast:* Tom Hanks (Jimmy Dugan), Geena Davis (Dottie Hinson), Lori Petty (Kit Keller), Madonna (Mae Mordabito), Rosie O'Donnell (Doris Murphy), Megan Cavanagh (Marla Hooch), Tracy Reiner (Betty Horn), Bitty Schram (Evelyn Gardner), Ann Cusack (Shirley Baker), Anne Elizabeth Ramsey (Helen Haley), Freddie Simpson (Ellen Sue Gotlander), Renee Coleman (Alice Gaspers), Robin Knight (Beans Babbitt), Patti Pelton (Marbleann Wilkenson), Kelli Simkins (Beverly Dixon), Neezer Tarleton (Neezer Dalton), Connie Pounds-Taylor (Connie Calhoun), Kathleen Marshall (Mumbles Brockman), Sharon Szmidt (Vivian Ernst), David Strathairn (Ira Lowenstein), Garry Marshall (Walter Harvey), Jon Lovitz (Ernie Capadino), Bill Pullman (Bob Hinson), Harry Shearer (Newsreel Announcer), Lynn Cartwright (Older Dottie), Kathleen Butler (Older Kit), Eunice Anderson (Older Mae), Vera Johnson (Older Doris), Patricia Wilson (Older Marla).

MR. BASEBALL

(1992) Outlaw Production Universal Pictures Color 100 minutes PG-13 *Director:* Fred Schepisi. *Writers:* Gary Ross, Kevin Wade, Monte Merrick, based on a story by Theo Pelletier, John Junkerman. *Producers:* Schepisi, Doug Claybourne, Robert Newmyer. *Cinematographer:* Ian Baker. *Editor:* Peter Honess. *Music:* Jerry Goldsmith. *Cast:* Tom Selleck (Jack Elliot), Ken Takakura (Uchiyama), Aya Takanashi (Hiroko Uchiyama), Dennis Haysbert (Max "Hammer" Dubois), Toshi Shioya (Yoji Nishimura), Kohsuke Toyohara (Toshi Yamashita), Toshizo Fujiwara (Ryoh Mukai), Mak Takano (Shinji Igarashi), Kenji Morinaga (Hiroshi Kurosawa), Joh Nishimura (Tomohiko Ohmae), Norihide Goto (Issei Itoi), Kensuke Toita (Akito Yagi), Naoki Fujii (Takuya Nishikawa), Takanobu Hozumi (Hiroshi Nakamura), Leon Lee (Lyle Massey), Bradley Jay Lesley (Niven), Tim McCarver (Himself), Sean McDonough (Himself), Art LaFleur (Skip), Greg Goossen (Trey), Nicholas Cascone (Doc), Larry Pennell (Howie Gold), Scott Plank (Ryan Ward), Charles Joseph Fick (Billy Stevens), Michael McGrady (Duane), Frank Thomas (Rookie).

SIMPLE MEN

(1992) Fine Line Features Color 105 minutes R *Director-Writer:* Hal Hartley. *Producers:* Hartley, Ted Hope. *Cinematographer:* Michael Spiller. *Editor:* Steve Hamilton. *Music:* Ned Rifle. *Cast:* Robert Burke (Bill McCabe), William Sage (Dennis McCabe), Karen Sillas (Kate), Elina Lowensohn (Elina), Martin Donovan (Martin), Mark Chandler Bailey (Mike), Chris Cooke (Vic).

Swell-Head: Dickie Moore (second from left) as Billy, Frank Moran (center) as the Rube, Wallace Ford (right) as Terry McCall.

223

The Slugger's Wife: Michael O'Keefe as Darryl Palmer.

BAD LIEUTENANT

(1992) Aries Film Releasing Color 96 minutes NC-17 *Director:* Abel Ferrara. *Writers:* Ferrara, Zoe Lund. *Producers:* Edward R. Pressman, Mary Kane. *Cinematographer:* Ken Kelsch. *Editor:* Anthony Redman. *Music:* Joe Delia. *Baseball adviser:* Josh Blum. *Cast:* Harvey Keitel (LT), Bob Murphy, Warner Fusselle (Play-by-Play Announcers).

THE SANDLOT

(1993) Island World Twentieth Century-Fox Color 101 minutes PG *Director:* David Mickey Evans. *Writers:* Evans, Robert Gunter. Producers: Dale de la Torre, William S. Gilmore. *Cinematographer:* Anthony B. Richmond. *Editor:* Michael E. Stevenson. *Music:* David Newman. *Cast:* Tom Guiry (Scotty Smalls), Mike Vitar (Benjamin Franklin Rodriguez), Patrick Renna (Hamilton "Ham" Porter), Chauncey Leopardi (Michael "Squints" Palledorous), Marty York (Allan "Yeah-Yeah" McClennan), Brandon Adams (Kenny DeNunez), Grant Gelt (Bertram Grover Weeks), Shane Obedzinski

(Tommy "Repeat" Timmons), Victor DiMatia (Timmy Timmons), Karen Allen (Mom), Denis Leary (Bill), James Earl Jones (Mr. Mertle), Art La Fleur ("The Babe"), David Mickey Evans (Voice of Adult Scotty).

DAVE

(1993) Northern Lights Entertainment/Donner/Shuler/Donner Warner Bros. Color 110 minutes PG-13 *Director:* Ivan Reitman. *Writer:* Gary Ross. *Producers:* Reitman, Lauren Shuler-Donner. *Cinematographer:* Adam Greenberg. *Editor:* Sheldon Kahn. *Music:* James Newton Howard. *Cast:* Kevin Kline (Dave Kovic/Bill Mitchell), Sigourney Weaver (Ellen Mitchell), Frank Langella (Bob Alexander), Kevin Dunn (Alan Reed), Ving Rhames (Duane Stevenson), Ben Kingsley (Vice President Nance), Charles Grodin (Murray Blum), Faith Prince (Alice), Jeff Tackett (Orioles' Catcher).

SLEEPLESS IN SEATTLE

(1993) TriStar Pictures Color 104 minutes PG *Director:* Nora Ephron. *Writers:* Nora Ephron, David S. Ward, Jeff Arch, from Arch's story. *Producer:* Gary Foster. *Cinematographer:* Sven Nykvist. *Editor:* Robert Reitano. *Music:* Mark Shaiman. *Cast:* Tom Hanks (Sam Baldwin), Meg Ryan (Annie Reed), Bill Pullman (Walter), Ross Malinger (Jonah Baldwin), Rosie O'Donnell (Becky), Gaby Hoffmann (Jessica), Victor Garber (Greg), Rita Wilson (Suzy), Barbara Garrick (Victoria), Carey Lowell (Maggie Baldwin), Rob Reiner (Jay).

ROOKIE OF THE YEAR

(1993) Twentieth Century-Fox Color 103 minutes PG *Director:* Daniel Stern. *Writer:* Sam Harper. *Producer:* Robert Harper. *Cinematographer:* Jack Green. *Editors:* Donn Cambern, Raja Gosnell. *Music:* Bill Conti. *Baseball adviser:* Tim Stoddard. *Cast:* Thomas Ian Nicholas (Henry Rowengartner), Gary Busey (Chet Steadman), Albert Hall (Sal Martinella), Amy Morton (Mary Rowengartner), Dan Hedaya (Larry "Fish" Fisher), Bruce Altman (Jack Bradfield), John Candy (Sportscaster), Eddie Bracken (Bob Carson), Robert Gorman (Clark), Patrick LaBrecque (George), Daniel Stern (Phil Brickma), Colombe Jacobsen-Derstine (Becky), Kristie Davis (Tiffany), Tyler Ann Carroll (Edith), Tom Milanovich (Heddo), Ross Lehman (Dr. Kersten), John Gegenhuber (Derkin), James "Ike" Eichling (Little League Coach), Josh Wagner (Little League Fielder), James Andelin (Wizard of Wrigley), Andrew Mark Berman (Ernie), Mark Doran, Neil Flynn, E. Milton Wheeler, Sam Sanders, Neil Fiala, Frank L. Wiltse (Cubs Players), W. Earl Brown (Bullpen Catcher), Barry Bonds, Bobby Bonilla, Pedro Guerrero (Three Big Whiffers), Jerry Saslow, Mike Bacarella (Bleacher Bums), Tim Stoddard (Dodger Pitcher).

TELEVISION FEATURES

IT'S GOOD TO BE ALIVE

(1974) Metromedia Producers Corporation/Larry Harmon Pictures CBS Color 100 minutes *Director:* Michael Landon. *Writer:* Steven Gethers, from the book by Roy Campanella. *Producer:* Gerald I. Isenberg. *Cinematographer:* Ted Voigtlander. *Editor:* John A. Martinelli. *Music:* Michel Legrand. *Cast:* Paul Winfield (Roy Campanella), Louis Gossett, Jr. (Sam Brockington), Ruby Dee (Ruthe Campanella), Ramon Bieri (Walter O'Malley), Joe DeSantis (Campanella's Father), Ty Henderson (David Campanella), Lloyd Gough (Surgeon), Eric Woods (Young Roy Campanella), Ketty Lester (Mother), Joe E. Tata (Pee Wee Reese), and Roy, Roxi, Joni, Tony, and Routh Campanella.

MURDER AT THE WORLD SERIES

(1977) ABC Circle Films ABC Color 100 minutes *Director:* Andrew V. McLaglen. *Writer-Producer:* Cy Cermak. *Cinematographer:* Richard C. Glouner. *Editors:* John F. Link II, Richard A. Harris. *Music:* John Cacavas. *Cast:* Lynda Day George (Margot Mannering), Murray Hamilton (Harvey Murkison), Karen Valentine (Lois Marshall), Gerald S. O'Loughlin (Moe Gold), Michael Parks (Larry Marshall), Janet Leigh (Karen Weese), Hugh O'Brian (The Governor), Nancy Kelly (Alice Dakso), Johnny Seven (Severino), Tamara Dobson (Lisa), Joseph Wiseman (Sam Druckman), Bruce Boxleitner (Cisco).

A LOVE AFFAIR: THE ELEANOR AND LOU GEHRIG STORY

(1978) Charles Fries Productions/Stonehenge Productions ABC Color 100 minutes *Director:* Fielder Cook. *Writer:* Blanche Hanalis, based on the book *My Luke and I,* by Eleanor Gehrig and Joseph Durso. *Producer:* David Manson. *Cinematographer:* Michel Hugo. *Editor:* David Newhouse. *Music:* Eddy Lawrence Manson. *Cast:* Blythe Danner (Eleanor Gehrig), Edward Herrmann (Lou Gehrig), Patricia Neal (Mrs. Gehrig), Gerald S. O'Laughlin (Joe McCarthy), Ramon Bieri (Babe Ruth), Jane Wyatt (Eleanor's Mother), Georgia Engel (Claire Ruth), Michael Lerner (Dr. Canlan), David Ogden Stiers (Dr. Charles Mayo), Gail Strickland (Dorothy), Valerie Curtin (Kitty), Jennifer Penny (Jennifer), Lainie Kazan (Sophie Tucker), Robert Burr (Joe Durso), James Luisi (Tony Lazzeri), Wynn Erwin (Yankee Executive), William Wellman, Jr. (Bill Dickey).

ONE IN A MILLION: THE RON LEFLORE STORY

(1978) Roger Gimbel Productions/EMI Television CBS Color 100 minutes *Director:* William A. Grahame. *Writer:* Stanford Whitmore,

Eight Men Out: John Cusack as Buck Weaver, David Strathairn as Eddie Cicotte, D.B. Sweeney as Shoeless Joe Jackson, Michael Rooker as Chick Gandil (top row, left to right); Charlie Sheen as Hap Felsch, Don Harvey as Swede Risberg, Perry Lang as Fred McMullin, James Read as Lefty Williams (bottom row, left to right).

Hot Curves: Rex Lease (without the catching gear) as Jim Dolan, Alice Day as Elaine McGrew.

based on the book *Breakout*, by Ron LeFlore with Jim Hawkins. *Producer:* William S. Gilmore. *Cinematographer:* Jordan Cronenweth. *Editor:* Aaron Stell. *Music:* Peter Matz. *Cast:* LeVar Burton (Ron LeFlore), Madge Sinclair (Georgia LeFlore), Paul Benjamin (John LeFlore), James Luisi (Jimmy Karalla), Billy Martin (Himself), Zakes Mokae (Pee Wee Parker), Larry B. Scott (Gerald LeFlore), Yaumilton Brown (Leroy), Walter King (Antoine), Jimmy Spinks (Umpire), James Butsicaris (Himself), John R. McKee (Ralph Houk), Matt Stephens (Mickey Stanley), Al Kaline (Himself), Norm Cash (Himself), Jim Northrup (Himself), Bill Freehan (Himself), James Karalla (Heckler).

THE KID FROM LEFT FIELD

(1979) Gary Coleman Productions/Deena Silver Kramer's Movie Company NBC Color   100 minutes *Director:* Adell Aldrich. *Writers:* Jack Sher, Katharyn Powers, from a story by Sher. *Producer:* Russell Vreeland. *Cinematographer:* Frank Thackery. *Editors:* Peter Kirby, Robert Hernandez. *Music:* David Frank. *Cast:* Gary Coleman (J.R. Cooper), Robert Guillaume (Larry Cooper), Gary Collins (Pete Sloane), Ed McMahon (Fred Walker), Tricia O'Neil (Marion Fowler), Tab Hunter (Bill Lorant).

AUNT MARY

(1979) Henry Jaffe Enterprises CBS Color   100 minutes *Director:* Peter Werner. *Writer:* Burt Prelutsky, from a story by Ellis A. Cohen. *Producer:* Michael Jaffe. *Cinematographer:* Hugh Gagnier. *Editor:* John Farrell. *Music:* Arthur B. Rubinstein. *Cast:* Jean Stapleton (Mary Dobkin), Martin Balsam (Harry Strassberg), Harold Gould (Dr. Hoxley), Dolph Sweet (Amos Jones), Robert Emhardt (Berwick), Philip Bruns (Det. Lamonica), Robbie Rist (Vernon), Anthony Cafiso (Nicholas Rocco), K.C. Martel (Billy), Hap Lawrence (Clyde Hopper), Ernie Harwell (Baseball Announcer).

THE COMEBACK KID

(1980) ABC Circle Films ABC Color   100 minutes *Director:* Peter Levin. *Writer:* Joe Landon. *Producer:* Louis Rudolph. *Cinematographer:* Ric Waite. *Editor:* David Newhouse. *Music:* Barry De Vorzon. *Cast:* John Ritter (Bubba Newman), Susan Dey (Megan Barrett), Doug McKeon (Michael), James Gregory (Scotty), Jeremy Licht (Paul), Dick O'Neil (Phil), Rod Gist (Ray Carver), Michael Lembeck (Tony), Patrick Swayze (Chuck), Kim Fields (Molly).

DON'T LOOK BACK: THE STORY OF LEROY "SATCHEL" PAIGE

(1981) TBA Productions; Satie Productions; Triseme ABC Color 100 minutes *Director:* Richard A. Colla. *Writer:* Ron Rubin, based on *Maybe I'll Pitch Forever*, by Satchel Paige as told to David Lipman. *Producers:* Jimmy Hawkins, Stanley Rubin. *Cinematographer:* Hector Figueroa. *Editors:* Bud S. Isaacs, La Reine Johnston. *Music:* Jack Elliot. *Technical consultant:* Leroy "Satchel" Paige. *Cast:* Louis Gossett, Jr. (Satchel Paige), Beverly Todd (Lahoma Brown Paige), Cleavon Little (Rabbit Thompson), Ernie Barnes (Josh Gibson), Clifton Davis (Cool Papa Bell), Hal Williams (Carl Roberts), Taylor Lacher (Announcer), John Beradino (Jake Wells), Jim Davis (Mr. Wilkinson), Ossie Davis (Chuffy Russell), Satchel Paige (Himself), Tommie Stewart (Mama Paige), Earle Willoughby (Dizzy Dean), Milton Stafford (Young Satchel), Bubba Phillips (Coach Hardy).

MILLION DOLLAR INFIELD

(1982) CBS Entertainment CBS Color   100 minutes *Director:* Hal Cooper. Writers: Dick Wimmer, Philip Mishkin, Rob Reiner, based on a story by Wimmer. *Producers:* Peter Katz, Rob Reiner. *Cinematographer:* Thomas Del Ruth. *Editor:* Jim Benson. *Music:* Artie Kane. *Cast:* Bonnie Bedelia (Marcia Miller), Robert Costanzo (Artie Levitas), Rob Reiner (Monte Miller), Christopher Guest (Bucky Frische), Bruno Kirby (Lou Buonomato), Candy Azzara (Rochelle Levitas), Gretchen Corbett (Carol Frische), Elizabeth Wilson (Sally Ephron), Shera Danese (Bunny Wahl), Harry Shearer (Jack Savage), Mel Allen (Himself).

TIGER TOWN

(1983) Walt Disney Productions The Disney Channel Color   76 minutes *Director-Writer:* Alan Shapiro. *Producer:* Susan B. Landau. *Cinematographer:* Robert Elswit. *Editors:* Richard A. Harris, John F. Link. *Music:* Eddy L. Manson. *Cast:* Roy Scheider (Billy Young), Justin Henry (Alex), Ron McLarty (Buddy), Bethany Carpenter (Mother), Noah Moazezi (Eddie), Mary Wilson (Herself), Sparky Anderson (Himself), Ernie Harwell (Himself), Al Ackerman (Himself), Ray Lane (Himself).

A WINNER NEVER QUITS

(1986) Blatt/Singer Production Columbia Pictures ABC Color 100 minutes *Director:* Mel Damski. *Writer:* Burt Prelutsky. *Producers:* James Keach, Lynn Raynor. *Cinematographer:* Joseph Biroc. *Editor:* Michael A. Stevenson. *Music:* Dana Kaproff. *Cast:* Keith Carradine (Pete Gray), Huckleberry Fox (Nelson Gary, Jr.), Mare Winningham (Annie), Dennis Weaver (Wyshner), Jack Kehoe (Bloom), Fionnula Flanagan (Mrs. Wyshner), Steve Rees (Young Pete), Andrew Lubeskie (Young Whitey), Ed O'Neill (Whitey), Dana Delaney (Nora), G.W. Bailey (Tatum), Charles Hallahan (Nelson Gary, Sr.).

LONG GONE

(1987) Landsburg Company HBO Color 110 minutes *Director:* Martin Davidson. *Writer:* Michael Norrell, based on a story by Paul Hemphill. *Producer:* Joan Barnett. *Cinematographer:* Robert Elswit. *Editor:* Gib Jaffe. *Music:* Kenny Vance. *Cast:* William L. Petersen (Cecil "Stud" Cantrell), Virginia Madsen (Dixie Lee Boxx), Dermot Mulroney (Jamie Don Weeks), Larry Riley (Joe Louis Brown), Katy Boyer (Esther Wrenn), Henry Gibson (Hale Buchman), Teller (Hale Buchman, Jr.), Panchito Gomez (Poco Izquierdo), David Langston Smyrl (Monroe Wright), Guich Koock (Bump Klein), Arthur Rosenberg (Peaches Cluff).

THE COURT-MARTIAL OF JACKIE ROBINSON

(1990) Von Zerneck-Sertner Films; Turner Pictures TNT Color 100 minutes *Director:* Larry Peerce. *Writers:* L. Travis Clark, Steve Duncan, Clayton Frohman, Dennis Lynton Clark, from a story by Clark and Duncan. *Producers:* L. Travis Clark, Cleve Landsberg, Susan Weber-Gold, Julie Anne Weitz. *Cinematographer:* Don Burgess. Editors: Eric Sears, Bob Wyman. *Music:* Stanley Clarke. *Cast:* Andre Braugher (Jackie Robinson), Ruby Dee (Mallie Robinson), Stan Shaw (Joe Louis), Kasi Lemmons (Rachel), Daniel Stern (William Cline), J.A. Preston (Wendell Smith), Bruce Dern (Ed Higgins), Paul Dooley (Willy Smith), Steven Williams (Satchel Paige), Don Hood (Major Foley), Ken Swofford (Coach).

BABE RUTH

(1991) Lyttle Productions NBC Color 100 minutes *Director:* Mark Tinker. *Writer:* Michael de Guzman, adapted in part from Robert Creamer's biography *Babe: The Legend Comes to Life.* *Producer:* Frank Pace. *Cinematographer:* Don Morgan. *Editor:* Stanford C. Allen. *Music:* Steve Dorf. *Baseball consultant:* Rod Carew. *Cast:* Stephen Lang (Babe Ruth), Bruce Weitz (Miller Huggins), Donald Moffat (Jacob Ruppert), Lisa Zane (Claire), Brian Doyle-Murray (Marshall Hunt), Pete Rose (Ty Cobb), Yvonne Suhor (Helen), William Lucking (Brother Matthias), Neal McDonough (Lou Gehrig), John Anderson (Kenesaw Mountain Landis).

THE COMRADES OF SUMMER

(1992) Grossbart Barnett Productions HBO Color 108 minutes *Director:* Tommy Lee Wallace. *Writer:* Robert Rodat. *Producers:* Tim Braine, David Pritchard. *Cinematographer:* Richard Leiterman. *Editor:* Stephen E. Rivkin. *Music:* William Olvis. *Cast:* Joe Mantegna (Sparky Smith), Natalya Negoda (Tanya), Mark Rolston (Voronov), John Fleck (Milov), Eric Allan Kramer (Boris), Ian Tracey (Andy),

The Bad News Bears Go to Japan: Marvin Lazar (Tony Curtis) reviews on-field strategy with young Mustapha Rahim (Scoody Thornton).

Michael Lerner (George Kennan), Jay Brazeau (Tom), Dwight Koss (Jack), Jim Lampley (Radio Announcer).

COOPERSTOWN

(1993) Brandman Productions, Inc./Amblin Television TNT Screenworks Color 90 minutes *Director:* Charles Haid. *Writer:* Lee Blessing. *Producers:* Leanne Moore, Steven Brandman. *Cinematographer:* William Wages. *Editor:* Andrew Doerfer. *Music:* Mel Marvin. *Cast:* Alan Arkin (Harry Willette), Graham Greene (Raymond Maracle), Hope Lange (Cassie Willette), Josh Charles (Jody), Ed Begley, Jr. (Dave Cormeer), Maria Pitillo (Bridget), Ann Wedgeworth (Lila), Paul Dooley (Sid Wiggins), Joanna Miles (Louise), Gailard Sartain (State Trooper), Charles Haid (Little Eddie McVee), Victoria Racimo (Isabel), Ernie Harwell (Baseball Announcer), Miles Perlich (Young Eddie), Byron Thames (Young Harry), Jason Orman (Young Pitcher), Juarez Orman (Catcher), Robbie T. Robinson (Umpire), Zahn McClaron (Young Raymond), Joe Spano (Minor-League Manager).

INDEX

230

ORDER NOW!
More Citadel Film Books

If you like this book, you'll love the other titles in the award-winning Citadel Film Series. From James Stewart to Moe Howard and The Three Stooges, Woody Allen to John Wayne, The Citadel Film Series is America's largest and oldest film book library.

With more than 150 titles--and more on the way!--Citadel Film Books make perfect gifts for a loved one, a friend, or best of all, yourself!

A complete listing of the Citadel Film Series appears below.
If you know what books you want, why not order now!
It's easy! Just call 1-800-447-BOOK and have your MasterCard or Visa ready.

STARS
Alan Ladd
Arnold Schwarzenegger
Barbra Streisand: First Decade
Barbra Streisand: Second
  Decade
The Barbra Streisand Scrapbook
Bela Lugosi
Bette Davis
Boris Karloff
The Bowery Boys
Brigitte Bardot
Buster Keaton
Carole Lombard
Cary Grant
Charlie Chaplin
Clark Gable
Clint Eastwood
Curly
Dustin Hoffman
Edward G. Robinson
Elizabeth Taylor
Elvis Presley
Errol Flynn
Frank Sinatra
Gary Cooper
Gene Kelly
Gina Lollobrigida
Gloria Swanson
Gregory Peck
Greta Garbo
Henry Fonda
Humphrey Bogart
Ingrid Bergman
Jack Lemmon
Jack Nicholson
James Cagney
James Dean: Behind the Scene
Jane Fonda
Jeanette MacDonald & Nelson
  Eddy
Joan Crawford
John Wayne Films
John Wayne Reference Book

John Wayne Scrapbook
Judy Garland
Katharine Hepburn
Kirk Douglas
Laurel & Hardy
Lauren Bacall
Laurence Olivier
Mae West
Marilyn Monroe
Marlene Dietrich
Marlon Brando
Marx Brothers
Moe Howard & the Three
  Stooges
Norma Shearer
Olivia de Havilland
Orson Welles
Paul Newman
Peter Lorre
Rita Hayworth
Robert De Niro
Robert Redford
Sean Connery
Sexbomb: Jayne Mansfield
Shirley MacLaine
Shirley Temple
The Sinatra Scrapbook
Spencer Tracy
Steve McQueen
Three Stooges Scrapbook
Warren Beatty
W.C. Fields
William Holden
William Powell
A Wonderful Life: James Stewart
DIRECTORS
Alfred Hitchcock
Cecil B. DeMille
Federico Fellini
Frank Capra
John Huston
Woody Allen
GENRE
Black Hollywood

Black Hollywood: From 1970 to
  Today
Classic Foreign Films: From
  1960 to Today
Classic Gangster Films
Classic Science Fiction Films
Classics of the Horror Film
Classic TV Westerns
Cult Horror Films
Divine Images: Jesus on Screen
Early Classics of Foreign Film
Films of Merchant Ivory
Great Baseball Films
Great French Films
Great German Films
Great Italian Films
Great Science Fiction Films
Harry Warren & the Hollywood
  Musical
Hispanic Hollywood: The Latins
  in Motion Pictures
The Hollywood Western
The Incredible World of 007
The Jewish Image in American
  Film
The Lavender Screen: The Gay
  and Lesbian Films
Martial Arts Movies
The Modern Horror Film
More Classics of the Horror Film
Movie Psychos & Madmen
Our Huckleberry Friend: Johnny
  Mercer
Second Feature: "B" Films
They Sang! They Danced! They
  Romanced!: Hollywood
  Musicals
Thrillers
The West That Never Was
Words and Shadows: Literature
  on the Screen
DECADE
Classics of the Silent Screen
Films of the Twenties

Films of the Thirties
More Films of the 30's
Films of the Forties
Films of the Fifties
Lost Films of the 50's
Films of the Sixties
Films of the Seventies
Films of the Eighties
SPECIAL INTEREST
America on the Rerun
Bugsy (Illustrated screenplay)
The "Cheers" Trivia Book
Comic Support
Cutting Room Floor: Scenes
  Which Never Made It
Favorite Families of TV
Film Flubs
Film Flubs: The Sequel
First Films
"Frankly, My Dear": Great
  Movie Lines About Women
The Greatest Stories Ever
  Filmed
Hollywood Cheesecake
Howard Hughes in Hollywood
More Character People
The Nightmare Never Ends:
  Freddy Krueger & "A Night-
  mare on Elm Street"
The "Northern Exposure" Book
The Official Andy Griffith Show
  Scrapbook
The 100 Best Films of the
  Century
The 1001 Toughest TV Trivia
  Questions of All Time
The "Quantum Leap" Book
Rodgers & Hammerstein
Sex in Films
Sex In the Movies
Sherlock Holmes
Son of Film Flubs
Who Is That?: Familiar Faces and
  Forgotten Names
"You Ain't Heard Nothin' Yet!"

For a free full-color Entertainment Books brochure including the Citadel Film Series in depth and more, call 1-800-447-BOOK; or send your name and address to Citadel Film Books, Dept. 1479, 120 Enterprise Ave., Secaucus, NJ 07094.